ON THE LINE

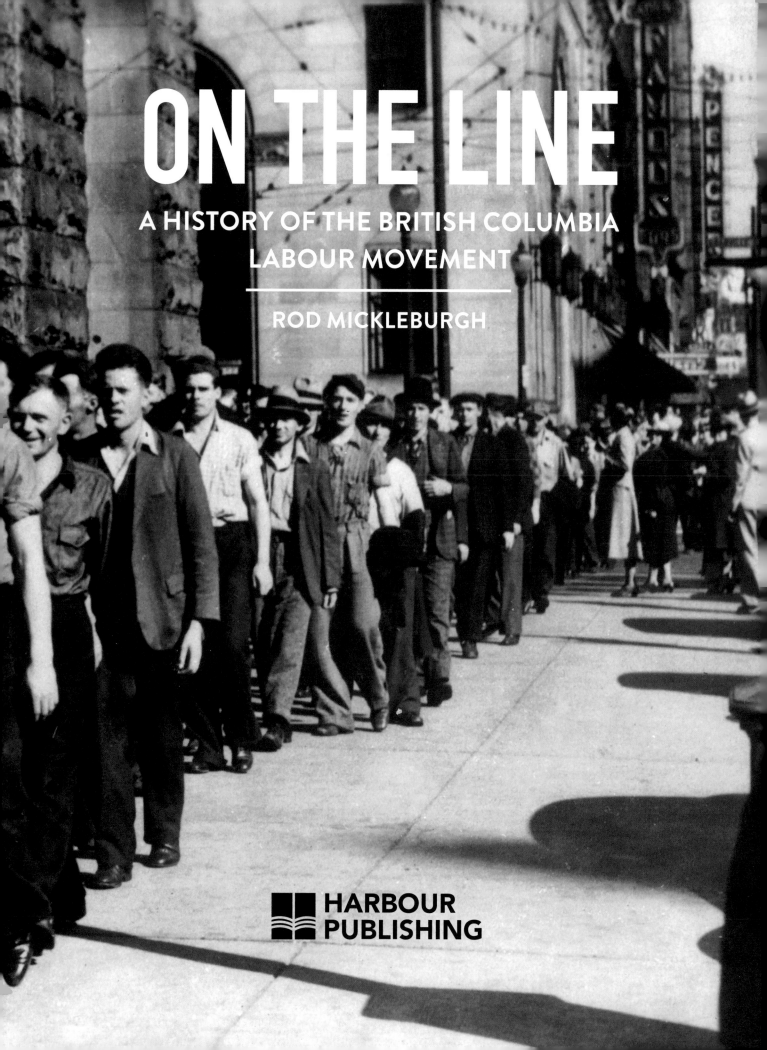

ON THE LINE

A HISTORY OF THE BRITISH COLUMBIA LABOUR MOVEMENT

ROD MICKLEBURGH

HARBOUR PUBLISHING

Title page:
Unemployed protesters take a break from their 1938 Vancouver Post Office sit–down. *Courtesy David Yorke.*

With thanks to the BC Labour Heritage Centre Society.

Harbour Publishing Co. Ltd.
P.O. Box 219, Madeira Park, BC, V0N 2H0
www.harbourpublishing.com

Developmental editor Silas White
Project editor Peter Robson
Copy editor Arlene Prunkl
Indexed by Ellen Hawman
Dust jacket design by Sari Naworynski
Text design by Roger Handling
Printed and bound in Canada

Harbour Publishing acknowledges the support of the Canada Council for the Arts, which last year invested $153 million to bring the arts to Canadians throughout the country. We also gratefully acknowledge financial support from the Government of Canada and from the Province of British Columbia through the BC Arts Council and the Book Publishing Tax Credit.

Library and Archives Canada Cataloguing in Publication
Mickleburgh, Rod, author
    On the Line : a history of the British Columbia labour movement / by Rod Mickleburgh.

Includes bibliographical references and index.
Issued in print and electronic formats.
ISBN 978-1-55017-826-5 (hardcover).--ISBN 978-1-55017-827-2 (HTML)

    1. Labor movement--British Columbia--History--20th century.
I. Title.
HD6529.B8M53 2018   331.809711   C2017-907054-1
                                    C2017-907055-X

In recognition of his fervent advocacy of labour heritage, *On the Line* is respectfully dedicated to Jack Munro.

CONTENTS

Opposite: Men and women workers at Vancouver Plywood gather for a union update toward the end of World War II. *Courtesy Gary Wong, IWA Local 1–217 Archives.*

FOREWORD

by Irene Lanzinger, president, BC Federation of Labour

The favourite photo of former BC Federation of Labour president Jim Kinnaird, taken in Vancouver on October 1, 1980, day three of a strike by federal government workers belonging to the Public Service Alliance of Canada. In BC, a picket line is a picket line. You don't cross. *Dan Scott photo,* Vancouver Sun.

On the Line: A History of the BC Labour Movement is a must-read for anyone involved in or interested in the labour movement today. It helps us to understand where we came from and why BC unions developed a national reputation for fight-back and militancy. Author and former labour journalist Rod Mickleburgh tells many stories of our struggles as workers—from the battles in mines, mills and the fishery to improve brutal conditions and paltry wages to the recent inspiring efforts of public sector unions in health care and education, backed by a co-ordinated labour move-

ment, taking on government in the streets and in the courts to defend the collective bargaining rights of union members. Mickleburgh makes it clear: no one ever gave working people the right to organize unions, the right to a safe and healthy workplace, the right to bargain for fair wages and decent working conditions—basic rights we take for granted today. Working people through their unions had to fight and in some cases suffer injury or death to achieve this. With skill and compassion, Mickleburgh weaves multiple stories of these many battles and struggles to put

together the essence of this book—how working people and their unions built a decent life for future generations with their sweat and dogged determination to take on employers and governments every time they tried to stop this progress. Mickleburgh tells the whole story. You can feel the sorrow of families with scant incomes on which to live being thrown out of their company-owned homes, the helplessness of striking workers forced to confront scabs brought in by employers to take their jobs, the horror of armed intervention by police or militia, always on the side of the employers—never on the side of working people. Mickleburgh brings our history to life.

You cannot read this book and not be overwhelmed by all the forces that opposed the progress of workers over more than a century of labour history. And you cannot read this book and not marvel at the tenacity and the capacity of workers to organize and fight back.

Mickleburgh recounts the work of Indigenous peoples, immigrant workers and women, and the additional challenges of discrimination these groups faced in their attempts to make a living. And it is important here to note, as Mickleburgh does, that our history is not always pretty. In any era, unions exist within the broader social and political context, and at times in the past they adopted the racist and sexist attitudes then prevalent. Mickleburgh also captures the many moments in our past when various political persuasions from socialists to communists to anarchists and others played a leadership role in organizing workers to fight back. And he pays heed to the battles workers sometimes waged against other workers because of racial, political or organizational differences.

Not since Paul Phillips wrote *No Power Greater* fifty years ago has anyone tried to tell the overarching history of unions in BC. *On the Line* is timely; and in the limited space provided, Mickleburgh has chosen those

stories that give us the big picture. Thus, not everyone may see themselves or their union in this history. But the book does capture the essence of how we got to where we are today. And because the story takes us right up to the present, we are quick to realize that the battles and struggles for rights and fairness for working people goes on. It is even more important for those still active in leading, working for, organizing or representing workers in the union movement to know our history. Knowing where we have come from will help us move forward in our continuing fight for a better BC in a better world.

This book is both entertaining and inspirational. As I reflected on Mickleburgh's capacity to completely engage the reader, I realized it is not only because of my role in today's labour movement; it is just because he tells such a damn good story. And that story is our story.

The Sisterhood at the canteen. Five shop stewards with the Marine Workers and Boilermakers Union share a happy moment during lunch at Burrard Dry Dock, 1942.
North Vancouver Museum and Archives, 8073.

SPONSORING PARTNER'S MESSAGE

Community Savings began in the imagination of woodworkers attending a union meeting. Following a guest presentation from the treasurer of the Common Good Credit Union, ten IWA members from the New Westminster local took up the cause. By May 18, 1944, less than two months after the project was first discussed, the IWA (New Westminster) Credit Union was born. Needless to say, this co-operative venture enjoyed considerable support. Today's observer might wonder why.

If one considers the stratification of early to mid-twentieth-century society, the need becomes obvious. Workboots and hard hats were rarely seen inside the oak walls and marble halls of BC's financial institutions. Banks were not serving wage earners well, if at all. Workers and their families needed a place where they could both save and borrow.

At the time, traditional savings accounts

"Yes, the long memory is the most radical idea in this country. It is the loss of that long memory which deprives people of the connective flow of thoughts and events that clarifies our vision, not of where we're going, but where we want to go."
—Utah Phillips, American labour organizer, folk singer, storyteller, poet

showed little or no return. Yet credit union members of the 1940s received patronage dividends averaging 5 percent and share dividends of 3 percent. These dividends were probably the first interest payments workers would have earned, and the rates certainly exceeded bank interest.

On the lending side, the co-operative

The Common Good Co–operative Association formed BC's first Credit Union in 1936. This Victoria Day Parade entry displays the credit union umbrella protecting working people from hard times, financial distress and sickness. *Simon Fraser University Library, Special Collections and Rare Books.*

credit union philosophy was unique in the financial world: credit was extended primarily based on character, not wealth. People banded together to save money but they loaned it too. While collateral was weighed, the fundamental issue was how your peers thought of you. That character counted was a powerful idea.

In the language of the day, IWA Credit Union members needed loans for "providential purposes" first. In response, their credit union offered them "accommodation loans" of $10 to $50, to tide them over until the next payday. Early records show loans were then made for car purchases, furniture, house repairs, construction, insurance, funerals and most telling of all, medical expenses. There were few delinquencies.

Following a membership vote to provide "temporary office space," Community Savings found its first home in the local union office. A month later IWA members voted to install a door, "so the credit union could be locked up." This "temporary" arrangement lasted for several years until the credit union moved to 12th Street in New Westminster, near where a branch exists to this day. By the end of 1945 the credit union was well on the way. Embracing the co-operative spirit, rank-and-file members elected their first woman officer, Ellen Mitchell, at the December annual meeting.

After those beginnings, Community Savings merged with other "union bond" financial co-operatives. The credit unions of the Distillery Employees, Longshoremen's & Warehousemen's Union, Federal Civil Servants, Victoria Labour Council, Utilco and Operating Engineers became part of the whole. In 1977 the credit union became "open bond," and in 1999 was renamed "Community Savings" to reflect the wider base of membership. With branches in New Westminster, Surrey, Port Coquitlam, Burnaby, Vancouver and Victoria, its geographic presence has grown as well. But Community Savings continues to be governed by the union members of its board and union principles in its practice.

While many union workers, leaders and their organizations are members of Community Savings, none was more beloved than Jack Munro. Long after his retirement from the presidency of IWA Canada, he remained active in the workers' cause. On a day not so long ago, Jack arrived at the Vancouver branch and announced the BC Labour Heritage Centre was going to write a history of BC workers. As always, his enthusiasm was infectious. Sadly, fate had other plans.

Jack Munro's passing was hard. He had always been there—tough and kind in equal measure. Genuine and smart, he was a working-class hero. In the wake of Jack's passing, Community Savings' board of directors passed a motion to fully fund this history. "It was the least we could do," they said, "for a brother who gave so much."

From founding to present day, Community Savings' story is but one of countless histories—lived and supported by the collective action of British Columbia's working people and their unions. We hope you will take inspiration and heart from their tale.

Members, Board and Staff
Community Savings Credit Union

PREFACE

*by Ken Novakowski, chair, BC Labour
Heritage Centre*

In early summer of 2013, Jack Munro, then chair of the British Columbia Labour Heritage Centre, convened a meeting at the West Georgia Street White Spot restaurant to begin the process that would lead to the publication of *On the Line: A History of the British Columbia Labour Movement.* Attending were Jack Munro; Scott McCloy of WorkSafeBC; Howard White, owner of Harbour Publishing; and me. The consensus of the meeting was that a book providing an overview history of the BC labour movement was not only overdue but feasible given enough support from the labour movement. Following the meeting, Munro, who was battling health issues that would soon prove fatal, asked me to chair the new initiative.

That summer, the BC Federation of Labour and the Simon Fraser University Labour Studies Program were drawn in as partners to the project, and with the assistance of a grant of $10,000 provided by WorkSafeBC as seed money, work began on the BC Labour History Book Project. A significant development occurred in early spring of 2014 when Community Savings Credit Union came on board as the financing partner to the book, committing up to $200,000 toward the project. This credit union was originally formed by members of the International Woodworkers of America union, including Jack Munro, and CSCU wished to sponsor it to honour Jack's memory.

To develop the initial framework for the book, to acquire an author and to provide ongoing editorial direction for the book, the partners formed a steering committee consisting of me (representing the BC Labour Heritage Centre), Joey Hartman (BCLHC), Irene Lanzinger (BC Federation of Labour), Jim Sinclair (BCFed), Kendra Strauss (SFU Labour Studies Program), Michelle Laurie (BCLHC) and Mervyn Van Steinburg (BCLHC). An early contribution to the project was provided by Andy Neufeld, assisted by Robin Folvik and Dale McCartney. Author Rod Mickleburgh, editor Silas White and publisher Howard White took part in most meetings as did project assistants Robin Folvik and, later, Donna Sacuta.

As chair of both the steering committee and the BC Labour Heritage Centre, I was responsible for the overall co-ordination of the project and for keeping the funding partner fully informed of developments through frequent meetings with Doug Eveneshen, then president and CEO of Community Savings Credit Union.

From the outset, the planned book was to be an overview history of how working people, through their unions, got British Columbians to where we are today. It was never intended to be a book that encompassed everything of note in the history of BC's working people; it would take many volumes to do that. Many fine books have already been published on individual BC unions and many excellent studies have been written looking at BC labour through lenses ranging from Marxism to feminism to racism to post-colonialism, but the intent of this project was simply to tell BC labour's amazing story in as straightforward and comprehensive a manner as possible.

INTRODUCTION

A MILITANT LABOUR MOVEMENT HAS BEEN PART of British Columbia's identity going back to earliest times. The region's resource-based, frontier economy produced a toughened brand of worker, the result of onerous conditions, low pay and hard, hard work. Confrontations, when they took place, were often rough. For years the BC labour movement was the most combative in the land, full of radicals and talk of general strikes. There was rarely a time when the drive to increase profits at the expense of workers went unchallenged.

As with most movements, the influence of unions has ebbed and flowed. It has suffered painful divisions and enjoyed inspiring periods of solidarity. Unions have endured fierce, often violent opposition: firings, jailings, and red-baiting, not to mention intimidation by vigilantes, militias, cops, courts and hostile governments determined to keep them in their place. Some activists sacrificed their lives. Yet against all odds, unions remain a vital force in today's world.

The scenes depicted in these pages are but snapshots—hopefully representative ones—from 150-plus years of working-class struggle in workplaces everywhere in BC. Collectively these examples represent a remarkable saga of workers and unions that stands with any in the province's history. The figures who people these stories are among the heroes of British Columbia—not merely the trade union leaders, but the millions of workers, their names forgotten, who confronted those who would deny their right to take collective action in pursuit of better lives. While we celebrate builders of industrial empires like Robert and James Dunsmuir—their name writ large on streets and in the province's chronicles—those who dared challenge their single-minded pursuit of wealth at the expense of workers are remembered minimally, if at all.

Workers organizing to improve their lot started early. In 1850, eight years before the province of British Columbia was formed, Scots miners imported to work in the Hudson's Bay Company coal mine at Fort Rupert went on strike to protest the employer's violation of their contracts. It was a sign of things to come. More than sixty years

Indigenous lumber handlers, along with some Chileans and Hawaiians, gather near the Moodyville Sawmill on the north shore of Burrard Inlet in 1889. The man with the laundry bag is William Nahanee; he worked many years on the docks, serving as president of the groundbreaking Bows and Arrows union local formed in 1906. Fifth from the left is Joe Capilano, later a prominent chief of the Squamish.

Charles S. Bailey photo, City of Vancouver Archives, Mi P2.

later, several thousand coal miners spent two years on strike fighting just for the company to recognize their union. Only when they had spent their last penny did they finally surrender to the multiple forces arrayed against them. Despite many more early defeats, softened by a few satisfying victories, the BC labour movement kept on growing.

In its formative years labour often reflected the same racial divisions that prevailed in general society, but organization proceeded regardless. Nikkei[1] (Japanese) fishermen, not always in solidarity with other fishermen, regularly banded together to press for higher prices. So too did Indigenous[2] fishermen, who eventually formed their own permanent organi-

zation, the Native Brotherhood, to take on the fish companies. And on Burrard Inlet's north shore, Indigenous longshoremen formed a legendary union local proudly known as the "Bows and Arrows." Nikkei lumber workers had their own union in the forest industry well into the 1930s. South Asians[3] were also prominent in the forest industry, bolstering strong locals on the sawmilling side of the International Woodworkers of America (IWA). One of the union's prime organizers in the great sign-up campaigns of the 1940s was firebrand Darshan Singh Sangha. The IWA also hired Joe Miyazawa and Roy Mah to bridge the gap between its predominantly white membership and Nikkei and Chinese[4] workers, who

1 Nikkei refers throughout to people of Japanese ancestry living outside Japan.

2 The terms Indigenous people, Aboriginal people and First Nations are used interchangeably in this text.

3 South Asian as used throughout describes immigrants from India, mostly Sikhs from the Punjab region.

4 Chinese is used throughout to indicate immigrants of Chinese descent before the Citizenship Act of 1947 made them Canadian citizens.

had already shown their union solidarity during a difficult strike by the IWA at Blubber Bay.

The province's women have been part of union struggles since Vancouver telephone operators formed a union in the early 1900s. Their willingness to fight for their rights was demonstrated many times, leading to such historic events as the drive of the tiny Service, Office and Retail Workers Union of Canada (SORWUC) to organize bank workers and actions like the 1981 strike by underpaid daycare and social services workers at the Ray-Cam co-operative centre in East Vancouver. Partly as a result of the relative shrinkage of private-sector unions and the rise of unions in the public sector, women now form a majority of BC's trade union membership.

Well into the second decade of the twenty-first century the need for collective action has remained great, as shown in battles by BC teachers in their long and ultimately successful struggle to recapture previously negotiated classroom working conditions, and limestone quarriers who fought off company demands to end their seniority rights near the same Blubber Bay site on Texada Island where previous quarry workers had taken a stand seventy-seven years earlier.

Often overlooked by the headlines of strikes and pitched battles is the important social role BC unions have played. Over the years many unions have quietly established credit unions to serve workers denied access to loans and other services by the big banks. They have partnered for years with the United Way to help ensure a better social safety net for those in need, run summer camps for union kids and those who are disadvantaged, apprenticed prospective skilled workers and fought for the unemployed. They have pushed hard for employee-assistance programs to deal with alcohol and drug problems. They have built co-op housing, extended help to oppressed workers in other countries and donated money and volunteers to myriad causes.

Some reactionary forces in today's world would have us believe unions have gone out of style and outlived their usefulness. Yet it is recognized that the greatest threat facing western societies today, British Columbia prominent among them, is the widening gulf between rich and poor. As this book definitively shows, no force in society has proven more effective at promoting fairer distribution of the fruits of all peoples' labours than unions—which makes them more relevant in today's world, not less. It is our hope that *On the Line: A History of the British Columbia Labour Movement* will improve awareness of the contribution that unions have made and continue to make to our province, one so aptly expressed in their aspirational principle of more than a hundred years' standing: "What we desire for ourselves, we wish for all."

Let the story begin.

1

BEGINNINGS

THE RICH CULTURE AND SOCIETIES OF BRITISH COLUMBIA'S First Nations did not collapse the moment British explorer James Cook sailed into Nootka Sound on a blustery March day in 1778. In fact, for the next hundred years, despite the toll taken by smallpox, alcohol and guns, many First Nations more than held their own. On the coast, with their sophisticated governance based on clans and an existence based on salmon and cedar, the First Nations were among the most advanced and diverse in the Indigenous world. When BC entered Confederation in 1871, Indigenous people outnumbered non-Indigenous people nearly three to one; not until 1891 did non-Indigenous residents represent a majority of the population. Missing from most history books has been the role Aboriginal people played in driving the pioneer economy. For much of the nineteenth century, in addition to sustaining the critical fur trade, First Nations provided the bulk of wage labour in British Columbia. Logging, sawmilling, longshoring, mining, farming, canning and fishing all featured significant numbers of Indigenous workers in the workforce, willing to trade their labour for wages to improve their own lives and communities. The importance of First Nations to the growing settler economy was made clear by the province's attorney general in 1871:

> Every Indian who could and would work was employed in almost every branch of industrial and domestic life, at wages which would appear ... high in England or in Canada. From becoming labourers, some engaged in their own account in stock breeding, in river boating, and in packing, as carriers of merchandise by land and water. Others followed fishing and hunting with more vigour than formerly to supply the wants of the incoming population. The government frequently employed those living in the interior as police, labourers, servants, and as messengers entrusted with errands of importance.

Cook was not the first European to land on the BC coast, but it was his arrival that set the wheels of change in motion. Once white traders discovered the value of sea-otter pelts in China, the demand for the sleek, luxuriant fur was insatiable. Scores of ships plied the West Coast seeking furs that the inhabitants provided in staggering numbers. Skilled First Nations traders accumulated iron chisels and other metal tools and adornments, blankets, clothing, cloth, molasses, rice, bread, biscuits, guns and alcohol. Within just a few decades, the once plentiful sea otter was hunted to virtual extinction, but the more traditional land-based fur trade continued. None of it would have been possible without the province's First Nations, both men and women, who fed, guided and mostly welcomed the early fur traders and explorers as well as providing the furs once trading posts were established.

As with coastal First Nations, whose first word to Cook was *makúk* ("let's trade"), trade was hardly new to the Indigenous people of the BC Interior. They had been trading for centuries via a network of age-old trails that elaborately wound through difficult terrain. In particular, there was the storied "grease trail" that carried precious oil from the oolichan to almost everywhere. Both West Coast and Interior Indigenous people had been quick to embrace trade in furs. Each new post, including the key colonial trading hub of Fort Langley, was quickly surrounded by native encampments anxious to barter whatever they had, including labour, for new possessions.

When Fort Victoria was erected in 1843, the Lekwungen (whom settlers called the Songhees) moved their biggest village close to the fort and even helped build its large stockade, receiving one blanket for every forty pickets they cut. With so few non-Indigenous people on hand, there was plenty of work to be had. By 1853, the Lekwungen had amassed sufficient wealth to host a massive potlatch attended by three thousand guests, sparking a seasonal migration of several thousand Indigenous people every year over the next three decades, some of them canoeing as many as a thousand kilometres to spend six months or so near Victoria. Governor James Douglas wrote in 1854 that they were drawn "by the prospect of obtaining employment as labourers and procuring by their industry supplies of clothing for themselves and families."

The opportunity for Indigenous people to trade goods enhanced many aspects of their daily lives without serious disruption. Throughout the fur trade, they retained control of their traditional territories. Fur traders were not settlers; most got along with those who permanently inhabited the land. When one fur trader tried to push his weight around against the "savages," Chief Kwah of the Dakelh Nation near Fort St. James, who supplied abundant salmon to the trading post, spoke for many with his dignified resistance when he reminded trader Daniel Harmon: "Do I not manage my affairs as well as you? When did you ever hear that I was in danger of starving? I never want for anything, and my family is always well clothed."

Vancouver Island became a Crown colony in 1849—not long before things began to change. Within a few decades, the economy of BC was taken over by the beginnings of a rampant capitalism reaping as much profit as possible from the province's rich resources—a formula that remains in place today. BC's abundant supply of timber, minerals and salmon was opened up for mass exploitation. Working for wages soon eclipsed the fur trade. Yet for most of the next fifty years—even as many of their villages were decimated by disease—Indigenous people continued to adapt. When jobs were to be had in the nineteenth century, they were glad to take them; their sweat and toil drove much of BC's early resource economy.

First Nations were in the thick of the

muddled, unassuming start to the fledgling resource boom. Members of the Kwagi-ulth subgroup of the Kwakwaka'wakw First Nation alerted the Hudson's Bay Company to the presence of surface coal near their village by present-day Port Hardy. With the advent of steamships, coal had become a valu-able mineral, and the HBC established Fort Rupert to extract it in 1849. The first miners were the local Kwagiulth inhabitants who mined the surface coal with axes and crow-bars, then transported it to offshore ships by canoe, receiving one large blanket for every two tons of coal. At the same time, the Kwa-giulth asserted their ownership of the coal-fields, forcing Douglas to negotiate a treaty to gain access.

A cockamamie scheme was hatched to import a group of experienced Scottish miners to sink shafts and mine the more lucrative underground coal seams. Most of them eventually deserted Fort Rupert for the California gold rush, with the help of a rival Kwakwaka'wakw group, the Nahwitti. Doug-las complained that the Scottish miners had not "turned out a single bushel of coal since their arrival, all the coal we have hitherto sold being the produce of Indian labour."

Among a group of Scotsmen hired to replace the deserters at Fort Rupert was a man who would dominate the BC coal-mining industry for more than thirty years. Robert Dunsmuir, as hard as the rock faces that made him wealthy, was perhaps the most merciless foe workers in British Columbia ever faced. Beset by scurvy, loss of life and harrowing sailing conditions, Dun-smuir's trip from Scotland lasted nearly eight

Snuneymuxw Chief Ki–et–sa–kun (centre) first alerted the Hudson's Bay Company to the presence of coal in the Nanaimo area, which proved far more bountiful than the meagre pickings of Fort Rupert. The Snuneymuxw were the area's first coal miners. Image D-07259 Royal BC Museum and Archives.

months—after he agreed to go on barely a day's notice with his wife pregnant. On arrival, Dunsmuir separated himself from the other miners, impressing his overseers by completing his contract. When coal petered out in Fort Rupert, the HBC dispatched him to Nanaimo, where local First Nations had identified an abundance of deeper, thicker seams. There, in time, Dunsmuir founded his empire.

As in Fort Rupert, the Indigenous inhabitants of the nearest Snuneymuxw villages were the first miners, gleaning surface deposits and loading the coal onto ships by canoe, lugged and transported by women who earned tickets for blankets and shirts at the company store. Like the Kwagiulth, they too claimed ownership of the coal seams, forcing Douglas to compensate them and negotiate another treaty to obtain clear access. The 1854 agreement with the Snuneymuxw was the last of the fourteen so-called Douglas Treaties signed with Vancouver Island First Nations. All received compensation, recognition of their existing village sites and surrounding fields, plus the unrestricted right to continue hunting and fishing on the large tracts of traditional territory they gave up.

In 1858, news of gold found along the Thompson River reached San Francisco, where hordes of penniless miners who had failed to strike it rich in the fabled California gold rush of 1849 still lingered. Soon, tens of thousands of unruly prospectors were making their way to the distant canyons and riverbanks of the Fraser and Thompson Rivers. There were no laws, no authorities, no regulations and plenty of Aboriginal people who had inhabited the region for eons. Alarmed, Douglas rushed to the region to assert sovereignty and in August the British government established a second colony, calling it for the first time British Columbia. But this did not head off a little-known brief but bloody conflict between the Nlaka'pamux First Nation and several vigilante militias formed by the gold-rush invaders. Numerous casualties occurred before the parties agreed to a truce

that promised tolerance for the rights of both sides.

By the end of the year more than twenty-five thousand rambunctious, predominantly American newcomers had pushed through Victoria and were strung out in makeshift camps along the Fraser and the Thompson. Rarely in any gold rush had so many arrived in such a short time. The pickings proved relatively modest, however, and most moved on to try their luck elsewhere, particularly in the Cariboo where a new gold rush erupted. But the sudden, dramatic influx of 1858 was the beginning of British Columbia's modern history.

Victoria became a bustling outpost overrun by thousands of miners waiting for their licences to prospect. Businesses emerged like mushrooms after a heavy rain to supply the miners with dry goods and materials. In the former wilds, crude transportation and horse-packing networks sprang up to deliver the miners and their bulky possessions to the gold fields. Local Indigenous people again showed their willingness to work. They panned and dug for gold, they were hired to help white miners work their claims, and they kept the miners fed and supplied, skillfully packing in goods through the harsh, rocky terrain by horseback. Indigenous labourers maintained their packing dominance until motor vehicles came along in the early part of the twentieth century.

For a brief time, during the larger and more lucrative Cariboo rush a few years later, the pop-up wilderness community of Barkerville was the continent's largest city north of San Francisco and west of Chicago. A significant number of the thousands who sought gold were Chinese. In addition to mining, some Chinese immigrants went into business, establishing BC's first Chinatown on the outskirts of Barkerville. Although the frenzy eventually died out, there were now roads and steamship services into the Interior and the beginnings of thriving settlements.

For the working people of British Columbia, the gold rush also launched the province

Indigenous family hard at work seeking gold in the latter years of the 19th century with sluice boxes and pans on the banks of the Thompson River, near its confluence with the Fraser.

Image D–O6815 Royal BC Museum and Archives.

on the journey from which it has never veered, an economy based on harvesting riches that only had to be found to be exploited. Alone among Canada's provinces, with only 4 percent of its large, forbidding land base suitable for growing, BC was not nurtured by agricultural roots. By and large, it was shaped by a capitalist thirst for natural resources and the sweat of industrial labour. Historian Martin Robin assesses BC as a province "primarily built by the working class," amid a corporate entrepreneurship that was "speculative, acquisitive and adven-

turesome." While it took thirty more years for Indigenous people to be supplanted as British Columbia's main workforce, the great transformation was now in motion. Settlers, not fur traders, were dictating the future.

The road to what became by far BC's number-one industry started in the 1860s with small-scale logging and sawmills to cut the timber. As the forest industry expanded, Indigenous people flocked to the mills and woods to do the work. On Vancouver Island and along Burrard Inlet, all newly built sawmills relied on Indigenous workers, many of

Indigenous workers running a drag–fishing operation for sockeye along the shores of the Nimpkish River, across from Alert Bay. Regulations eventually put an end to these fisheries that snared fish as they entered the mouth of a river.
Image E–O4636 Royal BC Museum and Archives.

whom travelled from far up the coast for the chance to earn wages there and across the border in Puget Sound. Pay was not all that bad for the time, said to be between at least $20 and $30 a month plus board at several Burrard sawmills in 1875.

Although claim to the province's seemingly infinite forests, featuring some of the tallest trees in the world, was unceremoniously taken from those who had frequented them for millennia, that didn't stop Indigenous loggers from harvesting them. Until increased mechanization and more regulated production methods cut into the industry, hand-logging was part of the work rhythm of many Indigenous labourers. Legendary Squamish chief August Jack Khatsalano

started in the forest industry at a young age in False Creek sawmills and developed a successful logging partnership that he ran into the 1930s.

On the docks, as the port of Vancouver developed to handle the province's budding export trade, nearly all the heavy lifting was initially done by members of the Squamish and Tsleil-Waututh Nations just across the waters of Burrard Inlet. As time went on, these longshoremen became famous for their ability to load lumber, a specialized niche of the trade they dominated for decades, praised by the likes of timber baron H.R. MacMillan for their speed. "They were the greatest men that ever worked the lumber," said veteran dock worker Ed Long.

Chief Joe Capilano worked lumber on the waterfront to help finance his historic trip to London in 1906 to present a petition of First Nations grievances to King Edward VII. The longshore tradition continued well into the twentieth century, producing three different incarnations (1906–07, 1913–16 and 1924–33) of a primarily Squamish and Tsleil-Waututh union local known to everyone on the waterfront as the Bows and Arrows, and providing Chief Dan George a living for twenty-seven years before he became a celebrated actor in the 1970s.

But no industry was more central to BC's Indigenous people than fishing. Celebrated in their art and culture, salmon drew Indigenous people to the coast and to the great rivers of the Interior. The West Coast's rich annual salmon runs, particularly of sockeye, sustained First Nations villages for almost the entire year. So when BC's post-Confederation resource boom began to recognize the value of salmon, Indigenous people were in the forefront. From the 1870s onward, thanks to the Industrial Revolution, cheap canned salmon found a huge market among millions of British workers driven from agricultural land to factory sweatshops. With so much money to be made and the salmon there for the taking, a second gold-rush mentality began to sweep the Fraser.

Some of the most prominent corporate tycoons in BC got their start in the business of canning salmon. By the end of the century, dozens of canneries dotted the coast and lined the banks of the Fraser and salmon rivers farther north. For the better part of that time Indigenous men did almost all the fishing, working from dawn to dusk in small gillnet skiffs supplied by the canners. Couples often worked together, the men catching salmon for $2.25 a day and their wives working the oars for a dollar.

Indigenous women were vital to the industry. Besides helping on the fishing grounds, they worked inside the canneries, sharing the labour-intensive processing and canning with Chinese immigrants. As vividly described by historian Rolf Knight, it was not easy work: "They worked amid a Rube Goldberg collection of steam vats, chutes, canning machines, hoses, pipes, steam, clanking transmission belts and other paraphernalia." Ten-hour days were the norm. When runs were at their peak, shifts were even longer.

The commercial fishing industry became part of the seasonal life for thousands of Aboriginal people. In *Makúk*, his thorough examination of the labour history of BC's First Nations, historian John Lutz estimates that a family of four working in the canneries could earn as much in three or four months as a skilled white tradesman over an entire year. Many travelled long distances for the work, camping on their own or housed in company-built cabins. Once the salmon runs were over, they would return to their communities for the winter to engage in a regular round of ceremonial dances, potlatches and renewal of their ancestral ways.

With their well-developed subsistence economies, Indigenous people were attracted to seasonal jobs: fishing, canning, logging and, toward the end of the century, harvesting hops. They sought wages as add-ons rather than as a means of survival. Yet with the fur trade's diminished importance, First Nations workers were important to the emerging economy of British Columbia. John Lutz concludes, "Coal would not have been mined in the 1840s and 1850s, export sawmills would have been unable to function in the 1860s and 1870s, and canneries would have had neither fishing fleet nor fish processors in the 1870s and 1880s without the widespread participation of aboriginal people."

In general, the wages Indigenous workers earned were used to enhance their traditions rather than to buy into "the white man's ways." Money allowed the accumulation of goods that were then given away at traditional potlatches. But non-Indigenous authorities considered the potlatch an affront to Christian-based materialism and a barrier to assimilation. They moved to ban the practice in the mid-1880s. Until then and for a spell thereafter, Indigenous culture and artisanship flourished. "There was never a time in the history of the Province when the Indians have been so prosperous as during the present year," wrote Indian superintendent Israel Wood Powell in his annual report for 1882.

It was not to last. In 1881, ten years after BC joined Confederation, Indigenous people were still a majority in the province; twenty years later, they constituted a mere 14.3 percent. Besides the loss of land, the banning of the potlatch and the ravages of disease, a succession of other calamities followed. After the Canadian Pacific Railway was completed in 1885, Indigenous people were crowded out by wave after wave of non-Indigenous settlers, the pell-mell drive for profit and outright discrimination by whites who wanted BC for themselves. In every industry where Aboriginal people had once laboured productively, they found themselves squeezed by new government restrictions on their hunting, fishing and trapping rights, and the desire by employers for year-round workers coupled with growing mechanization.

2 BRITISH COLUMBIA AND CANADA TAKE ROOT

———————

THE HEART OF THE SLOW BUT STEADY expansion of BC's emerging capitalism in the last half of the nineteenth century lay in the bounteous coalfields of Vancouver Island. And nowhere was working-class conflict more evident. From the beginning, the Island's miners waged a continuous, uphill battle for better wages, an end to hazardous working conditions and the simple right to join a union. Although their many strikes failed to achieve all their goals, the coal miners' tenacity passed on to future generations of industrial workers in BC a stout tradition of fighting hard to win the wages and workplace conditions they deserved.

The seeds of struggle had been sown at the Island's very first coal-mining operation at Fort Rupert in 1850, when the small group of miners hired from Scotland, aghast at conditions, downed their tools and refused to work. Two were clapped in irons for breaking their contract. Barely a year into its operation, the mine had already seen the province's first strike and the first punishment of workers for standing up for their rights.

Conditions in the early Vancouver Island mines were brutal, made worse by the paltry pay. Strikes occurred in 1861 (short), 1865–66 (six months) and 1870–71 (five months). The second dispute was a harbinger of things to come. For the first time, Chinese workers, many of them refugees from the end of the gold rush, were hired as strikebreakers. With the strike broken, they were kept on. Initially, the Chinese were paid the same wages as white miners. That didn't last long. Ordering their pay cut in half, the mine's general manager James Nicol explained, "If we are to pay the Chinaman the same rate of wage as the white men, there will be no use employing them." After that, the Chinese presence was consistently opposed by most white workers; almost all subsequent strikes featured a demand to ban Chinese workers from the mines.

Meanwhile, Lady Luck smiled for good on the determined Robert Dunsmuir. On one of his regular prospecting forays in 1869, he stumbled over a large tree root. When he took a second look, he saw that the root was laced with coal. The ambitious Scotsman had discovered the famous Wellington Seam that made his fortune. The instant coal-mining community of Wellington was soon BC's first company town. Small family homes, boarding houses for single miners and the general store were all built and owned by Dunsmuir, Diggle and Company. "A capitalist is one who lives on less than he earns," Dunsmuir liked to boast and in his case, what he earned was immense. He soon built a fine house for himself and his large family overlooking Nanaimo.

Conflict between the miners below, many of whom brought their British working-class sensibility with them, and their master on the hill was rarely absent. An attempt to resist a pay cut fizzled out in 1876, but the next year the miners had a union, the Coal-

miners' Mutual Protective Society, the second such miners' organization in Canada. This time, they took on Dunsmuir for real. When the mine owner rejected demands that their old rates be restored and the company fix a faulty scale, they walked off the job.

It was Dunsmuir's first serious labour dispute, and he responded with what became his standard hard-line response. Striking miners were ordered out of their company-owned homes, strikebreakers were brought in to keep the mine running and Dunsmuir served notice that anyone who dared strike against him would never be rehired. When the resolute miners began giving strikebreakers a difficult time, Dunsmuir added a fourth plank

Nanaimo coal miners gather at the pithead of one of the area's first mines in the early 1870s.
Image B–03624, Royal BC Museum and Archives.

to his strike strategy, convincing the government to send in the militia. This early alliance between capital and the state to impede BC workers from asserting their rights set the tone for industrial relations in the province for years to come.

In response, the miners had their courage, solidarity and a relentless quest for decent wages, safe mines and the right to join a union. They also had the active support of their wives and daughters. When a group of newly hired strikebreakers showed up during the 1877 strike, women gathered at the pithead, children clutching their skirts, and shouted, "Have you come to take the bread and butter out of our mouths?" When the militia first attempted to force miner families out of their homes, one cadet was thrown off a bridge while others were kicked and punched by a line of women as they passed by. But with dwindling resources and the mine still producing coal, the miners could not hold out forever. After four stubborn months, they called off their strike, managing to at least secure proper regulation over the scale that weighed their coal production for payment.

Not surprisingly, no one relished the chance to hire Chinese workers for abysmal wages and use them to maintain production during strikes more than Robert Dunsmuir. By 1878 a third of his 240 miners were Chinese, often working underground as runners who pushed empty coal cars to the rock face. Testifying before a Royal Commission on Chinese immigration, Dunsmuir praised their work habits and willingness to take on unappetizing tasks shunned by whites. Their low wages were also attractive to the mining magnate. Mine owners would be unable to compete in the coal marketplace if Chinese workers were not available "at much smaller pay," Robert Dunsmuir told the commission. "I consider their presence beneficial to the progress and development of the country."

By 1881 there were 4,350 Chinese immigrants in British Columbia. They hailed from a handful of counties bordering the city of Canton in southern China. Desperate poverty, overpopulation and a series of violent uprisings drove them to try their luck abroad, willing to pay agents hefty sums for the passage. Almost all were men. Thousands more arrived to work on the massive project that, like the gold rush, was to fundamentally change the BC economy. A key to BC joining Confederation, construction of the Canadian Pacific Railway galvanized the province, facilitating access to markets across Canada and establishing its terminus, Vancouver, as a major port for exports.

But first it had to be built. With towering cliffs plunging straight to the raging river below, no section, not even Rogers Pass, was more difficult and costly than the route through the Fraser Canyon. The major contractor, an American by the name of Andrew Onderdonk, said the railway could not be built through the canyon at an affordable cost without hiring Chinese labourers at a dollar a day. Dubbed "thundering grasshoppers" by white workers earning at least twice the wages, an estimated seventeen thousand Chinese immigrants worked at various times on the railroad.

Their heroic labour, under conditions that could hardly have been worse, was a major contribution to Canadian history. Working in gangs of thirty and often assigned the most dangerous tasks, including tunnel blasting, they died in the hundreds, usually without medical care. Head engineer Henry Cambie recorded Chinese deaths during a somewhat uneventful two-month period: one knocked into the river by a falling rock, one crushed by a rolling log, one buried in a rock slide, another smothered in a cave-in, while an unknown number drowned when their boat overturned in the Fraser River. Typical of white attitudes that did not take note of Chinese workers, the *Yale Sentinel* reported "no deaths" had taken place over the same period. Restricted to a diet of vegetable-free rice and ground salmon, shivering in drafty tents during the winter, more fell victim to scurvy and other diseases. All told, as many as six hundred Chinese workers are estimated to have died before the CPR's last spike was driven by the railway's well-dressed, top-hatted directors at Craigellachie in 1885.

From their princely pay of a dollar a day, Chinese railway labourers still had to pay for their passage from China, their contractor, clothes, tools and other incidentals. It was difficult to save more than $40 a year. Few made it back to China. Those in charge praised them as good, honest workers who mostly lived up to the terms of their contracts. But they were not passive. Brawls and work stoppages erupted if they felt they were being shortchanged or needlessly exposed to danger. It was estimated that hiring Chinese

On the same day, Nov. 7, 1885, that CPR railway tycoon Sir Donald Smith drove in the last spike of the national railway near Revelstoke (top), some of the workers who built the railway posed for their own last–spike ceremony (bottom). *Images E–02200 and C–00618, Royal BC Museum and Archives.*

"coolies" saved Onderdonk and the CPR between $3 and $5 million while helping to suppress wage demands from white railway workers. "Either you must have this labour, or you can't have the railway," declared Prime Minister John A. Macdonald.

As the railway neared completion, however, the establishment's real attitudes emerged. Once-valued Chinese workers were abandoned in their remote camps without transport and little food and water. Only intervention by some Vancouver charities rescued them from their plight. While the CPR was under construction, Macdonald had resisted persistent demands from British Columbians to restrict Chinese immigration. But when they were no longer needed, he moved quickly to impose a fifty-dollar head tax on Chinese immigrants. This made good on his avowal two years earlier that the federal government could stop Chinese immigration at any time "and therefore there is no fear of a permanent degradation of the country by a mongrel race."

Back on the mining front, Dunsmuir had bought out the last of his original partners in

WONG HAU-HON, RAILWAY WORKER

The thousands of Chinese immigrants who endured so much helping to unite Canada by rail left little record of their ordeal. But we do have one personal account written by former railway worker Wong Hau-hon in 1926. Following are some excerpts from his account:

"I first came to Canada in 1882," he wrote. "We debarked at Westminster. I set out on foot with about four hundred Chinese to join the railroad construction crews at Yale. We had worked only two days when the white foreman ordered our gang to move to North Bend. It rained all day. We were wet and cold. Some arrivals, unaccustomed to the Canadian climate, sickened and died, as they rested beneath the trees or lay on the ground. When I saw this, I felt miserable and sad."

"At China Bar, many Chinese had died from an epidemic. As there were no coffins, bodies were stuffed into rock crevices or beneath trees to await burial. Some were buried on the spot in boxes made of crude planks. Some were buried wrapped only in blankets or grass mats. The sight of these new graves dotting the landscape sent chills up and down my spine."

"We were ordered to Hope. The work there was very dangerous. On one occasion, a huge rock had to be removed by blasting. More than three hundred barrels of explosives were used. When blasting, the workers usually hid away in a safe place. But there was one, Leung, who had gone behind another hill, where he thought he would be safe. He lit his pipe while waiting for the blasting to proceed. Unexpectedly, a huge boulder thrown up by the blast landed on the hillside where Leung was sitting. It rolled down the slope, hitting him in the back. We heard a piercing shriek. By the time we reached him, Leung was dead."

"Another incident occurred west of Yale. Twenty dynamite charges were ignited to blast a rock cave, but only eighteen went off. The white foreman, thinking all the dynamite went off, ordered the Chinese workers to enter the cave to resume work. Just at that moment, the last two charges exploded. Chinese bodies flew from the cave as if shot from a cannon. Blood and flesh were mixed in a horrible mess. About ten or twenty workers were killed."

"So many Chinese labourers died from epidemics and accidents. I am now sixty-two and have experienced much hardship and difficulties in my life. I am proud of the fact that we Chinese contributed much to the development of transportation in Canada. Yet now the government is enforcing discriminatory immigration regulations against us. The Canadian people must surely have short memories!"

Source: Joe Huang and Sharon Quan Wong, eds., *Chinese Americans: Realities and Myths Anthology* (San Francisco: The Association of Chinese Teachers, 1997), 14–15.

1883 and brought his sons into the operation. James Dunsmuir, who became mine manager, was perhaps even more anti-union than his father. The Dunsmuirs, and the mines themselves, did much to stoke workers' militancy. Vancouver Island's nineteenth-century coal mines were dank, dirty and exceedingly dangerous. Fatalities were so commonplace that the primary purpose of many early miner organizations was providing funerals and pensions for the widows. The mines provided such a steady flow of customers that one local furniture manufacturer ended up focusing on caskets and undertaking. Suffocating gases, flooding, rock mishaps, roof collapses and accidental explosions exacted a terrible toll. Mine inspections were lax, the dangers of certain work practices and coal-dust accumulation not readily understood. Safety lamps tended to be shunned by the miners, who preferred open-flame lamps because they provided more light.

On May 3, 1887, deep in one of the Vancouver Coal Mining and Land Company slopes under Nanaimo Harbour, a poorly placed shot of black powder caused an outward blast that set off a series of escalating coal dust explosions that spread quickly through the entire mine. Those not killed immediately were trapped, scratching heartbreaking messages in the ground as their oxygen ran out: 150 men lost their lives, 46 women their husbands and 126 children their fathers. Among the dead were 53 Chinese workers, identified only by payroll numbers: "Chinamen 89, 100, 95, 84, 123 …" "I heard a sound like a heavy fall of rock, and then I felt the wind coming up the slope," survivor Jules Michael reported. "When I felt the rush, I said, 'My God, boys! What is coming on us now?'" Among the victims were many pioneers from the very beginning of coal mining on the Island, including Archibald Muir, one of those clapped in irons more than thirty-five years earlier in Fort Rupert. It remains the worst mining disaster in BC history and the second worst in Canada.

Barely eight months later, a second

So common were mine fatalities that the reverse side of early miners' union ribbons was black, so they could easily be turned into ribbons of mourning. *Courtesy David Yorke.*

calamity rocked the close-knit mining community, this one at Dunsmuir's operation in Wellington. A methane gas explosion ripped through the mine's eastern slope, taking seventy-seven lives. These two catastrophic explosions occurring so close together gave

FIRE DAMP.

Terrible Explosion at No. 1 Shaft,

Vancouver Coal Company, Nanaimo.

One Hundred and Fifty Men in the Mine.

Twelve Bodies Taken Out up to Midnight.

A Member of the Rescuing Party is Asphyxiated.

Little Hope Entertained for The Total Number.

The Mine is Now Burning Fiercely.

Heartrending Scene at the Mouth of the Shaft.

Medicines and Surgeons Telegraphed for to Relieve Sufferers.

A Special Train Leaves for the Scene at 1 This Morning.

tragic fuel to a long-simmering demand by the region's white coal miners. Although there was no evidence implicating Chinese workers in either disaster, the cry to ban them from the area's mines as a danger to safety soon swept aside any opposition. At a huge meeting in the opera hall, with emotions still raw from the heavy loss of life, not even Robert Dunsmuir could withstand the feelings of the community. To great cheers, he vowed to ban all Chinese workers from the payroll of his Wellington mine.

But the Dunsmuirs resolutely refused, even in the face of provincial legislation prohibiting all Chinese coal miners from working underground, to stop employing them at their large unionized mine in Cumberland.

Eventually, in a landmark constitutional case, the British Privy Council overturned BC's legislation, ruling that it was a matter of federal jurisdiction. In a brazen show of nerve, James Dunsmuir docked his Chinese miners fifty cents a month to help pay his court costs. They responded with a one-day strike and Dunsmuir relented.

In spite of their knock-downs, miners kept getting up off the mat and continuing to fight. They had struck and lost in 1883, and were again humiliated by Robert Dunsmuir in a short-lived dispute in 1889. When a miners' delegation tried to reason with him, he advised them, "Tell the men that I am a stubborn Scotchman, and that a multitude cannot coerce or drive me." The words could

Above: The front page of Victoria's *British Colonist* newspaper headlines the Nanaimo mine disaster in 1887, the second–deadliest in Canadian history.
British Colonist, May 4, 1887, p. 1.

Right: Crowds and families, including several Indigenous women, wait desperately for news after the lethal 1887 explosion at the Vancouver Coal Mining and Land Company's Number One Esplanade mine in Nanaimo. The blast claimed 150 lives.
Image C–03711, Royal BC Museum and Archives.

have served as his epitaph, notes historian Jeremy Mouat. Three months later Robert Dunsmuir was dead, and the reins of R. Dunsmuir & Sons were taken over by his son James.

By then, coal production in the Nanaimo area was at record levels, split among mines owned by the New Vancouver Coal Mining and Land Company (NVCMLC), the Dunsmuirs and the small East Wellington Coal Company. Nanaimo was no longer a rough, isolated frontier town of small houses and muddy streets. There was a railway to Victoria, steamship runs to and from Vancouver, a real estate boom, schools, manufacturing, a good newspaper, electricity, sports teams, a renowned brass band and an opera house. But class tensions were ever-present, fanned by the Dunsmuirs' fervent anti-unionism.

The difference between the Dunsmuir mines and those of the NVCMLC was stark. Rather than Dunsmuir-style company housing, their larger rivals provided five-acre lots to their workers, limited underground shifts to eight hours and recognized their union. The Dunsmuir mines had longer workdays, lower wages, no gas and pit committees to look after safety, and of course, no union. Strikers were blacklisted and union sympathizers regularly fired. Despite these conditions and their humiliation just a year before, Dunsmuir miners were ready to take on the company yet again in 1890. While there was some grudging respect and even admiration for the elder Dunsmuir, few had a good word for the thirty-nine-year-old, hard-nosed James Dunsmuir.

On February 1, 1890, a thousand boisterous miners packed the opera house to back a new union. The Miners' and Mine Laborers' Protective Association (MMLPA) represented a majority of all Nanaimo and Wellington miners for the first time. It was a heady start for the fledgling organization. Members successfully petitioned the legislature to ban Chinese underground miners. On May Day the union staged the grandest event in Nanaimo's young history, a gala gathering at the opera house. A train was chartered for the Wellington miners. Brass bands played and dancing went on until four in the morning.

A few weeks later after another spirited day of marches and music, the union was ready to take on Dunsmuir's Wellington mine for yet another round, demanding union recognition and an eight-hour day. "The day is [past] when we must go to the rich man's door and beg," vowed union leader Tully Boyce at a mass outdoor meeting. This time strike leaders had a strategy. In an impressive show of cross-border solidarity, union workers on the docks of San Francisco readily agreed not to handle Dunsmuir coal, strikebreakers were "talked to," convincing many to leave, and public sympathy soared when the miners peacefully complied with notices turning them out of their company homes. The mayors of New Westminster and Victoria offered money and tents, and the freshly formed Vancouver Trades and Labor Council (VTLC) held a large public fundraiser.

Still, despite the union's best efforts, Dunsmuir managed to hire enough strikebreakers to resume mining operations in early August. A few days later, several hundred strikers gathered to accompany the scabs to the pithead, then jeered them back to town. Dunsmuir and his government allies jumped on the minor incident. A day later, fifty-five militia men were dispatched by magistrates in Victoria to keep the peace that already existed. Although five strikers were arrested for intimidation, the push to discourage strikebreakers continued. Among the successes was a group of thirty black labourers brought in from Comox who refused to work, while a number of strikebreakers hired in San Francisco wound up in the pub sharing a pint or two with the strikers instead, and headed elsewhere.

The militia's presence actually increased local support for the strikers. Hotels offered the strikers free drinks, a travelling theatre troupe staged a benefit performance, and two thousand supporters participated in an exuberant September parade with myriad floats and banners proclaiming, "We Can Stand Cold and Hunger But Not Injustice." So much donated money flowed in, along with a siphoned 10 percent of wages from non-striking NVCMLC miners, that the union was able to double its strike pay. The MMLPA union worked feverishly to muster national and international support. Leaders sent a three-person delegation to Ottawa to seek help from the Trades and Labor Congress of Canada (TLC).[5] The group included Thomas Salmon, an Aboriginal union member who so impressed those he encountered that he met John A. Macdonald and was asked to chair a TLC committee.

The Nanaimo-based coal miners' union and its inspiring strike, along with a new desire to increase the political clout of the working class, led to the formation of British Columbia's first provincial labour federation toward the end of 1890. Twenty delegates from the labour councils of Vancouver, Victoria and host Nanaimo attended the gathering. MMLPA president Tully Boyce was elected to head the organization. Although the provincial federation did not last, it amplified the voice for key union issues such as the eight-hour day, opposition to Chinese immigration and expanding commitment to political involvement.

Farsighted strike leaders continued to work hard to expand union solidarity beyond Vancouver Island. Even legendary US craft union leader Samuel Gompers, not known for radical rhetoric, weighed in, calling the Dunsmuir operation "one of the most villainous, grasping corporations that ever lived." But the company's relentless efforts to import strikebreakers was paying off. Nearly three hundred were working at the Wellington mine by the end of the year. And the onset of rainy, chilly, sometimes snowy weather significantly worsened life in the strikers' tents, strung out in the words of one observer like "a second Gettysburg." When a procession of non-union members riding back to town was pelted with a flurry of hard-packed snowballs, the pro-Dunsmuir government responded by arresting sixteen strikers at their next march to the mine and charging them with intimidation.

Before the next union action could even begin, the Riot Act was read, making mass gatherings illegal. After a rousing version of "La Marseillaise," the miners dispersed. A large number of women responded with their own "March for Female Suffrage" through the streets of Nanaimo. When a taunting youth struck one of the women with the back of his hand, she took after her assailant, calling him "a blackleg son of a bitch" and threatening him with a rock. But the ban on union marches sapped the miners' spirits. Working miners began to question giving some of their wages to the strikers, whose ranks had dwindled as the strike dragged on into a second summer. Some hearts remained strong. "I am keeping the marrow on my bones, and not letting it go out," said one. Yet they knew the jig was up. In November, strikers voted by secret ballot to end their eighteen-month walkout.

It was a bitter defeat. More than twenty years were to elapse before the tough miners of Vancouver Island were ready to take on the Dunsmuirs one last time. In the meantime, they lost none of their class consciousness. Instead of strikes, they poured their energy into politics and the wave of socialism that was beginning to sweep the province. Nanaimo became a centre for radicalism and hostility toward the ruling class in British Columbia.

Although the fighting miners of Nanaimo spearheaded nineteenth-century labour resistance to the forces of capitalism, they had not been alone in the struggle to advance the cause of BC workers. In fact, the first appearance of a union occurred less than a year after the 1858 gold-rush flood engulfed Victoria, when a local newspaper notice announced formation of the Bakers' Society, which resolved to protect its trade and regulate "the wages of journeymen" so they did not have to work on Sunday. What happened to the society after that is lost in the mist of time, but no record exists of an earlier labour

5 For many years, the American spelling, labor, was predominant in the Canadian labour movement.

organization. Other unions followed, representing workers such as printers, shipwrights and construction trades. Almost all were relatively small craft unions organized around a specific skill rather than covering an entire work site.

It was only with the dramatic charge to the economy brought on by the transcontinental railway that jobs increased and workers outside Nanaimo began to rally around the flag of the proletariat. Much of the fervour came from the arrival of the Knights of Labor. The Knights started out as a secret holy order for working people in the United States. It soon progressed to a high-profile force that pressed for labour reform, particularly an eight-hour day, and raising the status of workers in society. Unlike closed-door craft unions, the Knights of Labor was open to anyone who was white and worked for a living. At its peak in the mid-1880s, one in five US workers belonged to the Knights, before internal divisions and structural problems precipitated a rapid decline.

The Knights also struck a chord with BC workers, who were frustrated by a succession of losing strikes and failure to make any headway on such broad issues as shorter working hours, mine safety and wage competition from increasing numbers of Chinese immigrants. These matters, they began to realize, needed to be addressed beyond their immediate workplace. The Knights' first assembly in BC was in 1883 in Nanaimo, where they operated a successful co-operative store providing members with goods that were cheaper than the Dunsmuir company store.

Over the next three years, a dozen other assemblies came into being, representing a cross-section of industrial workers stretched across the southern half of the province. The Knights had close ties with the province's first labour newspaper, *Industrial News*, published in Victoria. The Knights also backed the first organized attempt to elect pro-labour candidates. Two in Victoria and two in Nanaimo, including Knights' organizer Sam

Myers, were nominated by the new Workingmen's Party to run in the 1886 provincial election. Although all four were trounced and the party soon disappeared, historical researcher Thomas Loosmore points to its platform as the first political articulation in BC of conflict between "the toiling masses" and "the wealthier part of the community."

The strongest rallying cry in the Knights' growing ranks focused on putting a stop to Chinese immigration and their cut-rate wages. In testimony to a Royal Commission on Chinese immigration in 1885, Knights' representative F.L. Tuckfield said that with no families and able to live "on a few cents a day," the Chinese labourers "will make the white man powerless to compete against them for labor." This anti-Chinese hostility fired much of their political agitation. In the new Vancouver rising from the ashes of its devastating 1886 fire, the Knights demanded pledges from mayoralty candidates to ensure a Chinese-free city and pressured employers not to hire Chinese workers.

Sometimes these feelings instigated vigilante action. In November 1887, members of the Knights of Labor were widely thought to be responsible for painting black *X*'s on the windows of houses employing Chinese workers and on the sidewalks outside stores and offices doing business with them. Early the next year, emotions erupted into violence when a contractor brought in Chinese workers from Victoria to clear a large tract of land in Vancouver's West End. That night, in a precursor to the infamous 1907 Chinatown Riot, a large mob attacked and burned the Chinese camp, pummelling those who were slow to leave. As they dispersed under police orders, some rioters looted Chinese homes and set fire to a few buildings. Only the arrival of dozens of special constables dispatched by the provincial government allowed the land to be cleared and more Chinese immigrants to work in the city at other jobs.

During its relatively brief existence, the Knights of Labor attracted a diverse membership of miners, loggers and mill workers, teamsters, stevedores, railway workers and general labourers. As in the United States, the Knights of Labor soon faded, done in by its generalism and the rise of more specific unions. Despite its anti-Asian racism, it was nonetheless the first labour organization in the province to give workers a voice in fighting repression on a wider battlefield. The torch was there for the passing.

However short, the Knights' success attested to the outbreak of new industrial activity in the province. Sawmills dotted the shores of Burrard Inlet, logging crews ventured into the dark, wet woods to harvest immense cedars and Douglas firs, workers laboured on the roughly built docks of Vancouver to load ships carrying BC resources to markets in Europe and Asia, railway lines proliferated, and the discovery of silver and other precious metals was transferring the Kootenays into a mining hotbed. Yet none of these topped the surge of the salmon fishery; what began as a fishery conducted almost entirely by Indigenous people quickly became the province's number-two industry. Returning every year in numbers supplying both feasts and daily needs, the salmon were fundamental to First Nations' existence throughout BC. Now the colonizers had decided to get in on the action to meet the growing demand for canned salmon overseas.

Because of the need for capital, organization and some technology, the canning rush was initially confined to only a dozen or so entrepreneurs. They were a hard, diverse lot. The names of John Sullivan Deas, an adventurous black man from the United States, and short, squat T.E. Ladner remain a part of the Lower Mainland today. Another canner, Henry Ogle Bell-Irving, who hated strikes with a passion, was the patriarch of one of the province's most illustrious families of the twentieth century.

Despite their personality differences, the canning entrepreneurs shared a similar goal of amassing huge profits for themselves while keeping others out. These capitalists regarded free-enterprise competition as a virus to be avoided. In 1888 the wealthy canners formalized their oligarchy with the establishment of the BC Fisheries Association. Together they took on all comers: governments trying to regulate the fishery, newcomers wanting to get in on the action, and fishermen seeking better wages and prices. Subsequent cannery associations with similar goals followed for decades to come. Canning operations soon spread to rich salmon runs along the Skeena and Nass Rivers in the north and at Rivers Inlet on the central coast. By 1900 the Fraser supported forty-two canneries, the Skeena and Nass eleven each, and Rivers Inlet six.

Cheap labour was fundamental to the bottom line. The canneries provided an abundance of seasonal jobs for those at the bottom rung of the workforce: Chinese men and Indigenous women. Both groups were critical to the industry's rapid expansion and the boost it gave the BC economy. Under intense pressure to maintain production as the fish piled up, their work was beyond strenuous: long days spent in dark and noisy assembly-line sweatshops. Mostly, First Nations women did the cleaning, trimming and canning, while Chinese workers did the butchering. The vitriol aimed at them in other industries was absent in the canneries, because no whites wanted these jobs. The canners were appreciative. "But for cheap labour, I do not think there would be so many canneries in existence," canner Alexander Ewen told a second Royal Commission on Chinese immigration. Bell-Irving advised the commission that Chinese men, ostensibly content with rough accommodation, were less trouble and less expensive than whites. "I look upon them as steam engines or any other machine."

During the canneries' first fifteen years, Indigenous men did almost all the fishing. But as the demand for salmon soared and canneries multiplied, they gradually began to be crowded out by whites and fishermen from Japan. By 1893, Indigenous British Columbians made up but a third of the estimated 2,350 fishermen on the Fraser. The

canners had taken advantage of the numbers to switch to paying many fishermen per fish rather than a daily rate. With intense competition on the fishing grounds, they kept lowering the price, pumping up their substantial profits even more. When the canners offered a mere six cents a fish before the 1893 salmon runs, fishermen from all groups—white, Indigenous and Nikkei—realized they had to take a stand. The result was the first major strike in the BC fishing industry.

White fishermen now had a union, the Fraser River Fishermen's Protective and Benevolent Association. Numerous Indigenous fishermen also signed up. But racism complicated union resistance. Union members rejected their Nikkei counterparts' request to join. Instead, they called for a complete ban on Nikkei fishing licences. Although the numbers of immigrants from Japan never approached those from China, their arrival in

British Columbia had been both sudden and dramatic. From a mere handful before 1890, the number of Nikkei workers grew to several thousand in just a few years. Some worked in the Dunsmuir coal mine in Cumberland but most took up fishing on the Fraser, encouraged by the canneries to help squeeze prices paid to white and Indigenous fishermen.

On July 14, 1893, despite the racial split, all fishermen came off the river, demanding an increase to ten cents per fish from the six cents offered by the canners. There is nothing quite like the drama of a salmon strike. Salmon pay no attention to above-water picket lines, heading upstream to spawn on their own biological clocks. If boats are tied up when their peak run passes, both canners and fishermen lose out big time. Each day the run nears, pressure for a settlement ratchets up like a high-stakes poker game.

Stunned by the strike, the canners were

Cannery employees take a break from their hard work on the wharf at Alert Bay, where totem poles still stood in front of some oceanfront houses as the 19th century came to an end. *Image E–07419, Royal BC Museum and Archives.*

determined not to blink first. They immediately petitioned the local Nikkei consul to send in scab fishermen and Department of Indian Affairs officials to pressure Indigenous fishermen to abandon their tie-up. Although some Nikkei fishermen held out to the end, many were soon out on the fishing grounds after the canners agreed to a firm price of seven cents a fish. Most Indigenous fishermen continued to support the strike. At a large public rally in Vancouver, Indigenous union members told the crowd that Indian agents, who had been trying to pressure them back to work, should look after Indigenous interests and not those of the canners. A reporter's account of the rally in the Vancouver *World* concluded, "The Indians fully understood the grievances of the white fishermen and being in sympathy therein, had joined the union."

But with the big run approaching, with a worrisome number of Nikkei fishermen on the water and white fishermen also starting to trickle back, the union was out of cards to play. After a tough ten days leaders called off the strike. Among the last to return were militant fishermen from the Cowichan First Nation (who went on to form their own union local in 1900). Indigenous fishermen staged three further strikes on the Skeena and Nass Rivers before the century was out. As with many lost strikes in the nineteenth century, the 1893 fishing dispute was still a significant struggle. No longer would rapacious canners rule the rivers unchallenged. At the same time, the outcome revealed once more the difficulty of prevailing when workers were divided by race. These racial divisions were exploited by employers over and over.

Although certainly the most dramatic, the decline in their share of the salmon catch was not the only evidence of diminishing economic opportunities for the province's Indigenous people. As BC moved inexorably toward a functioning capitalist economy in the latter years of the nineteenth century, Indigenous workers were being swept aside by a flood of immigrants from everywhere, many with the colonialist attitude that the province was theirs. The accelerating demand for full-time, year-round workers, plus increased automation, loss of their rights and outright discrimination cut into the ability of First Nations people to earn a living. No longer were employers willing to adapt to Aboriginal employees coming and going with the seasons, leaving their jobs as winter approached for their annual round of village potlatches and ceremonial dances. Their right to vote had been extinguished. Deadly epidemics continued to slash their population and they were arbitrarily confined to small reserves, the only Indigenous people in Canada to have their traditional territories stripped away without a treaty. Slowly, their traditional hunting and fishing rights began to disappear too, victims of new regulations and requirements to have a licence. Indian superintendent A.W. Vowell put it bluntly in 1894: "The Indians do not now, nor can they expect to in the future, make as much money as formerly in any line of industry or business."

Unions on the other hand were becoming more numerous and willing to flex their muscles. Many had international connections, like the Victoria local of the American Brotherhood of Carpenters that staged a successful strike for a nine-hour day in 1884. Other newly organized craft unions with international charters included the iron moulders, typographers, painters, plasterers, bricklayers and masons. All were soon agitating for the same nine-hour day won by the Victoria carpenters. Whether eight or nine hours, a humane, defined workday was a central plank in all labour platforms. Strikes over the issue were common. To up their organized clout, unions began establishing community labour councils, most prominently in Nanaimo, Victoria and Vancouver. It was time for political action.

On a fine day in May 1890, a straight-shooting, Belfast-born coal miner stood before a crowd of eight hundred fellow miners and sympathizers at a mass public meeting

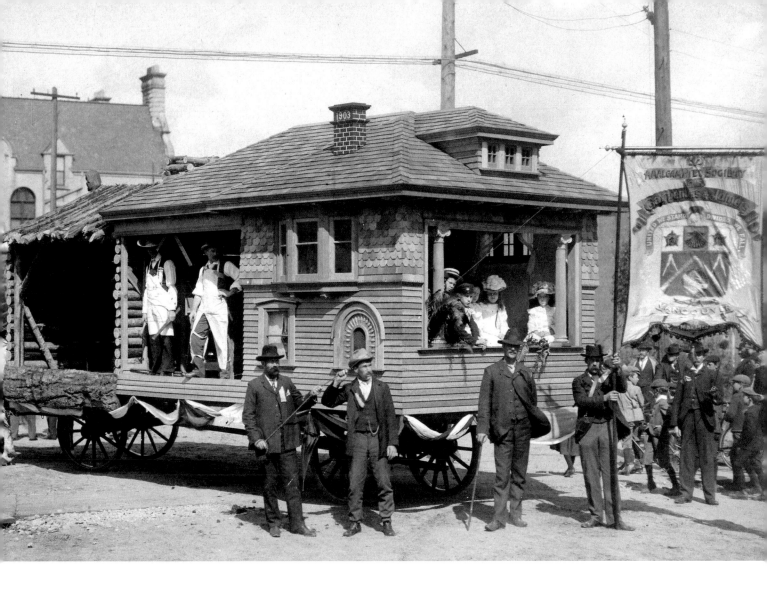

in Wellington. "Do not believe the capitalist will advance your interests and wants," he told the meeting, to great cheers. "The only man who will do this is the workingman." The gathering, organized by the new miners' union, and Thomas Keith's proclamation marked a turning point in the ongoing struggle of workers in British Columbia. After a succession of losing strikes to the Dunsmuirs and petition after petition ignored by the provincial government, Nanaimo-area coal miners concluded they needed to enter politics themselves.

The meeting chose Keith, former miner Thomas Forster and farmer C.C. McKenzie as labour-backed candidates for the three Nanaimo seats in the coming provincial election. The candidates ran on a platform calling for shorter working hours, safer work sites, tough anti-Chinese legislation and fairer taxation, including an onerous tax on public land given away to corporate interests and a then-radical proposal for a graduated income tax. All three were successful. When Thomas Keith took his place in the provincial legislature, he was the first member of the working class to do so. During his four years in Victoria, Keith showed the worth and shortcomings of electing your own, a conundrum that has not changed much over the past 125 years.

None of Keith's pro-worker actions succeeded, but the electoral triumphs of Keith and his associates and the raising of labour issues in the legislature did not go unnoticed by mainstream politicians. The government

Proclaimed a national holiday in 1894, Labour Day in Vancouver, a negotiated day off for all union workers, featured a celebratory parade with bands, floats and marching trade unionists. This horse–drawn float fronted the Amalgamated Society of Carpenters and Joiners contingent in 1903.
Alfred A. Paull photo, City of Vancouver Archives, F1 P2.

Right: Ralph Smith of Nanaimo—coal miner, union leader, gifted speaker, inveterate politician and moderate—pressed for labour reforms, including the eight-hour day, during his up-and-down career that straddled the 19th and 20th centuries. His wife, Mary Ellen, was a prominent pioneer of women's rights. *Image A-02467, Royal BC Museum and Archives.*

approved a few matters sought by labour, while opposition members began to espouse further restrictions on Chinese workers and more significantly, the principle of an eight-hour day. Although the three MLAS were blanked in the 1894 provincial election, the die had been cast; in the next five elections, Nanaimo returned pro-labour candidates to the legislature. The Vancouver Trades and Labor Council soon had some success of its own supporting candidates, and union forces in the newly emerging mining belt of the Kootenays chalked up other electoral victories.

Nanaimo miner Ralph Smith, a skilled orator who went on to play a significant role in labour and politics both provincially and nationally, was a key figure in these events. Although a relative moderate, Smith knew

which side of the class war he was on. During his successful campaign in 1898, he lashed out at R. Dunsmuir & Sons, reminding constituents that "the throats of the people of the province had been grasped by a corporation that was prepared to throttle them without mercy." The election resulted in a sharply divided legislature, giving Smith and a few other pro-labour MLAS leverage to bring about five pieces of legislation that were in the interest of workers.

One of them imposed an eight-hour day as the maximum underground shift in the mining industry. But miners found that once they had the eight-hour day, it was hard to keep, particularly in the heavy-metal mines of the Kootenays that had proliferated following the discovery of multiple rich ore bodies toward the end of the nineteenth century. Mine owners there bitterly resisted the change. "The world is made for the rich, and the poor are to work for them and be grateful for the privilege," said one. Miners were equally determined to retain the reduction in working hours.

Their fight was led by the Western Federation of Miners (WFM), then the most radical union in North America. At mine after mine throughout the western United States, the WFM had waged pitched, often violent war against special cops, Pinkerton agents, strikebreakers and ruthless mine owners to secure better pay and working conditions for union miners. As American miners spilled across the border to work the mines of the Kootenays, they brought their hard-rock union with them.

By the turn of the century, the Kootenays had thirteen WFM locals, bringing significant unionization to workers beyond the West Coast for the first time. Local 38 in Rossland, the first metal mines local in Western Canada, had been organized by the WFM in 1895. Rossland was a strong union town. Even the local newsboys were organized, staging three successful strikes in a single year. In 1898, Local 38 was strong enough to pay for and erect a substantial wood-frame union hall on

Rossland's main street that still stands. The eight-hour day was fundamental to the WFM cause. If miners were human beings "able to read, think, and appreciate the good things of life, as others do, then eight hours is sufficient for men to work underground," the WFM declared in a brief to the legislature.

As their first ploy against the shortened workday, mine owners cut the daily pay from $3.50 to $3.00. A hard-fought strike by WFM miners in the silver mines around Sandon managed to get the rate up to $3.25, but their efforts were hampered by strikebreakers brought in from the United States, in clear violation of the federal **Alien Labour Act**. Companies took a different tack in the mines around Rossland. To avoid the daily rate, they began hiring miners on contract with pay based on output.

By July of 1901, the Rossland miners had had enough. At a heated meeting in the union hall, tired of the owners' anti-union activities and lack of commitment to the eight-hour day, they voted to strike. Both sides knew the stakes were high. WFM president Ed Boyce came up to rally the strikers with a call for a fight to the bitter end. "I care not what it takes, nor how we win. I am in favour of winning," he declared, pledging $20,000 in strike assistance from the international union.

The mine owners were equally determined. Their spies and shotgun-toting police were everywhere in town. Trainloads of non-English-speaking immigrant strikebreakers began arriving from the United States to keep the mines running. As in Sandon, this contravened the **Alien Labour Act**. But the government refused to enforce the act. When two strikers had the effrontery to heckle arriving scabs, they were sentenced to two months of hard labour. Increasingly desperate and running low on funds, the union invited future prime minister William Lyon Mackenzie King, then a twenty-six-year-old deputy labour minister, to Rossland to investigate the company's willful violation of the **Alien Labour Act**. King quickly fell under the sway of the owners, shrugging off voluminous

Opposite: Members of Local 119 of the Western Federation of Miners take time out from their union meeting to pose for a group photograph, complete with a baby, in April 1901, in the West Kootenays town of Ferguson.
Vancouver Public Library, 100.

A heart-rending funeral procession through Fernie in the Crowsnest Pass, transporting 28 victims of the 1902 Coal Creek Mine disaster to the community's small cemetery. The explosion and resulting fire killed a total of 128 miners. *Image D–01630, Royal BC Museum and Archives.*

evidence of illegally imported scabs and advising the union to call off its strike. The Sandon *Paystreak* newspaper slammed King as "a cultural dub with a university education, a picturesque name and a thrilling ignorance of labor as a concrete sociological force."

The new year brought defeat. After nine months, with no more strike pay and the law stacked against them, the miners, some close to starvation, voted to return to work. "No man living outside Rossland can imagine the troubles [we] have been through," said one union miner. The mine owners weren't finished. In the imposing courthouse purposely built opposite the miners' hall, the companies were awarded $12,500 in damages from Local 38, forcing it into receivership. Afterward, concluding that laws made by the workers were the only way forward, many Kootenays miners became ardent socialists, pursuing victory by the working class and an end to capitalism. They would fight more battles in the years ahead, not a few of them over the ongoing quest for a permanent eight-hour day.

Farther east, the rich coalfields of the Crowsnest Pass were being opened up to give the province a second major coal-mining resource. But it was just as susceptible to tragedy as the underground mines of Vancouver Island. During the night shift on May 22, 1902, a horrific explosion and coal-dust-fed fireball ripped through the mine at Coal Creek eight kilometres east of Fernie. The first victim carted out was thirteen-year-old Will Robertson. By the time rescuers had finished their grim task, the official death toll was 128, the province's second-deadliest mining disaster. Over the next few days, Fernie was consumed by the building of coffins, the digging of graves and a series of sad funeral processions down its frontier main street. Grief and anger were rife. When a new police constable was overheard expressing a cruel wish that more had died, hundreds of miners and residents gathered outside the police station, refusing to leave until he was put on the next train out of town. It was the first example of the class solidarity that would turn Crowsnest Pass coal-mining communities into a resolute left-wing stronghold for many years.

A NEW CENTURY
AND NEW LABOUR
AWARENESS

3

———————————

WITH THE NEWLY EUROPEAN-DOMINATED POPULATION of 170,000 people, the province's industrial muscle was in full swing. Settlers, workers and entrepreneurs poured in. Exports had soared from about $3 million in 1885 to $17 million by 1900. In 1901, fifteen years after burning to the ground, Vancouver had supplanted Victoria as the province's largest city, with twenty-seven thousand residents. The end of the line for Canada's transcontinental railway and the gateway to Asia, the city continued growing at a phenomenal rate, more than quadrupling its population over the next ten years. As for BC itself, by the outbreak of World War I nearly half a million people lived in the province.

The scattered skirmishes of the previous twenty-five years—when only the resistance of Vancouver Island's coal miners stood out—were replaced by a harder edge that spread to most regions of the province. It was marked by a growing embrace of socialism by the working class that went beyond reforming capitalism to overthrowing capitalism and waves of industrial strife.

Unions deployed new weapons to fight for change: direct and political action, provincial and city-wide labour organizations to foster solidarity, civil disobedience, sympathy walkouts and general strikes—and on occasion, violence. They were stronger too, with organizers more committed than ever before. And socialism made its first appearance as a political force beyond impassioned rhetoric at rallies and meeting halls.

The fiery James W. Hawthornthwaite, first elected as a labour candidate in a 1901 Nanaimo by-election, soon became a committed socialist. Running under their anti-capitalist banner, he was returned to Victoria four more times by the coal miners of Nanaimo. During his first year as an MLA in 1902, Hawthornthwaite mustered enough votes for the passage of Canada's first Workmen's Compensation Act. Covering only railway, factory, mine, engineering and construction workers, the act nonetheless provided

Successful labour and socialist politician James W. Hawthornthwaite from Nanaimo was elected five times to the BC legislature. He was a sponsor of Canada's first Workmen's Compensation Act in 1902 and a founding member of the Socialist Party of Canada in 1904.
Image A–02210, Royal BC Museum and Archives.

compensation levels for injured workers regardless of fault, and benefits equivalent to three years' salary for families of workers killed on the job. Although there were holes

in the act that ultimately lessened its effectiveness, it was a significant step forward for workers and an example of what could be achieved through political action.

The Socialist Party of BC—with a platform calling for female suffrage, old-age pensions, an eight-hour day for all workers, exclusion of Asians and an end to capitalism—elected members in each succeeding provincial election until 1916. In 1903, socialist and labour candidates received an impressive 15.9 percent of the total popular vote despite fielding far from a full slate, declining only slightly to 14 percent in 1907. Hawthornthwaite's longevity was matched by fellow socialist Parker Williams, who was elected five times by working-class voters in the adjacent Nanaimo riding of Newcastle. Despite labour's stepped-up fervour, nothing came easily. Arrayed against them were ever more prosperous and ruthless companies, pro-business governments, an anti-union press and authorities easily persuaded to

Chinese fish plant workers unload salmon for a cannery along the Fraser River in 1897.
Stephen Joseph Thompson photo, City of Vancouver Archives 137–57.

unleash soldiers, police and special constables to preserve the existing order. Inevitably, setbacks occurred.

There was also the downside of labour's ongoing campaign against Asian immigrants, a campaign that commonly included overt racism and once, in 1907, along with other citizens, a frightening rampage through Vancouver's Chinese and Nikkei areas. While some, notably the Industrial Workers of the World (IWW), preached that workers were workers regardless of race, that tolerance did not prevail. As shown by strikes in the fishing industry and other disputes where Chinese strikebreakers were used, this deep-seated racial division continued to be used by employers to keep unions at bay.

The Fraser River Fishermen's strike of 1900 was the first major confrontation of the new century in British Columbia and the province's first significant strike outside the mining industry. It marked not only the beginning of two years of open warfare on the water, but the start of twenty years of unsurpassed radicalism in the province's long history of union struggle. After their defeat in 1893, fishermen were determined to reverse their fortunes, particularly with the dramatic changes that had overtaken the Fraser River fishery. Canners had lost their campaign to restrict fishing licences, and by 1900 they were being handed out like candy at Christmas. Close to thirty-seven hundred licences had been issued, more than triple the number in 1893. Most fishermen were now paid per fish.

Since there were only so many salmon, the licence explosion meant lower catches for everyone. Hardest hit were Indigenous fishermen, who had seen their share of the fishery severely diminished by the dramatic influx of fishermen from Japan. In seven short years, the Nikkei had gone from a few hundred licences to become the largest fishing group on the Fraser. Indigenous fishermen were left with only a third of the allotted licences. But tensions were inflamed among all fishermen when canners organized themselves into the Fraser River Canneries Association to set fixed quotas for each cannery and to unilaterally impose a maximum price for caught salmon.

The BC Fishermen's Union emerged in the spring of 1900. Its many locals included Aboriginal fishermen from Cowichan and Port Simpson. Frank Rogers, a driven twenty-eight-year-old longshoreman and socialist, was hired to prepare for the looming confrontation. Rogers was a rare trade unionist with no outward racial animosity toward the Nikkei. Knowing no strike could be successful without their support, he quickly set to work to bring them on board. With an interpreter, he made the rounds of their rough bunkhouses, urging them to join the union and explaining the need to stand firm on prices. Instead, the Nikkei formed their own association, the Japanese Fishermen's Benevolent Society. Although less a union than a cultural and social welfare group working to build a hospital and school for the swelling Nikkei community in Steveston, the society also functioned as an advocacy group for their fishermen.

But Rogers's efforts bore some fruit. All three ethnic groups—Nikkei, whites and Indigenous—united on a demand for twenty-five cents a fish throughout the season. When the canneries stuck to their usual guns of refusing to negotiate, the historic strike was on. By the time it ran its course nearly a month later, the dispute had seen just about everything. Shortly after the strike began on July 8, 1900, a group of Nikkei fishermen went out to fish anyway. Union patrol boats herded them back. A parade of union fishermen, accompanied by an interpreter, repeated Rogers's bunkhouse visits to explain the strike. The next day, all Nikkei boats remained on shore.

The strike remained solid for the next two weeks. Fundraising and food donations helped feed hundreds of strikers every day, many of them Nikkei. Regular meetings at the Steveston Opera House buoyed spirits, and a large, uplifting demonstration in

Vancouver drew more than a thousand marchers led by the famous First Nations brass band from Port Simpson. Stunned by the solidarity, the canneries became increasingly anxious. After attempts to have the militia sent in failed, they reluctantly appointed a negotiating committee and began talks with the union. At one point, the gap narrowed to a mere two cents per fish—eighteen cents from the canneries to twenty cents demanded by the fishermen's committee. But talks broke off when the companies declared their offer final. Nikkei, white and Indigenous fishermen all rejected the canners' ultimatum; never before had so many, across all races, held out for so long to force a better price for the fish they caught.

The pace of events began to quicken. On the evening of Friday, July 20, one of the Bell-Irving canneries deliberately sent two non-union boats out to fish, protected by three tugs carrying ten special constables. A union patrol boat went after one of the vessels and forced it to shore, where Frank Rogers and an agitated crowd awaited. Rogers hauled the skiff's boat-puller up on a soapbox and cuffed him about, amid loud jeers of "Scab!" The strikebreaker was then jostled by the fishermen before being let go. The trivial incident prompted a flurry of hysterical pleas to Victoria urging that forces be sent in to curb a "state of lawlessness" on the river that risked "a great loss of life and property."

The canneries were also preparing another final offer. This one promised twenty cents each for the first six hundred fish caught each week, and fifteen cents per fish after that. More than thirty-five hundred Nikkei community members, by far the largest crowd in Steveston's short history, gathered to consider the new offer. After ninety minutes of speeches, including a forceful

A mass march of fishermen toward the village of Steveston during the big showdown with Fraser River canners in 1900. *Henry Joseph Woodside/Library and Archives Canada/A016346.*

address by the driven, outspoken secretary of the Japanese Fishermen's Benevolent Society, Yasushi Yamazaki, the offer was accepted unanimously. The ensuing cheers could be heard a mile away. A huge, spontaneous procession wound through the muddy streets of Steveston to celebrate. Once again, the canneries had managed to drive a racial wedge between their adversaries.

Two hours later, members of the BC Fishermen's Union marshalled a force of their own. On short notice, six hundred white fishermen crowded into an angry meeting, calling for hundreds of trade unionists from Vancouver to rally to their aid. More than a few threatened to throw any Nikkei found fishing into the Fraser. The boats of white and Indigenous fishermen would remain tied up after an overwhelming secret-ballot vote to hold out for twenty-five cents. It was a critical turning point in the most intent effort thus far by Fraser River fishermen to crack the stranglehold that the corporate canneries had imposed on the rich salmon fishery.

The canneries quickly cajoled three compliant local justices of the peace to requisition two hundred militiamen to protect the Nikkei fishermen the next morning. Ammunition was handed out and the troops took up positions around the docks. Out sailed the Nikkei fleet, likened by a reporter to "a large and beautiful crowd of butterflies, against the western sky." Somewhat less entranced, striking fishermen watched helplessly from shore. With fifteen hundred Nikkei boats now hauling in salmon, the strike appeared lost. But there was no loss of spirit. White and Indigenous fishermen amassed on a local meadow that afternoon, vowing continued resistance.

Several chiefs were among those who addressed the crowd. Other speakers made a point of praising Indigenous fishermen for standing firm. When Frank Rogers suggested it was time for their own march to match the militia's parading about, one of the more colourful events of the strike ensued. Up to five hundred fishermen proceeded to the

main military post outside the Gulf of Georgia Cannery. In a festive mood, they spent the afternoon parading around the soldiers. Mocking them as the "Sockeye Fusiliers," they jeered and ridiculed the young, straw-hatted troops and serenaded them with a derisive rendition of "Soldiers of the Queen."

Surprisingly, the canneries continued to fret, despite the Nikkei return to fishing. Many were failing to bring in much of a catch. As well, the salmon run stayed light. With more than half the fleet remaining on strike, the canners were still short of fish and worried they would be unable to take full advantage once the largest run of salmon hit the Fraser. They were also under intense pressure from an angry public, newspaper editorials and the legislature, miffed by the canners' underhanded role in summoning the militia against mostly peaceful fishermen. Much against their will, they approached the white and Aboriginal fishermen once again.

Rogers, a realist and skilled strategist, knew it was time to settle. He persuaded the fishermen to propose a new bottom line of twenty cents per fish for the full season, plus recognition of the union. During two days of tense talks, the fishermen reduced their demand to nineteen cents, a cent less than the Nikkei were receiving for their first six hundred fish of the week, but it would be a firm price with no reductions. The canners agreed. Even then, hungry and broke, the strikers did not stampede back to the fishing grounds. In what historian Keith Ralston called "a last display of the discipline and loyalty to their organization that had brought them to a negotiated settlement," the fishermen delayed their return for a day to allow for a formal vote on the agreement. They started fishing at the crack of dawn on July 31, 1900.

While the union failed to win union recognition and the price they wanted, unwilling canners had been forced for the first time to negotiate a fixed price per fish for the entire season. When the salmon run proved heavier than expected, the union's deal turned out to be better than that accepted by the Nikkei. Heartened by their relative success, union leaders began plotting strategy for 1901. This would be what the industry called a "big year," when the four-year cycle of salmon hits a peak, flooding BC rivers with astronomical numbers of fish returning to spawn.

In the fall of 1900, the Grand Lodge of BC Fishermen emerged as BC's first coast-wide fishing union. First Nations fishermen from Cowichan and Port Simpson, with their ever-popular brass band, were among the most militant of the many locals. In fact, First Nations played a much stronger role in the 1901 showdown than they had in 1900. Following a large meeting in Chilliwack, thirty-three chiefs agreed unanimously to reject the canners' offer of twelve and a half cents to start the season and a lower price once the heavy run began. The Nikkei settled first, accepting twelve and a half cents, but with a 250-fish daily limit after August 3, 1901. White and Indigenous fishermen held

out for a firm price of twelve and a half cents for the full season. "At one time, the Indians owned the whole country, the rivers, everything," declared Chief Jimmy Henry as he supported the call for strike at a mass union meeting in late June.

The resulting tie-up was shorter but far more intense than the previous year's confrontation. Desperate to cut off delivery of fish by the Nikkei, striking fishermen went all out on the water. After one crew was severely beaten, a score of armed patrol boats sailed out to protect the Nikkei fishermen, rumoured to have been given guns. Frank Rogers called on picketers to arm themselves in self-defence. During the next few days, picketers boarded a number of Nikkei boats, cut their nets, tossed their weapons overboard and brought the men ashore, setting their boats adrift. On July 10, gunfire broke out on the waters off Point Grey. Six strikers found to be carrying four shotguns and a revolver were arrested by police on board

The celebrated Tsimshian brass band from Port Simpson marches along Hastings Street in Vancouver during a holiday parade in the city, likely Dominion Day. In mid–July, the same band led a thousand–strong march in support of striking fishermen, whose ranks included many Indigenous members. A few days later, the band was in Nanaimo to help rally local union coal miners to the cause.
John Tyson photo, City of Vancouver Archives, P120.1.

one of the Nikkei vessels and charged with intimidation.

Not long afterward, union picketers abducted as many as a dozen Nikkei fishermen and marooned them on Bowen Island. News of the kidnappings became a newspaper sensation. The drama was then heightened even further thanks to the ubiquitous Yasushi Yamazaki. After arranging their rescue, Yamazaki brought the abducted Nikkei fishermen to court, where they fingered Frank Rogers as one of the culprits. There to support the six strikers, Rogers was quickly arrested and charged with kidnapping and possession of a concealed weapon. The union leader was held without bail for six months as the Crown tried and failed twice to convince a jury to convict him. After the first trial, held in Vancouver, the Crown's lawyer complained that it was impossible to convict Rogers in "a union town."

But with Rogers in jail, Nikkei boats fishing and a massive salmon run on its way,

union fishermen resentfully accepted the canneries' terms and headed out to harvest what turned out to be the greatest run in the recorded history of the Fraser River. Despite a breakthrough in establishing the practice of negotiating fish prices, the fishermen's bitter struggles of 1900 and 1901 ended with the canners ruling the Fraser. The next year many canneries consolidated into the formidable BC Packers Association, which would dominate the industry for the next ninety-five years.

Alone, it seemed, Indigenous fishermen kept fighting back. They regularly denounced weak union agreements and continued to demand Nikkei fishermen be gone from the fishing grounds. A major confrontation took place on the Skeena and Nass Rivers in 1904. Close to eight hundred First Nations fishermen refused to fish for the offered prices. As in all strikes involving the First Nations, Indigenous women cannery workers also refused to work. Once again, many

Nikkei fishermen at the old Ewens cannery on Lion Island in the south arm of the Fraser River, 1913. Many of their sons and grandsons became members of the Fishermen's Union.
UBC Rare Books and Special Collections, 1532–1324.

Nikkei eventually began fishing and the strike died out. But three years later, with a labour shortage in the canneries, Indigenous women struck successfully for a higher wage on the production line.

But ethnic divisions among all BC fishermen continued to plague solidarity on the grounds. A 1912 strike by Indigenous dragseine fishermen on Vancouver Island was undermined by white fishermen willing to fish for less. And a strike by Nikkei fishermen in 1913 foundered after Indigenous and white fishermen accepted the companies' deal. According to newspaper reports, the Nikkei strikers used violence and intimidation to keep other fishermen from setting their nets.

Such incidents were telling. There would be no chance of standing up to the fish companies on an equal basis as long as the industry was wracked by what fishing historian Geoff Meggs called "the corrosive effect of racism."

The early twentieth century also brought another influx of Asians from across the Pacific that drew white labour's ire. Enticed by reports from visiting South Asian soldiers that British Columbia was a good place to work and live, upwards of five thousand immigrants from India, mostly South Asians from the Punjab, had made their way to the West Coast by 1908. Many found employment in sawmills, establishing themselves as hard-working, dependable and, yes, cheap

Most early South Asian immigrants made their way in the province's booming forest industry. In 1910, these men worked for the North Pacific Lumber Company at Barnet (today part of Burnaby). *Phillip Timms photo, Vancouver Public Library, 7641.*

labour. Their growing numbers set off the same racism and union opposition that dogged immigrants from China and Japan. Both the Victoria and Vancouver Trades and Labor Councils protested the entry of "Hindoos" into the workforce. Levelling the familiar charge that they undercut wages and conditions for white workers, the labour organizations called for banning "the hordes of Asiatics" from the forestry, mining and fishing industries.

Although citizens of the British Empire, South Asians were denied the right to vote by the provincial government in 1907, the same basic right Asian immigrants from China and Japan had lost earlier. The next year, an extraordinary order-in-council by the federal government restricted future immigration to those making a direct, nonstop passage from India. No such passage existed. When 376 South Asian passengers, many of whom boarded at ports outside India, boldly tried to challenge the restriction in 1914, they were left marooned in Vancouver Harbour for two months aboard the *Komagata Maru* before being escorted back out to sea by Canada's only warship. A century later, the incident is widely recognized as a black mark on Canada's and British Columbia's racist past, along with the Chinese Head Tax, Nikkei internment and residential schools. All have generated formal government apologies.

Barely a thousand South Asians remained in 1920. But they continued to be a fixture in coastal sawmills, typically assigned to arduous tasks on the green chain or otherwise moving lumber while being paid significantly less than non-Asian workers, even at mills run by South Asians themselves. Only with the admission of women and children under a grudging family reunification program did BC's tightly knit South Asian communities begin to grow.

The years following the fishermen's strikes

South Asians on board the *Komagata Maru* during their ill–fated attempt in 1914 to secure landing rights in Vancouver. Expedition leader Gurdit Singh is at the top left, identifiable by his white beard and light–coloured suit. *Canadian Photo Company, Vancouver Public Library, 136.*

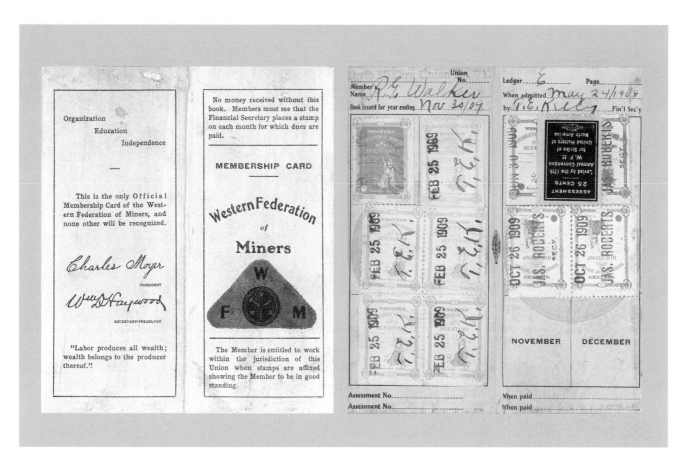

Above: A Western Federation of Miners union card with payment of dues stamps carried by R.G. Walker, who worked at the Moyie silver mine in the East Kootenays. The card is dated 1909 and signed by union secretary–treasurer Big Bill Haywood. *Images 0531.0019 and 0513.0020, Moyie House High Museum & Columbia Basin Institute of Regional History.*

Right: Frank Rogers's death was front-page news in the *Vancouver Daily Province*. *Daily Province, April 15, 1903, p. 1.*

FRANK ROGERS DIED THIS AFTERNOON

WAS HE SHOT BY POLICEMAN ?

Officer Allan Is Under Arrest in the Waterfront Firing Case--No Dying Deposition Was Made by the Unfortunate Union Man.

Frank Rogers, who was fatally wounded by a shot in the abdomen, fired during a fusillade at the wharf end of Abbott street on Monday night, died at the City Hospital at 3:30 o'clock this afternoon.

From the first it was practically certain that the unfortunate union man was mortally hurt, and that it was but a question of a day or two at the most before he would pass away. The bullet, entering his abdomen, tore through the intestines and lodged somewhere in his back. The internal hemorrhage shortly after the shooting, was in itself sufficient to cause death.

To-day Rogers was still conscious, and he believed himself that he might possibly recover. For that reason no deposition was taken from him, and all the authorities have is the general statement which he made yesterday morning to Provincial Constable Colin Campbell and Magistrate H. O. Alexander. Late last night the Magistrate was called again to take a dying deposition, but Rogers did not feel that his case was hopeless, and under those conditions could not make an official statement that might be used as evidence after death.

Every one in Vancouver who knew Rogers will learn of his death with regret. He was a union man of strong feelings, but as a matter of fact he often counseled against exhibitions of force or anything like riots. The funeral arrangements will be in the hands of the union.

The Police Court was crowded this afternoon when the case against Alfred Allan was called. Allan is the special constable arrested last night, with the charge against his name of having shot Rogers. Mr. G. F. Cane, Crown attorney, appeared to prosecute, and on his request a remand was granted until Friday.

Mr. C. B. Macneill appeared for the accused, and called attention to the revolver that was found on him after he was arrested. Mr. Macneill claimed that the gun was loaded, and it could be easily seen that it had not recently been discharged, he said. He asked to have it examined by a gun expert, and this would probably be done.

Chief North, on the other hand, is of the opinion that the gun has been discharged recently.

The revolver is of .32 calibre, much smaller than the .38 which the doctors believe inflicted the wound in Rogers' stomach.

were relatively good ones for BC's trade union movement. As industry boomed, the working class also expanded. Union membership rose to a record fifteen thousand workers in 175 separate unions. Strikes abounded. When the United Brotherhood of Railway Employees (UBRE) struck in 1903 for union recognition, their walkout for the first time sparked widespread sympathy action by other unions including Vancouver longshoremen, two hundred local teamsters, the BC Steamshipmen's Society, and the Western Federation of Miners in the Kootenays, who refused to process coal shipments to the CPR. But the familiar litany of an employer importing strikebreakers protected by private security agents prevailed once more. After four months, the UBRE walkout collapsed.

In the meantime, the strike had also produced BC's first labour martyr. Frank Rogers, who played such a prominent role in the recent fishing disputes, was felled by a shot fired from the CPR side of the tracks during the UBRE strike, when he approached the

FRANK ROGERS

There are no pictures, no precise descriptions of what he looked like and only the skimpiest details of his back-ground. But during the first few years of the twentieth century, no BC trade unionist was as feared by employers and as well known as Scotland-born Frank Rogers, a strong socialist who hit Vancouver in 1897. His effective leadership was pivotal in the dramatic fishermen's strikes on the Fraser in 1900 and 1901, making him a target for the canners and their friends in government. Although never convicted, he was arrested and jailed during both strikes. The second time he spent nearly four months at New Westminster's notorious BC Pen while awaiting various trials.

Incarceration took a toll on Rogers's health. He cut back on his activism, working quietly as a longshoreman until an acrimonious strike by the United Brotherhood of Railway Employees against the CPR in 1903 rekindled his trade unionism. Rogers helped organize a support strike by fellow longshoremen to hamper the CPR's dockside operations. Shortly after 11 p.m. on April 13, he and two friends wandered to the waterfront to check on a group

Workers on the CPR pier in Vancouver in the early 1900s, not far from where union activist Frank Rogers was fatally shot during a strike by CPR railway workers in the spring of 1903. *Phillip Timms photo, Vancouver Public Library, 2987.*

down by the tracks. As Rogers passed under a street light, shots rang out. He fell to the ground, mortal-ly wounded, dying two days later. The fatal bullet tore through his overcoat, his copy of the longshore union's constitution and bylaws, and into his abdomen.

Rogers was the BC labour movement's first martyr. The culprit was almost certainly a CPR special constable brought in from Montreal, but a witness who changed his testimony led to the strikebreaker's acquittal. After a solemn funeral service at the Labor Hall, and oblivious to a driving rainstorm, close to a thousand workers from all trades in the city marched in a huge funeral proces-sion to accompany his body to its final resting place in Mountainview Cemetery. Today his grave is marked by a plaque erected in 1978 that reads, "Frank Rogers/ Mur-dered by a Scab/ In Strike against CPR/ Died April 15, 1903/ Union Organizer and Socialist."

docks late at night to see what was going on. He died shorty afterwards in hospital. His rain-soaked funeral procession was the largest union gathering the city had ever seen.

Around the same time, while women workers remained rare outside the canneries in the new century's first decade, those who did join the workforce showed that they, too, were not always prepared to turn the other cheek. No group carried the torch of female resistance higher than Vancouver's telephone operators. They were all women, preferred by phone companies because they were considered hard-working and polite to customers. They could also be paid less than men. Local switchboard operators did not accept that view. As early as 1902, they formed a women's auxiliary of the International Brotherhood of Electrical Workers. Before the end of the year, they were on strike. For the first and only time in more than a century of subsequent labour turmoil, phone service was completely cut off by union job action, prompting another one-and-only occurrence: strike support from a business community desperate to have its phones back in operation.

With pressure from the Board of Trade, solidarity from other trade unions and public sympathy, the phone company caved in. Operators won a wage increase, paid sick leave and, most significantly, a closed shop. Four years later the phone company was ready to counterattack. This time, when telephone workers walked out, the company maintained service with strikebreakers and a few union members who stayed on. The strike collapsed after a few months and the "hello gals," as they were known, said goodbye to their union. But not forever.

It was tough to sustain a strong labour movement in BC's ever-cyclical economy so dependent on export markets. Union successes went up and down with the economy. At the same time, employers, government, the hysterical press and hired thugs took turns beating up on unions and workers who dared to stand up and fight for a better life. If they played by the book, they lost. If they took action into their own hands, they lost.

Switchboard operators at the BC Telephone Company in Vancouver, not long after the company broke their union in 1906. They reorganized in 1918.
City of Vancouver Archives,
BU P498.

Working-class views hardened. The system seemed stacked against them.

For hard-done-by members of the proletariat, the red card of the Industrial Workers of the World (IWW) was a badge of resistance, hidden from employers but waved proudly over a beer. During the first two decades of the twentieth century, no one promoted class struggle more vigorously than the IWW. The "Wobblies," as members were known, did not achieve the same inroads in BC that they did in the USA, but they certainly made their presence felt for a brief few years. For a time the IWW was the province's largest union. The Wobblies also staged what was then BC's biggest strike and were at the centre of one of Vancouver's fiercest confrontations with civic authorities.

The Wobblies spread to BC after two miners from the Kootenays attended the IWW's founding convention in 1905 in Chicago. One of them, John H. Riordan, was elected to the national executive and later took a leading role in the union's shift to greater militancy. The IWW soon chartered half a dozen BC locals including the famous Bows and Arrows Local 526 representing mostly Indigenous lumber handlers on the docks of Vancouver. Except in scattered pockets such as Nelson, which

became an IWW stronghold, there was not much Wobbly activity for the next few years. But many travelling and unemployed workers found a home in the union. Its premises in Vancouver served as a mail depot, job mart, reading room, lecture hall, dormitory, and a warm, dry place to chew the fat and share stories of life on the road.

The popularity of the IWW was also indicative of growing resentment of the prominence of the craft unions championed by one-time cigar-maker Samuel Gompers through his American Federation of Labor (AFL) and the Trades and Labor Congress of Canada. Organized on the basis of specialized trades, craft unions were mostly closed to unskilled and industrial workers. Their approach to trade unionism, political agitation and anything that smacked of socialism was cautious. To many of the workers toiling in factories, mines, the woods and other workplaces where sweat counted for more than the narrow skill of a trade, craft unions seemed part of a labour elite.

These feelings were particularly acute in British Columbia, where even the craft unions tended to be on the left. When Gompers came to Vancouver for a public meeting in 1911, he was shouted down, sub-

THE BOWS AND ARROWS

History does not tell us why a group of Indigenous lumber handlers on the Vancouver waterfront decided to form a union in 1906, nor why they opted to join the revolutionary Industrial Workers of the World as one of its first locals in BC. The Wobblies' acceptance of all workers regardless of race might well have been the reason. Forming one of the waterfront's first unions, most of its sixty or so members belonged to the Tsleil-Waututh and Squamish Nations on the North Shore of Burrard Inlet. Union meetings took place at a hall on the Squamish reserve across the water. The local was known to everyone on the docks as the "Bows and Arrows," a tag applied to all subsequent union locals

representing Indigenous lumber handlers stretching into the 1930s.

Unfortunately, little more is known about one of the IWW's most intriguing locals. After losing a strike in 1907, Local 526 disappeared. However, one can safely say its brief existence was symptomatic of the resistance by many First Nations to what was happening to them as their rights were steadily eroded. Among those who worked on the docks at the time (though as a foreman) was well-known Squamish chief Joe Capilano, who used his waterfront earnings to help finance an expedition to England to press King Edward VII on Aboriginal land claims.

jected to what the union leader called "the vilest language I have ever heard." His raucous reception had been organized by local members of the IWW. The Wobblies argued that only when capitalism and its inherent "wage slavery" were exterminated once and for all could workers share properly in the fruits of their labour.

The IWW's first big BC confrontation erupted in 1911 in Prince Rupert. The union led several hundred private sewer and road workers out on strike to demand wage parity with civic employees doing the same work. When the contractors imported scabs, the Wobblies organized a day of marches that coaxed many of the scabs off the job. At a site called Kelly's Cut, however, strikebreakers refused to leave. Rocks were soon flying through the air, first thrown, many believe, by undercover Pinkerton agents who had infiltrated the union. Police and armed citizens counterattacked with clubs and scattered gunfire. One of the strikers was shot in the stomach, another in the shoulder. Many others on both sides were bloodied in the melee,

which came to be known as "The Battle of Kelly's Cut." Scores of strikers were arrested. Since the local jail had only two cells, union carpenters were summoned to build a makeshift pen to hold all the Wobblies. At least, said a Wobbly wit, it was a union job.

Amid the IWW's sporadic, often spontaneous strikes, nothing came close to matching the scope of the union's effort to organize thousands of scattered, ill-treated, underpaid railway construction labourers. Most were recent immigrants from Europe, unskilled and with minimal English. They toiled long, back-breaking hours while living in deplorable camps provided by unscrupulous, profit-hungry contractors. No one disputed that their living conditions were a disgrace, not even a shocked parliamentary committee that looked into them. Established unions ignored them as too transient and too difficult to organize. But they were ideal for the Wobblies' roving activists. The worst conditions existed along the Canadian Northern line. "Words can hardly describe the situation. It is almost beyond imagination," said

As much a social organization as a union, the Industrial Workers of the World hosted this smoker for Prince Rupert longshoremen at the IWW hall on Christmas night, 1911. *Courtesy ILWU Local 505, Prince Rupert.*

one occupant. "The air was so foul at night it was not uncommon for men to arise in the morning too sick to work."

By 1912, CN labourers were not prepared to take it anymore. All that winter, IWW organizers had been signing them up and laying the groundwork for a strike. As spring approached, they were ready. To the amazement of contractors and other unions, nearly eight thousand railroad construction workers from Hope to Kamloops walked off the job. Although their demands included a nine-hour day and a minimum daily wage of $3, the driving force was the unspeakable state of their overcrowded, filthy work camps.

The Wobblies implemented tight discipline. In Yale, which served as the chief command post, hotels were warned not to serve more than two drinks a day to anyone on strike. Guns and ammunition were banned. To further keep the peace, Wobbly patrols walked the streets, backed up by a "people's court" that handed out penalties to those who broke the rules. The leadership knew any trace of trouble or unruly behaviour would bring in cops and special constables to break up the strike. The union established its own camps, serving two meals a day. The local constable said he had never seen the town so law abiding. A journalist described Yale as "a miniature republic run on socialist lines, and it must be admitted that so far it has been run successfully."

A week or so into the strike, legendary Wobbly songwriter Joe Hill showed up. It was his only known visit to BC, attesting to the admiration American Wobblies had for the railroad labourers' stand. Hill hung around long enough to raise the strikers' spirits with several on-the-spot songs, including his well-known "Where the Fraser River Flows." They would certainly have been delighted at such verses as "For these gunny-sack contractors have all been dirty actors,/ And they're not our benefactors, each fellow worker knows./ So we've got to stick together in fine or dirty weather,/ And we will show no white feather, where the Fraser River flows." The Vancouver

Trades and Labor Council, impressed by the IWW's groundbreaking walkout, rallied to the cause too. They donated money. *The British Columbia Federationist*, the comprehensive weekly labour newspaper published jointly by the VTLC and the fledgling BC Federation of Labor, became the strike newspaper.

But a fierce counterattack was soon afoot. A month into the strike, hard-line BC Attorney General W.J. Bowser, who had never shown a whit of concern over conditions in the contractors' camps, dispatched provincial health inspectors to the IWW camps. They were ordered shut for health reasons. When the strikers stayed put, police and contractor goons sworn in as special constables stormed in, ripped down the tents and marched the workers out by gunpoint. Following Bowser's instructions to "prosecute and imprison on every possible occasion," hundreds were arrested.

Judge Frederic William Howay demonstrated what BC workers were up against when they dared to challenge the boss. "We are a free and law-abiding people, and above all, we will not tolerate the red flag of anarchy," he raged at IWW members brought before him. Despite no evidence they had seriously flouted any laws, many were jailed for terms the judge deliberately varied to thwart welcoming demonstrations if workers were released on the same day.

Contractors were bringing in more and more strikebreakers from the United States. The Wobblies responded with an astounding "one-thousand-mile picket line," which had members picketing employment offices from San Francisco to Seattle to Minnesota to try to stem the flow of scab hires. But they continued to arrive. With newspapers regularly whipping up alarmist flames over non-existent armed strikers and calling for the government to repel the "invasion of the most despicable scum of humanity," the IWW was beset on all sides. It became impossible to maintain the strike's original solidarity. The union's call for mediation was ignored. As fall neared, the strike petered out. A walkout in July by three thousand railroad construction labourers on the Grand Trunk Line up north met a similar fate. Thanks to their fight, however, workers hired back did return to camps that were much improved.

Although occasional strikes and organizing continued in other industries, even as the railway construction boom ended, the IWW was never to come close to the stature it had in BC in 1912. Overall, BC labour conflict peaked that year, with a record 490,726 workdays lost to disputes. The Crowsnest Pass area straddling the Alberta border had been convulsed the year before by an eight-month strike involving nearly seven thousand members of the United Mine Workers of America (UMWA) who toiled in the region's deep coal mines, coke ovens and smelters and also worked for the railways. At the end of a historic struggle, the union won a small wage increase but not the union shop requiring all mineworkers to join the UMWA that they had been seeking.

For the Wobblies, the tone for 1912 had

been set earlier that year with a renowned fight for free speech in Vancouver. One of the union's most effective recruitment tools was speaking directly to workers from street-corner soapboxes. Outraged by the public airing of such radicalism, civic authorities would usually ban the practice even as they allowed religious street preaching to go on unimpeded. The IWW traditionally answered with a procession of speakers. As each was arrested, another would take his place until city jails and the courts were clogged, driving municipal budgets haywire. More often than not, authorities capitulated.

The battle in Vancouver was more pronounced. Thousands of workers and free-speech supporters were caught up in battle against the city's newly elected law-and-order mayor James Findlay, who had vowed to crack down on IWW soapbox preaching. In early January, the city banned all outdoor public meetings. Ten Wobblies were arrested for speaking out. The rest of the union movement viewed the arrests as an attack on them all.

Bobby-like Vancouver police patrol the Powell Street Grounds after charging into a peaceful free-speech rally with clubs and horsewhips to make arrests on Jan. 18, 1912.
Image D-06368, Royal BC Museum and Archives.

On January 28, 1912, at a large protest rally on the Powell Street Grounds (now Oppenheimer Park), prominent labour leader Parm Pettipiece was arrested the moment he began to speak. A large force of waiting police brandishing clubs and horsewhips charged into the crowd. Those unable to flee "went down like ten pins before the irresistible onslaught," a *Province* reporter wrote. Thirty protesters were arrested with bail set at a vindictive $500. More street meetings produced more arrests. Someone then had what seemed like a good idea at the time. To subvert the ban, protesters hired a boat and constructed a large megaphone to address crowds at Stanley Park from the water. But strong currents carried the craft off-course and those on board were arrested as soon as they came ashore, their message lost in the blowing wind.

But support for the IWW's free-speech campaign kept growing. Labour and Socialist Party leaders scheduled another mass rally February 18 at the Powell Street Grounds.

They dared city officials to shut it down. Nearly ten thousand people packed the park and adjoining streets to hear a dozen speakers, including several from the IWW. This time, the police stayed away. The crackdown on street meetings eased, and the right to speak freely in parks had been confirmed.

The free-speech struggle and the heroic railway strike were high-water marks for the IWW in BC. Once World War I broke out, patriotism trumped the Wobblies' relentless opposition to the "capitalist war." Their influence began to wane. The IWW was among those organizations that were banned outright. Every now and then, Wobbly activity would rumble in the lumber camps, but their glory days were done. They left behind a legacy of radical leaders, martyrs and a treasure trove of hard-hitting union songs that are still heard today, including labour's standard, sung at every convention and picket line: "Solidarity Forever."

Alone among labour organizations of the time, the IWW saw class as the issue,

A large group of strikers is arrested near Savona in April 1912 during the battle by IWW railway construction workers against the Canadian Northern Railway. Their only crime seemed to have been their effrontery in going on strike.
Image E–00230, Royal BC Museum and Archives.

not race. "When the factory whistle blows, it calls us to work as wage-workers, regardless of the country in which we were born or colour of our skin," said a Wobbly from Prince Rupert. It was a message that struck home among vast numbers of immigrant and itinerant workers who had been shunned by established unions—and would be again for decades to come. And the IWW's brand of revolutionary industrial unionism was soon taken up by others.

For the province's Indigenous people, the early years of the twentieth century were increasingly grim. Smallpox and other fatal diseases had taken a devastating toll. Estimated at seventy thousand strong in 1835, the Indigenous population of British Columbia had fallen to 25,488 in 1901. The Haida Nation was down to fewer than six hundred people. By the time the terrible scourge had run its course, a third of the province's First Nations had died. "My grandmother told me she lived through it. Not many did," elder Mary Augusta Tappage recalled in her memoir. "They died like flies." Smallpox wasn't the only disease. W̱SÁNEĆ elder Dave Elliott remembered tuberculosis "running like wildfire" through his community. He would wake every morning to the sound of someone "crying or wailing" and the sawing and hammering of casket making.

As well, after many years in which their labour had played a significant role building the BC economy, they were slowly being squeezed out of activities where they had previously flourished. The seal hunt, which brought a measure of wealth for the bold Nuu-chah-nulth sealers on the west coast of Vancouver Island, was banned by all countries in 1911. And BC's dramatic economic expansion led inevitably to more demand for a stable, year-round workforce. Employers were less willing to tolerate the seasonal employment preferred by most Aboriginal workers, who would often head back to their home villages for traditional dancing, ceremonies and feasting that occupied the winter months. Government policies were put in place to make it exceedingly difficult for Indigenous workers to share in the economy beyond a subsistence living. These policies were deliberate. Few made it clearer than Premier Richard McBride. When whites in Ootsa Lake, calling themselves the "bona fide" settlers, complained in 1909 that too many Indians were being hired for government road work, McBride replied, "Have issued instructions to our officials [that] white settlers must be considered first."

Similar anti-Indigenous measures were applied in occupation after occupation. Despite a decline in Indigenous sawmill workers from the days when they were the backbone of the fledgling industry, hand-logging had continued to be a major source of income for coastal First Nations. They would take their saws, axes and other tools into the woods to harvest timber. In 1904, however, the province unleashed a major giveaway of accessible forest land while cracking down on hand-logging without a licence. Most licences went to non-Indigenous people, freezing out Indigenous loggers. Rubbing salt into the wound, the province prevented Indigenous people from logging without permission even on their own reserves.

At the same time, Indigenous people also lost the right to hunt whenever they wanted. They were now confined to specific seasons set by BC game wardens hostile to First Nations hunters. There was no need for Aboriginal people to hunt deer out of season in the fall, the province's game warden told a Royal Commission in 1913: "In many places there is work for Indians haying and harvesting. Giving Indians permits to hunt deer at this time of year simply encourages them to do nothing else."

There were pockets—such as the Vancouver docks, the northern fishing and canning industry, and Fraser Valley hop fields—where Indigenous labourers remained a significant part of the workforce. But new fishing restrictions were another hardship. Upstream fishing weirs, traps and reef nets that Indigenous fishers had used for centuries

INDIGENOUS SEALERS

For forty years, the prowess of First Nations' hunters dominated the risky but immensely profitable quest for fur seals on the wild, open waters of the Pacific. At the height of this quest, up to one hundred schooners would follow the great sealing herds on their annual migration from California to the desolate Pribilof Islands in the Bering Sea. When they came across a herd, hunters went after them in canoes lowered over the side of the ship into the heaving sea. No one was more skilled at this bloody trade than the Nuu-chah-nulth on the northwest coast of Vancouver Island, who slew the seals with their own handmade harpoons. When guns were banned for conservation, Nuu-chah-nulth hunters virtually took over. Although returns could vary, many Nuu-chah-nulth made pots of money, killing thousands of fur seals every year. Their village potlatches were renowned along the coast for their abundance.

But the hunt often came at a grim cost. Ships foundered. Crews were lost. Between 1886 and 1895, thirty-three sealing schooners went down in the stormy Pacific. Even safe voyages were difficult, with long stretches spent in dim, cramped quarters. Indigenous hunters sometimes travelled to sea with their wives, who cooked and steered the ocean-tossed canoe for their spear-wielding partners. In 1891, 40 percent of adult Nuu-chah-nulth males listed sealing as their main occupation. By 1911, however, few seals were left to hunt. Britain, which represented Canada in international matters, was one of four countries to sign a treaty outlawing open-water seal hunting on the West Coast. The North Pacific Fur Seal Convention is considered the first international treaty to address conservation of wildlife. The era of the great Nuu-chah-nulth seal hunters was over.

Indigenous fur seal hunters pose with their equipment, including spears, long lines and paddles, aboard the sealing ship *Forward* in 1894.
University of Washington Libraries, Special Collections, NA3062.

A traditional Indigenous salmon weir across the Cowichan River in the late 1860s. They were later banned as part of a deliberate strategy to drastically reduce the Indigenous share of salmon they once had all to themselves.
Image C–09260, Royal BC Museum and Archives.

to catch returning salmon were banned. Indigenous people were prohibited from selling salmon caught during their food fisheries, which were heavily regulated as well. And the large majority of commercial fishing licences were now issued to individuals rather than through canneries; Indigenous fishermen found it hard to acquire these licences, granted almost willy-nilly to whites and Nikkei. Noting the bewildering array of regulations that governed their once untrammelled right to hunt and fish, elder Peter Webster lamented, "All of these things made it easy to get into trouble with the law.

I think a lot of us became 'criminals' without really knowing the reason."

Ironically, amid all the division, there was a consistent call by union leaders during the first decade of the new century for greater unity to confront the forces of capitalism. On May 2, 1910, twenty-six delegates met in Vancouver to form labour's first province-wide organization, the BC Federation of Labor. Although the Federation would have several reincarnations in the years ahead, it was radical from the start. Pledging itself to unceasing struggle for the eight-hour day, the new organization declared that the

future belonged "to the only useful people in human society—the working class." Unions rushed to join. Within a year, it was able to take a 50 percent interest in the VTLC's labour newspaper, *The Western Wage Earner*, and rename it *The British Columbia Federationist*, which became one of the most comprehensive labour publications in North America.

Delegates and officers of the BC Federation of Labor's historic first convention at the Labor Hall in Victoria, March 13–15, 1911.
UBC Rare Books and Special Collections, 1429–1.

4 THE GREAT VANCOUVER ISLAND COAL STRIKE

VANCOUVER ISLAND COAL MINERS HAD NOT LOST their burning sense of injustice over their treatment by the Dunsmuirs. Their deep-seated hostility had been further powered by another dreadful gas explosion, this one south of Nanaimo at Extension in 1909. The tragedy claimed thirty-two lives. One miner's wife remembered bitterly, "You don't forget when you see thirty graves, all new, dug in a row waiting to be filled with men you've known all your life."

Despite their past defeats, many felt the time was right to take on the owners yet again. In 1911, the miners had called in the tough, seasoned United Mine Workers of America in hopes of triumphing at last in their long fight for union recognition. Hundreds flocked to join. With antagonism toward the company sky-high, the stage was set for the Great Vancouver Island Coal Strike. Lasting just short of two years, the confrontation turned into the most protracted, fiercely fought labour dispute in the province's history. It was bare-knuckled class warfare of the old school, with neither side willing to give an inch. It all began with a member of the miners' safety committee named Oscar Mottishaw.

In June 1912, Mottishaw reported gas in one of the shafts at the deadly Extension mine. By then, James Dunsmuir's coal-mining operations had been bought out by Canadian Collieries, a conglomerate dominated by the Canadian Northern Railway. But there was no shift in the company's ruthless anti-unionism. Although a mines inspector confirmed Mottishaw's report, the veteran union man was soon out of work. Shortly after he hired on in September as mule driver for a contractor at the company's mine in Cumberland, Mottishaw was sent packing once more. This dismissal ignited the strike.

While seemingly a trivial matter to set off such a reaction, his firing underscored two issues Island coal miners had been fighting for since they first rose up against the Dunsmuirs in 1870: mine safety and the right to join a union without being blacklisted. On September 16, miners at Cumberland and Extension called a one-day "holiday" to demand Mottishaw's reinstatement. The company told them not to bother coming back. Within three days, sixteen hundred Canadian Collieries workers were off the job and the war was on.

The owners quickly unleashed the tried-and-true tactics of the Dunsmuirs. Miners in Cumberland were evicted from their company-owned homes, forcing families into crude tents. Chinese miners initially stayed out too. Faced with threats that they too would be thrown out of their homes and already ostracized by the strikers, they soon went back to work. Strikebreakers were also brought in along with special constables to protect them. As usual, the government knew which side it was on. Brushing off entreaties from union and socialist MLAs to intervene, Premier Richard McBride told a confidant he believed it "intolerable" for coal miners to make demands of the mine owners.

Arriving strikebreakers were greeted by raucous protest parades, and were further harassed on their way to work by loud, discordant music and relentless heckling. Strike pay was $4 a week with extra money for wives and children. A multitude of activities were organized to keep the restless strikers out of the saloons as much as possible. In Ladysmith, where most Extension miners lived, the union rented a large hall with games rooms, a library and a piano for regular concerts. There were sports days, and at Christmas the hall hosted a large, festive gala with music and dancing to the wee hours for the adults and toys, candies, clothes and oranges for the children. Premier McBride donated the grand sum of $10 to the miners' Christmas fund to show what a merry old soul was he.

Wives, daughters and sisters turned the Women's Auxiliary into a formidable force. They raised money, staged support marches and social events, and harassed authorities and strikebreakers. Two fiery women were fined $20 by the courts for persistently calling the pit bosses "scabs." Many women also took on work outside the home to help their

A small boy holding a union newspaper near the beginning of the coal strike in 1912. *Cumberland Museum and Archives, c110–128.*

families survive. Their strong backing of the strike, accompanied by growing agitation for women's suffrage, was critical to keep the union pot boiling. After eight months, however, with no budge from the mine owners, matters were becoming desperate. Staffed by Chinese labour and other strikebreakers from as far away as Italy, the Cumberland mine was back to normal production. The mines at Extension were running too, albeit with limited production. The union decided it had to expand the strike.

Miners' wives and children parade behind the union's brass band as part of a mass procession down the main street of Ladysmith in 1913 during the Great Coal Strike of 1912–14. Their support was crucial to maintaining the long, difficult dispute. *Image E–O2631, Royal BC Museum and Archives.*

On May Day 1913, thousands of miners, their families and union supporters converged on Ladysmith for the largest parade and display of community solidarity the Island had ever seen. A brass band led the way. Children marched behind a banner proclaiming themselves "The Hope of the Future," while miners and their wives followed with defiant banners declaring "In Union There Is Strength" and "Workers of the World Unite." The day culminated that evening in Nanaimo. A thousand miners packed the town's Princess Theatre for a tumultuous meeting that endorsed the union's decision to broaden the strike to all three Nanaimo-area mines: Western Fuel, Pacific Coast Coal Colliery and the small Jingle Pot mine. The next day, thirty-seven hundred miners were off the job from Cumberland to Nanaimo.

Yet more and more strikebreakers arrived. After eleven months on strike and determined to take on the scabs in pitched battle, the miners finally snapped. The turbu-lence began in Nanaimo when a large crowd of miners and their families swarmed the pit-heads to dissuade strikebreakers from going to work. Several were injured in the scuffles that broke out. The next day at Pacific Coast's South Wellington coal mine, hundreds of miners drove strikebreakers and their families out of town and into the woods. On their way back, they attacked company property and the bunkhouses of Chinese workers.

On the night of August 13, jeering strikers massed outside the Temperance Hotel in Ladysmith, where a number of scabs were staying. When police arrested one of them for singing, "Hurray, hurray, we'll drive the scabs away," the crowd hurled rocks through windows of the hotel and houses belonging to strikebreakers and mine supervisors. A short time later, someone tossed a small stick of dynamite into the bedroom of strike-breaker Alex McKinnon, where his five children were sleeping.

As McKinnon rushed to toss it outside, the dynamite exploded, blowing off his right hand and burning his face. (It emerged later that the culprits were not strikers but three non-union local men caught up in events after more than a few swigs of the bottle.) Miners also ransacked Ladysmith's Chinatown, ordering its residents to get out of town. Crowds continued to surge through the streets all night and into the next day, prompting the mayor to call for the militia.

Back in Nanaimo, strikers forced the steamer *Princess Patricia* to return to Vancouver with its human cargo of strikebreakers and twenty-five special constables. Feelings reached a fever pitch on a false report that strikebreakers had shot and killed six strikers in Extension. Miners rushed to the scene. A tense standoff followed between strikebreakers holed up in a mine pithead and union men massed outside. Shots were fired at the strikers. Some strikebreakers retreated down the tunnel while others snuck away into the surrounding forest. Miners headed into the village when darkness fell, plundering and burning homes owned by the company, scabs and Chinese immigrants.

Once this violent outburst was out of their systems, strikers resumed peaceful picketing. That didn't matter to Attorney General William Bowser, who immediately ordered in the militia complete with a pair of mounted Maxim machine guns. The deployment of the militia actually re-energized the miners, attracting an outpouring of support from the public and other unions. In a rhetorical outburst, BC Federation of Labor vice-president Jack Kavanagh told a large rally in Vancouver that mining communities were being

Top left: After the mass arrests of striking Vancouver Island coal miners, an outpouring of support came from the BC labour movement, particularly in Vancouver. This fundraising tag day outside the city's Labor Temple on Dec. 20, 1913, was organized by the hastily formed BC Miners' Liberation League.
City of Vancouver Archives, 259–1.

Bottom left: This mounted Maxim machine gun was part of the force brought in by the militia against unarmed striking coal miners after trouble flared in August 1913, one year into their strike. The gun was manned by members of the Royal Canadian Garrison Artillery.
Image A–03159, Royal BC Museum and Archives.

"terrorized by half-clad barbarians armed with rifles and bayonets … No reptile ever evolved from the slime of ages resembles the spawn of filth now on Vancouver Island known as the militia."

The speedy crackdown on those suspected of fomenting trouble during the few days of violence was harsh. At Nanaimo's Athletic Hall, bayonet-wielding soldiers stormed into a meeting of more than a thousand miners and ordered everyone out. To ensure no one escaped out the back, the rear door was guarded by one of the Maxim machine guns. A number of union leaders and ordinary miners were marched off to jail while soldiers ransacked the empty hall for weapons. They found none. Similar round-ups took place in Ladysmith and Extension. All told, 213 strikers were arrested, charged with such offences as assault, obstruction of police, unlawful assembly and the heinous crime of picketing. Most were held without bail until their trials. In Ladysmith, Judge Frederic Howay imposed sentences that were severe even for those law-and-order times. Five men got two-year sen-

tences, twenty-three received a year and many others three months in jail. When dozens of the prisoners returned from Oakalla prison to Ladysmith the next spring, they were joyfully paraded through the streets to a loud rendition of "La Marseillaise."

Striker Joseph Mairs was not among them. Tragically, he died in Oakalla two weeks short of his twenty-second birthday, a victim of poor medical treatment after he fell ill. A funeral procession reportedly nearly a mile long accompanied his body to the Ladysmith cemetery, where he joined those killed in the Extension mine explosion of 1909. A large memorial commemorating Mairs still dominates the cemetery today. Part of the inscription reads, "A martyr to a noble cause—the emancipation of his fellow men."

In spite of all their setbacks, the miners' spirits remained strong even as the strike entered its second year. Sending in the militia was widely regarded as a declaration of war by workers throughout the province. That November, unions and left-wing organizations joined together to form the BC Miners' Liberation League. Its elected president

Striking Ladysmith coal miners are marched off to jail by armed soldiers with bayonets fixed in place. Although some faced assault charges, most were charged only with unlawful assembly and picketing. All were held without bail until their trials. Many received prison sentences.
Image E–01194, Royal BC Museum and Archives.

Mass Protest Meeting
DEMANDING RELEASE OF VANCOUVER ISLAND MINERS
DOMINION HALL, Pender Street, Near Homer.
Monday, 8 p.m., November 10th
ADMISSION FREE.

Auspices B. C. Miners Liberation League.

Speakers representing Federations of Labor, Trades Unions, Mine Workers, Industrial Unions and Socialist Parties.
Thos. Greenall M.P., Representing Great Britain Miners

(Over)

Above: A postcard for the public meeting organized by the BC Miners' Liberation League to demand the release of arrested Vancouver Island coal miners. A featured speaker was British coal mining trade unionist and Labour Party politician Thomas Greenall. *Courtesy David Yorke.*

Left: Young cyclist and coal miner Joseph Mairs died in Oakalla prison in early 1914, three months into a harsh sixteen-month sentence for activities during the coal miners' strike. This postcard was sold to raise funds for a large memorial headstone in the Ladysmith cemetery, saluting Mairs as a martyr to a noble cause. *Courtesy David Yorke.*

was a prominent member of the IWW. The League dedicated itself to raising money and public support for its beleaguered brothers on the Island and the release of those in jail. Public pressure grew for a fair deal to end the strike. Even McBride weighed in.

But the coal companies, by then enjoying near normal production, saw no need to bend. A visit in June by the famous American union firebrand Mother Jones briefly buoyed the miners. Local historian John R. Hinde speculates that her scorching rhetoric may have motivated their rejection of a status quo offer by the companies. Still, as the months continued to roll by, nothing could change the bleakness of the miners' situation. The gathering war clouds in Europe doomed the Liberation League's agitation for a forty-eight-hour general strike to back the miners, and the union began to run out of money. In July the UMWA local made a painful decision to cut off strike pay. A month

later, two weeks after the outbreak of World War I, miners voted to return to work after twenty-three months of heroic struggle that remain unrivalled in the annals of BC labour.

"MOTHER" JONES IN CANADA.
Dominion Admits Strike Leader, Overruling Immigration Officials.

SEATTLE, Wash., June 6.—"Mother" Mary Jones, organizer for the United Mine Workers of America, left for Victoria, B. C., by steamer last night without hindrance, arriving there today, the Canadian immigration officials who prevented her from embarking on the previous day having been overruled by their superior officers at Ottawa.

The British Columbia Government ordered the exclusion of "Mother" Jones, who had announced her intention of addressing the strinking coal miners of Vancouver Island, on the ground that she would be likely to "stir up trouble."

"Mother" Jones at once left Victoria for the centre of the coal mine strike district at Nanaimo.

The visit in 1914 to Vancouver Island by the famous "friend of the miners" made *The New York Times.*

MOTHER JONES

Mention Mother Jones today and thoughts immediately turn to the prominent muck-raking journal of the same name. But one hundred years ago, the world knew a different Mother Jones. Mary Harris Jones was regularly denounced by authorities as the most dangerous woman in America. A diminutive firebrand well into her senior years, undeterred by jailings and frequent arrests, Jones preached a fierce, anti-capitalism gospel of resistance and socialism wherever she travelled, which was usually wherever miners were on strike.

In June of 1914, she responded to a union request to buoy the spirits of Vancouver Island coal miners in the second year of their desperate struggle against the mine owners. After making her way from the strike-bound Colorado coalfields to Seattle, Canadian officials branded her a troublemaker and barred her from the ship to Victoria. The feisty seventy-six-year-old retorted that she had friends in high places. Sure enough, US Labour Secretary William B. Wilson intervened on her behalf, and she was soon on her way. The hard-pressed miners gave her a rapturous reception.

Mother Jones, the famed mine workers' organizer and radical who grew up in Toronto, returned to Canada in June of 1914 for a series of solidarity rallies to boost the morale of striking coal miners on Vancouver Island.
Archives of Ontario, F1405-15, #1871.

As she recounted in her autobiography, "A regiment of Canadian Kilties met the train, squeaking on their bagpipes. Down the street came a delegation of miners [who] wore the badge of the working class—their overalls. I held a tremendous meeting that night, and the poor boys who had come up from the subterranean holes of the earth to fight for a few hours of sunlight, took courage. I brought them the sympathy of the Colorado strikers, a sympathy and understanding that reaches across borders and frontiers."

She finished her BC visit with a miners' rally in Cumberland and a rousing speech at the Labor Temple in Vancouver. Before an overflow crowd, she called for unity and a general strike if necessary to win the battle of the coal mines. "Capitalism," she told cheering trade unionists, "has danced too long on the hearts of the aching miners."

THE GREAT WAR AND CANADA'S FIRST GENERAL STRIKE

5

T HE OUTBREAK OF THE GHASTLY "WAR TO END ALL WARS" in 1914 had a profound impact on the BC labour movement, as it did on almost every aspect of provincial life. Among the fifty-five thousand British Columbians who went off to the butchery in Europe were many workers, motivated both by patriotism and a deep recession that made jobs hard to find. The war and a slumping economy cut BC union membership in half, from twenty-one thousand in 1913 to less than eleven thousand in 1915.

The longer the war went on, however, the more matters began to change. Labour shortages increased unions' bargaining power, while paycheques eroded by wartime inflation whetted an appetite for fighting back. Workers not in the trenches flocked to join unions once again. By 1917, BC union membership was back over twenty-one thousand, a trend that continued until 1919, when an impressive forty thousand workers, representing 20.8 percent of the workforce, held union cards. At the same time, the terrible death toll in a conflict that seemed to have neither point nor end hardened class attitudes. What could be more unjust than an economic system allowing capitalists to profit from a war that was killing millions of workers?

Inspired by the 1917 Russian Revolution as well, many workers—particularly in the West—became increasingly militant and radical. The federal government's promotion and eventual enactment of conscription was a tipping point. At the 1917 convention of the BC Federation of Labor, delegates elected a socialist slate bitterly opposed to conscription, a key rallying point in the growing class war. They were further infuriated by the Trades and Labor Congress of Canada, powered by eastern-based craft unions, which had swung behind mandatory military registration. "The Labor movement of the east is reactionary and servile to the core," stormed *The BC Federationist*. A resolution to fight conscription with a general strike received

VOTE TO STRIKE IN VANCOUVER OVER CONSCRIPTION

VANCOUVER, B. C., Nov. 15—At the trades and labor meeting tonight a motion to call a general strike on December 17 was substituted for one declaring a holiday on that date in order that organized labor might register its vote against the Military Service act.

"Ginger" Goodwin

overwhelming support from Vancouver trade unions. Although the conscription strike didn't happen, workers were downing tools throughout BC, from the mines of the Crowsnest and Kootenays to the shipyards, laundries and shingle mills of Vancouver. All told, upwards of fourteen thousand BC trade unionists hit the bricks in 1917, followed by more than sixteen thousand in 1918. Such labour turmoil was unprecedented to that point in the province.

This simmering anti-capitalist anger erupted into out-and-out rage when charismatic union activist, socialist and organizer Albert "Ginger" Goodwin was fatally shot on July 27, 1918, by special constable Dan Campbell in the woods overlooking the working-class bastion of Cumberland. Goodwin, a vice-president of the BC Federation of Labor, had been hiding out to avoid a politically suspicious order that he report for military duty. The order, which followed his equally dubious reclassification from unfit to fit for service, took place during a strike he led for an eight-hour day by Trail smelter workers. The Dominion Police had been tracking him for months. Although the precise circumstances of Goodwin's killing remain inconclusive, there is no doubt he died a martyr to the cause of working-class struggle, pursued solely for his trade union leadership.

Remembered for his role in the 1912–14 coal strike, Goodwin was revered by the people of Cumberland, who had helped him survive his clandestine existence. Already a veteran of nearly nine years in the mines of Yorkshire and Canada, Goodwin had come to Cumberland the year before the strike began, five months shy of his twenty-fourth birthday. His solid play for the local soccer team and growing espousal of socialism and worker rights soon made him a community fixture. On a hiring blacklist after the strike, Goodwin managed to find work at the smelter in Trail, where he significantly upped his activism. He ran for the Socialist Party in the 1916 BC election, winning 20 percent of the vote. He helped organize and was elected full-time secretary of the local smelter workers' union. He was also chosen as a vice-president of the BC Federation of Labor. His prowess as a Socialist orator, urging "the wage slaves" to rise up and overthrow "the master class," led to many speaking engagements. A reporter for the *Vancouver Daily World* covering a Goodwin speech at the Rex Theatre on August 19, 1917, praised his socialist knowledge and calm delivery. Six months later, he was on the run.

His sombre funeral procession, led by the municipal band, stretched from one end of town to the other. "The casket was packed shoulder-high right through Cumberland," miner Ben Horbry recalled years later. "When one bunch of men got tired, another bunch took over." Police were told to make themselves scarce. "The miners were so incensed over it," Horbry said. "It was a good thing for [Dan] Campbell that he got out and disappeared when he did. He would have been hung or shot."

In Vancouver, news of the shooting hit like a thunderbolt. At noon on August 2, the day of Goodwin's funeral in Cumberland, close to six thousand workers walked off the job across the city to mourn Goodwin and protest his fatal shooting. Shipyards and the docks were shut tight. Trolleys were taken off the streets by their drivers. Construction trades, linemen, garment workers and other

The funeral procession accompanying the white casket of slain union leader Ginger Goodwin to the town's cemetery stretched more than a kilometre along the main street of Cumberland on Aug. 2, 1918.
Hayashi/Kitamura/ Matsubushi Studio, Cumberland Museum and Archives, c110–001.

JOE NAYLOR

Student and mentor. Martyr and saint, some say. Together they lie virtually side by side in the historic Cumberland Cemetery. Ginger Goodwin, with a memorable headstone, a mountain named after him, books, graphic comics, films, songs and so much else commemorating his labour martyrdom, is as familiar to British Columbians as anyone who died a hundred years ago could possibly be. But Joe Naylor is remembered by few, his grave marked for years only by a small metal plate.

Yet without Joe Naylor, Ginger Goodwin might not have become the labour leader he did. The two immigrant miners forged a bond in Cumberland during the epic 1912–14 coal strike. Naylor, the stolid, forty-year-old head of the local miners' union, took young Goodwin under his wing. By the end of the strike, Goodwin had fully embraced Naylor's strong socialist politics. Blacklisted after the strike, Goodwin moved on to Trail, where he led an unsuccessful strike at the smelter, before returning to Cumberland to evade the military draft and meet his fate, tracked down and killed by a special constable in the woods above town.

Naylor stayed in Cumberland. In 1917 he was elected president of the BC Federation of Labour on an anti-war, anti-conscription platform, with Goodwin as vice-president. At the end of the war, barred from further employment in the Cumberland coal mines, Naylor threw himself into the One Big Union movement. A member of its central committee, his outspoken rad-

This is the only known portrait of coal miner, union leader, Socialist and the pride of the Cumberland working class, Joe Naylor (1872–1946).
Cumberland Museum and Archives, C192–030

icalism put him on the RCMP's list of Canada's "chief agitators."

Naylor stood out from other trade unionists by opposing Asian exclusion. He sympathized with Asian workers forced by mine managers to work as strike-breakers during the coal strike. "The white men ... are the real curse in this province," Naylor told the BC Federation of Labour convention in 1914, referring to owners and non-Asian strikebreakers. "It isn't the Asiatics at all." Instead of supporting a ban on Chinese immigrants to keep them from undercutting rates of white workers, he urged a minimum wage for all workers regardless of race. A passionate advocate of mine safety, Naylor was also among those credited with pushing the province to pass its landmark Workmen's Compensation Act in 1917.

Naylor was eventually allowed back in the coal mines. But it wasn't until 1937, when he was sixty-five, that the Cumberland mines were organized for good and he could again become a union member. Spurning both the Communist Party and the CCF, Naylor remained a socialist until his last breath in 1946, still hoping for workers to one day overthrow "this damnable system."

assorted groups also took part. The shutdown lasted twenty-four hours. It was Canada's first general strike.

The business community reacted hysterically to the show of union force. Branding strike leaders as both pro-Bolshevik and pro-German, they incited hundreds of ex-soldiers into a frenzy. The vets, some fortified with booze, proceeded to ransack the Labor Temple at Dunsmuir and Homer Streets. They destroyed records, broke up furniture and assaulted several VTLC officers. Secretary Victor Midgley only just avoided being tossed from the building's second floor when switchboard operator Frances Foxcroft bravely stood in front of the window to protect Midgley as he crouched on the outside ledge. The mob did not leave until the union men knelt and kissed the Union Jack.

The next day, with many workers still off the job, the same veterans tried to invade the Longshoremen's Hall. This time, union members were ready, beating back all attempts by the soldiers to get inside. The strike was a resounding success, giving unions a strong taste of collective action.

The intensive class struggle and political action that permeated much of the first two decades of the twentieth century in British Columbia did not leave women sitting on the sidelines. Many had already shown their mettle during early strikes in the coalfields of Vancouver Island, hectoring strikebreakers and helping to hold their families together with little income. In Vancouver, which had emerged as an increasingly working-class community, women resisted the prevailing view they should remain at home with no part in industrial work. They joined existing male unions. In occupations where women dominated, they formed their own unions. As on Vancouver Island, they also backed the struggles of male workers while playing a major role in union label campaigns to push goods produced by union workers.

Toiling long hours in small, scattered

Angry crowds, including many WWI soldiers, mass in front of the Labor Temple in Vancouver, headquarters of Canada's first general strike, called to protest the killing of Ginger Goodwin. Urged on by a uniformed officer at the back of the crowd, they soon charged through the doors of the Temple, ransacking offices and threatening those inside.
Stuart Thomson photo, Vancouver Public Library, 18266.

work sites, with little access to child care or even public transportation, Vancouver women were far from a union organizer's dream. Yet as labour historian Star Rosenthal points out, the fact that some organized at all "argues either a large degree of class-consciousness, or a large degree of desperation, or both." Much of the activity was stoked by Helena Gutteridge, the city's most prominent woman activist almost the moment she arrived from England in 1911. Relentless in her drive for women's suffrage, she was also a social reformer and active trade unionist.

By 1914 Gutteridge was president of Local 178 of the Journeymen Tailors' Union of America and the first woman elected to the executive of the Vancouver Trades and Labor Council. Later that year, as the city was swept by unemployment, she organized an exceptional co-operative to provide work for impoverished women struggling to make ends meet. The Carvell Hall Cooperative Settlement made toys, dolls and puddings, rushing them into production in time for Christmas sales. Scores of women found work at the "toy factory," earning $3.50 a day,

three days a week. Others did sewing work. At the end of the year, proceeds amounted to more than $2,500. Although hostility by business operators and some male workers eventually did in the co-operative, the tireless Gutteridge barely paused for breath.

Gutteridge was in the forefront of the successful 1916 referendum that at last gave British Columbia women the right to vote. (Asian and Indigenous men and women remained barred from voting.) During the campaign, prompted by fears that increasing numbers of women replacing men in wartime factories would become low-wage competition, the labour movement reversed its previous support for women's suffrage. A wrong-headed editorial in *The BC Federationist* predicted that once women had the vote, they would help keep the establishment in power, while their presence in the workforce would enable employers to roll back fifty years of trade union gains.

Despite her anger at this turnabout, Gutteridge continued to work with the VTLC. In 1918 she and several other women led a spirited campaign supported by the labour movement that resulted in BC's, and Canada's, first minimum-wage law for women workers. Although the law fell short of guaranteeing a living wage, it did result in significant pay increases for women in many areas of employment. The measure had been piloted through the legislature by another female pioneer, Mary Ellen Smith. The widow of union leader-turned-politician Ralph Smith, she was BC's first woman MLA, elected in a by-election as an independent Liberal with the slogan "Women and children first."

Mary Ellen Smith subsequently became the first female cabinet minister and first female Speaker in the British Empire. A true social reformer, albeit with the era's prevalent prejudice against Asian immigrants, Smith also spearheaded legislation establishing social welfare for abandoned wives, mothers' pensions, workplace protection for women, female appointments to the judiciary, and

Helena Gutteridge in 1911, the year she arrived in Vancouver at the age of thirty-two. A campaigner for women's right to vote, social activist, trade unionist and organizer, Gutteridge quickly became one of the city's most prominent women, and later the first woman elected to city council.
City of Vancouver Archives, CVA 371-2693.

juvenile courts. In 1929 she represented Canada at the International Labour Organization.

In September of 1918, Helena Gutteridge headed a gutsy strike by city laundry workers, almost all of whom were women. They walked out at seven laundries after managers threatened to fire them if they didn't quit their union. The owners quickly agreed to boost their pitifully low wages, but refused their demand for a closed shop, requiring them to hire only union members. At a lively meeting punctuated by cheering and wild applause, the strikers voted unanimously to reject the owners' offer.

With solid backing from other unions, the women redoubled their efforts. They built wooden picket shelters, organized whist and dance nights to raise money, and rallied awareness at public meetings, unde-

terred by the death of four of their members from the worldwide outbreak of Spanish flu. "The laundry workers have decided to fight to the last ditch," wrote Gutteridge in *The BC Federationist*. Alas, after four months on the picket line, the laundry workers voted to return to work. As in so many strikes, management simply refused to budge on the matter of a closed shop. Eighty women and twenty men were not hired back. Still, their militancy yielded real gains for those who were rehired. The new Minimum Wage Board awarded the laundry workers higher wages than their original demand.

Less successful were attempts to form a waitresses' union and the Home and Domestic Employees Union (HDEU) of British Columbia. But the latter union did raise awareness of the plight of domestic workers,

The annual picnic of Pioneer Laundry Employees on Bowen Island in June of 1918, with uniformed WWI soldiers among them. Several months later, the employees were on strike.
City of Vancouver Archives, 99–5199.

forced to work up to fourteen-hour days for just $30 a month and room and board. With policies that were both radical and feminist for the time, the union was led by Lillian Coote. She rejected the idea that domestics were mere service workers, viewing them as industrial workers under the capitalist system. During its two years of existence, the HDEU operated from an office in the Labor Temple, campaigning for a nine-hour day, a minimum wage and a union hiring hall.

Women retail clerks, described by the Vancouver Trades and Labor Council as "among the most exploited classes of labor on earth, subjected to the whims and idiosyncrasies of both customers and petty bosses," also drew union attention. The Retail Clerks International Protective Association (RCIPA) was one of the first labour organizations to welcome women into its ranks, going to bat for earlier closing times, higher pay and an end to wage discrimination. "Every trade unionist whose female dependents … work in stores should see that they are made acquainted with the aims and objectives of the Clerks' Union," said organizer W.H. Hoop.

Not strong enough to combat tight-fisted merchants head on, the RCIPA did have some success encouraging union members to shop at stores employing union clerks. One was the pioneer family shoe store Ingledew's. An ad listing pro-union stores in *The Federationist* referenced Ingledew's as "Two soles with but a single thought. The Union Man and The Ingledew Shoe." The RCIPA also exposed some of the shortcomings of the new Minimum Wage Board for female workers. After an investigation, the board proclaimed a minimum wage of $12.75 a week for women clerks, a level decried as ludicrous by the union.

Helena Gutteridge, whose laundry workers had received a much more favourable ruling, produced evidence showing $16 a week was the bare minimum a female clerk needed to get by. But efforts to raise wages by organizing more women retail workers were hampered by store-owner intimidation. Five pro-union women were fired by Spencer's Department Store in late 1917, and Woodward's sent managers to spy on union meetings at the Labor Temple to make sure none of its employees were present. Three years later, the clerks' union in Vancouver was mostly dormant, not to resurface until the tail end of the Depression, but the foundation had been laid.

In the midst of all these struggles, the workers of BC achieved a significant milestone. In 1917, after many promises and strong protestations by labour, the government passed a meaningful Workmen's Compensation Act. Rather than forcing injured workers to fight for compensation against deep-pocketed employers in the courts, the act guaranteed them 55 percent of their average earnings, and monthly payments of $20 plus $5 per child to widows of employees killed on the job. The act allowed employers to escape being sued over workplace deaths and injuries, but workers welcomed the security of knowing they would be compensated. The new act was also the first in North America to provide comprehensive medical aid for injured workers. And it covered almost all workers, rather than restricting it to select occupations as did the trailblazing but imperfect 1902 compensation act. During its first year, the new Workmen's Compensation Board (WCB) registered six thousand employers covering seventy-five thousand workers.

ONE BIG UNION 6

WHEN WORLD WAR I FINALLY CAME TO AN END on November 11, 1918, the spirit of resistance was soaring in Western Canada, especially among industrial unions. Despite double-digit inflation eating into workers' pay while unregulated profiteering thrived, government and owners continued to reject workers' rights to negotiate better wages and working conditions. Anger was particularly acute in BC, which had the highest inflation and unemployment in Canada. A record number of strikes hit the province in 1919. Union membership was at an all-time high.

The first two years after the Great War were the high-water mark of radical trade unionism in Western Canada. The temper of the times was reflected during a labour hall meeting in Victoria. Hobbling to the front of the hall on his crutches, a veteran of World War I demanded that the Union Jack draping the speaker's podium be replaced by the red flag. "The realization is growing that there is a class war, a war in which there is no discharge," chimed in a supportive William Yates of the city's Street and Electric Railway Employees.

Having lost vote after vote at the annual convention of the middle-of-the-road Trades and Labor Congress of Canada in 1918, the radicalized Western Canadian union leaders' frustration could not be contained. The TLC leadership's decision to support conscription was the last straw. They decided to forge their own path. Western union representatives met in Calgary in the spring of 1919 to map out industrial unionism in a big way, free from the dominant craft unions they derided as too rigid and conservative. This division between industrial workers and those in craft unions with specific skills was to plague the labour movement for years to come.

One-third of the 239 delegates had made the journey to Calgary from British Columbia. Most had attended the BC Federation of Labor's convention purposely held in Calgary just the week before, where moderate views were brushed aside. The Federation also abandoned its long demand for Asian exclusion. "This body recognizes no aliens but the capitalist," delegates declared. "Asian workers should be encouraged [to join] white unions, for it is a class problem, and not a race problem that confronts the white mill-worker in BC," exclaimed *The BC Federationist*. Finally and most significantly, the Federation announced its intention to embrace a single workers' organization to take on the forces of capitalism, once and for all.

Delegates at the socialist-dominated Western Labor Conference that followed saw no need to spend any more time lobbying politicians and trying to elect their own representatives. They embraced direct action and general strikes as the way to end political repression and win breakthrough measures such as a six-hour day. The conference called for workers to rally behind a new, militant and radical organization called simply One Big Union (OBU). Industrial workers across the West stampeded toward the OBU as their organization of choice. By the end of the year, nearly twenty thousand BC workers were paying two cents a month in dues to the OBU: teamsters, metal workers, construction workers, railway workers, shop craft workers, miners and, significantly, loggers.

Given the low pay, dangerous work and grim accommodation early loggers endured, the province's largest industry had always seemed ripe for unionization. But isolation and the transient nature of logging were rough terrain for union organizers, regularly rousted out of the camps by obdurate operators. Loggers liked to say there were three crews in the camps: one coming, one going and one working. Although the IWW had managed some inroads, it was not until the emergence of the Lumber Workers Industrial Union (LWIU) in 1918 that a union was able to take on the forest companies. Within a year, enhanced class attitudes brought on by the war, continued inflation and the misery of camp life had prompted eleven thousand BC woodworkers to join the LWIU, an enthusiastic supporter of One Big Union and its preferred weapon to achieve progress: the general strike.

The same mood prompted a five-day general strike in February 1919 by sixty-five thousand Seattle workers. Three months later, Canadian working-class fervour exploded into the historic Winnipeg General Strike. For six weeks, thirty thousand public- and private-sector workers withdrew their labour in a united bid to force Winnipeg employers to recognize unions and the right to collective bargaining. The breadth of the walkout, its disciplined non-violent organization and the harsh measures unleashed by authorities to crush it aroused workers across the country. Solidarity walkouts took place in more than two dozen Canadian municipalities from Victoria to Amherst, Nova Scotia, where more than a thousand workers shut down the town for three weeks.

While the Winnipeg General Strike remains a pivotal, much-studied event in Canadian history, these dramatic "sympathy strikes" are relatively forgotten today. Although Victoria came late to the struggle, five thousand mostly industrial unionists left their jobs for four days to protest the arrest of the Winnipeg strike leaders. Workers in Prince Rupert also walked out, as did miners in the Kootenays. And in Vancouver, ten thousand union members were off the job for an entire month in a sustained general strike to back workers in Winnipeg. Even after the Winnipeg General Strike ended in late June, Vancouver workers stayed out for another week.

Labour historian Elaine Bernard suggests their walkout was arguably more radical than the Winnipeg General Strike: "While the Winnipeg strikers were supporting workers engaged in a struggle with the local captains of industry, the Vancouver strike was remarkable in that it was motivated by solidarity for workers more than a thousand miles away." The strike in Vancouver had gradually expanded in response to the city's threats to fire its own employees for walking out and to the city allowing private vehicles to carry paying passengers. By mid-June those off the job included stevedores, shipyard workers, streetcar drivers, telephone operators and linemen, CPR workers, woodworkers, teamsters, brewery workers and city employees including non-emergency police and firefighters. Vancouver strike leaders soon issued their own set of demands, including compensation and pensions for veterans and their dependents, nationalization of food storage plants to combat postwar hoarding, and a legislated six-hour day for all industries hit by unemployment.

The city's women telephone operators, regrouped as IBEW Local 77A, had been called off the job on June 14, 1919. After locking the doors and dropping keys through the window of BC Telephone's Seymour Street headquarters, more than three hundred operators and supervisors joined the general strike. BC Telephone responded by recruiting seventy-six strikebreakers, many of them society women, to maintain service. As the strike continued, the financial pinch on the striking women was acute. "My landlady didn't come looking for rent money. She kept me going," operator Leona Copeland told *The Federationist*. "I was pretty close to brass tacks. Most of us who stayed out couldn't afford to stay out, but we did."

Not only did they stay out, but the Vancouver telephone operators were the last of the sympathy strikers across Canada to return to work. In an ultimately unsuccessful effort to prevent supervisors from being disciplined for joining the picket line, they remained off the job for another thirteen days after the general strike officially ended. Afterward, *The Federationist* doffed its hat to the operators' resolve. "The action of the telephone girls in responding to the call for a general strike has placed them in a class by themselves amongst all women workers in this province," lauded the labour paper. "These girls have won the admiration of all those who admire grit and working class solidarity."

Another unusual feature of the Vancouver general strike was a censorship board set up by the International Typographical Union (ITU), whose members printed the city news-

papers. Prevented from striking, the ITU set up a committee "to ensure the publication of the strikers' views and [to prevent] deliberate misrepresentation ... under penalty of cessation of work." They made good on their vow by shutting down the *Vancouver Sun* for five days over its anti-strike diatribes. The *Vancouver Province* also lost an edition because of an anti-strike ad that ITU members refused to print.

With unions having no inkling that any of their demands would be met, coupled with growing threats of government-backed vigilante violence, momentum eventually faded. The Vancouver general strike officially came to an end on July 4. All told, forty-five union locals had taken part, a remarkable response

This labour cartoon ridicules high society Vancouver matrons who scabbed on telephone operators after they left their jobs in support of the 1919 general strike. "She doesn't understand that we are out for a principle—or she wouldn't do that," the striking operators observe. Even the cat sneers *Scab!* *Courtesy Elaine Bernard.*

Labour leader, socialist and bricklayer Ernest Winch, in 1917, is wearing his *L* for Labour pin. As president of the Vancouver Trade and Labor Council, he prevailed over city-wide general strikes in 1918 and 1919. A founding member of the CCF, he and his son Harold were two of the first seven MLAs elected by the new party in 1933. *City of Burnaby Archives, 514-028.*

considering that the original vote by union members in favour of the strike was hardly a landslide: 3,305–2,499. The strike committee ran up a grand total of $462 in expenses.

An ardent socialist and president of the Vancouver Trades and Labor Council, Ernest Winch had been in the forefront of the city's general strikes in 1918 and 1919. He was also the energetic head of the expanding Lumber Workers Industrial Union. With LWIU offices springing up across BC, the province's first "war in the woods" ensued. Over the next two years, government records list eighty-one separate walkouts by disgruntled lumber workers. Most resulted in substantial on-the-job improvements. The union was also One Big Union's largest affiliate, constituting more than 40 percent of its total membership.

The popularity of the OBU's revolutionary industrial unionism set off alarm bells in the ruling class. In Vancouver, police staged night-time raids on the homes of socialist labour leaders such as Winch, Bill Pritchard, Jack Kavanagh and Victor Midgley. Offices of *The Federationist* and other left-wing publications were ransacked and BC Federation of Labor records seized. Most companies

refused to negotiate with OBU locals, while the national Trades and Labor Congress, egged on by international craft unions, cancelled the charters of unions and local labour councils that joined or supported the OBU. These counterattacks, along with the usual media and government hysteria over "Bolshevism," were effective. At the same time, the BC Federation of Labor surrendered its charter voluntarily to the TLC in 1920, mistakenly thinking One Big Union was the future. And Vancouver's grand Labor Temple, its financial resources crippled by the split, was bought by the province.

Nothing illustrated the hurdles faced by the OBU more vividly than what happened to the fighting coal miners of the Crowsnest Pass area in BC and Alberta. After voting more than 95 percent to leave the United Mine Workers (UMW) and join the OBU, six thousand miners went on strike in May of 1919, seeking higher wages, cost-of-living protection and better working conditions. But the UMW, which revoked the miners' union charter, made a backroom deal with the companies, grouped together as the Western Coal Operators' Association. There would be wage increases for the strikers, but only if they rejoined the UMW. At the same time, with the active support of the government-appointed director of coal operations, the companies imposed a UMW closed shop at all organized coal mines, meaning no one but UMW members could work there. One Big Union was blindsided, and the United Mine Workers regained control over a bitter membership.

There was also active opposition to the OBU by union moderates. In Vancouver, Helena Gutteridge and other leaders remained loyal to their international craft unions. They established their own labour council separate from the Vancouver Trades and Labor Council, which supported the OBU. As in the Crowsnest, employers united with international unions to freeze out the OBU. Its adherents were blacklisted, left to press demands that had no hope of succeeding. Inevitably, there were ideological divisions too, amid a

ONE BIG UNION
OFFICIAL MEMBERSHIP RECEIPT

N.º 651 Cst C

Date May 20 1920

Received from H. Treacher

Occupation Lumber-Worker O.B.U. No. 53-481

Address Hdqtrs Ledger No.

For Mar - June 1920 the sum

of 2.00 Dollars. Signed J Clarke Secretary.

This receipt is issued by the Lumber and Camp Workers' Industrial Unit of the O. B. U. It can be issued to any wage worker in any unit of the One Big Union. State if Lumber or Camp Worker, Miner, Transport, Construction, Fisheries, Food Supply, General Worker, etc. etc.

Duplicate No. 651C Cst Issued by Delegate

A One Big Union membership receipt issued to H. Treacher in 1920 by the lumber workers' union, by far the largest affiliate of the short-lived OBU. *Courtesy David Yorke.*

worsening economy. After internal conflict over Ernest Winch's plan to begin organizing workers in other occupations, the lumber workers dropped out of the OBU in 1920. They were not alone. Within a year the organization was a shell of its former self, reduced to running a lottery to stay afloat.

The revolution didn't happen. Yet it would be wrong to see the rapid rise and fall of One Big Union as a historical blip. The attempt to build the OBU paved the way for the eventual rise of the US-based Congress of Industrial Organizations (CIO), which spearheaded an unprecedented union organizing drive across North America, including BC, from the late 1930s well into the 1940s. Labour historian David Frank observed that "the OBU was not so much an institution as an idea. It had an influence that went well beyond its high, short-lived membership."

In contrast, the International Longshore-men's Association had been a fixture representing Vancouver dock workers since 1912. Continuing the waterfront workers' combative tradition that predated the turn of the century, the ILA was a strong union with solid membership support. It could point to real achievements: wages were now competitive with other West Coast ports and the union had established regular shifts. Dockside labourers no longer had to spend long, unpaid hours waiting in all kinds of weather for a ship to arrive and a chance call to work by a straw boss who regularly played favourites.

But in 1923, the Shipping Federation decided it was time to break the union. When the ILA advanced a series of modest demands for its next contract, the companies refused to negotiate. Not knowing this had been the Shipping Federation's game plan all along, ILA members voted overwhelmingly to strike, setting up picket lines on

The Tools and Tree logo of the Lumber Workers Industrial Union of Canada, headed by Ernest Winch, which organized thousands of BC lumber workers in the early 1920s. *Courtesy BC Labour Heritage Centre collection.*

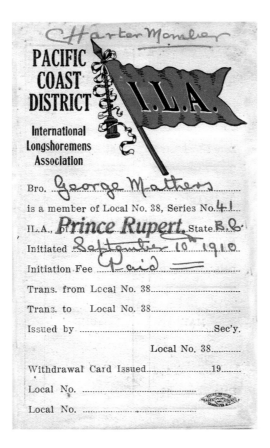

October 8. The companies were ready. Protected by several hundred armed security guards who patrolled the waterfront day and night, hordes of strikebreakers were imported to load and unload the ships.

The strikers fought back. Teenager Albert Stock witnessed an onslaught on the strikebreakers at the Great Northern Railway Pier: "I heard all these longshoremen coming. They were pushing one of the tank cars from the Sugar Refinery. They pushed it right through the barricade, and it went to the end of the dock, just balancing over the end. The union guys were getting the men to leave. Every time one did, he got a big cheer." Several union attackers were charged in the melee, which sent nine men to hospital. The ILA's defence lawyer was none other than Gerry McGeer. A dozen years later as mayor of Vancouver, his union past forgotten, McGeer would unleash squads of mounted police against a march of unarmed union longshoremen.

The strikers held firm until December, but nothing, including pressure from a federal government conciliator and pared-down union demands, could move the companies. After nine weeks, members voted 584–337 to end their strike. The defeat was complete. The ILA disappeared from the waterfront. The Shipping Federation established its own hiring hall and a company union with a constitution that proclaimed, "Workers [must] support the existing form of government in Canada and resist all revolutionary movements." A decade later, the Vancouver and District Waterfront Workers' Association (VDWWA) developed into a strong union, shedding its company unionism and rising up to bite its employer overseers in the rear end.

After the strike, most ILA members were blacklisted. The Shipping Federation's tough labour manager, Major William Claude David Crombie, could not resist rubbing it in when a striker asked for his old job back. "Well, young Will, do you know what the initials ILA stand for?" Crombie asked. "Yes, International Longshoremen's Association," the man replied. "You are wrong, Will," gloated Crombie. "ILA stands for: I Lost All."

Most of the Tsleil-Waututh and Squamish Nations' lumber handlers from the North Shore, who had been reluctant supporters of the strike, survived the carnage. They regrouped the next year as the Independent Lumber Handlers' Association (ILHA). Led by Andy Paull, the Bows and Arrows local was back. The ILHA had a three-storey union hall on the east side of Vancouver with a shop on the first floor, a bootleg joint called "Tween Deck" on the second floor and a dispatch centre on the top floor. Before merging with the VDWWA in 1933, the union negotiated several contracts that improved conditions for its members.

But the fact the powerful ILA could be swept away was a reminder of the precarious status unions had in the first decades of the twentieth century. "Organized labour is in a death [fight]," rued ILA business agent Bill Pritchard. The same anti-union back-lash tore into the lumber workers' union, as the big coastal logging operations set up their own hiring hall in Vancouver, carefully weeding out anyone identified as pro-union. The companies also began to realize that the better loggers were treated, the less likely they were to join a union. Camp food improved, as did health care, sanitation, bunkhouse conditions and grievance processes. A downturn in the forest industry, an ideological split and the union's inability to organize sawmill workers also contributed to a fall in membership. A few years later the ambitious Lumber Workers Industrial Union had all but vanished.

For LWIU leader Ernest Winch, it became tough just to earn a living. He returned to the docks, only to be frozen out by employers after the ILA strike collapsed. With few jobs available elsewhere, his family was reduced to living over a shoe factory in a single room separated by blankets. Meals were often sheep heads or fish-head soup. According to his son Harold, who went on to head the BC Co-operative Commonwealth Federation (CCF) political party for fifteen years, a businessman once offered his father a job if he would renounce his socialist politics. Ernest refused.

After the demise of the OBU, the newly reconstituted Vancouver Trades and Labor Council resumed its hostility to Asian immigration as a threat to non-Asian workers. This ignored the fact that Chinese lumber mill workers had taken part in the city's two general strikes, while staging several walkouts of their own during the heyday of the OBU. With high unemployment and a recession in full swing, a VTLC committee proclaimed Asian immigrants "the most serious social menace facing the citizens of BC."

The council, seven unions, five veterans' groups and the Retail Merchants' Association together reconstituted the notorious Asiatic Exclusion League. Among the league's goals was educating "the white population to the terrible menace of Oriental immigration." In 1923, supported by the BC labour movement, the federal government

WILLIAM PRITCHARD

On a wintry March morning in 1920, William Pritchard stood in a packed Winnipeg courtroom far from his home in spring-like Vancouver to defend himself against six charges of seditious conspiracy. For two full days, the BC union leader gave a riveting discourse on why workers were driven to resist those who oppressed them, why the charges against him were a fundamental breach of the right to freedom of speech, and why the working class yearned for a better world where production was for use, not for profit. "Did you ever consider, gentlemen of the jury, that you cannot kill ideas with a club?" Pritchard postulated in his closing arguments. "You cannot drive theories into oblivion by machine guns. If an idea be healthy, sunshine will help it grow. If it is not healthy, sunshine will help to kill it."

The son of a British miner, Pritchard had edited the Socialist Party's *Western Clarion* from 1914 to 1917, then found work in a sawmill and on the Vancouver waterfront (he was also the grandfather of former NDP MLA and cabinet minister Bob Williams). Pritchard, by then a foremost socialist, had spent only a few days in Winnipeg to make some speeches and offer support near the

Vancouver socialist and trade unionist Bill Pritchard shown here (back row, far right) with other defendants at Manitoba's Vaughan Street jail, waiting for trial on seditious conspiracy charges connected to the 1919 Winnipeg General Strike. *Archives of Manitoba,* N12322.

end of the Winnipeg General Strike. Yet he was nabbed and charged with the same "seditious conspiracy" as those actively involved.

At the end of his long oration, close to collapse from the strain, the thirty-two-year-old Pritchard told the spellbound courtroom, "Standing on the threshold of the parting of the ways, one path leading to concrete and iron-bound walls of the penitentiary, and the other to freedom, I say I have done nothing for which I feel I need apologize. What I have done, I have done in good faith with sincerity and the purest of motives." As he concluded his remarks, the normally restive court fell silent.

A day later, the jury found him and six other defendants guilty. All were sentenced to a year in jail. On Pritchard's release from prison, an estimated ten thousand people turned out to greet his returning train to Vancouver—more, it was said, than showed up for the Prince of Wales' visit in 1919.

enacted the **Chinese Exclusion Act**, closing the door to any further immigration from China. The impact of the act was immediate. The "Oriental" share of the labour force fell from 20 percent in 1918 to just 12 percent by 1925. Over the next twenty-four years, until the act was repealed, no more than fifty Chinese emigrants managed to make their way to Canada. The province's Chinatowns lost much of their vibrancy, dominated by aging, "single" males, many of whom continued to send money back to China for wives and children they were never to see again.

Matters were somewhat different for the Nikkei. Although immigration was restricted, it was not cut off completely. Hundreds of "picture brides" sent for from Japan helped ease the loneliness of the predominantly male immigrants and enhanced domestic life. But racism remained. Like the Chinese, Nikkei workers continued to be paid significantly less than non-Asians for

similar work, and the Nikkei share of Fraser River fishing licences began to decline. With limited English, many immigrants were exploited by both white owners who padded their profits by paying poor wages and predatory Nikkei labour contractors, who got them jobs in return for a cut of the action. This double victimization was rarely understood by white workers. As they showed in the fishing industry, however, Nikkei immigrants were not always willing to turn the other cheek.

They were encouraged by the resourceful Suzuki Etsu, an acclaimed activist, journalist and translator who arrived in Vancouver from Japan in 1918. Suzuki soon began writing a column for the local *Tairiku Nippo* (*Continental Times*) that regularly called for common cause with non-Asian workers. During a 1920 strike at the Swanson Bay sawmill not far from today's Hartley Bay south of Prince Rupert, Chinese and Nikkei workers joined

Nikkei loggers in the 1920s working at the Rice Lake sawmill in North Vancouver. The young boy in front, Shigeo Kato, was later one of a handful of Nikkei volunteers allowed to enlist in the Canadian armed forces in 1941.
North Vancouver Museum & Archives, 26–19E–7.

other strikers to protest arbitrary wage cuts. About thirty Nikkei workers left on the next steamship to Vancouver. Although company pressure on the remaining workers led to the strike's collapse, Suzuki sensed an opportunity. He organized a meeting of the Swanson Bay strikers at the Japanese Language School, where they were applauded by the Nikkei consul among others for uniting with white workers.

Out of that meeting came the Japanese Workers' Union with Suzuki as its chief adviser. Not surprisingly, the Vancouver Trades and Labor Council refused the JWU's request to affiliate. Yet the new union quickly made its presence felt, supporting a strike by Nikkei employees at the Alberta Lumber Co. sawmill in Vancouver. There, the racial tables were turned. White war veterans were hired as strikebreakers and the conflict was lost.

Suzuki continued to advocate for Nikkei workers. *The Labour Weekly*, a new paper he edited, targeted unscrupulous labour contractors. After the paper accused several Nikkei companies of making excess profits from supplying cheap food to camp workers, the publisher succumbed to strong pressure from wealthy Japantown merchants to shut it down. (During the Swanson Bay strike, a Japantown department store had sponsored newspaper ads for strikebreakers.) The dedicated Suzuki then began his own paper. Although boycotted by advertisers and forced to operate on almost nothing, *The Daily People* had many readers in the province's isolated mills and lumber camps.

With more than a thousand members, the renamed Japanese Camp and Mill Workers' Union was finally accepted by the Trades and Labor Council as its first Asian labour organization. Although Suzuki is not much remembered today, even by the Nikkei, historian Michiko Ayukawa concludes that Suzuki and his followers "had a tremendously positive impact on the community."

Punctuated by the rapid rise and fall of the OBU, the 1920s were a challenging time for BC unions and those who believed in social change. Anti-union governments and hard-nosed employers were in the ascendancy. Union membership dipped dramatically while socialist/worker political candidates fared poorly. To put the cap on a difficult decade, Indigenous workers suffered another tragic loss. Not content with curtailing their hunting, fishing, logging and other traditional rights, authorities moved in on trapping. Northern First Nations had operated traplines since the beginning of the fur trade. Now, there were new registration requirements. Indigenous people would show up on traplines their ancestors had worked for generations and find non-Aboriginals there. George Archie of the Secwepemc lost a line he had trapped for twenty-five years. "The white people are taking Indian traplines, and the Indians cannot trap," he wrote Indian Affairs inspector W.E. Ditchburn in 1927. "I would like you to help me get back my trapline, so I can support my family." His plaintive plea fell on deaf ears.

THE ON-TO-OTTAWA TREK 7

NO ERA IN CANADIAN HISTORY IS AS WELL-DEFINED as the Depression. Even the dates are precise, from the spectacular Wall Street crash on October 29, 1929, to the beginning of World War II on September 3, 1939. The bottom fell out of the economy, inflicting untold misery and poverty on millions of Canadians—whether ill-fated Saskatchewan farmers, eastern factory workers or labourers in BC's once humming woods and mines. By the time it ran its course, the Depression had shown once and for all the inadequacy of an unregulated free market and the need for government action to ensure a decent life for ordinary people.

The ten lost years were characterized by government indifference. There was nothing like the New Deal of US president Franklin Delano Roosevelt that did so much to limit the plight of millions of hard-hit Americans. Instead, those unable to find work in Canada were provided with extremely meagre relief payments if they had a family—or if single, forced into work camps for a pittance. Both R.B. Bennett and William Lyon Mackenzie King, the country's two prime ministers during the 1930s, were more concerned with balancing the budget than helping citizens in desperate need. Those who protested were more often than not clubbed or thrown into jail. "The image of a policeman's truncheon bringing a shabbily dressed man to his knees was to become familiar," wrote Pierre Berton in his angry book *The Great Depression*.

The Depression seemed to come out of nowhere. As the Roaring Twenties neared their end, prosperity continued its multi-year roll. Investors were making fabulous riches on paper from the ever-rising stock market, financing their wealth by loans and buying on margin. Production was at record highs. But consumers couldn't buy everything. Worrisome stockpiles of unsold products began to accumulate. Then in the fall of 1929, the stock market's Black Thursday, October 24, was followed by the even more catastrophic Black Tuesday of October 29, and the house of cards collapsed.

When the Depression hit, hundreds of thousands of Canadians were thrown out of work. Jungle camps became home to many unemployed with nowhere else to go. These three men found space in a camp near the Vancouver city dump.

W.J. Moore photo, City of Vancouver Archives, RE N8.2.

capital of Canada. In the fall of 1931, Andrew Roddan, minister of the First United Church, told a visiting federal cabinet minister that his church's bread lines were feeding more than 1,200 people a day. Hundreds were sleeping in shacks made of bits of tin and wood, while others slept outside, often in the rain, among rats "as big as kittens," Reverend Roddan reported. When a local restaurant began handing out bags of bread crusts at the end of the day, a hundred men would show up every evening for the scraps.

As most labour unions focused on their own members, and politicians with no answers tried to pass responsibility to other levels of government, the country's Communist Party (CP) came to the fore. From its founding at a 1921 clandestine meeting in an Ontario barn, where the twenty or so delegates slept in the hayloft, the party had grown in influence during the 1920s. Although ever subject to the policy whims of the Moscow-based Communist International (Comintern), the CP had developed a base of skilled, committed organizers, who found the country's hard-pressed industrial workforce and hordes of single unemployed men tailor-made for action. Ordered by the Comintern to abandon its previous policy of working within established unions, the CP established its own radical federation in early 1930, just as the Depression hit. The Workers' Unity League (WUL) was to hold its red banner high for the next five years and play a major role in confronting authorities and the forces of capitalism.

A union of the unemployed affiliated with the WUL was soon leading regular protests and hunger marches demanding, with some initial success, better relief. Still, assistance remained barely above subsistence levels and predominantly restricted to families. For the masses of unemployed single men, many of whom washed up on the West Coast, there was nothing but charity. The WUL's involvement in organizing the unemployed made authorities nervous. "Communist agitators," they feared, were stirring up revolu-

Billions of dollars were lost in a single day. The Great Depression was on, triggered at its most basic level by overproduction, under-consumption and a sea of credit based on expectations of endless growth.

Products moving through BC's formerly busy ports declined nearly 60 percent. Lumber production, critical to the province's economic health, fell 30 percent. A scourge of horrendous poverty and unemployment fell over the land, never seen before or since. By 1933 one-third of all eligible wage earners, 1.5 million Canadians, were without work, many with no social safety net. For hundreds of thousands of mostly young Canadians, riding the rails, occupying jungle camps, visiting soup kitchens and bumming a meal became part of the rhythm of daily life. Large numbers of Prairie families driven from their land by dust storms, drought and plagues of grasshoppers added to the desperation.

Before long, with its relatively mild climate, Vancouver became the unemployment

tion among the throngs of jobless hanging around Vancouver and other cities.

To get them off the streets and away from the clutches of the Workers' Unity League, the federal government devised a network of relief camps, perhaps the most mean-spirited of all the country's responses to the ravages of the Depression. Most were wilderness work sites far from the city, where single unemployed men received bare-bones accommodation, skimpy food and paltry compensation in return for their labour. The first camps provided $1.15 a day. The men worked building roads, parks and other public facilities. A year later, pay was down to $7.50 a month. A year after that, all relief camps were taken over by the Department of National Defence. The daily stipend was further reduced to the derisory sum of twenty cents, and the trouble began.

Rather than squelching unrest, the camps proved fertile ground for communist organizers. While few camp workers had any interest in Stalin, they appreciated efforts to improve their lot and fight back against the camps' harsh military-like rule. The Relief Camp Workers' Union, a direct charter of the Workers' Unity League, became a force in all eighty-three BC camps. Braving blacklists, camp residents staged numerous strikes and protests to demand better conditions, keeping abreast of activities in other locations through the union's popular, surreptitious newsletter, the *Relief Camp Worker*. Much of the successful organization could be attributed to the efforts of one driven individual: Arthur H. "Slim" Evans.

In short order, Evans would become a household name across Canada and a red flag to governments, police and the courts

NOVELIST OF THE DEPRESSION

There is no Canadian equivalent to John Steinbeck's powerful Depression novel *The Grapes of Wrath*. But British Columbia did have Irene Baird and *Waste Heritage*. Her stark, uncompromising account of single unemployed men protesting in Vancouver and Victoria for government relief is as good as social realism got in Canada in the 1930s. And it was written by the most unlikely of authors for such a subject. Baird was an aspiring upper-middle-class writer from Victoria who became fascinated by the 1938 sit-down strikes in Vancouver. When the protest moved briefly to Victoria, she convinced the city's medical officer to let her tag along as he inspected their grim lodgings.

She listened intently to what the men were saying. Her observations provided the foundation for *Waste Heritage*. The novel focuses on a group of protesters consumed by anger and despair over their plight, unable to find a way clear to salvation even with their well-led protests and a savvy political organizer. "I found those jobless people irresistible, urgent, challenging," she wrote nearly thirty years later.

Critics praised her portrayal. A *Globe and Mail* re-

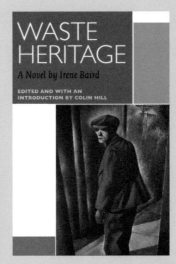

Irene Baird's compelling novel of the Depression details the anger and hopelessness of a group of unemployed men in Vancouver.
University of Ottawa Press.

viewer compared it favourably to *Grapes of Wrath*, while eminent writer Bruce Hutchison proclaimed it "one of the best books that has come out of Canada in our time." Alas, *Waste Heritage* emerged just as World War II began, making the Depression old news. Baird's book more or less disappeared until its republication in 1973. Yet for all the speeches, protests and organizing that took place during the Dirty Thirties, few gave a better voice to those on the bottom than Irene Baird.

wherever he led a fight on behalf of workers or the unemployed. Fiercely committed to working-class struggle, the lean carpenter in his mid-forties had already been wounded once and jailed three times for his role in union battles, including most recently in Princeton. There, a miners' strike provoked cross burnings and frightening threats by a local chapter of the Ku Klux Klan, violent attacks on peaceful pickets, a late-night vigilante attack on a local union leader and the kidnapping of Evans himself. Yet it was Evans who went to prison, serving more than a year in jail on a charge of advocating the overthrow of the Canadian government during the strike. When he rejoined the relief camp protests in late 1934 as district organizer of the Workers' Unity League, protests began in earnest.

Responding to growing strife in the camps, Evans and the Relief Camp Workers Union declared a strike on April 4, 1935. Their rallying cry, "Work and Wages," was to resound for the rest of the Depression. Nearly fifteen hundred camp workers answered the summons to Vancouver, pouring into the city by rail, road and foot. The presence of so many young, restive unemployed men with no money and nothing to do, under the leadership of communists, unnerved civic leaders. Flamboyant mayor Gerry McGeer bombarded Ottawa with demands that they be rounded up and sent back to the camps.

But organizers displayed an astounding ability to feed and billet the strikers, keep them occupied and, most importantly, maintain order and discipline. In defiance of civic ordinances, they raised funds with regular tag days. Men wearing sashes that read "When Do We Eat?" worked four-hour shifts at busy street corners, holding out tin cans for donations. A sympathetic public showered them with cash. On one bumper Saturday, tin-canners brought in a record-breaking $5,500. With a sense of mischief, Evans, who had been up for forty-eight hours organizing the all-out blitz, asked police to safeguard the tidy sum until the banks opened Monday morning. When two officers arrived to carry off the money, he told them it was "Moscow Gold."

Little was left to chance. The men were organized into four divisions, each with its own leader. There were committees for just about everything. All reported to the central strike committee headed by Evans. "We couldn't slice a loaf of bread into five bologna sandwiches without appointing a committee to see it was done according to plan," division leader Steve Brodie joked later. Hunger marches, demonstrations, tin-canning, large public rallies and boisterous snake dances through downtown streets became as familiar to Vancouverites as the North Shore mountains. May Day produced the largest parade in the city's history.

Mother's Day was even better. The Mothers' Council, a broadly based, left-wing women's group that was formed to muster sympathy for "our boys," led a large Mother's Day march to Stanley Park. There, they formed a giant heart around the young relief camp workers. That night, mothers across the city invited strikers to their homes for a meal. It was, said one event planner, "something of real value instead of the usual bourgeois, maudlin sentimentalism associated with Mother's Day."

The only trouble occurred during an impromptu snake dance through the aisles of the Hudson's Bay Company on April 23. When police arrived to evict the protesters, a large glass display case was shattered and merchandise strewn about. Hundreds then marched down Georgia Street to the Victory Square cenotaph, where squads of RCMP, provincial police and city police surrounded them in a tense stand-off. A delegation of strikers was dispatched to the mayor's office to try to defuse the situation. The twelve-member delegation got nowhere with the bullheaded Gerry McGeer. As they left his office, all but one was arrested for vagrancy. McGeer proceeded to a corner of Victory Square for a much-ridiculed reading of the Riot Act.

Six weeks into the strike, however, despite

Opposite top: Federal relief camps, run by the Department of National Defence, were accurately described as slave camps by the single unemployed men who wound up there. Like all camp workers, this road crew near Kimberley toiled six days a week for a princely daily stipend of twenty cents.
Dept. of National Defence/ Library and Archives Canada, AO36O89.

Opposite bottom: In 1935, the unemployed participate in a May Day protest parade along Hastings Street in Vancouver. Marchers are pulling a wagon mocking Mayor Gerry McGeer's reading of the Riot Act at the cenotaph a week earlier, dressing him as a German soldier, labelled with a sign reading IN HITLER'S FOOTSTEPS.
Vancouver Public Library, 8811.

On Mother's Day, May 12, 1935, mothers from across Vancouver showed their support for single unemployed men and their strike for better relief by forming a giant heart around them and hosting a picnic at Stanley Park. *Glenbow Archives, NA–3634–10.*

Snake dances, so named because they formed a snakelike *S*, were a common feature in downtown Vancouver streets during the strike by members of the Relief Camp Workers Union in the spring of 1935. *Vancouver Sun.*

waves of public sympathy, there was no sign of either the city or Ottawa granting relief, providing "work and wages" or forcing them back to the camps. Running low on food, the stalemated strikers needed something different. On May 18, their four divisions marched off in different directions. Two headed to local department stores, one went to the West Vancouver ferry depot, while the fourth followed a familiar route toward Main and Hastings. But this time, catching police off guard, they strolled into the city library on the corner, headed up the spiral staircase of what is today the Carnegie Centre and began occupying the civic museum on the third floor. Barricading the door, they posted a large sign on the window: "When Do We Eat?"

Large, supportive crowds gathered in the streets below. Well-prepared, the men lowered baskets on a string. Citizens filled them with bread, pies and pastries from neighbourhood bakeries, jugs of coffee, cigarettes, chocolate and sweets. The bounty proved too much for some, who hadn't eaten well in days. Bottles of pills were sent up to ease their stomach discontent. As police fumed, jubilant snake dances took over Hastings Street, accompanied by lusty renditions of the strike's rallying song, "Hold the Fort." ("Hold the fort/ For we are coming,/ Union men be strong./ Side by side keep pressing onward,/ Victory will come.") For the first and only time in the protracted protest, Gerry McGeer gave in. By phone from the Vancouver Yacht Club, he agreed to have the city feed and lodge the fifteen hundred strikers over the weekend. The occupiers emerged from the library in triumph.

The tactic was typical of Slim Evans. He had a genius for maintaining momentum. "You can't go on marching and singing and begging with tin cans," he would say. "You've got to do something new." Two weeks later, as the passage of time began to thin ranks, sap morale and cut into public support, Evans hit the strategic mother lode. At a mass meeting called to discuss the future of the faltering strike, someone put forward the idea of taking the protest to Ottawa. Evans seized on the idea. When the proposal was endorsed, the strikers nearly took the roof off the joint with their roars of approval. It was as if a huge jolt of electricity had revitalized their flagging spirits. They had a mission once again.

The ensuing On-to-Ottawa Trek remains one of the defining events of the Depression in Canada. It caught the fancy of the country in a way that not even Slim Evans could have foreseen. The journey came to epitomize everything that was wrong with the federal government's hard approach to those

brought low by forces beyond their control. The public saw it that way too. The farther the young BC trekkers travelled on top of swaying boxcars—many attaching themselves with belts or ropes—in their quest for a fair deal, the more they were embraced by Canadians as doing the right thing.

The idea was mad to begin with, of course. With a mere four days to prepare, little money and scant arrangements along the way, more than a thousand men had to be supplied and kept together for a three-thousand-mile journey to the lair of Prime Minister R.B. Bennett. Certain that it would quickly fall apart, governments and police could barely stifle a yawn when the trek was announced. But the relief camp strikers were charged with excitement by the sheer audacity of the plan. "Suddenly there was a new level of struggle. It was as if everything we had done up to that point was preparing for [this]," said trekker Willis

On May 18, 1935, relief camp strikers occupied the Vancouver civic museum on the top floor of the Carnegie Public Library at Main and Hastings. They used ropes to haul up supplies of hot coffee, bread and pastries from supporters below. Their occupation ended when the city granted them two days' relief.
Vancouver Sun.

Shaparla. Half a century later, Shaparla, a veteran of the D-Day landing, considered his participation in the On-to-Ottawa Trek the highlight of his life.

Yet no one knew what lay ahead the night of June 3, 1935, as hundreds of men clambered atop a line of CPR freight cars by the Vancouver waterfront and headed off into the darkness. Crowds had gathered to see them off. More than 800 left on the first train, another 200 boarded a later Canadian National Railway freight, and 350 more moved out the next evening.

The trek had a rough beginning. In Kamloops, the strikers' first stop, civic officials were unfriendly, and many men grumbled over the poor arrangements. At the small mountain community of Golden, however, things turned around. Sooty, begrimed, exhausted and hungry after a chilly night ride through the Selkirk Mountains and smoke-filled Connaught Tunnel, men staggered down from their perches and marched toward a local auto park. "I was so cold, I could have fallen off the roof of the box car," remembered Red Walsh. As dawn broke, there waiting for them was a bathtub suspended over a fire and a grey-haired woman stirring its contents—a vast beef stew—with a three-foot-long ladle. Other stew-filled washtubs were nearby. "Good morning, boys," she hailed them. It was a stew the men never forgot. Long tables laden with bread and eggs added to their wonderful breakfast.

On they went to Calgary, passing a handful of relieved provincial police at the BC–Alberta border, who gave them a cheery wave. The swirling, acrid smoke that filled the many Rocky Mountain tunnels blackened faces, stung the eyes and made breathing difficult. But Calgarians cheered from their housetops as the sooty trekkers marched to the city's exhibition grounds. Thumbing their nose at the city's refusal to grant them a permit, they raised $1,300 in a tag day. And when authorities denied them temporary assistance, they occupied the provincial relief office until the government gave in.

New recruits arrived on boxcars from Edmonton. One of them was Phil Klein, father of future Alberta premier Ralph Klein. (During a fiftieth-anniversary re-creation of the trek, Ralph Klein, who was mayor at the time, welcomed surviving trekkers to Calgary and formally guaranteed them safe passage through the city. He then invited them to lunch.) Fulminations by politicians that the men were being led by communists cut less and less ice. "To be quite frank, we don't care very much," said an editorial in the *Calgary Albertan*. The public saw the protest as just, and the protesters as disciplined young men who wanted a better deal, not revolution. Before leaving Calgary, they were feted at picnics and flooded with food and clothing. Hundreds gathered to say goodbye.

Back in Ottawa, Bennett was stunned by the trek's growing popularity. Over five hundred more men had joined the venture since Vancouver. Bennett determined that it must be stopped. He chose Regina. As communities continued to bend over backward to feed and lodge the eighteen hundred men on their overnight stops, the RCMP began drawing up a

battle plan. Having learned of Bennett's plans, the trekkers held a mass meeting attended by three thousand people in Moose Jaw. The mood was defiant. "If they attack us, we are not going to lay down and take it," warned twenty-four-year-old Matt Young. That determination quickened their departure to Regina on the next evening freight.

The overnight journey was terrible. A violent prairie storm replete with thunder and lightning lashed the men all night. But the strikers maintained their discipline. Arriving just after dawn on June 14, they made their way down from the boxcars, lined up in their divisions and proceeded in good order, four abreast, to the local exhibition grounds. Later that morning, they put on a show for the welcoming citizens of Regina, parading

Many On-to-Ottawa trekkers identified themselves and their cause on the backs of their jackets. These read VANCOUVER TO OTTAWA and B.C. STRIKER TO OTTAWA. *Winnipeg Evening Tribune, June 15, 1935. p. 1.*

The eight-person delegation of trek leaders who took the train to Ottawa to meet with Prime Minister R.B. Bennett, at Bennett's invitation. From left: Tony Martin, Arthur (Slim) Evans, Bob (Doc) Savage, Red Walsh, Mike McCauley, Paddy O'Neil, Jack Cosgrove and Peter Neilson. *Courtesy David Yorke.*

in a long line down Eleventh Avenue. "On to Ottawa" was chalked on the back of many flimsy jackets, and the men chanted, "Where are we going? *Ottawa!* Who's going to stop us? *Nobody!*"

The RCMP had other ideas. Despite opposition from Premier Jimmy Gardiner and strong backing for the trekkers from the citizens of Regina, the Mounties moved hundreds of reinforcements into the city with the intent of stopping the boxcar cavalcade and arresting the leaders. Bennett leaned on the railways to no longer accommodate the trekkers. They were trespassing on private property, he reminded them. Nevertheless, Evans set June 17 for their departure to Winnipeg, where hundreds more single unemployed men were waiting eagerly to join up.

But Bennett put the trek on hold with a cagey invitation to the leadership committee to meet with him in Ottawa; in the meantime, the government promised the trekkers a week's worth of meal tickets. Although Bennett's invitation was clearly a delaying tactic to help the RCMP prepare, Evans felt they had

no option but to accept. The meeting was a stage director's dream. Dressed in their worn, rumpled clothes of the road, Evans and his committee sat opposite the corpulent R.B. Bennett, wearing a swallow-tailed coat and winged collar, with a diamond stick pin in his tie. It quickly degenerated into a bout of schoolyard name-calling. Bennett began by charging that the trekkers' goal was not work but the overthrow of the government. If he believed that, Evans retorted, Bennett wasn't fit to be leader "of a Hottentot village." Furious, the prime minister shot back that Evans was an embezzler of union funds. Evans snapped that Bennett was a liar. "You are not intimidating me one bit." The meeting came to a quick close. The verbal donnybrook between the two men was headline news across the country, setting the scene for the tragedy that followed.

By the time Evans and the delegation returned to Regina on June 26, the city was full of police with riot sticks. Their ranks included seventy-five Mounties freshly arrived from taking part in a bloody crack-

down against striking dock workers in Vancouver. The trekkers were trapped, followed by police wherever they went. Assistant RCMP Commissioner Stuart Wood warned that any citizen assisting the trekkers would be subject to arrest. Donations dried up. Access to the radio airwaves ended. When only a sparse crowd turned out for a Saturday picnic on June 29, Evans realized there was no way forward.

He began to negotiate a resolution with Premier Gardiner, who was furious with Bennett and the RCMP for proceeding with no regard for the wishes of the province. The men were prepared to call off the trek and return west, Evans said, but they would not go to an alternate work camp in Saskatchewan as Bennett insisted. There matters stood on the Dominion Day holiday, July 1. In the circumstances, no one thought much about a rally scheduled that night for the city's vast Market Square. The resulting Regina Riot remains one of Canada's most widely known civil disturbances.

At 8:17 p.m., as a modest crowd of fifteen hundred listened to the rally's first speaker, two loud blasts from a police whistle split the early evening air. Within seconds, police were charging through the terrified crowd, clearing a path to the speakers' platform by knocking over anyone in their way with truncheons. Willis Shaparla called the sudden whistle and police charge "the most fearful moment of my life." As people desperately took flight to escape the riot sticks, Evans and co-leader George Black were quickly collared and taken to jail. After a brief lull, the fracas turned into a riot.

The unprovoked attack on a peaceful gathering released an outpouring of bottled-up rage from the trekkers and equally angered citizens. Rocks, bricks and other projectiles rained down on police. A few attacked isolated officers with clubs and other weapons. Plainclothes city detective Charles Millar was struck and killed, his assailants never identified. The battle continued in Regina's darkened downtown streets. Police advanced with tear gas, billy clubs, gunfire and fierce charges on horseback. Nick Schaack, an

Nursing their cuts and bruises, trekkers march in good order toward the train that will carry them in comfort back to Vancouver, but not without their accordionist, who had led them on so many versions of their stirring signature anthem: "Hold the Fort."
Saskatchewan Archives Board, R−A21749−1.

On–to–Ottawa trekkers gather at Vancouver's Victory Square on a spring day in 1985 to mark the fiftieth anniversary of their great venture. Standing is Jack Geddes, with Ray Wainwright to his right and Willis Shaparla in the middle of the three men in front of the banner.
MSC160–1139_06, Pacific Tribune Photo Collection, Simon Fraser University.

unemployed farmhand, received several blows to the head. He died in hospital three months later. Despite their numbers and firepower advantage, police did not manage to secure an edgy calm until 11 p.m. The city's two hospitals treated more than a hundred victims, including some police and at least a dozen patients with gunshot wounds.

The next morning, outraged by the RCMP onslaught, Premier Gardiner wrested control of the situation from police and the federal government by arranging the strikers' orderly departure. After their frustrating three-week stay in Regina, trekkers began to register for the trip home. All told, 1,358 men accepted the offer to leave—this time inside the trains and "on the cushions." Two-thirds were from British Columbia, half from

Vancouver. Although falling twenty-six hundred kilometres short of its goal, the On-to-Ottawa Trek, hatched in Vancouver, is remembered today as one of the country's most inspiring protests. Sixty-six years later, at the age of ninety-two, trekker Harry Linsley told an interviewer, "All we ever wanted was work and wages."

Two years after the trek ended, a number of participants were fighting in Canada's Mackenzie–Papineau Battalion as part of the international contingent of volunteers against Franco's fascist forces in the Spanish Civil War. Two who died, Peter Neilson and Paddy O'Neil, had been members of the trekkers' delegation that met with R.B. Bennett in Ottawa.

BALLANTYNE PIER AND OTHER BATTLES 8

T
HE HARSH PUTDOWN OF THE ON-TO-OTTAWA TREK was the last nail in the political coffin of R.B. Bennett. On October 14, 1935, William Lyon Mackenzie King and the federal Liberals cruised to a crushing electoral victory. The Liberals soon closed the federal relief camps and repealed Section 98 of the Criminal Code, which had been used to jail communists. On the union front in BC, there had been few bright spots. As demand and prices plunged, hard-pressed employers wasted little time slashing wages, imposing longer hours and reducing workplace standards. Rare was the union or worker who complained. Most felt lucky to be employed at all when so many were not.

But there were occasions when the boss went too far, and workers showed their fight. One of the most significant battles took place early in 1931 at Western Canada Lumber in Fraser Mills, just east of Vancouver. One of the world's largest timber operations, WCL tried to impose a fifth wage cut in twenty months. The mill workers said no. They were also angered by the firing of employees who refused to work overtime. Many had joined the revived Lumber Workers Industrial Union, now an affiliate of the Workers' Unity League, still trying to secure a toehold in the province's number-one industry.

The workforce at Fraser Mills was one of the most diverse in British Columbia. While white workers predominated, a large number of them were French Canadians, their BC roots stretching back more than twenty years when the company had recruited a large number of employees from Quebec. They were now well ensconced in their own nearby community, Maillardville. Contingents of Nikkei, Chinese and South Asian labourers also worked at the mill.

It was the kind of ethnic division that had doomed so many strikes in the past, but that did not happen at Fraser Mills. Unlike the Vancouver Trades and Labor Council, which continued to campaign for Asian exclusion, the Workers' Unity League welcomed workers of all races. Only half the six hundred workers carried union cards when the strike began, but membership from all groups grew significantly during the hard-fought conflict.

Following strong rejection of the company's wage cut, picket lines went up at the sprawling site on September 17, 1931. The head of the strike committee was shingle weaver Harold Pritchett, already an experienced union activist at the age of twenty-seven. Demands included a 10 percent wage increase, time and a half for overtime, union recognition and an end to the nefarious contract system for Asian workers. On the first morning, spirited picketers popped the cigar from the mouth of company manager Henry Mackin before allowing him to pass.

Tension mounted on day two. The union's picket line was bolstered by 150 recruits from the National Unemployed Workers' Association, another WUL affiliate. Melees broke out, bringing squads of provincial police to the scene. They were aided by a "Special Watch" of armed company guards who patrolled the grounds night and day. The mill entrance was further protected by a mounted machine gun.

The next day, police plunged into the hundreds of picketers to make ten arrests, while the usual suspects trotted out their familiar accusations of political troublemakers stirring up the workers. Premier Simon Fraser Tolmie warned of "agitators and communists," while Attorney General R.W. Pooley said the government would not stand for "imported radicals" to foment trouble. Neither the strikers nor their families were cowed. When those arrested appeared in court, fifty schoolchildren walked out of class to join a demonstration in front of the courthouse, "led by a determined looking lady with a stout stick," according to the *British Columbian* newspaper.

An uneasy truce took hold. But three weeks later, hurt by the shutdown of a subsidiary mill in Comox, the company blinked. Mackin agreed to rescind the wage cut, increase shingle rates, cap weekly hours at forty-eight and meet regularly with a committee of mill workers. All in all, it was not a bad offer. But there was no union recognition—and the strikers, their combativeness sharpened by the company's original intransigence, were not ready to settle. At a raucous meeting, they voted unanimously to reject the proposal.

Spirits and resources were bolstered by dances, picnics, sports events, a relief

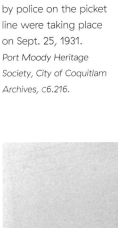

Fraser Mill strikers mass outside the Coquitlam municipal hall, where trials of those arrested by police on the picket line were taking place on Sept. 25, 1931. *Port Moody Heritage Society, City of Coquitlam Archives, c6.216.*

kitchen run by women supporters to provide meals for single men, a "Bumming Committee" to solicit donations of food and money, and organized bartering of skills and services such as haircuts, shoe repair and cutting wood for fuel.

In its minutes, the strike committee noted, "[A] Japanese comrade was appointed to the Relief Committee, also a Hindu and a Chinaman. They were very successful." Nikkei farmhands in the region donated vegetables, while others raised cash within their own communities. The tightly knit French Canadians were the strike's greatest strength. Even an outrageous intervention by the local parish priest could not fracture their solidarity. Denouncing "communists and radical revenge," Father François-Xavier Teck told his flock he would not grant absolution to anyone holding a union card. Few complied, and the union arranged transportation for Sunday mass to a more welcoming church in New Westminster.

Yet there was no more give from the company, and the loss of regular pay gradually reduced the strikers' willingness to carry on into the winter. On November 20, they voted by a large margin to return to work under the company's October offer. Still, in a precarious economic environment, they had made real gains against a stubborn employer. Although there were far more hurdles to overcome, the Fraser Mills strike was the first step forward in the arduous but ultimately successful unionization of the BC forest industry.

The result was also a tribute to the leadership of the strike, which pulled together the many disparate elements of the workforce to take on a powerful timber company. It didn't matter to the men that the struggle was led by members of the Communist Party. They backed whoever would support their fight for a better deal. Said LWIU president George Lamont as the strike began, "We intend to fight the Fraser Mills company and the Federated Timber Mills of BC, not on the basis of communism but on the basis of bread and butter." It was a recipe CP trade unionists fol-

lowed with considerable success over the next decade and a half in the push to organize the province's major industries.

Despite the party's wealth of activity and organizing, most socialists steered clear of communism. Although just as convinced by the Depression that capitalism had broken down and a new system was needed to deliver prosperity for all, they had no interest in a dictatorship of the proletariat. In late July 1932, a group of left-wingers from a quilt-like variety of organizations met at the Calgary Labor Temple to hammer out a less extreme socialist alternative to the Communist Party. In the forefront was Independent Labour MP J.S. Woodsworth. He had deep roots in BC, including several years as a union longshoreman in Vancouver, while his daughter Grace had just married his House of Commons seatmate, Vancouver South MP Angus MacInnis.

Over a mere two days, the one hundred or so delegates put aside their many differences to choose Woodsworth as leader and form a leftist political party that continues today as the NDP. The ungainly titled Co-operative Commonwealth Federation was soon referred to far and wide as simply the CCF. A year later, the CCF held its first national convention to build a party platform. The famous Regina Manifesto, hailed by leading British socialist Harold Laski as the best democratic-socialist document ever put together, called for public control of key industries, publicly funded health care, universal pensions, income-based taxation, abolition of the Senate, a planned economy, an end to profit-driven chartered banks and a national labour code that would "secure for the worker maximum income and leisure, insurance covering accident, old age, and unemployment, freedom of association and effective participation in the management of his industry or profession."

"I am convinced that we may develop in Canada a distinct type of socialism," said Woodsworth. "I refuse to follow slavishly … the Russian model." Workers and others beaten up by the system rallied to the CCF's paler red flag in a way they never had to the hammer and sickle. The fresh approach was soon felt in BC. In its first crack at an election, the CCF won enough seats to form the province's official opposition in 1933.

Among its seven new MLAS were Ernest Winch and his twenty-six-year-old electrician son, Harold. At the local level, successful CCF candidates included long-time trade unionist Helena Gutteridge, the first woman elected to Vancouver city council. Although there were no official ties until its 1961 alignment with the Canadian Labour Congress (CLC) as the New Democratic Party (NDP), the CCF was considered "labour's party" from the beginning, consistently attracting widespread support from workers and unions in BC.

Far from the provincial legislature, there were other labour flare-ups in the Dirty Thir-

ties. Miners in the isolated town of Anyox, far up the Portland Canal north of Prince Rupert, joined the left-wing Mine Workers' Union of Canada (MWUC) and walked off the job in early 1933 to protest a wage cut and the high cost of room and board. Intimidated by large numbers of armed police sent in by boat from Prince Rupert who arrested strikers and strutted menacingly about the

community's wooden boardwalks, the miners voted to go back to work. But more than three hundred single men soon left, robbing Anyox of its heart.

Not long after that was the courageous miners' strike in Princeton, and in 1934, twenty-five hundred fallers on Vancouver Island revolted against their low pay, long hours and abysmal working conditions. The dispute featured a celebrated long march by more than a hundred strikers over a mountain and through the bush to escape company detection and confront a bunch of strikebreakers. When they arrived, they found machine guns and "a cop for every [scab] they had," said union leader Ernie Dalskog. "There was no way we could force them out." The logging companies eventually agreed to a wage increase, but the fallers' bid for more fell short after ninety-six days off the job. Industrial disputes peaked in 1935. Days lost from strikes and lockouts were nearly double the previous year's total, and that did not include the two-month strike by relief camp workers.

The familiar recipe was played out in particularly harsh terms yet again early in 1935 in Corbin, a small coal-mining community tucked into the southeast corner of the province. The Corbin Miners' Association, formerly supporters of the OBU and now affiliated with the radical MWUC, had been agitating for some time to improve their rock-bottom company housing. Miners were also angry about recent pay cuts and worried the American-owned company was about to shut its underground operation, throwing many of them out of work. But pickets did not go up until January 22, after the company fired union secretary John Press. Over the next few months, Corbin was riven with tension over the presence of provincial police brought in to spy on the strikers and guard the narrow ledge of a road leading to the mine.

Matters came to a boil in mid-April. A large number of picketers led by a group of wives headed through the snow toward the mine. As they approached, a bulldozer suddenly drove forward into the middle of the

women, running over their legs and dragging one of them three hundred feet before she could get free. Enraged miners began hurling rocks at the police who followed the bulldozer, swinging clubs as they advanced. Several dozen strikers and fifteen police were injured. For three days, seventeen arrested strikers were confined in two tiny cells. But the injuries suffered by the miners' wives caused the most outrage. A picture of eight women taken a few days after they were mowed down showed some with bandaged feet and crutches, others with their heads wrapped in bandages.

Fundraising campaigns sprang up in BC and nearby coal-mining communities in Alberta. An independent commission headed by three CCF MLAS exposed the miners' dreadful living conditions, but the provincial government was unmoved. Predictably,

the trouble was blamed on the usual outside agitators and the Workers' Unity League. Six strikers were eventually jailed for up to six months for their role in the confrontation with police. The bulldozer driver was not charged. In the face of growing public anger, the owners announced the closure of mining operations in Corbin. Although the skeptical miners, buttressed by outside funds, maintained their strike for many more months, the government hastened the town's demise by cutting off funds to its only doctor, who had no choice but to leave. When the CPR tore up the tracks leading to the mine, the miners accepted their fate. They scattered to find work where they could, and Corbin died.

In Vancouver, meanwhile, the hundreds of striking relief camp workers were not the only headache for the city's excitable mayor, Gerry McGeer, during the spring of 1935.

Women recovering from their injuries during an intense strike by coal miners in the East Kootenay community of Corbin. They were hurt when a company bulldozer drove into their midst as they led a union march toward the strikebound mine on April 17, 1935. *Glenbow Archives, NA–3479–2.*

Trouble was also brewing on the waterfront. Just as during the relief camp strike and other disputes, the dreaded "Reds" were in the thick of it. On the docks, a surprising thing had happened to the company union formed by the Shipping Federation after wiping out the International Longshoremen's Association in 1923. As the Depression deepened and waterfront companies increasingly squeezed their workers, the Vancouver and District Waterfront Workers' Association (VDWWA) had become militant.

Resentful of a poor three-year agreement they had accepted reluctantly in 1934, union members chose a strong new executive. Business agent Oscar Salonen belonged to the Workers' Unity League. So did Ivan Emery and George Brown, who had been elected president and secretary respectively of the Longshoremen and Water Transport Workers of Canada, a federation representing maritime worker organizations all along the BC coast. Its largest affiliate was the VDWWA. Each of the three men had at least ten years' experience on the docks.

The union began pressing for a wage increase and an end to company control over the longshore hiring hall. The latter issue was critical. Vancouver was the only West Coast port without a fair, union-run dispatch system. Stevedores in the United States had won control of their halls the previous year after an exceptionally violent three-month strike that cost six union lives. But Vancouver companies were resolved not to relinquish their right to pick and choose who got to work. No wonder two-thirds of those who took part in the 1923 strike never worked another shift on the waterfront.

The two sides continued to butt heads through the spring of 1935. The ongoing strike by relief camp workers added to the tension. Waterfront workers were strong supporters of the strike, staging an hour-long sympathy walkout on April 29, and booking off for an entire shift two days later to head the large May Day parade.

With relief camp strikers already in the streets and a waterfront shutdown looming, McGeer believed revolution was nigh. Over the radio, he railed about the need for citizens to make a choice between the "constituted authority" and "communism, hoodlumism and mobs." The next day, the mayor led four hundred police on a show of force. At the Beatty Street Drill Hall, military instructors began training squads of police to combat insurrection. On May 29, a vigilante group of prominent residents organized by the Shipping Federation bought full-page newspaper ads swearing that "ruthless Radicals" would not be allowed to imperil prosperity.

When the relief camp strikers made their spur-of-the-moment decision to launch the On-to-Ottawa Trek, McGeer, the Shipping Federation and police were now free to focus completely on the waterfront. On June 4, 1935, a day after the first contingent of trekkers headed east, Vancouver longshoremen refused to unload a shipload of "hot" newsprint from the strikebound docks of Powell River, where dock workers and seamen had walked out in mid-May. The companies quickly dispatched boats from the Vancouver Yacht Club carrying strikebreakers to handle the load and cancelled their union contract, and the fight was on. As in 1923, the Shipping Federation relished the opportunity to crush a union for having the temerity to stand up for its members' rights. This time they were also able to harness the anti-Red hysteria of police commanders and the mayor.

On day one, the province agreed to send McGeer two hundred more provincial police to aid his crusade against communism. *Vancouver Sun* columnist Bob Bouchette was one of the few in the media to see through the mayor's vitriol. "The strike isn't about communism," wrote Bouchette. "It's about working conditions and whether the union will be broken." He noted that most union members were married with families and with many years' experience on the docks. "Are these the men who, we are told, are helping fomenters of revolution? The question does not merit a reply."

But the companies' ability to keep the port operating was a problem. At a union meeting on June 16, members decided to march *en masse* to the docks to "talk" to the scabs. In a blistering speech, Ivan Emery avowed, "[This strike] will be won by going down on ships and taking off strikebreakers … If we are refused [by police], we are going through anyhow." Referring to the number of World War I veterans in the union, Emery added with a flourish, "We have heard the rattle of machine guns. I believe we have enough ex-servicemen on the waterfront who are prepared to listen to them again." Emery too was a vet, having served in the same battalion as Vancouver Police Chief William Foster.

Early on the afternoon of June 18, 1935, a thousand strikers and supporters marched down Heatley Avenue toward Ballantyne

Pier. At the head of the grimly determined demonstrators carrying the Union Jack was the city's war hero, Victoria Cross winner Mickey O'Rourke. Said to be the second-most decorated Canadian soldier after flying ace Billy Bishop, the fifty-six-year-old casual dock worker had won the foremost award for military valour in World War I as a stretcher bearer during the horrendous Battle of Hill 70 that followed Vimy Ridge. A group of fellow vets followed behind, their war medals pinned prominently to their shirts and sweaters. As they marched, the men sang songs from the war. The defiant Ivan Emery was missing from the march. He'd already been carted off to jail and charged with inciting a riot. But business agent Oscar Salonen was there, right beside O'Rourke.

A host of edgy cops, two manning machine guns, waited at the tracks. "Just a

Striking longshoremen march to the waterfront on June 18, 1935, determined to roust strikebreakers from the docks. Medalled WWI veterans were at the front, headed by Victoria Cross winner Mickey O'Rourke (bottom left), carrying a Union Jack flag. The Battle of Ballantyne Pier erupted shortly afterward, when mounted police with truncheons turned them back.
City of Vancouver Archives, 417–1.

minute, boys," Chief Foster told the marchers. Not another step, he warned. Salonen was not deterred. "This strike has been going on long enough," he told the chief. "We're going in there, and we're going to take these scabs off the boats." A small scuffle broke out. Foster lowered his raised gloved hand, and all hell broke loose. For the first time, volleys of tear gas were deployed in Vancouver. The marchers, gasping for breath, their eyes stinging, began to flee. Police charged after them, swinging their clubs. They were joined by provincial police and RCMP reinforcements who had been hiding behind some boxcars.

The chase went on through the streets, alleys and yards of East Vancouver. A newspaper photo showed a lone striker on an empty street, no threat to anyone, about to be hit by a whip brandished by a cop on horseback. Other police rode their horses right to the front steps of houses to pursue and beat their prey. Some strikers responded with rocks. One officer was dragged out of his car and beaten. Another was knocked off his horse and attacked. But by and large, the Battle of Ballantyne Pier was a one-sided affair. "They'd hit you over the head. They'd hit you anywhere," remembered striker Ted Hovi.

A temporary first-aid station hastily set up at the Ukrainian Labor Temple treated dozens of injured strikers. Some bystanders were also injured, including a woman just doing her shopping. Police launched tear-gas attacks on the offices of the VDWWA and the Workers' Unity League. Still, police were unable to gain total control of the streets until 5 p.m. As for Mickey O'Rourke, police claimed they hustled him away from the chaos to safety. O'Rourke had a different story: "When I saw we were beat, I beat it, but not before I heaved a brick at a mounted policeman's head."

The next day, a triumphant McGeer cut off relief payments to strikers' families. Emery and Salonen each received three months in Oakalla prison for unlawful assembly. Fifteen rank-and-file strikers were given sentences ranging from three months to a year. Despite the mounting odds against them, members maintained the strike. Those who could pitched in to help. Some caught fish. Others grew vegetables. Volunteers cut hair and repaired shoes. There was a strong Ladies' Auxiliary to rally support, including the formidable Mildred Dougan. Given the option of a $25 fine or thirty days for assaulting police officers while on the picket line,

Below left: Mounted provincial police and other police gather at the foot of Heatley Avenue to keep union dock workers away from Ballantyne Pier during their hard-fought strike in 1935. *Vancouver Public Library, 8828.*

Below right: During the Battle of Ballantyne Pier, club-wielding police on horseback pursued and bloodied defenceless union dock workers throughout the Strathcona area of Vancouver. Front steps proved no obstacle for the determined cops. *City of Vancouver Archives, 371–1127.*

Dougan chose jail. "The money is needed for relief more than it is by the police court treasury," she said.

But with hundreds of strikebreakers keeping the port open, police guarding the waterfront, the Vancouver Trades and Labor Council taking a hands-off attitude and money shortages becoming acute, the strike was called off on December 9. After a valiant five-month struggle, the VDWWA was broken, as were all other coastal locals. The Shipping Federation retained its iron grip on the province's ports. Hundreds of workers were again blacklisted from employment on the docks, and another company union replaced the VDWWA. Every year on the anniversary of the Battle of Ballantyne Pier, union dock workers gather at a waterfront memorial to remember those who marched for union rights on that bloody day in Vancouver history.

The fishing industry also showed fight during the Depression. After their epic strikes at the turn of the century, BC fishermen had garnered few of the riches that continued to fill the pockets of the province's powerful can-

ners. The same was true of fish-plant workers. The situation worsened just before the Depression. A major industry consolidation thrust BC Packers Ltd. into a dominant position, claiming nearly 50 percent of the 1929 salmon catch. The company used its enhanced

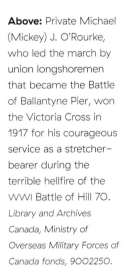

Above: Private Michael (Mickey) J. O'Rourke, who led the march by union longshoremen that became the Battle of Ballantyne Pier, won the Victoria Cross in 1917 for his courageous service as a stretcher-bearer during the terrible hellfire of the WWI Battle of Hill 70. *Library and Archives Canada, Ministry of Overseas Military Forces of Canada fonds, 9002250.*

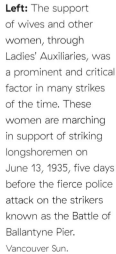

Left: The support of wives and other women, through Ladies' Auxiliaries, was a prominent and critical factor in many strikes of the time. These women are marching in support of striking longshoremen on June 13, 1935, five days before the fierce police attack on the strikers known as the Battle of Ballantyne Pier. *Vancouver Sun.*

prominence to pad profits by offloading more and more costs onto fishermen. At the same time, owing to a big rise in the number of licences, individual fishermen were bringing in fewer fish, further cutting into their incomes. In 1934, *The Voice of the Fishermen* calculated that with all the expenses and fees imposed on fishermen, their return for five weeks of labour was a loss of $30.

In the canneries, with a workforce 15 percent Chinese, 15 percent Nikkei and the remainder almost all Indigenous women, workers toiled eleven to twelve hours a day under onerous, piece-rate contracts. For two hard months, their average take-home pay was $80 to $100, not enough to keep anyone off relief.

Anxious to challenge the industry, many fishermen joined the Fishermen's Industrial Union, formed in 1932. Another affiliate of the Workers' Unity League, the FIU was the first in a long string of communist-led unions in the fishing industry. "Is it any won-

der that many fishermen are radicals?" one observed, pointing to the canners' unstinting efforts to exploit them. Two years later, the FIU became the Fishermen and Cannery Workers Industrial Union, accepting fishermen and shore workers of all races. By 1936 in the salmon-fishing hot spot of Rivers Inlet, the union was ready to take a stand. After the industry cut the price per fish from fifty to forty cents, a thousand Central Coast fishermen voted 85 percent to strike; they tied up on July 6.

On the water, it was undeclared warfare. Strikebreaker nets were cut, their catches seized. Police aimed guns at striking fishermen to protect the scabs. Kitchens in the communal village of Sointula turned out bread and other provisions to help feed isolated fishermen who were denied access to company stores. The strikers, many Nikkei and Indigenous fishermen among them, held firm for a full month. But the companies refused to budge, and the season was essen-

Members of the Salmon Purse Seiners' Union raise their arms in victory after their fleet tie–up in September 1938 forced canners to recognize their union and agree to a minimum price for fall chum salmon.
Fisherman Publishing Society Collection, Simon Fraser University.

tially lost. The result was particularly devastating to the First Nations. "What we lost was not just a job," said skipper Billy Assu, whose son Harry's seine boat was featured for years on the $5 bill. "Fishing is our living, our way of life. We own these waters and we have to be able to fish them." Convinced they could no longer trust non-Indigenous organizations to safeguard their interests, Aboriginal fishermen formed the Pacific Coast Native Fishermen's Association.

Not lost, however, was the value of sticking together. After winning an arbitrated settlement in 1937, fishermen struck again in 1938. This time it was a seine-boat show centred in Johnstone Strait. Indigenous and non-Indigenous vessel owners alike backed the tie-up. But the canneries continued their usual hardball, cutting off credit at company stores and ordering fishermen to return their equipment. They did, but not before carefully dismantling the gear to make the nets useless for further fishing. Unbowed, the striking seiners headed for Vancouver, famously sailing into port under the new Lions Gate Bridge in two grand columns of thirty boats each. What appeared to be another season-long standoff suddenly turned in the union's favour when many coastal gillnetters joined the strike. In a rare capitulation, the canners signed the first-ever coast-wide pricing agreement.

Although choppy waters remained ahead, the bold strikes of 1936 and 1938 far up the coast from the busy Fraser River set unionization of the BC commercial fishing industry on a course that would only go forward in the years ahead. In a verbal confrontation during the 1938 strike that became union lore, one-eyed fisherman John Hanson corrected a company negotiator who had inquired what price fishermen were asking. "We are not requesting," Hanson proclaimed. "We are making our demands." Whipping open the drapes of the company's dockside office, he pointed to the idled fleet outside. "And there's our solidarity. You get on the phone and tell Vancouver that."

The Japanese Camp and Mill Workers' Union also showed spunk during the difficult decade. Despite ongoing hostility from some within the Nikkei community who backed Japan's rightward drift, membership in the union remained relatively strong. By the end of the decade, the JCMWU had eight locals, representing two-thirds of the province's eighteen hundred Nikkei lumber workers.

9 BLUBBER BAY, BLOODY SUNDAY

LABOUR HISTORY IS OFTEN A TALE of the unpredictable. Certainly, no one could have foretold that a former whaling station on Texada Island with the unglamorous name of Blubber Bay would be the site of the first critical strike by a newly formed organization that for decades would be the province's largest and most important union. The eleven-month strike in 1938–39 by the International Woodworkers of America resonates still, with its combination of workers fighting hard for their union—and company and police actions that were shocking even for those repressive times.

The roots of the bitter confrontation go back to 1935. Even beyond its many strikes and protests, the year saw two key decisions that made it one of the most pivotal years in the history of the Canadian labour movement. Despite their profound implications for Canada, both decisions took place outside the country's borders—in Washington, DC, and far-off Moscow. Meeting in the Soviet capital, the Seventh World Congress of the Communist International ordered communist-led unions in Canada to abandon their outsider status and throw their red caps in with the mainstream labour movement. It was time, the Comintern proclaimed, for a common front against fascism. That meant the abrupt dissolution of the Workers' Unity League, which had spent five gainful years organizing and fighting for the unemployed and the country's industrial workers. The WUL's radical unions were now ordered to fold themselves into craft unions headquartered in the United States. At the same time, escalating tension between industrial unions and the craft union leadership of the American Federation of Labor (AFL) blew wide open into a complete rupture. The split was inevitable once the mercurial, charismatic leader of the United Mine Workers of America, John L. Lewis, punched out "Big Bill" Hutcheson, the pro-Republican head of the Carpenters Union, at the AFL's stormy 1935 convention that summer in Atlantic City. Lewis and

The dues and membership books of Harold Pritchett, who became the International Woodworkers of America's first international president in 1937, as well as the first Canadian to head an international union. *UBC Rare Books and Special Collections, 1449–1–14.*

other industrial union leaders had made a pitch at the convention for the AFL to help them organize millions of employees in the nation's mass-production industries. But the craft union members, proud of their status as skilled tradesmen, wanted no part of worker groups that one AFL leader derided as "riff-raff [and] good-for-nothings." After he and his industrial allies lost every vote, Lewis's frustration boiled over into fisticuffs.

That November in Washington, Lewis presided over a historic gathering of fed-up industrial union leaders to form a new organization within the AFL, which became the Congress of Industrial Organizations (CIO). Quickly turfed from the AFL and galvanized by the Roosevelt administration's far-reaching Wagner Act that enshrined union rights, the CIO began organizing millions of workers into powerful, industrial unions throughout the United States. Without a northern equivalent to the Wagner Act, the CIO took longer to have a similar impact in Canada. But eventually, the robust CIO changed the face of labour here too.

Under pressure from the AFL, the Trades and Labor Congress of Canada expelled its industrial union affiliates in 1939. Ousted industrial unions soon merged with the relatively small All-Canadian Congress of Labour to form a more powerful Canadian Congress of Labour (CCL). Although minus much of the animosity that characterized the AFL and CIO feud in the United States, the TLC and CCL also operated as two separate, rival labour organizations. When the BC Federation of Labour re-emerged in 1944 (with a "u" in *labour*), it was for CCL affiliates only. And in Vancouver, each body had its own labour council.

The disappearance of the Workers' Unity League, coupled with the rise of the CIO's American-based unions, meant that for the next fifty years almost all private-sector unions in Canada had their headquarters in the United States. Although the pros and cons of this became a subject of heated debate in the years ahead, it was hardly an issue at the time. Only the CIO had the resources and the charisma to bring unionization on a massive scale to Canada.

In BC, the Lumber Workers Industrial Union was first to be affected by these dramatic developments. The battle-scarred WUL affiliate obediently enlisted in the United Brotherhood of Carpenters and Joiners. It was not a good fit. Snubbed and forced to sit as second-class, non-voting delegates at the Carpenters' annual convention, union lumber workers from Oregon, Washington and BC did not take long to map a different course. On July 17, 1937, at Tacoma, Washington, after receiving overwhelming support for the move in a union-wide referendum, heady delegates voted to join the CIO as the brand-new International Woodworkers of America. Harold Pritchett, the thirty-three-year-old committed trade unionist and communist who had led the Fraser Mills strike six years earlier, was elected president, the first and for many years the only Canadian to head a major international union.

In the United States, the move sparked an immediate organizing battle, laced with violence, between the Carpenters and the IWA. There, with companies compelled by the Wagner Act to recognize unions chosen by local bargaining units, the IWA managed to secure a majority of American lumber workers. But with no **Wagner Act** in British Columbia, it was tough sledding.

Along with other governments across Canada, the province aligned with powerful business interests and police to clamp down on union organizing at every turn. While thousands joined the IWA in Oregon and Washington, encouraged by US labour legislation, BC's twenty-five thousand woodworkers remained virtually unorganized, stymied by persistent company refusals to recognize any union or bargain collectively. And why not? There was no legal compulsion to do either. When a union did strike for recognition, police were regularly dispatched to protect strikebreakers and break up union protests, while company blacklists ensured that pro-union loggers found it difficult to obtain work. In this imposing environment, successful strikes were few and far between.

Finally, in 1937, with a stated goal of furthering labour harmony in BC, the Liberal government of Thomas Dufferin "Duff" Pattullo passed the **Industrial Conciliation and Arbitration Act** (ICA). The legislation mandated conciliation, then arbitration, to settle labour disputes. It also recognized a few union rights. But tellingly, it put company unions and ad-hoc employee groups on the same legal footing as legitimate unions. Employers remained free to ignore unions chosen by the workers, a situation unchanged since the first organizing efforts of Nanaimo-area coal miners in the early 1870s. Still, as part of its recent embrace of reform over revolution, the BC IWA decided to give the ICA a chance at Blubber Bay.

The one-time landing spot for removing blubber from captured whales on the northern end of Texada Island was now the site of a small sawmill and an enormous open-pit limestone mine. For thirty years workers, many of them Chinese, had quarried the 250-foot-deep "glory hole" with little labour turmoil, despite wretched working conditions. But an obstinate new manager and a wage cut spurred the workers to join the IWA. A six-week strike brought a modest wage adjustment and promises by the Pacific Lime Company not to single out union activists. Instead, once production resumed, PacLime fired local president Jack Hole and twenty-two other pro-union workers.

These Chinese immigrants in 1912 were among the first to be hired to quarry limestone on Texada Island. Twenty–six years later, Chinese and white workers joined together in a fight for union recognition at the Blubber Bay limestone operation.
University of Washington Libraries, Special Collections, UW5761.

Rather than strike again, the IWA opted for the ICA. After lengthy hearings, the arbitration board appointed under the act recommended reinstatement of those fired. But the board refused to recognize the IWA as the workers' union, allowing PacLime to brush off the recommendation. The ICA had proven useless. On June 2, 1938, after an angry public meeting, two-thirds of the company's 156 employees walked off the job. For the union's credibility, this was a fight the IWA had to win.

It turned into a strike like no other, where authorities acted as a law unto themselves, reminiscent of the Deep South. Along with the usual trappings of a company store and company housing, PacLime owned virtually all property and every facility in the community. During the strike, schoolchildren had to obtain a pass to cross company roads merely to attend school. Strikers were denied access to telephone and telegraph services. When union leaders were able to find a phone, police monitored their calls. Strikers were followed and often thrashed by company thugs if they wandered too far astray. High

barbed-wire fences surrounded PacLime production sites. The officer in charge of the squads of provincial police sent in to protect strikebreakers helped recruit the scabs from provincial relief rolls.

Chinese strikers were ordered out of their bunkhouses. When union lawyer John Stanton entered the bunkhouses to retrieve some of their belongings, he was arrested. Other workers were evicted from their small family homes. On an island under police and company rule, union members had to find a way to survive. One of the few private property owners allowed members to set up camp on his meadow just outside town. Donated provisions, including tons of vegetables, had to be brought in from Vancouver. The Chinese strikers were particularly resourceful. By travelling in groups and letting it be known they were not afraid of a fight, they were left alone by company vigilantes. They slept in shifts in tents, deftly scrounging Texada for food.

In the unfortunate vernacular of the day, the IWA's John McCuish saluted their resolve: "There was a lot of Chinamen. They went out on the docks and rocks, and caught

English and Chinese–language signs warning strikebreakers to stay away attest to the solidarity between white and Chinese workers during their determined strike at Blubber Bay on Texada Island in 1938.
Kaatza Station Museum & Archives, IWA Local 1–80/Wilmer Gold Photo Collection ©United Steelworkers Union Local 1–1937.

rock cod. They killed deer. There were quite a few pheasants on the island, and they lived mostly on that ... Them Chinamen were solid. I never seen such a bunch as solid as they were." The IWA took pains to ensure Chinese strikers attended and voted at union meetings. "There can be no differentiation between a worker, whether he be white, yellow or black," a union rep told the ICA hearings. Union demands included a base rate of forty-five cents an hour for all employees.

Success depended on stopping the flow of strikebreakers. Whenever Union Steamship delivered a group of new workers, confrontations erupted on Blubber Bay's government wharf as police physically prevented strikers from stopping them. At times emotions boiled over. The worst incident took place in mid-September, three and a half months into the strike. As the steamer *Chelohsin* lowered its gangplank, local vice-president Bob Gardner yelled, "Here come the scabs among us!"

Strikers rushed forward, trying to get at them through heavy police lines. Clubs and tear gas drove them back. Police continued the chase along local roads, while strikers and company employees hurled rocks at one another. Eleven wound up in hospital in Powell River. Twenty-three strikers were arrested. That night, Bob Gardner, one of those arrested, was taken into a private room and beaten by Constable Andrew Williamson, suffering four broken ribs.

The next day, forty members of the Pulp and Sulphite Workers journeyed over from Powell River to warn police commander T.D. Sutherland that if police didn't cool it, four hundred of them would be back "and we won't fool with you bastards." The day after that, sixty striking seine-boat skippers dropped anchor at Blubber Bay on their way to Vancouver. They left in the morning, buoying the strikers with a chorus of defiant horn blasts.

Despite the strikers' resolve, the arrests from the dockside fracas did them in. Not only did they lose their leadership, defending those charged sapped the union of funds

and energy. Charged with rioting and unlawful assembly, strikers were tried in groups of four, giving proceedings an aura of show trials. Twelve were convicted, sentenced to four to six months of hard labour at Oakalla prison. In a rare turnabout of justice, Constable Williamson also got six months at Oakalla for his brutal assault of Gardner.

With local leaders in jail, its coffers drained and PacLime operating normally, the IWA decided further resistance was futile. After eleven months, picket lines came down and the IWA virtually disappeared. While organizing drives thrived in the United States, BC remained a burial ground for industrial union aspirations. It took the coming war for seventy years of government anti-unionism to loosen and finally provide a fairer playing field for workers to organize. Bob Gardner would not be around to celebrate. Sentenced to four months in Oakalla, the forty-four-year-old former train engineer, still ailing from his injuries, contracted influenza while in prison and died.

As the worst of decades neared its end, it seemed as if the forces of law and order had become hooked on bashing anyone who rose up to demand change. For those who were not British subjects of the Commonwealth, there were arbitrary deportations with no right to appeal, regardless of their roots in the province. In Princeton, Vancouver, Anyox, Corbin, Blubber Bay and even in Regina, the recipe was the same: British Columbians who challenged the existing order were to be trampled. In Vancouver, this shameful period concluded with yet another calculated, cold-blooded attack on peaceful protesters. It remains known today as Bloody Sunday.

After the decisive ousting of Prime Minister R.B. Bennett, the economy took a marginal upturn. Premier Duff Pattullo, elected on his own "work and wages" program, unrolled a public works program that included the Fraser River bridge that bears his name. But toward the end of 1937, when the economy slowed once more, governments showed they had learned nothing from the turbulence of previous years. As before, no one wanted to pay for the rising numbers of unemployed. Ottawa cut grants to the provinces, including its 50 percent share of funding BC's relatively successful forestry camps.

Unwilling to absorb the added financial burden, BC closed the camps down in the spring of 1938, driving six thousand unemployed men to Vancouver with little means of support. Organized tin-canning and communist leadership of the unemployed were back. Once again, the men were organized into divisions, causing familiar headaches for authorities with their constant marching. This time there was no Slim Evans to lead them; he was busy organizing. The man in charge was Steve Brodie, a few years shy of thirty but a veteran of the On-to-Ottawa Trek.

Brodie had lived the hard times of the Depression. Blown from his job on a farm by Prairie dust storms, Brodie rode the rails and suffered the indignities of the relief camps. After the trek came to its violent end in Regina, he drifted from job to job. His experiences had turned him into a communist. But Brodie preferred action over ideology. He felt tin-canning had run its course. "It

no longer had nuisance value, nor could it provide enough for two fifteen-cent meals per man," he recalled. Brodie opted for a bold strategy to bring the desperation of the unemployed right into government front yards. On the afternoon of May 20, he sent all four unemployed divisions on various downtown marches, spreading word that they were headed to Stanley Park.

Only division leaders knew the real plan. Brodie had meticulously timed and measured their routes to the last centimetre. At

Below: A postcard of the unemployed sleeping on the floor of the post office they occupied for thirty days was issued after the police crackdown on Bloody Sunday. The postcard is labelled "Forgotten Men." *Courtesy David Yorke.*

Left: Another postcard, titled "Homeless at Home," shows post-office sit-downers stretching their legs with an orderly march past the federal building. *Courtesy David Yorke.*

2 p.m., seven hundred men marched through the doors of the imposing granite post office at Granville and Hastings Streets and sat down. Fifteen minutes later, as police hurried to the post office, three hundred men moved into the unguarded lobby of the Hotel Georgia at the corner of Howe Street. Another two hundred men strode farther west along Georgia Street to set up camp beneath the paintings of the Vancouver Art Gallery, then four blocks from its current site across from the Hotel Georgia. The fourth division simply paraded through downtown streets in a successful ploy to baffle police. The hat trick of occupations targeting federal, city and private-sector locations fired up the public's imagination. Occupants were inundated with sandwiches, tinned goods, money and endless cups of coffee from nearby cafés.

Brodie shrewdly challenged police: if the occupiers are breaking the law, arrest them. It was his hope that mass arrests would finally force governments to accept responsibility for the long-suffering unemployed. But the mayor, the premier and the prime minister all stuck to their well-worn insistence that the

unemployed were not their responsibility. Prime Minister Mackenzie King, who professed pride in his grandfather William Lyon Mackenzie for taking up arms in 1837 to fight for responsible government, denounced the protesters as "a bad lot. They do not want to work. They want trouble." Authorities, however, blanched at the prospect of more than a thousand men clogging the city's jails. They waited for the occupations to wither away. It was not to be.

Early on at the Hotel Georgia, nervous management agreed to pay the men $500 if they left. They took the money and left. But sit-ins at the other two locations stayed solid. Wickets remained open for business at the post office. Although art gallery officials opted to close their doors, there was not a hint of damage to any of the displayed artwork. A month in, the unemployed occupants had provided no reason to be evicted other than their cheek at being there. Finally, however, authorities ordered in the police, hitching their excuse to a health officer's warning that disease might break out in the cramped, crowded quarters. MLA Harold Winch persuaded the men at the art gallery to leave if city police let them go free, which they did. There was no such resolution at the post office.

In the pre-dawn haze of Sunday morning, June 19, police massed menacingly on adjacent street corners. At 5 a.m., RCMP Colonel Cecil Henry Hill entered the building and ordered the men out. Brodie calmly replied that the protesters remained willing to be arrested, if they had broken the law. Hill's cold response sealed their fate: "I have no orders about arrests." Moments later, volleys of tear gas were fired into the midst of the protesters, and the onslaught began. Frantic, the men broke every window they could to bring in fresh air and rushed for the doors, blinded and choking from the gas. Gauntlets of police waited for them. As they emerged, a terrifying cascade of whips and riot sticks came crashing down on their heads. Brodie, easily visible in his bright orange sweater,

After using tear gas to end the unemployed workers' month–long occupation of the Vancouver Post Office on Father's Day, 1938, police beat them with billy clubs as they emerged. Scores were injured, several seriously. *Image C–O7969, Royal BC Museum and Archives.*

was among the last to leave. Police singled him out for special attention. Blow after blow rained down on the defenceless protest leader. A chilling newspaper photo showed Brodie surrounded by police, his hands over his head in a futile effort to protect himself. He woke up at St. Paul's Hospital twenty-four hours later, one of his eyes permanently damaged.

Thirty-seven other post office occupants were also hospitalized. Scores more were treated at the Ukrainian Labor Temple, its front yard covered with bloodied and bandaged victims. Livid by what had happened, those who had escaped injury and angry citizens raged along Hastings Street, shattering windows as they went. A spontaneous rally at Oppenheimer Park drew ten thousand people. Hundreds then massed outside the nearby police station, demanding the release of those arrested. Winch intervened again as a peacemaker. Climbing onto a light standard, the CCF MLA calmed the crowd, urging them to take their protest to Premier Pattullo in Victoria.

A one-hundred-strong delegation left on the midnight ferry, cheered on by large crowds of supporters. In Victoria, the answer was the same cold-hearted "no" that echoed just about every other government response to pleas from men at the end of their economic rope. "There comes a time when too much sympathy can be shown the men," said the unfeeling Pattullo. Not long afterward, many of these men enlisted to fight for the same country that had shunned them when they needed help.

After nearly ten years of economic adversity, the dark days of the Depression showed few signs of brightening. In the early summer of 1939, unemployment remained stubbornly high, production levels in BC were still 12 percent below those of a decade earlier, and governments continued to resist spending money on social assistance. A million Canadians were on some form of pitifully low relief. Many others scrabbled to survive on nothing.

Thronged by thousands of homeless, unemployed men, Vancouver had taken on the look of a shabby, beaten city.

Although the bleak situation drove many British Columbians to the political left, there was no significant breakthrough by the trade union movement. Without legislation compelling companies to recognize unions, overcoming determined anti-union employers—who had the help of police and governments—was simply too difficult. Workers were left with little love for the system that had done them wrong. "There were people who became leaders of the labour movement, who grew out of those days, and stuck with it all their lives," said Syd Thompson, who himself became a long-time leader of the IWA's Vancouver local and the city's labour council. He was permanently scarred by his grim experiences during the Depression. "I have a hatred for this system that, in some ways, has never left me," Thompson told an interviewer in 1978. "How could it be otherwise, I guess, after nine years on the bum?"

The brutal police eviction of unemployed men occupying the post office on Bloody Sunday, June 19, 1938, produced an outpouring of rage. Hundreds of protesters rallied outside the Vancouver police station, vowing to free those arrested, until CCF MLA Harold Winch defused the situation by climbing a light standard and persuading them to pursue their protest in Victoria.
Image c–O7959 Royal BC Museum and Archives.

10 WORLD WAR II

THE ASSERTION IS OFTEN MADE THAT CANADA CAME OF AGE as a nation during the Great War of 1914–1918, but it was World War II that profoundly transformed the country. On September 3, 1939, Britain and France declared war on Germany after Hitler had ordered German troops into Poland two days earlier. Canada issued its own declaration of war a week later, plunging the country into a six-year conflict that traversed the globe, claiming tens of millions of lives. As in World War I, British Columbia had the highest enlistment rate in the country.

While Canadians fought for democracy in Europe, workers left behind fought to make sure that democracy at home included union rights. The time was ripe. Governments saw the need to avoid the class turmoil sparked by World War I and end their standoffish approach of the Depression. They were open to reform. Labour's decades-long demand for federal unemployment insurance was realized in 1940. Universal family allowances were introduced in 1944. And at long last, after seventy years of struggle, the fight for compulsory recognition of unions and collective bargaining was finally won, first in British Columbia and then across Canada.

In 1943, amendments to BC's flawed **Industrial Conciliation and Arbitration Act** gave the government authority to recognize a union and force employers to bargain. They were the most advanced in Canada, giving BC workers virtually the same organizing rights US workers had had since the 1935 **Wagner Act**. Bogus company unions and the use of police-protected strikebreakers to thwart a union fighting simply for the right to be recognized at the bargaining table were now anomalies. The amendments were brought in by the province's first coalition government, an uneasy alliance between the Liberals and Conservatives put together when neither party won a majority in 1941. (The CCF, which topped the popular vote, remained on the outside.) The amendments were promoted by the coalition's reformist labour minister George Pearson, a sixty-one-year-old wholesale grocer from Nanaimo and a carry-over from the administration of Duff Pattullo. Although imbued with the anti-Asian racism of the day, Pearson was a rare friend of labour among his cabinet minister peers.

A grander breakthrough came early in 1944, when the federal government further enshrined union rights with its landmark order-in-council bearing the banal title of PC 1003. As in BC, the federal measures introduced under the War Measures Act gave unions legal bargaining rights for the first time, forcing companies to recognize and bargain with unions chosen by a majority of their workers. PC 1003 applied to all Canadian workplaces under federal jurisdiction, which had been extended early in the war to every major industry in the country. It gave certainty to BC's amendments, and other provinces had no option but to comply.

Since PC 1003 also removed the right to strike during a collective agreement, some have referred to the sweeping changes as a historic compromise. But for unions, it was a compromise to be welcomed. For generations, they had seen governments either stand by or actively participate as employer after employer stymied their aspirations. Thanks to the war, the ground had shifted.

Governments assumed a new neutral role, at least on paper, still trying to settle disputes through compulsory conciliation, but otherwise letting union organizing and legal strikes take their course. It was a fundamental change. Meanwhile, the federal government's obsession with balancing the budget, which had shortchanged millions of suffering Canadians throughout the 1930s, had suddenly disappeared with the first shot in Europe. By the fiscal year 1943–1944, federal spending skyrocketed to $5.3 billion, eight times what it was a mere four years earlier when the war began.

BC was in the thick of the booming wartime economy. From fewer than a thousand employees in 1939, Vancouver and Victoria shipyards grew to more than thirty-one thousand workers, turning out hundreds of merchant ships and naval vessels at breakneck speed. Burrard Dry Dock in North Vancouver became the busiest shipyard in the country. There, it was said, one could walk half a kilometre on ships under

Women were an integral part of the wartime workforce, building Catalina flying boats at Boeing's plant on Sea Island in Richmond.
City of Vancouver Archives, Air P1.3.

construction without touching the ground. Ferries carrying workers to and from their shifts across Burrard Inlet were often so crowded that passengers had to hang off the outsides of the vessels.

Boeing established aircraft plants in Vancouver and built a major factory on Sea Island in Richmond that produced "flying boats" for Canadian and US air forces, and later, sections of B-29 bombers. Mines, sawmills, logging operations, pulp and paper plants and the huge smelter at Trail maintained a feverish pace to meet the insatiable demands of war. Agriculture expanded too. And in the north, the building of the historic Alaska Highway opened up the Peace River region. By 1943, all this activity gave British Columbians the highest per-capita income in Canada.

On the union front it was full bore ahead. Bolstered by compulsory union recognition at last and the need for large, stable, industrial workforces to spur production during the war, union organizing took off. No longer could employers turn their backs on workers demanding improved wages and working conditions. For the first time, governments accepted that unions were vital partners in the economy, their yearnings legitimate. The craft union dominance of the labour movement also began to wane, challenged by the rising clout of industrial workers and their unions.

Three months after the declaration of war, the country had a new national labour organization. The Canadian Congress of Labour resulted from a merger of the CIO's expanding Canadian affiliates and the weakening All-Canadian Congress of Labour (ACCL), which had been founded in 1927 as a rival to the craft-led Trades and Labor Congress of Canada. Privately, ACCL president Aaron Mosher and Charles Millard of the Ontario Steelworkers, with CCF national secretary David Lewis prominent in the background, were anxious to curb the influence of industrial unions headed by members of the Communist Party. But for the moment, all factions united around the goal of organizing the unorganized under the CIO's philosophy of one union in each industry.

The Communist Party of Canada was banned early on under the War Measures Act. Prominent CP members were even interned for a time because of their initial opposition to the war. That changed the moment German tanks poured across the Soviet border in June 1941. After that, no one was more eager for the conflict than the suddenly pro-war communists, to the extent of adopting a no-strike policy and urging support for the Mackenzie King government in Ottawa. They were allowed to regroup in 1943 as the Labour Progressive Party (LPP).

In BC, far less fearful of being fired and blacklisted for joining a union, waves of workers took out union cards. Local 1 of the Boilermakers and Iron Shipbuilders' Union of Canada led the charge. Representing more than fourteen thousand Vancouver and North Vancouver shipyard workers, Local 1 became the largest union local in the country. "During the war, governments were forced to seek labour's goodwill with favourable labour legislation," recounted Bill White, the Boilermakers' tough president at the time, in his colourful memoir *A Hard Man to Beat*. "Many companies, with cost-plus contracts, found it cheaper to give in rather than lose production with a strike. We made big gains."

Besides across-the-board wage increases, those big gains in the shipyards included extra pay or "dirty money" for working in cramped, fume-filled quarters (won after a series of sit-down strikes), the first holiday pay for BC workers, longer rest periods, a good minimum wage, equal pay for women and a virtual union shop. On the job, the Boilermakers also pioneered a number of new labour practices, enforcing them with a very strong system of elected shop stewards. "When I look back, I realize I was seeing the formation of the modern labour movement," said White.

At the same time, in a sign of the fierce ideological battles to come after the war, the union's left-wing leadership had to fight off interference from the CCL's anti-communist

On behalf of the union, Harvey Murphy (right) signs the first collective agreement between the Consolidated Mining and Smelting Company and its Trail smelter workers, represented by the International Union of Mine, Mill and Smelter Workers, in 1944. Directly behind Murphy is union negotiating committee member Leo Nimsick, later a cabinet minister in BC's first NDP government
UBC Rare Books and Special Collections, BC1449–49j.

president Aaron Mosher. When a left-wing executive slate was elected by mail referendum in December 1942, Mosher voided the vote and put Boilermakers Local 1 under trusteeship. Turmoil swept the union. Backed by packed membership meetings, the deposed leadership and a three-hundred-strong shop stewards' committee refused to surrender control. When Mosher reappointed former executive members who had been voted out, more than a hundred shop stewards blocked their entry to union offices in downtown Vancouver. The Boilermakers then upped the ante, winning membership approval to leave the CCL and holding new elections that returned ousted leaders to their posts.

The battle moved to the courts, where Supreme Court Justice Sidney W. Smith ruled that the CCL's suspension of Boilermakers Local 1 was illegal. He ordered yet another round of elections to determine the membership's wishes once and for all. Close to six thousand members amassed in Vancouver's Athletic Park to elect a new executive. "All streets leading to the stadium were lined with parked cars," *The Daily Province* reported. "The huge crowd crawled along the sidewalks from south, east and west for an

hour, showing their cards at the gate before being admitted." A shipyard pipe band added to the memorable occasion. When the ballots were counted, anti-Mosher candidates held every position on the union executive. After another Supreme Court decision went the local's way, Mosher threw in the towel.

Elsewhere, union organizers spread throughout the province, signing up workers in industries that had long resisted unionization. The militant International Union of Mine, Mill and Smelter Workers' (Mine Mill) launched a successful drive to organize the large workforce at the Consolidated Mining and Smelting Company's huge smelter in Trail in 1944. Labour minister George Pearson, who became friendly with Mine Mill's larger-than-life communist leader Harvey Murphy, acknowledged its triumph at Trail as "one of the greatest accomplishments of BC unions in recent years."

In addition to its success at Trail, Mine Mill organized thousands of Kootenays metal miners. In the Okanagan, the Fruit and Vegetable Workers established the province's first agricultural-based union in 1943. Office workers and even newspaper reporters joined unions for the first time. The upsurge also swept over the Vancouver waterfront. After twice losing their union following grievous strikes in 1923 and 1935, the city's resilient stevedores overthrew their company union once again. Four hundred waterfront workers voted unanimously at a special meeting toward the end of the war to join the CIO's International Longshoremen's and Warehousemen's Union. This union stuck.

The organizing outburst spurred new and rejuvenated Canadian Congress of Labour unions to join in common cause. The Vancouver Labour Council, set up as a rival to the craft unions' Vancouver Trades and Labor Council, grew from a handful of unions to include thirty-eight affiliates with twenty-eight thousand members in just four years. Other new labour councils were set up in Victoria, Prince Rupert, the Okanagan and Nanaimo. But the biggest move came in 1944 when CCL affiliates revived the BC Federation of Labour. The original Fed had fallen apart in 1920 during the brief ascendancy of One Big Union. The founding convention of the second Federation of Labour took place on September 30 at the Boilermakers' union hall on Pender Street in Vancouver, attracting seventy-three delegates from unions affiliated with the CCL.

CCL regional director Dan O'Brien, who

pledged to steer an even course between the CCF and the communist LPP, was chosen as president. Radical left-wingers Harvey Murphy of Mine Mill and Harold Pritchett of the IWA were elected as vice-president and secretary-treasurer respectively. More than half the delegates were from the IWA, along with significant numbers from Mine Mill and the Boilermakers. Despite its leftward tilt, the convention generally avoided ideological matters and concentrated on the need to pressure government for better labour legislation. The born-again BC Federation of Labour quickly jumped into action.

On February 25, 1945, a mass delegation of 180 lobbyists from the Fed travelled to Victoria to pressure MLAs with a set of demands: compulsory deduction of union dues from pay cheques of unionized employees (known as dues check-off), rigorous safety standards, improvements to the Workmen's Compensation Act, BC support for a national health insurance plan, a sweeping government housing program and nationalization of the BC Electric Company. Lobbyists were delegated to buttonhole individual MLAs on the ambitious platform and report back on their reaction. They stayed three days, receiving extensive media coverage and establishing

The first convention of the new BC Federation of Labour, after the defunct organization was revived in 1944. *UBC Rare Books and Special Collections, BC1429–202.*

high-profile labour delegations to Victoria as a regular ritual.

The changed circumstances in BC galvanized the International Woodworkers of America. Drained of resources, its membership down to a paltry few hundred and no contracts in place, the future of the IWA at the onset of World War II had appeared bleak. Now, with the desperate fight against fascism intensifying, workplace harmony was required as never before. The IWA had leverage. With workers unwilling to toil for the war effort in poor working conditions at sub-par wages while forest companies profited, organizing took off. The result was the greatest union organizing drive in BC history. By the end of 1946 the IWA was the third-largest union in Canada, with more than twenty-five thousand members.

The union's campaign to organize the large Chemainus mill on Vancouver Island pointed the way to what was to come. Off and on since 1936, organizers had stood outside the gates to leaflet workers at quitting time. Half the leaflets were tossed on the ground, some spit on or thrown back. But in June of 1943, a three-week blitz reaped signed union cards from four hundred mill workers. Their certification as an IWA bargaining unit was a turning point for the province's unorganized sawmills. "When [Chemainus] went over, she went with a bang," recalled organizer George Grafton. "Everything [began to go] at the same time. You see, it was the war, the removal of fear from people's minds, of losing their job."

A similar pro-union mood prevailed among coastal loggers. This too was sweet reward for the many hardships endured by dedicated organizers over the years. Surviving on meagre income and grub, they had flitted into isolated camps in all kinds of weather, forever on the run from foremen and company stooges. In a typical incident, the camp superintendent at Elk River trailed two organizers on their bunkhouse rounds as they handed out copies of the *BC Lumber Worker*, snatching the paper away from each

man. When they were through, he angrily handed back the entire bundle. Not a single logger protested. "They had no rights, and they accepted it," said Grafton. These were gruelling times for IWA organizers. "The continual walking or rowing into the camps with the knowledge that the membership was dwindling everywhere else made it tough," Myrtle Bergren observed in her engaging book on those difficult times, *Tough Timber*. "It was an arduous routine."

It was during these years that the Loggers' Navy was born. A way had to be found to visit the many logging camps scattered along ocean inlets, particularly on the Queen Charlotte Islands (now Haida Gwaii). The union scraped together some cash, bought an old but seaworthy cabin cruiser and learned to sail it. In no time, the *Laur Wayne* was known up and down the coast by loggers who looked forward to its visits as a welcome break from work. If a hard-nosed

IWA organizer John McCuish at the window of the union's celebrated Loggers' Navy boat, otherwise the refitted cabin cruiser *Laur Wayne*, during a 1945 stop in Prince Rupert. The vessel was key to union efforts to organize loggers in isolated West Coast camps, accessible only by boat or seaplane.
Courtesy Rod Mickleburgh.

superintendent barred access to the camp, the crew blasted the vessel's horn and the men gathered on the dock to hear the union gospel preached from the deck.

The key breakthrough took place on the lush, heavily forested Queen Charlotte Islands. In 1943, four logging companies had federal contracts to supply manufacturers with Sitka spruce for the famed high-speed Mosquito fighter-bomber, yet conditions for felling the tall timber were often abysmal. With the help of the Loggers' Navy, the IWA had established a firm foothold in the camps. A federal conciliation board confirmed the IWA as the loggers' accredited bargaining choice and recommended that the companies settle with the union. But the employers dug in their heels, vowing to never sign a contract with a communist-led IWA no matter what the board said.

Facing provincial legislation compelling companies to negotiate with certified unions, coastal forest operators feared an IWA victory would fling the gates wide open to organizing throughout the industry. They decided to draw a line in the log-strewn sand of the Queen Charlottes. Representing 75 percent of the industry, forty-two coastal forest companies threw their weight behind the Islands' camp owners. They wired their support to the federal labour minister and took out large newspaper ads attacking the union. To dodge the labour legislation, they had adopted a strategy of agreeing to negotiate and even reach settlements with the union, but not put their names to an actual collective agreement. The tactic left the IWA with nearly ten thousand members throughout the province and only one signed contract. "We hate to have a knock-down, drag-out fight, but we cannot get anything at all," complained IWA leader Nigel Morgan.

On the Queen Charlottes, the industry hoped to stall proceedings until the winter shutdown, or pressure the union into calling a strike, a move they were certain would bring down the wrath of government and the public for disrupting a key wartime indus-try. A strike would also be a quandary for the union, which had a no-strike policy as part of the LPP's all-out support for the war effort. But after more than a year of company intransigence, the loggers were too restless to keep on the job. The union set a strike deadline of October 8, 1943.

The labour movement rallied to the IWA's side. They took out their own newspaper ads. Endorsed by almost all major unions in BC, the ads lambasted the "so-called dollar patriots running the vital aeroplane spruce industry companies" for their refusal to sign an agreement with the IWA. By then the loggers were so fed up they jumped the deadline. On October 6, ninety woodworkers stormed out on a wildcat strike at Skedans Bay. Word flashed quickly to the other camps. Loggers' Navy skipper John McCuish remembered: "As soon as [news] was received by delegates at a big camp, they went up to the engineer and said, 'Blow the whistle, the camps are out on strike.' So they blew the quittin' whistle and that was it."

In short order, more than five hundred loggers at eight camps were off the job. The strike was solid. No one left the camps. Supplies had been stocked up. Deer hunting and military exercises were organized "to keep the boys busy." After two weeks, the operators ran up the white flag. Much to the industry's surprise, public sentiment saw through their anti-communist ruse and backed the union. Reluctantly, the companies signed a one-year agreement providing a wage increase, progress toward an eight-hour day, seniority, grievance procedures, joint safety committees, travel rebates and union recognition.

R.V. Stuart, who co-ordinated bargaining for the forest companies, tried to put a positive spin on their surrender. The employers realized "the vital danger to the war effort was more important than their own private interest," said Stuart, a realization that took nearly two years. The industry abandoned all resistance after that and fell in line. In early December, District Council No. 1 of the IWA signed its first coast-wide

Massive timbers are stacked and rafted on the Queen Charlotte Islands (now Haida Gwaii) in 1944, ready to be towed to sawmills farther south. The loggers there were now unionized, after a successful IWA strike the year before.
City of Vancouver Archives, 586–3401.

forest agreement, a one-year deal covering eight thousand employees in twenty-three camps and mills. Five years after the debacle at Blubber Bay, it was an extraordinary achievement. Not only was the great leap forward a victory over the forest companies, the contract was won against a backdrop of fierce internal battles with the IWA's own international leaders in Portland.

The IWA triumph was not the only major advancement on the worker front during World War II. Women entered the industrial workforce for the first time. With so many men in the armed forces, their labour was critical. The influx was particularly dramatic in the shipyards. Beginning in late 1942, hundreds of women stormed the yards' all-male ramparts. Jonnie Rankin was hired at Burrard Dry Dock. "It wasn't like a women's lib hiring. They needed our labour power, that's all," she recalled decades later. But the Boilermakers Union made sure women received fair pay for doing much the same job as men. Rankin was soon making more money than the average wage earner in the city of Vancouver, a Canadian equivalent to the USA's ubiquitous "Rosie the Riveter."

Rankin worked as a passer, fielding red-hot rivets tossed her way by using a slender cone with a handle, then using tongs to pass the rivets to a bucker for installation by a riveter. After a harrowing first day, when a smart-aleck youth purposely tossed the rivets close to her face, at one point burning off some skin, she mustered the courage to come back for a second day. "The next day I felt a little better, and all of a sudden I wasn't afraid at all. The bucker showed me how to catch, how to move my bucket. I got so fast at it, and so good at it, that I was one of the first called when I walked into the yard. That was the highest egoism I ever had."

Alice Kruzic was hired on as a sweeper for sixty cents an hour at the South Burrard shipyards. She embraced the chance to work, impressing male workers by rolling her own cigarettes. Kruzic, who kept her old shipyard overalls and cap for years, also appreciated being able to aid the war effort. "We were told we could go down to see [one of our ships] launched," she recalled in the 1970s. "When I saw that ship slide down the ways, I was so proud. I felt that I had helped to build it. I wanted so much to win the war against the fascists."

Of the huge workforce at BC Shipyards,

The IWA Shows the Way

HIGHER WAGES · UNION HIRING · NO DISCRIMINATION · NO BUSH LING · UNION RECOGNITION · Contract

THIS BUNKHOUSE IS 100% UNION

Above: During its all-out organizing in the 1940s, the IWA portrayed itself as a beacon showing the way to a better working life. Loggers were given signs to put up in their unionized bunkhouses. *Courtesy IWA Archives.*

Right: There were no high-profile Canadian versions of the United States' iconic Rosie the Riveter, but that didn't mean women shipyard workers didn't handle rivets in the grimy holds of vessels under construction at Burrard Dry Dock—they did. *Jack Lindsay photo, City of Vancouver Archives, 1184–1057.*

6 percent were women, the most of any ship-building operation in the country. In addition to rivet passers, they were plate makers, jitney drivers, painters and lathe operators. Some became welders and charge hands. Because of company concerns that they might mingle too much with the men, there were separate lunchrooms, lockers and gate entrances for women. Rankin relished it all. "I worked in the deep tanks and I was slimy. We'd get on those old street cars, filthy dirty. They wouldn't let me sit down, so I'd hang off the back," she said. "But I didn't mind how dirty it was, or how rough it was. I just felt great."

Union consciousness took hold among the women shipyard workers. Alice Kruzic and Jonnie Rankin both became strong union supporters. "The old Wobblies and those who had helped organize the union talked to me about their struggles," said Rankin. "I got more of an education than you could get in three universities." In June of 1943, a group of them staged a brief strike to protest the firing of a woman for altering her company-issued overalls. "We cannot let an act like this go unchallenged," one striker told the *Vancouver Sun*.

Solidarity echoed elsewhere as well. Alice West helped organize a union at the Fraser River plywood plant where she was hired at sixteen. "My father believed in strong unions. It was something I breathed in quite early," West reminisced many years later. "I still have friends from that plywood plant."

Peggy Kennedy was hired by Boeing. She

COMPLIMENTS OF BURRARD DRY DOCK CO. LTD
AUGUST 1945

worked in the aircraft company's 1-A plant down by Coal Harbour in Vancouver. "We were all broke, and I felt I should do my part for the war effort," she recalled. "There were a lot of women working there. It was a first job for many of them, a way to get ahead after the Depression." The women did sub-assembly work and inspections while mostly staying off the machines. But like the Boil-ermakers, the International Association of Machinists insisted that women employees receive the same wages as men for similar work. Kennedy earned more during the war than her older brother Bill, who worked as a radio announcer. She also got involved in her union, serving as a shop steward and writing a column for the union's plant newspaper.

There were workplace issues at Boeing. As the pace of production sped up, the work-ers demanded two five-minute rest periods a shift. When Boeing refused, they staged a sit-down strike. After two weeks, the com-pany gave in. Union members also lobbied to get rid of lousy supervisors. "I think we were

"Boy! was I scared, there was a mouse right under my bed".

Above: Hundreds of women working at Burrard Dry Dock gather for this historic photograph taken at the end of the war in August 1945. They were soon laid off as shipyard orders dwindled and industrial jobs like those at Burrard went back to men.
North Vancouver Museum and Archives, 1421.

Left: This cartoon appeared in the July 1944 edition of the Vancouver local newsletter put out by Aircraft Lodge 756 of the International Association of Machinists, which had many women members during the war.
UBC Rare Books and Special Collections, 756 Review, July 1944, p. 4.

more interested in production than management. They were more interested in profits," said Kennedy. "It was a stimulating time. Many people who'd never considered joining a union were drawn into the movement, and it changed them." As for the job itself, Kennedy was not as enamoured as Jonnie Rankin. "Women work for the same reason men do, not so much 'cause they love it, but that they gotta."

In the forest industry, women worked as timekeepers in the woods and in mills. No operation was as welcoming to women as the Alberni Plywood plant, rushed into production to supply plywood for ammunition boxes, Mosquito warplane components and other war needs. As it expanded to a round-the-clock operation, the mill hired more and more women. Eventually, women made up 200 of the plant's 250 workers. Most were young and single. Many had relocated to Port Alberni from the Prairies, where they left behind family farms hit hard by the Depression. "The mill was a lifesaver for us girls," recalled one worker from Saskatchewan. The women were soon known throughout the community as "the Plywood Girls." They formed a softball team, dominated local dances and had a memorable time just hanging out together, a godsend for those who had grown up isolated in rural Saskatchewan. "When you're with a whole bunch of other ladies, it's always going to be great," remembered one former worker fondly. "We were happy. We had a lot of fun in that place."

By 1944, more than seven thousand BC women were members of a union, up from fewer than two thousand just three years earlier. It would not last. When Johnny came marching home, almost all women industrial workers were dismissed. Society dictated that veterans returning to the workplace had to be accommodated. As overseas fighting neared its end, Peggy Kennedy's aircraft union knew the wartime plants were in jeopardy. "We tried to find alternative uses, pre-fab housing or something," she said. "But everyone was laid off after the war. The layoffs were just massive." Women were no longer welcomed as industrial workers.

A return to domestic life was accepted, but not happily. A survey by the US Women's Bureau, likely reflecting attitudes in BC as well, found that 75 percent of female production workers wanted to continue working for wages after the war, and 86 percent of those wanted to stay in their same occupation. Now they had to resign themselves to either staying at home or earning lower wages for more traditional female employment. "There was no other place to work," complained a laid-off woman shipyard worker. "You went back as a waitress or worked in an office, or something like that … Nobody would hire a woman to weld anything. That was a man's job again."

During the war, close to a third of adult women in Canada were part of the workforce. That percentage of working women was not to be reattained for another twenty years. Yet all was not gloomy. Their integration into the workplace during the war

As men headed off to war and orders piled up, Alberni Plywood on Vancouver Island rushed to recruit women for its expanding workforce. Many were young single women from the Prairies, glad of a chance to work at a real job for decent wages. *UBC Rare Books and Special Collections, BC1930–103.*

remained a beacon for women in the years ahead. And they hardly disappeared from the workplace. Many took up jobs in the expanding clerical, retail and service sectors. Although their wages were less than those earned by women in wartime industries, they were nonetheless part of a significant new stream of women into the workforce, an evolution that author Judith Finlayson called one of the greatest social changes since the Industrial Revolution.

The need for unity to fight a common enemy had done little to stem the racism that continued to permeate British Columbia. Ethnic Chinese and Nikkei were still barred from most professions, rebuffed when they tried to enlist and remained unable to vote. Far worse was to come. Over four decades, people of Japanese descent had worked hard to stake their claim to a share of the province's economy through fishing, farming and working in the forest industry. Despite rampant prejudice and ostracism, they had mostly done well. That changed in an instant. On December 7, 1941, Japan attacked the US fleet anchored at Pearl

Harbor. Canada declared war against Japan the next day. Without a shred of evidence that they posed any sort of security threat, all twenty-three thousand Nikkei in British Columbia were soon branded "enemy aliens."

The first targets were fishermen. The very night of the Pearl Harbor attack Tsuguo Mineoka, secretary of the Japanese Fishermen's Union, was arrested by the RCMP at his home in Steveston. Hundreds of other fishermen were also rounded up and sent to camps. But first they were ordered to surrender their cherished fishing boats. From Prince Rupert on down the coast, a forlorn procession of Nikkei-owned vessels sailed its way south. The boats were tied up at the mouth of the Fraser, left to the Custodian of Enemy Property to be auctioned off for a fraction of their value. All told, 887 seiners, gillnetters, packers, trollers and cod boats came under the auctioneer's hammer. Most were bought by canners, who resold them to other fishermen. Others went to Indigenous fishermen.

The fishermen's union welcomed the sale. The union newspaper *The Fisherman* said its

The saddest of round-ups. Hundreds of Nikkei–owned fishboats tied up at the mouth of the Fraser River after being impounded by authorities from their owners all along the coast. They were soon sold off for a pittance of their worth.
UBC Rare Books and Special Collections, JCPC_12b_001.

workers supported "the taking of stringent precautions against dangers they have long recognized, even though such precautionary measures work hardships upon Japanese loyal to our country." Forgotten were the earnest words of Tatsuro "Buck" Suzuki in the same *Fisherman* paper just four months before Pearl Harbor. Already a leader of Nikkei fishermen at twenty-six, Suzuki urged unity between the two divides. "Most of us have been in the industry for years. We are average human beings, with the same likes and dislikes as every other human being," he wrote. "We are the weak link in the long chain of Canadian workers, not because we want to be, but because of the way other Canadians look at us and treat us. What we need is a real get-together of white Canadian and Japanese Canadian fishermen."

On February 4, 1942, the federal government announced that all people of Nikkei ethnicity living within one hundred miles of the West Coast would be removed, either to work camps or to flimsy wood and tarpaper shacks scattered among the mining ghost towns and small settlements of the Kootenays. Their possessions, homes and land met the same fate as Nikkei-owned fishboats, sold off for criminally low sums. Of those caught in the authorities' shameful scoop, an estimated fourteen thousand had been born in Canada. Not one Nikkei was found guilty of a single disloyal act. "I was fingerprinted, photographed and issued an 'alien' registra-

The poignant writing on the blackboard says it all as Hide Hyoto, BC's only Nikkei public school teacher, keeps up lessons, despite her removal along with thousands of other Nikkei from their homes to Hastings Park at the PNE, before being interned.
Toronto Star Photographic Archive, Toronto Public Library.

tion number," remembered Canadian-born schoolgirl Mary Haraga. "The worst part was being declared an enemy alien by my own country. I was a patriotic Canadian, but I had the face of the enemy."

When the war ended, few wanted the Nikkei back, no matter the terrible times they had endured. "For security reasons alone, I believe no Japanese should be allowed in BC for years after the war," said North Vancouver Liberal MP James Sinclair, grandfather of current prime minister, Justin Trudeau. More than four thousand unhappily agreed to return to Japan. The rest were scattered across Canada, barred from their home province until 1949, their lives shattered. Slowly, some Nikkei eventually drifted back to BC but nowhere near pre-internment numbers. Once thriving Nikkei communities in Vancouver and Steveston never returned to what they were.

The fishing industry was as resistant to their return as everyone else. But Buck Suzuki, who had enlisted with the British after Canada turned him down, was determined. Against strong opposition, union president Homer Stevens went to bat for him and other Nikkei fishermen. When they were threatened and harassed, Stevens lectured local union fishermen and enlisted their support. "He saw to it that we would be protected," Suzuki told author Barry Broadfoot. "That's the way it happened. Suddenly, the canneries took licences out of their back pocket [for us]. But it was because of the union guaranteeing our safety on the coast that we came back." Suzuki became a revered figure within the union. A founding member of the Society Promoting Environmental Cooperation (SPEC), his passion for preserving fish habitat and the environment led the union in 1981 to establish the T. Buck Suzuki Environmental Foundation, an ongoing charitable organization dedicated to fish habitat protection.

As for British Columbia's original inhabitants, as if governments had not done enough to strip them of rights, territory and

Under pressure from the British, Nikkei fisherman Buck Suzuki was accepted into the Canadian Intelligence Corps, willing to serve a country that had interned him and confiscated his fishboat. After the war, he spearheaded reconciliation between Nikkei fishermen and the United Fishermen and Allied Workers' Union, winning renown for his work to preserve salmon habitats. *Nikkei National Museum, 2010.23.2.4.682.*

economic opportunities, Ottawa singled them out again. At the height of the war, the federal government extended conscription to the country's First Nations, Métis and Inuit, obligating them to fight for a country that was forcing their children into residential schools and taking their land. Ottawa further proclaimed that Indigenous fishermen would now have to pay income tax on all off-reserve earnings, which is where the commercial fishery took place. Since Indigenous people didn't have the vote, it was a classic case of taxation without representation, on a resource fundamental to their culture and economic self-sufficiency.

Furious over both moves, the Native Brotherhood of BC and the Pacific Coast Native Fishermen's Association merged into a stronger, better-financed Native Brotherhood with an office in Vancouver and a full-time business agent. Although the two federal measures stood, the Brotherhood emerged as one of the most effective Indigenous voices in the country, pressing for better education, health services, cultural renewal and Aboriginal rights—especially to land taken without treaties. The organization had first come together among northern coastal First Nations groups in 1931, spurred by Haida elder Alfred Adams and his vision of tribal unity. Women formed a separate Native Sisterhood of BC, supporting the Brotherhood through door-to-door canvassing, bake sales, raffles and a thrift shop in Alert Bay. The Sisterhood was also active promoting education and health. Some members trained as midwives. Where possible, they provided daycare for female cannery workers.

In its enhanced role, the Native Brotherhood began negotiating with the canneries on behalf of First Nations commercial fishermen. The Brotherhood's first two business agents, Andy Paull and Ed Nahanee, were experienced hands in resistance by Indigenous workers. Both had been active in the Bows and Arrows longshoremen's local on the Vancouver waterfront. The Brotherhood took part in many strikes over the years, usually in conjunction with non-Indigenous union fishermen. Increasingly, however, they felt excluded from strategy and settlements, left "holding the bag," as one Brotherhood activist termed it. At times this led to tension with the larger United Fishermen and Allied Workers' Union, which had singularly managed to unite cannery workers and fishermen up and down the coast. The UFAWU tended to be more militant than the Brotherhood, whose members were more closely tied to the canneries and included seine-boat owners.

But overall, the two organizations worked hard to maintain their common front against the canneries. Leaders attended each other's conventions and joint negotiations prevailed, with a few hiccups, into the 1980s. Nonetheless, the Brotherhood rebuffed UFAWU entreaties to merge. Past distrust of non-Indigenous unions was difficult to shake. The Brotherhood wanted to remain distinctly

The early grassroots nature of the Native Brotherhood is still evident at its no-trappings annual convention in 1964. *UBC Rare Books and Special Collections, BC–1532–65–8.*

First Nations. "We supported their demands for complete legal and social equality and the works," said long-time UFAWU leader Homer Stevens, whose grandmother was Cowichan. "[By and large,] our relationships were good."

Although their federal voting door stayed shut until 1960, Indigenous people won the right to vote in BC in 1949, leading to the election of hereditary Nisga'a chief Frank Calder for the CCF, the first status Indian to be elected to a legislature in Canada. At about the same time, legislated discrimination against Asians, which had stained the country's history for so many years, came to an end. The vile Chinese Exclusion Act was repealed in 1947, and citizens of Chinese, South Asian and Japanese ethnicity finally got the right to vote. "When I voted, I felt like I could finally join the human race," said one elderly Nikkei man, whose internment during the war was only the most recent example of the marginalization and discrimination he had suffered since arriving in 1910. At the same time, a new Citizenship Act removed, at last, country of origin as a bar to citizenship.

These moves were part of a new Canada, far from perfect but moving forward, no longer steeped in the past. By the time the war was over, the country had become a respected mid-level world power on the verge of unprecedented prosperity, with burgeoning social programs and one of the best economies on the planet.

Labour's long hostility toward Asian workers was also transformed. The International Woodworkers of America showed the way by hiring organizers Roy Mah, Joe Miyazawa and Darshan Singh Sangha to help break down the barriers of race during the union's intense organizing drives of the 1940s.

Mah, later an acclaimed leader of Vancouver's Chinese Canadian community, was hired by the IWA in early 1944. In addition to organizing, he put out a Cantonese edition of the union newspaper, the first of its kind in North America. After serving in the war for a country that denied him the vote, Mah returned to the IWA for two more years. He is credited with bringing as many as twenty-five hundred Chinese Canadian workers into the union.

Miyazawa got his union start during internment, helping to organize the Kamloops sawmill where he and other Nikkei found work. Afterward, he signed on as an IWA organizer in the West Kootenays, where many Nikkei remained from internment. "Wherever I was, I knew somebody, and then we'd call a meeting at the farmers' or ladies' institute hall or some damn thing," he recalled of his fruitful time in the region.

Darshan Singh Sangha, son of a poor farmer, emigrated to BC as a nineteen-year-old student in 1937, but sought work in a series of sawmills instead. Dismayed by the discrimination and poor conditions experienced by Asian workers, he turned to communism and the IWA. His Punjabi pamphlets and fiery rhetoric soon had South Asian sawmill workers flocking to join the union. Sangha rose to become an IWA district trustee, the first non-white to hold such a position. In 1947, he opted to return home to be part of India's new independence. Before leaving, he saluted the IWA's "great achievement uniting all woodworkers—white, Indian, Chinese, Japanese—irrespective of race and colour." Back in India, he purposely changed his name to Darshan Singh Canadian.

11 POSTWAR POLITICS

WHEN IWA CONTRACT TALKS GOT UNDERWAY in 1946, the union's demands were ambitious, but familiar: a forty-hour week, union security and dues check-off, plus a wage hike of twenty-five cents an hour. This time, however, there was a difference. The union claimed an astonishing eighteen thousand members, and its wartime no-strike policy was gone. When the companies offered an hourly increase of twelve and a half cents, provided the union dropped its other demands, the union wasted little time pussyfooting around. On May 15, 1946, the vital BC forest industry was shut tight by the largest strike the province had ever seen. The prodigious walkout extended from the coast through to the Interior, closing logging and sawmill operations from Vancouver to Port Renfrew to Prince George.

In a surging show of solidarity, non-union employees joined their union co-workers on the picket line. Within a week, thirty-seven thousand woodworkers were off the job. As in the Queen Charlotte Islands dispute, no one scabbed. Even remote logging camps such as Blue River, where no union organizer had set foot, went out. The union had prepared well, with its dynamic Ladies' Auxiliary playing a key role. Far from a tea and crumpets organization, Auxiliary women bolstered picket lines, staged marches, helped fundraise and solidified support for the union's demand for a shorter workweek. "I didn't marry a meal ticket," said one Auxiliary member, "but that's what it amounts to if my husband works more than forty hours a week. We just never see our husbands when they work such long hours." When the City of Vancouver refused permission for a union tag day, the IWA held one anyway, raising buckets of money from a supportive public.

Halfway through the strike, federally appointed arbitrator Gordon Sloan, a chief justice of the BC Supreme Court, handed down his contract recommendations. He proposed a wage increase of fifteen cents an hour, a limited reduction of working hours that nonetheless set the union on the road to a five-day, forty-hour week, and some improvement in dues check-off, though short of a complete union shop. The companies accepted Chief Justice Sloan's report. The IWA did not. Fearing the provincial government was

The unprecedented 1946 strike by the IWA hit logging operations and mills across the province, including the large operation of the Western Canada Lumber Company at Fraser Mills, now part of Coquitlam.
UBC Rare Books and Special Collections, BC1485–1–2.

about to legislate Sloan's recommendations to end the dispute, the union mounted a mass march on the legislature by three thousand strikers and supporters.

They came by ferry from Vancouver and by car and bus from all over Vancouver Island. Jonnie Rankin was inspired by the sight of scores of women boarding the midnight boat to Victoria. "You know, it was a wonderful thing," Rankin told interviewer Sara Diamond. "They came from all these mills all over New Westminster and they were just ordinary working girls, and they walked on that boat singing, 'You Can't Scare Me, I'm Sticking to the Union,' and militant, you know. They just lifted the whole thing."

After bunking overnight in local armouries, the demonstrators were led by a large group of women from the Lake Cowichan chapter of the Ladies' Auxiliary, carrying signs and banners backing demands for more take-home pay and particularly the forty-hour week. Cheered on by the citizens of Victoria, they marched toward the Parliament Buildings. As union leaders met inside with members of the cabinet, the protesters

paraded around, chanting, "25–40 Union Security!" and singing union songs, their voices clearly audible to those within the legislature's thick walls. But the stirring protest failed to soften the government's attitude, and the IWA's first major strike soon came to an unexpected close.

Members of the Lake Cowichan Ladies' Auxiliary led a mass march on the provincial legislature by IWA strikers and their supporters during the union's province–wide strike for the forty–hour workweek in 1946.
Courtesy United Steelworkers.

Influenced by complaints from Okanagan fruit growers, who feared their crops would rot because the strike had cut off their supply of wooden shipping crates, the federal government ordered Okanagan mill workers back to work at their old wage rates. At this point, the IWA was beginning to feel some heat, worried the back-to-work order would be extended beyond the Okanagan and sensing some wavering within the membership. On June 20, the union leadership decided to call off the strike and accept Chief Justice Sloan's recommendations.

Yet the overall results were positive. There were clear gains in the Sloan report, even if they were short of the union's hopes. The thirty-seven-day strike solidified the IWA's position as the strongest union in BC. With the addition of ten thousand new recruits who signed up during the strike, the IWA now claimed twenty-eight thousand members. Its militant leadership had shown an ability to take on the might of the province's major industry. The fifteen-cent pay hike smashed federal wage controls, setting a pattern for other industrial unions both in BC and across the country, and it would not be long before most woodworkers could look forward to weekends without work.

The strike was a watershed event. During all the years BC workers had been fighting for their rights, such a province-wide walkout would have been beyond the wildest dreams of union organizers. Now, it had happened. The strike also convinced the province's anti-union employers there would be no rolling back of workers' wartime gains. For the moment, employers focused on opposing labour's drive for legislation to impose a union shop and dues check-off on all bargaining units. Such measures, the Canadian Manufacturers' Association told cabinet, would produce a "tyranny of the majority" in violation of an individual's right to work.

Already up to 29.8 percent of the non-agricultural workforce in 1945, unionization surged even more during the immediate postwar years, fuelled by a booming econ-

IWA strikers in 1946 pose outside the Western Crown Manufacturing plant at Fraser Mills. The company's vintage wooden ironing boards are now highly sought collector items.
UBC Rare Books and Special Collections, BC1485-9.

omy. Toughened by the Depression and six years of war, workers were not content to accept a lesser share of the pie. This time the craft unions, which had lost initiative during their rancorous split with the muscular industrial unions, were in the forefront. Not only did the building trades expand as construction increased across the province, but other unions within the craft union orbit—belonging to the Trades and Labor Congress of Canada—also took off.

The International Pulp and Sulphite Workers regrouped at large pulp and paper mills in Ocean Falls and Powell River, where managers had fired all "left-wingers" and "foreigners" in the mid-1930s. Union membership also rose among teamsters, transit workers and the fishermen's union. As workers in the public sector began to attach themselves to the labour movement, their organization of choice was also the TLC. The BC Teachers' Federation brought five thousand members into the congress, the BC Government Employees' Association four thousand and the National Union of Public Employees, a forerunner of the Canadian Union of Public Employees (CUPE), another two thousand.

Industrial unions suffered a slight, temporary membership dip, with a decline in coal mining and the province's once mighty shipbuilding industry. But they lost none of their fight. In the dying days of the war, just before the bombings of Hiroshima and Nagasaki, 450 members of the United Steelworkers of America struck American Can, the Vancouver factory that produced all metal containers in the province, in a forceful bid for a union shop. Later in the year, thousands of Crowsnest coal miners staged a month-long wildcat walkout over, of all things, inadequate meat rations. They demanded more fresh meat and an end to rationing of bologna for their lunchtime sandwiches. The baloney brouhaha finally ended when the miners secured concessions from the Wartime Prices and Trade Board.

The next year, just as the IWA had taken on the province's forest industry, the Mine, Mill and Smelter Workers' Union went head to head with BC's obstinate mining companies. Having secured a good agreement for its several thousand members at the Consolidated Mining and Smelting Company's large smelter and mining operations in Trail and Kimberley, Mine Mill sought industry-wide bargaining for its twelve metal mines in the province. When the companies refused, two thousand Mine Mill members walked out on July 3, 1946, shutting down the province's metal mines except those run by Consolidated. Chief Justice Sloan, fresh from his similar role in the forestry strike, was quickly appointed as a conciliator. After ten days he quit, declaring that the mining companies' refusal to bargain as an industry made a settlement impossible. In a blunt message to the mine owners, the chief justice told them, "If 147 lumber operators can sign an agreement, so can you."

Instead, the companies kept up a steady barrage of propaganda against the union and its spirited leader Harvey Murphy. With regular radio broadcasts, they also raged against BC's allegedly union-friendly labour legislation. New laws were necessary, proclaimed the *Western Miner*, "to cope with the rapidly increasing power concentrated in the hands of union leaders … so communists will be deprived of their most potent weapon." Despite their bluster, the employers' solidarity shattered first. In mid-October, two copper mines settled with the union, followed shortly afterward by two silver-lead-zinc mines. A month later, the Hedley Mascot gold mine signed a union agreement. The remaining mine operators accepted settlement terms on December 5, and the strike was over. Although wage gains by the union were modest, their members had stuck together and broken the mines' resistance to any form of industry-wide negotiations.

It was an impressive display of union strength, which only hardened the owners' determination to see the last of labour minister George Pearson, whom they blamed for creating a climate in which unions could persevere. BC employers began pressuring the shaky ruling coalition to tilt the legislative balance in their favour once more. The fact that company representatives received an advance look at the new **Industrial Conciliation and Arbitration Act** (Bill 39) while labour was left in the dark showed which way the wind was blowing. Introduced in March 1947, the bill contained two key employer demands: government-supervised votes on all conciliation reports and making unions liable to heavy fines and lawsuits for any activity deemed to be illegal. Rather than quell job action, labour leaders predicted these measures would only lead to more strikes. "Where [the Act] puts one tooth in, it puts in a pair of pliers to yank it out," said Federation of Labour president Dan O'Brien.

The labour movement's fight against Bill 39 marked the beginning of a new era in industrial relations. Now that the fight for basic rights such as certification, compulsory collective bargaining and union recognition had largely been won, union energy was increasingly directed against a steady stream of legislation that restricted them in other ways. They found themselves fighting off employer actions in the courts and shoring up structurally to take on the battles ahead. Advances continued, but the struggles were different.

Not long after the war, employers had discovered to their delight that the courts could be just as effective as truncheons for thwarting unions. For the next twenty-five years, police on horseback and the billy club were replaced by the court injunction to keep labour in its place. Injunctions could be obtained against almost any union picketing that kept customers and other workers away from the work site. The vast majority were issued after one-sided hearings on the basis of employer affidavits without any union representation in the courtroom. Not only did these *ex parte* injunctions tie up resources as unions fought to overturn them, they also led to many trade unionists going to jail for defying them.

The pattern was set in 1946 during a violent strike at the *Vancouver Province* newspaper. Members of the International Typographical Union struck the paper on June 5 to support ITU members in Winnipeg, whose strike against that city's two dailies was not going well. Both the *Province*, then Vancouver's largest-circulation newspaper, and the *Winnipeg Tribune* were part of the Southam chain of papers. The union was not above using muscle to try to keep the *Province* from publishing. Four strikebreakers brought in by the paper were forcibly evicted from the company building across from Victory Square. Others were harassed and manhandled, their hats grabbed and put on display at the front of the *Province* building with a label "Rats' Hats."

When the *Province* tried to resume publication on July 22, delivery trucks leaving the loading docks were confronted by crowds of union supporters. One vehicle was overturned. Copies of the paper were burned or scattered about surrounding streets. Photos of strikebreakers, including their names and addresses, were published in the ITU's publication, the *Typo Times*. Labour forces in the city carried out an intense boycott campaign against the *Province*. Some news vendors were warned their stands would be overturned if they carried the paper. Other newsstands were picketed. Signs read, "It is easy to help the union printers. Don't buy the *Daily Province*." Many didn't. Thousands of readers cancelled their subscriptions and turned to the *Vancouver Sun*, which supplanted the *Province* as the city's number-one newspaper.

But the ITU strike led to BC's first significant court injunction against union activity. After the initial attack on strikebreakers, the company obtained an injunction preventing the union and its supporters from gathering in large numbers, from accessing the *Province* building and from "watching and besetting" the paper's premises. In short order, the injunction became a blueprint for the courts, its terms often copied word for word in other far less violent cases where companies applied for relief against picketing.

The first attempt by the 1946 strikebound *Vancouver Province* to publish a paper using non-union workers ended with overturned delivery vehicles, copies scattered in the street and some set on fire. The incident led to a court injunction which became a template for similar picketing restrictions over the next twenty-five years. *Jack Lindsay photo, City of Vancouver Archives, 1184–2559.*

"Watching and besetting," a term lifted from the Criminal Code, became a key phrase in injunction after injunction. Not long after the *Province* case, an injunction against striking employees of the Aristocratic Restaurant in Vancouver seemed to outlaw legal and peaceful picketing merely for being effective.

Court injunctions gave employers a powerful new weapon. Since almost all applications were *ex parte*, with only the employer allowed to present evidence, they were almost never denied. Nor did they have any time limit. Unions had to challenge *ex parte* injunctions after the fact, when it was often too late to do any good. Worse, anyone disobeying an injunction could be found guilty of contempt of court and sent to jail. When emotions ran high during a bitter strike, complying with an injunction was not always easy, especially when the courts rarely gave any thought to the root causes of a dispute or considered behaviour of the employer. For the first time since the 1930s, labour leaders were finding themselves behind bars.

Dan O'Brien's prediction that Bill 39 would lead to more rather than fewer strikes proved correct. A few months after its passage, a major flare-up took place in Nanaimo over unionized laundry worker Violet Dewhurst's decision to book off work to attend a BC Fed convention in Vancouver. When Dewhurst returned, she was fired along with another worker who had taken time off to care for her sick mother. Twenty-eight employees walked out in protest. They had strong backing from the labour movement, which saw the dispute as the first fightback against Bill 39's prohibition of spontaneous strikes. There were mass pickets and a large parade through the streets of Nanaimo featuring Bill 39 hung in effigy and one-day sympathy strikes by local coal mine and sawmill workers.

Authorities quickly laid charges under the new ICA Act against all twenty-eight strikers, the Nanaimo Laundry Workers' Union, regional CCL director Dan Radford and the United Mine Workers' Percy Lawson. This time the courts were sympathetic. Judge Lionel Beevor Potts pointed out that the wildcat walkout had nothing to do with collective bargaining procedures. "It's a great pity this thing ever arose," he said, adding the relevant provision in the act was "cumbersome and long drawn out." Although he found most of the strikers guilty, he fined them a token one dollar each.

A month later, it was the Steelworkers' turn to defy the legislation, striking five Vancouver-area iron and machinery companies without holding a government-supervised vote. On September 2, 1946, 114 workers, two officials and two union locals were charged with violating the ICA Act. This case also drew withering comments from the judiciary. With charges pending against packinghouse and furniture workers who had also ignored the act, punctuated by a widespread, month-long transit strike and a walkout by Vancouver Island coal miners, the government bowed to growing consensus that its legislation needed to be amended. Legal proceedings came to a halt.

Although the amended ICA Act contained a few changes sought by labour, its overall thrust restricted unions even more than the original. Not only was the hated supervised strike vote retained, the Labour Relations Board (LRB) was given added power to order a membership vote on any "bona fide" settlement offer made by an employer. As well, unions were now more liable to be sued and even decertified for an illegal strike. They also lost their chief ally in the coalition government's labour minister George Pearson, who made no secret of his opposition to supervised union votes. His departure was cheered by the business community, which had long agitated for someone less sympathetic to labour in the job. In his thorough study on the ICA Act, UBC graduate student Paul Knox observed, "The life work and philosophy of one reformer (Pearson) proved no match for the organized forces of a dominant class."

The labour movement's ability to fight the legislation was further compromised by the ongoing internal struggle between communist-led unions and those supporting the CCF. From the beginning, the main labour opposition to Bill 39 had been spearheaded by unions with communist leadership, whose membership numbers gave them control of both the Vancouver Labour Council and the BC Federation of Labour. But most communist leaders, like the IWA's Harold Pritchett, knew enough not to let their left-wing politics get in the way of representing workers under capitalism. "It would be foolish—and impossible—for us to try and force socialism into Canada, until the people want it," he told a *Vancouver Sun* reporter in 1947. In the meantime, Pritchett said, the IWA was "willing to operate within the framework of capitalism ... The forest industry means our livelihood ... We need it every bit as much as the operators do."

But the writing was on the wall for communist leaders and their unions, both in BC and the rest of Canada. A Cold War between the western democracies and a newly powerful Soviet Union was being waged on the international stage, rife with fears of home-grown spies and communists. It was a period of witch hunts for alleged "Reds," blacklists, and purges of organizations where communists were prominent, notably in the labour movement. Anti-communism began earlier and took hold more intensely in the United States. Even before the US's entry into World War II, communists had been hounded out of many unions. Pritchett himself had felt its sting when he had to resign as international president of the IWA in 1940 after US authorities refused him a visa for speaking at the funeral of a BC communist. In 1947 Republicans and southern Democrats rammed through the odious Taft-Hartley Act, which piled numerous new restrictions on unions including a requirement that all officers take an oath affirming they were not members of the Communist Party.

The Canadian Congress of Labour and the rival Trades and Labor Congress also worked to expel unions with communist influence. In the most singular example, the Canadian government, shipping companies, AFL "roadmen" in Canada and eventually the TLC gave a green light to the US-based Seafarers' Interna-

A button from the BC Federation of Labour campaign against Bill 39, legislation brought in by the coalition government in 1947 that curbed union rights to free collective bargaining.
Courtesy David Yorke.

tional Union (SIU) to break the storied Canadian Seamen's Union (CSU). The CSU was an all-Canadian, communist-led union that had organized freighters on the Great Lakes and the country's extensive fleet of deep-sea vessels. The SIU was led by the notorious Hal Banks, who had served four years in San Quentin prison for forgery and whose connections to the American mob were shrugged off by those who wanted the CSU gone.

When the CSU launched an unprecedented strike against Canadian deep-sea shipping companies in 1949 that tied up ships at ports around the world, Banks used orga-

nized thuggery on vessels docked in Canada, including Vancouver, to help break the strike. Strikebreakers were herded through CSU picket lines by SIU goons wielding axe handles, chains and sawed-off shotguns. With the assistance of sweetheart contracts signed behind the backs of the Seamen's Union, Banks and the SIU soon controlled the waterfront from coast to coast.

TLC president Percy Bengough, who got his trade union start as secretary of the Vancouver Trades and Labor Council at age sixteen, resisted for a time. Complaining to the federal government about AFL interference in

Top left: Members of the Seafarers' International Union boarding the SS *Riverside* docked in Vancouver after a court injunction ordered crew members of the Canadian Seamen's Union off the ship during their worldwide strike in 1949. *Vancouver Sun.*

Top right: Striking members of the Canadian Seamen's Union don their formal best to greet Prime Minister Louis St. Laurent with their picket signs on his arrival at the CNR station in Vancouver in 1949. *Courtesy William Mozdir papers.*

Bottom: Ships at the Terminal Dock in Vancouver were among Canadian merchant vessels in ports around the world struck by crew members belonging to the Canadian Seamen's Union in 1949. *Courtesy William Mozdir papers.*

Jack Phillips, communist leader of the independent Vancouver Civic Employees Local 28 until it merged with CUPE in the late 1960s, is speaking at a convention in 1973. Known in labour circles as the man with the cigar, Phillips was an effective backroom strategist, seeking to exert left-wing influence on the labour movement without becoming a target. *UBC Rare Books and Special Collections, BC–1532–2076.*

Canadian union affairs, Bengough declared, "[We] will accept domination no more readily from Washington than from Moscow." But once he fell in line, under intense pressure from the AFL's threat to withdraw its affiliates from the TLC, there was barely a ripple of protest from the non-communist labour movement.

The Canadian Seamen's Union disappeared, albeit with a reputation as one of Canada's most inspiring rank-and-file unions. Now that he had cleaned out the CSU, Banks showed no sign of stopping. Under his direction, the SIU began expanding its empire, moving in on other Canadian maritime unions with the same tactics of violence, sweetheart deals and support from the AFL in Washington. Battles took place in Vancouver and other ports across the country. Too late, the TLC realized the SIU medicine was far worse than the cure. Only when the burly Banks went on the lam to the States in the mid-sixties, to escape a criminal charge of assaulting a rival union leader, did an uneasy calm descend on the Canadian waterfront.

After barring eighteen left-wing delegates from attending its 1950 convention, the TLC adopted its own Taft-Hartley-like policy banning communists, members of the Labour

Progressive Party "or any person advocating the violent overthrow of our institutions" from holding office in unions affiliated with the TLC. One of the targets was crafty, cigar-smoking communist Jack Phillips, who headed Vancouver Civic Employees' Union Local 28. The TLC ordered him to resign. Instead, Phillips led the union out of the TLC. Backed by the membership, Local 28 survived an onslaught of legal and raiding challenges by TLC unions before finally joining CUPE as Local 1004 in the late 1960s.

The United Fishermen and Allied Workers' Union was another target. Amid fending off a raid by the SIU in line with Hal Banks's determination to organize "everything that floats," Bengough suspended the fishermen's union because of its "very definite leaning toward communism." As with the Vancouver Civic Employees' Union, members of the UFAWU backed their leadership, flourishing outside the "house of labour," as the mainstream labour movement called itself, for the next twenty years.

The rival Canadian Congress of Labour was equally eager to purge its communist-led unions. Firm supporters of the CCF, the CCL's national leaders loathed communists within their ranks, not for their trade unionism but for their willingness to co-operate at times with the federal Liberals, their convention resolutions conforming with the Soviet Union's view of the world and their resistance to embracing the CCF as Canada's labour party. Nowhere was the militant Left stronger than in British Columbia, where communist-led unions had played a dominant role organizing the province's industrial workers. In 1947 the congress appointed the brash thirty-year-old Bill Mahoney of the United Steelworkers of America as its Western director, giving him two years to "clean out the communists." It took him less than one.

Mahoney scored an early success at the Vancouver Labour Council. He rounded up eligible delegates from every local, no matter how small and obscure, that had mostly shunned the left-wing council. Under his direction, they drew up a slate of non-communist candidates for the council's twenty-one elected positions and won every one. The triumphant Mahoney next turned his sights on the BC Federation of Labour. He began by dabbling in the internal affairs of its largest affiliate, the IWA, working with its relatively small anti-communist "white bloc" to challenge the supremacy of Pritchett and other officers. This venture failed. Pritchett's slate trounced the white bloc in union elections, retaining all executive positions and maintaining control of every local but New Westminster.

Then Mahoney was handed an unexpected plum by Mine Mill leader Harvey Murphy. At the time, that union represented almost all BC metal miners, plus several thousand smelter workers in Trail. "[Murphy] was the soul of the union," remembered lawyer John Molson, who did legal work for the union during its fierce raiding battles with the Steelworkers in the 1960s. "He was all for the worker, and the men loved him. A real straight shooter, a good talker and he could be very funny. I liked him immensely. I would call him a rough diamond."

Unfortunately for Murphy, his rough side came to the fore at a labour banquet in Victoria in the spring of 1948. Upset over CCL support for the deportation of Mine Mill's international president Reid Robinson because of his communism, and having had by his own admission too much to drink, Murphy lashed out at CCL officials, ridiculing them as "phonies" and "Red-baiting floozies." He went further, causing his speech to go down in labour lore as Harvey Murphy's "Underpants Speech." Referring bitterly to CCL president Aaron Mosher and secretary Pat Conroy, both hard-line anti-communists, Murphy suggested that if asked to kiss the boss's arse, their only request would be for the boss to first pull down his underwear.

Mahoney pounced. He immediately laid charges against both Murphy and Pritchett, who had emceed the banquet without censuring his comrade-in-arms. While Pritchett

Bill Mahoney, on left, of the United Steelworkers of America was sent to BC by the Canadian Congress of Labour in 1947 to end control of the province's labour movement by communist–led unions. He returned a year later, task accomplished, and remained Canadian leader of the Steelworkers until his retirement in 1977. *Courtesy United Steelworkers.*

and other Federation officers were merely reprimanded, Murphy was decked with a two-year suspension from all meetings of the Canadian Congress of Labour and its chartered organizations, including the Federation of Labour. Even better for Mahoney's mission was Mine Mill's suspension from the CCL over an attack on Mosher in the union newspaper. This cost the communist side twenty-two key voting delegates at the Fed's forthcoming convention.

After a summer touring the province to round up convention delegates, Mahoney was ready for his *coup de grâce*. The Fed gathering that September, fought over political attitudes rather than specific trade union issues, turned into one of the most dramatic labour conventions ever. For two days, the two evenly split sides battled it out at the microphones. To paraphrase Abraham Lincoln's famous statement, never was a house of labour more divided against itself.

Voting was even more intense. Left and right sides fielded full slates for all executive positions. Mahoney, a backroom master, was confident his side had one more vote. So he was stunned when communist Bill Stewart of the Shipyard Workers edged

The Woodworkers
Industrial Union
of Canada held its
founding convention
in 1948 at the
Boilermakers' union hall,
where Fraser Wilson's
famous workers' mural,
now at the Maritime
Labour Centre, can be
seen on the right–hand
wall. The communist–
led breakaway from the
IWA stemmed from the
bitter left–right fight
that split the union after
WWII. The WIUC lasted
only a year.
Courtesy David Yorke.

the Steelworkers' Pen Baskin 66–65 for first vice-president. Positive he had left nothing to chance, Mahoney surmised someone had double-crossed him. For the next ballot, he assigned CCL officer George Home to "assist" the suspected vote-switcher in his vote for second vice-president. Sure enough, this time the same, razor-thin 66–65 tally was in favour of Mahoney's candidate, Stewart Alsbury. With Mahoney's men continuing to ride shotgun on the delegate, communist titan Harold Pritchett was toppled from the key post of secretary-treasurer, again by 66–65. When voting ended, Mahoney's slate had control of the BC Federation of Labour. The communists were vanquished.

In the meantime, Mahoney had continued to zero in on the BC IWA, whose communist leadership was under increasing pressure from the union's international officers in Portland. Working with the International, Mahoney vigorously played up some sloppy but not fraudulent bookkeeping by the BC District, which showed $150,000 unaccounted for. The district's representative on the international executive was fired for refusing to take an oath that he wasn't a communist, and thirty-three of their international convention delegates were refused entry to the United States. BC District leaders felt the walls closing in on them. Fearing trusteeship would be next, they made a fateful decision

in the fall of 1948 to break away from the IWA and form their own union, the Woodworkers Industrial Union of Canada (WIUC). Officials quietly moved their assets to secret accounts. Files and office equipment were moved to an equally secret location.

But the white bloc also moved quickly. That same night, with the help of the *Sun*'s Jack Webster, an ally of Mahoney's throughout, two union officials worked until dawn to produce their own copy of the union *Lumber Worker*, which went out in the mail. The next day, international president James Fadling and New Westminster white bloc leader Stewart Alsbury applied to the courts to freeze the IWA's BC assets. Alsbury was appointed provisional president of District Council No. 1, and the International undertook to secure all its local charters and certifications.

Three weeks later, the new forestry union held its first convention, full of bluster and bravado. "The Woodworkers' Industrial Union is here to stay," proclaimed Harold Pritchett, who had privately opposed the breakaway. But legally, certifications remained with the IWA and rare was the company willing to switch to the WIUC. Dues check-off became a serious problem. Whenever the new union did manage to reorganize a workforce and apply for certification, the Labour Relations Board often stalled proceedings long enough to stymie the union's drive.

The fate of the WIUC seemed to boil down to a critical stand at Iron River, a MacMillan logging camp controlled by the union south of Campbell River. In mid-November, after a flare-up over the firing of two loggers, the WIUC shut down the entire operation. Both sides considered the dispute a key opportunity to prove their mettle. The WIUC went all out to support the wildcat walkout; the IWA tried to break it. On an application from the IWA, the LRB declared the strike illegal, prompting Stewart Alsbury and a few other IWA officers to escort a group of twenty-five IWA loggers in to work across the picket line.

Amid the pre-dawn glare of car headlights, the picketers turned on them. In the resulting mayhem, Alsbury had his ribs broken. Two others were also sent to hospital. The next night, twenty-six provincial police and a gang of 150 men recruited by the IWA—many from south of the border—made sure the loggers got in to work, daring the small band of WIUC picketers to take them on. When the picket-

ers wisely opted to stand aside, the swarm of IWA men burned down their picket shelter instead. Five WIUC picketers were charged with assaulting Alsbury and the others. On the witness stand, Alsbury admitted that the company had invited him to bring loggers into the camp. He also testified that the IWA had enlisted white bloc volunteers to infiltrate WIUC operations on Vancouver Island. Defendant Mike Farkas confessed to beating up Alsbury and throwing him to the ground "because [he] had tried to lead scabs through a picket line." His cause was not improved by defence witness Danny Holt, who recounted for the court that when Alsbury "yelled for mercy, I told Farkas, 'Hit him again, Mike.' And Mike did."

Unable to maintain the strike, the WIUC picket line came down in April. By then, the union had managed to secure just nine certifications through the slow-moving labour board. The union's stalwart vice-president, Ernie Dalskog, spent nearly a month behind

Logs are being loaded into a truck by spar tree at Iron River on Vancouver Island in 1947. A year later, the operation was hit by a violent wildcat strike that put breakaway members of the IWA against those in control of the international union.
Museum at Campbell River, 13310.

bars until he complied with a court order to return the IWA's $130,000 strike fund. As difficulties mounted, leaders of the WIUC realized success was not in the cards. They began to soften their vilification of the IWA, stressing the need once more for "one union in wood." Less than a year after its bold separation, the WIUC closed its doors.

Bill Mahoney returned to Ontario, where he eventually became Canadian director of the United Steelworkers of America and a major advocate for AFL-CIO unions in Canada. WIUC leaders were blacklisted by the IWA. Pritchett returned to his old trade as a sawyer and shingle weaver, never allowed back into the union he had done so much to build. Ernie Dalskog could find work only as a first-aid man in non-union logging outfits.

Still, with the white bloc at the helm, IWA members did not shirk from strikes. Not all produced the benefits that were sought, especially some long, bitter disputes in the Interior and northern BC. But on the coast, centralized bargaining produced good overtime rates, paid statutory holidays, compulsory dues check-off, medical insurance and other benefits, and a healthy fifty-cent raise in the base rate to $1.59 an hour. Other unions continued to look to the IWA to set wage and benefit patterns for BC industrial workers.

Bitterness from the deep political division in the IWA eased over time. Eventually there was appreciation of the communists' contribution to the union, although its blacklist of so-called "errant members" took fifty years to erase. The move at the 1998 convention was "far, far overdue," said president Dave Haggard. "They were workers, and they were IWA members, and they helped build this union." Former BC Communist Party leader Maurice Rush used the occasion to return the original charter of Local 1-85 from Port Alberni, stressing what a mistake the WIUC was. "It did not strengthen workers," said Rush. "It divided and weakened them in their struggle with the employer." And some could laugh about it. One veteran of the ill-fated decision with a taste for graveyard humour liked to tell the story about a membership meeting near the end, when WIUC numbers were dwindling. Looking around at all the empty seats, an old Swedish logger observed, "Well, at least we got rid of all those phonies."

At the national level, the Canadian Congress of Labour kept up its drive against communist-led unions. Although Mine Mill had been allowed back in the CCL after its suspension, higher-ups now wanted the troublesome union expelled for good. This would be a boon to the Steelworkers, who had an eye on the union's certifications in the mines of BC and metal refineries and nickel smelters of Ontario. At the urging of the congress's executive council, delegates to the CCL convention in the fall of 1949 voted overwhelmingly to throw them out perma-

PUBLISHED BY THE INTERNATIONAL WOODWORKERS OF AMERICA (CIO-CCL)

Vol. 1. No. 3   October 8, 1948   Vancouver, B. C

LAUGH THIS ONE OFF, DALSKOG!
Supreme Court Grants International Order to Freeze Funds

Power of the law went into action to protect the interests of IWA members —International President J. E. Fadling (right) and Stewart Alsbury, President Local 1-357, mounting the steps of the Court House to secure court order.

Singer Paul Robeson performing at his legendary Peace Arch concert straddling the US–Canada border in 1952 after he was denied entry into Canada because American authorities had confiscated his passport. On stage to his right is event organizer Harvey Murphy of the Mine, Mill and Smelter Workers' Union. *Pacific Tribune Photo Collection, Simon Fraser University Library.*

nently. The next year, with the expulsion of the United Electrical Workers and the Fur Workers, the CCL's purge of communist-led unions was complete.

Mine Mill remained a force outside the Canadian Congress of Labour. Attempts by the Steelworkers to raid its large smelter workforce in Trail were rebuffed by a membership that stayed faithful to Mine Mill despite its communist leanings. Most of the union's mines stayed too. Harvey Murphy also carved a place for himself in left-wing lore by organizing a legendary Paul Robeson concert. The famous American singer had been invited to perform at Mine Mill's 1952 convention in Vancouver but was denied entry into Canada because of his politics. Murphy invited Robeson to a substitute concert at Peace Arch Park, straddling the border between Canada and the United States. Robeson famously sang from the back of a

flatbed truck on the US side to an estimated crowd of ten thousand people on the Canadian side.

Ousting unions simply because their elected leaders took a different view of the world was not a glorious chapter for the labour movement. Few questioned the communists' commitment to trade unionism. But their ejections played out against the anti-Red hysteria of the Cold War—from which the trade union movement was not immune— and a very real, intense political antagonism between the CCF, backed by a large majority of the country's labour leaders, and those sympathetic with the Soviet Union. Perhaps, given the highly charged emotions of the times, the fracture was inevitable.

12 BAD NEWS BENNETT

O UTSIDE THE CONFLICT RAGING IN BC UNION HALLS, a political shock loomed that was to consume and bedevil the province's labour movement for the next two decades. After ten years in office, the Liberal-Conservative coalition government was fraught with tensions that could no longer be smoothed over. The two parties went their separate ways to fight the next election in 1952. Still worried about the steady strength of the CCF, however, coalition masterminds imposed a transferable ballot, which took into account second and even third choices until a candidate had a majority of the votes cast. They estimated that most people's first and second choices would be split among the Liberals and Conservatives, keeping the CCF out of office. They didn't foresee the unexpected appeal of an upstart Social Credit Party.

Tapping into a strong mood for change, Social Credit was many voters' second choice. After a month of complicated calculations on the electoral abacus, the final totals stunned the province. With 31 percent, the CCF had the highest popular vote. Social Credit garnered 27 percent, the Liberals 23 and the Conservatives 17 percent. But the transferable ballot gave the Social Credit Party nineteen seats, one more than the CCF. The Liberals had six seats, the Tories four and independent labour candidate Tom Uphill had once again captured Fernie, as he had in every election since 1920.

Once confirmed as Social Credit party leader and premier, former Conservative W.A.C. Bennett parlayed BC's polarized politics into a historic string of electoral triumphs, forever campaigning on keeping the socialists out of office. William Andrew Cecil Bennett was an ambitious, politically astute appliance store owner from Kelowna driven to open up the province with new roads, big dams and an expanding resource sector. With his customary eloquence, esteemed political writer Bruce Hutchison summarized W.A.C. Bennett's stamp on booming British Columbia in the *Vancouver Sun*: "The fixed neon smile, bustling salesman's assurance, ceaseless torrent of speech, undoubted talents of a small-town hardware merchant writ large and a certain naïve, boyish charm are ... the emblem and hallmark of a new province."

But Bennett and Social Credit were bad news for the province's trade unions. The new government was dominated by an outsider's spirit of unrestrained free enterprise that worshipped profits and the bottom line and hated anything that smacked of unions or socialism. The labour movement soon found itself locked into long, bitter combat with a government that made its battles with the coalition benign in comparison.

Ironically, perhaps, given the forces grouped against them, the 1950s and 1960s were also good times for BC's organized workers. Apart from bashing labour, Social Credit fanned the province's expanding economy with its all-out building program. Well-paying union jobs abounded. In 1958, unionization hit an all-time high, never to be surpassed, of 53.9 percent of the workforce. In reaching this plateau, unions were also aided by widespread adoption of the so-called Rand formula, which resolved dues check-off as an issue after more than half a century of contention. The formula

THE UNSINKABLE TOM UPHILL

When Thomas Aubert Uphill retired in 1960 at the age of eighty-five, he was far and away the most successful MLA in BC history, elected eleven straight times as the member for Fernie. Boer War vet, coal miner, insurance salesman, union official, multi-term mayor and jokester, Uphill was a bit of everything. But through seven premiers and a multitude of changes in the labour movement, he never wavered in his passion for the cause of the working class.

Uphill was first elected as one of three successful candidates for the socialist Federated Labour Party in 1920, at a time when the One Big Union was frightening the bejeebers out of the establishment. Re-elected in 1924 for the short-lived Canadian Labour Party, Uphill ran thereafter under various independent labour party banners of his own making, spurning the CCF as not Left enough. Though never a member, he was closer to the communists, visiting and praising the Soviet Union in the 1930s, speaking at their rallies, attending the Communist-backed World Peace Congress in 1952 and regularly addressing May Day gatherings in the coal-mining communities of Michel and Natal.

As an MLA, Uphill campaigned for pensions, better workers' compensation and mine safety and against any curbing of the sale of beer, which he likened to "mothers' milk" for toiling miners. During the Depression, he pressed for higher relief, while urging government to take over the means of production and use them for "the common good." He railed against the "fat lawyers and millionaires" who had made their fortunes "by

Tom Uphill (1874–1962) was a legendary independent labour MLA for Fernie. His passionate advocacy of beer for workers led a Victoria craft brewery to concoct a Thomas Uphill Amber Ale in his honour.
Image B-06782, Royal BC Museum and Archives.

bleeding their workers and their customers." As the years passed, Uphill lost some of his rhetorical fire but never the support of the Crowsnest Pass miners. Political columnist Bruce Hutchison summed him up as "not red, not a Communist, not a pink Socialist even. He is simply a working man, out to help the underdog."

Premier W.A.C. Bennett used his perpetual crusades against unions and the socialists, populism and BC boosterism to preside over the province for twenty years. Bennett loved grandiose projects, like the opening up of the Pacific Great Eastern Railway to the Peace River in 1958, marked by a photo op and a big wave.
Image I–32387, Royal BC Museum and Archives.

compelled all members of a bargaining unit to pay dues regardless of whether they belonged to the union.

Despite hostility from government, corporations and the courts, the need for workers gave unions good leverage at the bargaining table. In addition to healthy wage gains, unions began to hone in on fringe benefits, winning more paid holidays, better overtime pay, disability provisions, pensions and other improvements. But this did not bring labour peace. Industrial relations under Social Credit were to be marked by confrontation, jailings of many union leaders and class bitterness.

After winning a strong majority in the 1953 follow-up election, Social Credit brought in its first labour legislation a year later. Bill 28 set the tone for all the years the Socreds were in power. Under the **Labour Relations Act**, powers of the courts and the labour minister were enhanced, those of the Labour Board curtailed. There were new restrictions on strikes and heavy penalties for contravening them. "[Bill 28 brought] industrial relations more into the political sphere," observed labour historian Paul Phillips. They were to remain there for a long time.

Setting aside their differences, more than three hundred delegates from CCL and TLC affiliates gathered in Victoria to protest Bill 28 and lobby MLAs for changes. One of the delegation's strongest demands, prompting some to call for a general strike, was an end to *ex parte* injunctions, which had become such a boon to strikebound employers. At the very least, unions contended, both sides should be heard before any injunction was issued. The government ignored them.

One of the more egregious examples of injunction injustice befell Tony Poje, business agent of the IWA's Duncan local. During the union's big coastal strike in 1952, Poje oversaw picketing of a bridge leading to a dock in Nanaimo that prevented union dock workers from loading lumber onto a waiting cargo vessel. The ship owners quickly obtained an injunction, ordering the picketers to cease and desist. The next day, two hundred angry picketers showed up to keep the longshoremen away, ignoring a sheriff's reading of the injunction and copies posted on the bridge. Six days later, the company summoned the longshore crew a second time. Again the injunction's order was read out by the sheriff and again IWA picketers thronged the bridge. Poje was charged with contempt of court.

Before his case could be judged, however, the strike ended. As part of the settlement, companies petitioned the court to drop the charge against Poje. The chief justice of the BC Supreme Court, Wendell Burpee Farris, paid no heed. Declaring that defiance of court injunctions could not be bargained away, he sentenced Poje to six months in jail. Union members showed their appreciation of their business agent's sacrifice by electing him president of the local even while he was locked up. (Three years later, Tony Poje switched to management, and was regularly heckled by union negotiators whenever he showed up on the company side of the bargaining table.)

As unions' pursuit of better wages and worker rights accelerated, health and safety had tended to take a back seat, despite a growing toll in workplace tragedies. Yet some unions, with the backing of CCF MLAS, did keep up a steady outcry over such basic matters as adequate compensation for injured workers, better pensions for widows of husbands killed on the job and independent medical reviews to consider appeals of denied claims.

In 1949 Gordon Sloan, the chief justice of the Court of Appeal, was appointed to head a Royal Commission on workers' compensation. By then Bill White of the Marine Workers and Boilermakers Union had made this a personal cause. He began fighting back on individual cases where he felt the Workmen's Compensation Board had made a particularly bad decision to deny a worker's compensation claim. Gradually, White acquired a grasp of medical matters, along with a group of doctors he could rely on for unvarnished opinions.

The Boilermakers president prepared for commission hearings for months. He spent days on the witness stand, detailing more than forty individual cases in which workers had suffered disabilities but been denied compensation. He called eighteen doctors, including eight medical specialists, to support his contention. "We were setting out to show that the board was absolutely rotten," White explained. "Our basic demand was an appeal board where a fella could go to some outside authority and have his case re-examined, if the Board rooked him." Dissatisfaction with the board was so rife, two years of hearings were needed to accommodate the hundreds of fed-up workers and many doctors who wanted to air their complaints.

As part of his comprehensive report, Justice Sloan urged the establishment of medical review panels, as advocated by White and other trade unionists. Unfortunately, his report came down shortly before the pivotal 1952 election, and the recommendation was left to the Social Credit government to implement. To White's dismay, instead of instituting full-fledged review panels, the Socreds tinkered with the concept. Only after yet another Royal Commission in 1966 were effective and viable medical review panels put into place. White was also critical of the government's attempt to head off complaints by appointing a form of compensation ombudsman, which he termed "about as much use as a pocket in your underwear."

Benefits to workers were improved, however. Social Credit agreed to Justice Sloan's call for higher compensation, better widow pensions and improved travel and therapy subsidies. Further, after considerable political pressure, the government made the increases retroactive to the start of the Royal Commission. "In the first year, monies paid out to BC injured workers by the Compensation Board increased by three million dollars," White recalled with pleasure. While the outspoken trade unionist was hardly the only advocate on these issues, his leadership showed how one person can make a difference on an issue that gets few headlines but affects thousands of workers.

Despite the best effort of White and other advocates, however, the WCB maintained its regimen of denial. If the board could find a reason to shortchange or reject a pension to an ailing worker, it did. Nothing illustrated

After more than five years of fighting for her ailing husband, on February 23, 1956, Bea Zucco went public. She camped out for a day at the WCB. Four days later, accompanied by three of her children, she staged a sit-down protest on the steps of the legislature in Victoria. The determined miner's wife captivated the media. Even the Social Credit government was sympathetic. Labour minister Lyle Wicks ordered another review. The WCB didn't budge. Evicted from her home, relying on donations, Bea Zucco took off on a province-wide "Car Crusade for Silicosis" to raise awareness. On September 11, Bea Zucco became a nationwide *cause célèbre* when she again camped out on the legislature steps, this time for nine days. Her sign read, ONE SICK HUSBAND. ONE MOTHER— BC PRODUCT. FOUR CHILDREN—ALSO BC PRODUCTS. SEVEN YEARS OF STRUGGLE—A BC DISGRACE!! She won the hearts of the public but could not sway the WCB. Rules were rules.

With Bea holding his hand, Jack Zucco breathed his last in early April 1958. Three weeks later, an autopsy confirmed what the couple had known all along. His lungs had been ruined by "advanced silicosis." The WCB could not fudge any longer. Expressing "deep regret" over its previous rulings, the board awarded Bea Zucco retroactive compensation of $12,998.87, carefully itemized lest she get a penny more, plus a monthly pension of $75 and $25 for each of her children. After so many years of grinding adversity, Zucco declared it "a hollow victory," but she was nonetheless proud of her perseverance. "They just can't do this to ordinary people, not in Canada. I know they can't," she said. "I didn't know anything at the beginning. All I had was the spirit."

The impact of her indomitable spirit went beyond Bea Zucco's personal mission. She had exposed the WCB as a cold, unfeeling bureaucracy that shortchanged workers. Unions renewed their attacks on the board at a large special conference, slamming its use of "rigid and legalistic formalism" to reject

In 1956, the indomitable Bea Zucco camped out with her children on the steps of the legislature in a heartfelt effort to secure a pension from an unyielding Workmen's Compensation Board for her dying husband, who was stricken with silicosis. Her campaign became news across Canada, but only after her husband died were regulations changed to give ailing miners a better deal.
Bill Halkett photo, Victoria Daily Times.

the board's stringent approach more than its attitude toward the deadly mining disease of silicosis. Its hard-heartedness burst into public view in 1956 thanks to a courageous personal crusade by Bea Zucco, whose husband, Jack, was slowly dying of the disease. Although his condition was first diagnosed in 1949, the board repeatedly denied his petition for a pension. The WCB based its decision on X-rays showing he was suffering from tuberculosis, not silicosis. The board ignored the fact that tuberculosis often afflicted victims of silicosis and overshadowed its evidence in the lungs. A series of outside doctors, including a specialist in Bellingham, reaffirmed his silicosis, but the WCB continued to rule "no evidence."

legitimate claims by injured and ailing workers. Qualifications for silicosis pensions were finally overhauled, ending their sole reliance on X-rays and providing suffering miners like Jack Zucco the benefit of the doubt.

Concurrently, a sea change in attitude was taking place among the country's trade unions. The more governments rolled back labour's wartime legislative gains, the more labour realized they could only fight back effectively by calling off the historic conflict between craft and industrial unions. It happened first in the United States. Unions headquartered there had long played a dominant role in Canada's labour movement, as most workers considered the border irrelevant to their struggle against the boss. Positively, American-based CIO unions spurred the great industrial organizing drives of the 1940s. Negatively, the bitter split between the AFL craft unions and the CIO industrial unions spilled over into Canada, resulting in two national union organizations, the craft-dominated Trades and Labor Congress and the Canadian Congress of Labour, bastion of industrial unions. In BC, the rift compromised solidarity on a growing number of issues as Social Credit fastened its grip on the province.

Under far heavier fire from anti-union forces in their country, US unions realized their rivalry was hurting no one but themselves. In 1955, the AFL and CIO patched up their deep divisions and made peace. The newly merged AFL-CIO claimed a membership of fifteen million workers. Once their merger was complete, the way was open for labour unity in Canada. Facilitated by a no-raiding pact, ongoing talks between TLC and CCL leaders culminated with the formation of the unified Canadian Labour Congress in April 1956. More than a million Canadian workers, representing 80 percent of the country's trade union membership, belonged to union affiliates of the new national organization.

The 1956 merger of the Canadian Congress of Labour, dominated by industrial unions, and the craft union–oriented Trades and Labor Congress ended years of enmity between the two rival labour organizations. In BC, that soon led to a historic, unified convention of the BC Federation of Labour. TLC delegates gather for one last separate photo before the convention began and they joined CCL delegates in a single labour body. *UBC Rare Books and Special Collections, 1902-05-02.*

Unity followed in British Columbia as well. Rival local labour councils merged across the province, and the founding convention of the third reincarnation of the BC Federation of Labour, with craft and industrial unions together for the first time, was held in Vancouver in November 1956. They united around a socially progressive platform calling for, in addition to extensive labour reform, universal health care, post-secondary colleges across BC and nationalization of BC Electric. The exercise was not without rancour. Some unions stayed on the outside, including the United Mine Workers, several rail unions and the BC Teachers' Federation, which decided it was more a professional association than a trade union. Also missing, of course, were the unions that had been tossed out of the CCL and TLC for their communist leadership.

Politically, the industrial unions were big on supporting the CCF, the craft unions not so much. There was also tension over how activist the Federation should be. The more autonomous-minded craft unions initially preferred leaving political action to individual unions, but they too had been affected by operating in a province with a long history of union resistance. It did not take long for the new BC Federation of Labour to resolve these matters and emerge as the most effective, hands-on, centralized labour organization in the country. With unions under persistent attack from hostile employers and government, the Fed was soon taking a new, heightened interventionist role in the province's labour disputes. Strike co-ordination, beefed-up picket lines, "hot" declarations proscribing union members from handling goods produced by a strike-bound company and threats of a general strike became regular weapons in the Federation's arsenal.

There were changes in the public sector too, particularly for the BC Government Employees' Association (BCGEA) as it tried to grapple with the tight-fisted Socreds. The union was led by Ed O'Connor, a Dublin-born son of a soldier who had been working for the government as a court registry clerk since 1928 and delighted in wearing Homburg hats. His mettle was tested almost from the moment W.A.C. Bennett came to power in 1952. For the next twenty years, Social Credit policy was unyielding: keep government employees under thumb, with no say in determining their wages and working conditions.

Within two years, O'Connor was complaining that the Socreds had "all the earmarks of fascism, Nazism and communism." As he did whenever he felt that the BCGEA was getting uppity, Bennett punished the association for O'Connor's remarks. In a fit of pique, he cut off all meetings with the organization, vowing no resumption until the BCGEA had leaders more akin to his liking. Thus began the annual ritual of government unilaterally ordaining wage increases for the coming year. There was no collective bargaining, not even talks. Instead, Bennett notified employees of their modest annual raises through the media, without a word to the association. The BCGEA and the provincial Civil Service Commission made competing cases to the government through written presentations, dubbed by union historian Bruce McLean as "the battle of the wage briefs." Even commission head Dr. Hugh Morrison admitted the process was nothing more than "legalized paternalism."

The association did manage to gain a five-day week in 1955, plus improved vacations and sick pay. But pay hikes remained stuck around 2 percent a year, well below those won by government employees in other provinces and leaving them ever further behind wages in the private sector for similar work. It seemed as if the words of civil service commissioner W.E. MacInnes to a small gathering of government workers back in 1919 were still relevant nearly forty years later: "Blessed are they that expect little, for they shall not be disappointed."

In 1957, fed up with their low wage rates and armed with an 89 percent strike vote, the BCGEA threatened to strike for the first time. Taken aback by their resolve and cognizant of public support for underpaid civil servants, Bennett agreed to bump up their small raise, albeit minus six months' retroactivity. That set the stage for 1959, when the BCGEA took on the government in earnest. Demanding a 10 percent wage increase and full collective bargaining rights, the association called a strike for March, Friday the thirteenth. Once again, on the eve of a walkout, the government wavered, doubling its previous wage increase to an acceptable 7.5 percent. But there was no give on collective bargaining, so the association went ahead with its first-ever full-scale strike.

At 7 a.m., carrying signs that read "On Strike. Sorry for the Inconvenience," thousands of union members began picketing government buildings across the province. Three and a half hours later, the government had an injunction ordering pickets to stop "watching, besetting or picketing" any of its premises. Half an hour after that, the association complied. The historic strike was over. O'Connor said there was simply not enough solidarity to maintain what the *Vancouver Sun* called "the most genteel strike in British Columbia labour history." "A few people crossed our picket line, but we were too polite to call them scabs," said first-time striker Dorothy May.

Notwithstanding the *Sun*'s description, the sight of nattily dressed men and smiling women in their long coats and fur-trimmed boots wearing picket signs enraged blustery highways minister Phil Gaglardi. No government in a free country could give its employees full union status, he bellowed. "[Association leaders] are [only] interested in power so that they can abuse those civil servants, use them as pawns, [and] take over from the elected representatives." A few days later, the Socreds passed an amendment to the **Constitution Act** making it illegal to picket government buildings. Later, they explicitly banned civil servants from striking at all.

Despite the strike's speedy end, association members were energized by having

BC government employees went out on strike for the first time on March 13, 1957. Although their walkout was short-lived, they displayed cleverly worded picket signs, derived from the province's ubiquitous SORRY FOR THE INCONVENIENCE highway construction signs.
BC Government and Service Employees' Union.

stood up to the government, for however short a time. "It was a sad task convincing [some] members that the strike was over in four hours," said Roy LaVigne, an employee at the Essondale (later Riverview) mental health facility. "But we had closed them down. You couldn't get married, buried or buy a bottle of booze. If there is a next time, pray God that the union tells them to stick their injunction where Paddy put his sixpence." Nancy Hamilton, who went on to serve many years as the organization's treasurer, said the strike was an emotional experience for members at the Woodlands psychiatric facility. "It was a miserable morning, snowing and blowing. We were all keyed up. It was a disappointment to have to go back in the afternoon," Hamilton recalled. "But I was relieved, because I had seen some nurses and aides in tears on

The sudden, horrific collapse of the Second Narrows Bridge being built across Burrard Inlet on June 17, 1958, claimed nineteen lives. It remains the worst industrial accident in the history of Vancouver. Province *newspaper photo, Vancouver Public Library, 3042.*

the picket line, really worried about their patients. There was a lot of heartbreak."

The previous summer, a horrifying tragedy had befallen members of Local 97 of the International Association of Bridge, Structural and Ornamental Ironworkers. On the hot afternoon of June 17, 1958, the lead crew of ironworkers on the massive Second Narrows Bridge under construction across Burrard Inlet laboured to put one more section of steel in place to complete the last anchored span jutting out from the north shore. Just before quitting time, with a terrifying roar that could be heard all over East Vancouver, the span collapsed, bringing previously built sections of the bridge down with it. In six seconds, seventy-nine men were pitched more than a hundred feet into the deep, swirling water amid a lethal cascade of massive steel girders.

"I went right down to the bottom, right

down to the soil. I thought I was gone. Goodbye. Adios," recalled Norm Atkinson on the fiftieth anniversary of that fateful day. But just the year before, a new safety regulation had required all those working above water to wear a life jacket. Somehow, the veteran ironworker managed to undo the quick release on his heavy tool belt, and his mandatory life preserver brought him to the surface. "As I came up, I remember the water getting lighter. Finally, I hit air. What a wonderful feeling that was." Atkinson and other survivors surfaced to a scene of horror: maimed, mangled bodies and terribly injured men trapped in the twisted steel and rising tidewater, screaming for rescue. "I saw a hell of a lot of things that day, and I forget nothing," said Atkinson. "Bodies going by like corks, like pieces of wood. They were your mates, but you couldn't do anything. It was awful."

Gordy MacLean remained alive after hitting the water but he was trapped in the cab of his small shuttle locomotive that shunted steel along the bridge. Divers tried frantically to free the well-liked engineer, who was hollering for help as his cab filled with water. One was sixteen-year-old scuba diver Phil Nuytten. As he prepared to make yet another rescue dive, Nuytten looked over to see MacLean's blond hair floating under the surface. He was gone. Continuing to dive, Nuytten found two ironworkers still upright on the bottom of the inlet, anchored by the weight of their tool belts. When he arrived, he noticed three bodies laid out on the wharf. "By the time I left two hours later, there were twelve."

Eighteen lives were lost that day, most of them ironworkers. A diver later died during a search for victims, bringing the final death toll to nineteen. Another twenty workers were seriously injured. It was by far the worst industrial accident in Vancouver history. The catastrophe was front-page news across North America. Hundreds showed up at Empire Stadium for an emotional outdoor service. Country star Jimmy Dean and Stompin' Tom Connors wrote heartfelt songs about the tragedy. The provincial government wasted no time striking a Royal Commission into the disaster, headed by BC Chief Justice Sherwood Lett, a veteran of both world wars with a reputation for no-nonsense jurisprudence.

It did not take long to identify engineer John McKibbin's inadequately designed falsework as the cause of the collapse. It had buckled under the weight of the outer span. Both McKibbin and his direct overseer Murray McDonald died in the collapse. But why had his mistake not been noticed? In his comprehensive report, Lett found contractor Dominion Bridge guilty of negligence for failing to submit the falsework plans to higher-up consulting engineers and "leaving the design to a comparatively inexperienced engineer, with inadequate checking." Although he stopped short of citing Vancouver-based Swan-Wooster Engineering, the overall bridge designers, for neg-

ligence, Chief Justice Lett singled out the company for "lack of care." No blame was attached to any of the workers who perished.

The media moved on to highlight the sad state of WCB pensions provided to widows and families of the dead workers: $75 a month for their wives and $25 for each child, amounting to barely a quarter of what their husbands or fathers had earned. Although a public trust fund amassed some extra money, most widows had to find ways to work to provide for themselves and their families.

Since 1994, the collapse has been remembered by renaming the bridge the Ironworkers Memorial Second Narrows Crossing. But few are aware of the dramatic events that followed for Local 97. As survivors returned to the job, Local 97 was locked in tough negotiations with Dominion Bridge. Armed with a strong strike mandate, including a 79–4 "yes" vote among those building the Second Narrows bridge, the union was seeking a wage increase to reflect the dangers they faced on the job, improved travel pay and a ban on using workers imported from neighbouring Alberta. On June 23, 1959, mere days after the first anniversary of the collapse, ironworkers were on strike at Dominion Bridge construction sites across the province.

The year after the calamitous 1958 collapse of the Second Narrows Bridge, a strike by Ironworkers Local 97 left this unfinished section of the bridge hanging over a busy road. The ensuing dispute over its safety led to a dramatic series of events that changed the union. *Otto F. Landauer photo, Jewish Museum & Archives of BC, LF–36342.*

At Second Narrows, the striking ironworkers left behind an expanse of steel balanced on falsework that was hanging over the road and railroad tracks leading to the "old" bridge farther east, which was still open to traffic. Declaring the overhang hazardous, Dominion Bridge asked the union to allow a crew to finish the span until it was anchored to the next pier. When Local 97 business agent Norm Eddison refused, the company went to court, where the drama really began to unfold. Submitting affidavits claiming the jutting span was a risk to the public, Dominion Bridge sought an *ex parte* injunction, ordering the ironworkers to resume work until the span was "entirely safe."

The application came before Justice Alexander Malcolm M. Manson, who had begun his BC legal career in 1906. He had a reputation as an exceedingly prickly anti-union judge who didn't hesitate to harangue lawyers he found annoying. Without much ado, Justice Manson ordered the ironworkers to return to work on the southern section of the bridge. Although pickets came down forthwith, ironworkers continued to stay away. Referring to company claims that the span was liable to plunge onto the roadway in a small earthquake or other tremor, Eddison asked, not unreasonably, "If the bridge is unsafe for the public, why is it safe for our members?" He avowed he would rather rot in jail than imperil their lives by ordering them back to work.

Justice Manson reconvened the court to consider the ironworkers' appeal. There, he first clashed with the union's brash twenty-six-year-old lawyer Thomas Berger, who argued it was not up to a judge to order men on a legal strike back to work. It was the job of the legislature. Berger got nowhere and Justice Manson upheld his injunction. Sheriffs trying to serve copies of the injunction found few ironworkers at home. Eventually eighteen were served, but the site stayed idle. When Manson summoned them to appear before him, none showed up. He ordered their arrests. Berger later wrote in his auto-

biography, "The judge was inventing his own procedure, because none in the books suited his purpose."

On July 13, 1959, seven ironworkers finally complied with the angry judge's summons. Union supporters crowded the courtroom, jeering the judge when he threatened Berger, later a BC Supreme Court justice himself, with contempt of court for his interjections. Eric Guttman, the first ironworker to take the stand, told Justice Manson he had been instructed by the union to return to work. "But it is a free country and nobody can force me to go to work to build a bridge if I don't want to." The judge got much the same answer from the others. In the end, union officials Eddison, Fernie Whitmore and Tom McGrath were fined $3,000 for criminal contempt of court, then hauled off to Oakalla until they paid. Justice Manson also fined the union $10,000 and Guttman $100 for his defiance, a penalty the rank-and-file ironworker described as a badge of honour. The union leaders were soon free, after the BC Federation of Labour raised money to help pay their fines.

George North was not so fortunate. In a jaw-dropping sidelight to the legal furor surrounding the ironworkers, the editor of the *Fisherman* newspaper was also charged with contempt of court for what he wrote about Justice Manson's original judgment. Calling the ruling prejudiced and collusive, North's editorial appeared under the headline, "Injunctions Won't Catch Fish nor Build Bridges." For that effrontery, North was fined $3,000 and sentenced to thirty days in prison.

The BC Court of Appeal quashed all fines levied by Justice Manson against the ironworkers' union and its leaders. The superior court also admonished the judge for his legal threats against Berger. But the jailing of George North was upheld. After the legal dust had settled, a new regulation, clearly motivated by Justice Manson's judicial vendetta against the ironworkers, compelled BC Supreme Court judges to retire at

George North, editor of the union newspaper *The Fisherman*, is welcomed home in 1959 after spending thirty days in Oakalla prison. The sentence was imposed by a judge who found him guilty of contempt of court for a defiant editorial declaring that court injunctions will not build bridges or catch fish.
Ralph Bower photo, UBC *Rare Books and Special Collections,* BC–1532–2–1.

seventy-five. "Judge Manson was no hypocrite. He hated unions," wrote Berger. "He was out to get you, and he did."

After a fifty-day shutdown, Local 97 settled its dispute with Dominion Bridge and work resumed on the Second Narrows Bridge. Almost two years to the day of the collapse, the last linking girder was lowered into place. First across was survivor Norm Atkinson. "Atta boy, Norm," a workmate called out. *Vancouver Sun* reporter John Arnett wrote, "Atkinson's grimy face creased into a wide grin, as he called back, 'Bring on the cameras.'" It was the most bittersweet of moments.

There was more to come. As Atkinson strode jauntily across the twelve-ton girder, his local union was anything but united. Not long after the strike ended, the local's international overseers came riding into town. Fed up with criticism from the local, the International charged Eddison, Whitmore and McGrath with organizing an unauthorized strike. After a one-sided hearing that found all three guilty, their punishment was harsher than anything handed down by Justice Manson. Not only were they fired, the three were banned for life from belonging

Top right: Labour was always involved in CCF election campaigns. Gathered to talk strategy ahead of the 1960 election were, from left to right, CLC political action director George Home, IWA District Council #1 president Joe Morris, BC party leader Bob Strachan, BC Federation of Labour secretary–treasurer Pat O'Neal and CCF campaign director Grant MacNeil.
UBC Rare Books and Special Collections, 1902–21–19.

Bottom right: Later, in the 1970s and 1980s, following the demise of his Canadian Ironworkers Union, Tom McGrath became a hero to exploited Third World seamen. As the Vancouver representative of the International Transport Workers' Federation, he had the power to order foreign ships tied up until crew grievances were resolved. In this 1976 photo, McGrath is in a ship's kitchen, after winning thousands of dollars in back pay and monthly pay increases of four hundred dollars for seventeen crew members.
UBC Rare Books and Special Collections, 1365–19–1–25.

to the union, making them ineligible to earn a living as construction ironworkers. Dismayed by the punishment, Pat O'Neal of the BC Federation of Labour noted the three men had organized "one of the most successful strikes conducted in this province for many years."

Tom McGrath hadn't waited for the decision. Calling the hearing against him "a vivid example of international gangsterism," McGrath simply quit. The feisty, bantam-sized trade unionist had cut his union teeth at the age of sixteen during the Canadian Seamen's Union strike against Canada's deep-sea merchant marine fleet in 1949. Coloured by the Seafarers' International Union's crushing of the CSU and what had just happened to him in Local 97, McGrath felt it was time for all-Canadian unions, free of international entanglements.

He formed Canadian Ironworkers Union Local 1 to take on the International directly.

Sid Stewart (the father of Alan Stewart, who died in the Second Narrows Bridge tragedy) signed on as business agent. A majority of Local 97 members joined up, and McGrath asked the Labour Relations Board to cancel four certifications held by the International, including Dominion Bridge. But McGrath's dream of a Canadian union foundered on the same shoals of reality as the breakaway Woodworkers Industrial Union of Canada. The International held the contracts, certifications and resources to oppose all attempts by the Canadian Ironworkers Union to secure collective agreements with unwilling contractors. At the same time, open supporters of McGrath's union found themselves kicked out of Local 97. Some were threatened with violence, although none took place.

Bled dry by ongoing legal battles, Local 1 eventually ceased to function as an effective union. One victory remained, however. Too late for it to make any difference, the courts awarded the Canadian Ironworkers Union $30,000 in damages from the International for its underhanded tactics. After paying off debts, McGrath donated the remaining $2,500 to another independent Canadian union, the Canadian Association of Industrial, Mechanical and Allied Workers.

Meanwhile, the country and the labour movement had a new political party. The CCF was gone. Taking its place was the New Democratic Party, unveiled to great fanfare at a founding convention in Ottawa in August 1961. The result of collaboration between the CCF and the Canadian Labour Congress, the NDP sought to distance itself from the rural roots of the CCF and attract new voters in Canada's bourgeoning industrial workforce. Tommy Douglas, the long-time CCF premier of Saskatchewan, took over as leader. The BC New Democratic Party was formalized two months later. Carpenter Bob Strachan headed the provincial party with Tom Berger, fresh from his ironworker legal battles, as president. The significant involvement of unions, which now had an official party for the first time, did not go unnoticed. Premier Bennett hastily pushed through a bill banning unions from donating any portion of dues money to a political party.

The New Democratic Party held its founding convention in 1961, a collaboration between the Canadian Labour Congress and the CCF to give Canadians a new socialist alternative at the polls.
Courtesy Ray Haynes.

13 A NEW NATIONALISM

THE 1960S USHERED IN A NEW SENSE OF NATIONALISM and confidence, capped by the outstanding success of Expo 67 to celebrate Canada's centennial. The inferiority complex of the postwar years, when the country fell under the large shadow of the United States, was shunted aside. Aided by a new flag, Canadians found that they too could be a proud country, able to stake their own place in the world. These feelings also played out in the country's labour movement. Some Canadian trade unionists belonging to international unions, which made up the bulk of organizations within the Canadian Labour Congress, were becoming dissatisfied with top-down rule from their unions' American leaders. Some began looking for alternatives, as Tom McGrath had with his Canadian Ironworkers Union. They wanted autonomy to make their own decisions, without being second-guessed or overruled by union officials in the United States.

No union in BC was more challenged by this emerging sentiment than the International Brotherhood of Pulp, Sulphite and Paper Mill Workers, which represented almost all of the province's pulp and paper workers. Angus Macphee, a self-proclaimed socialist mill worker from Prince Rupert, and Orville Braaten, a bright, committed, left-wing trade unionist from Vancouver, were part of a cross-border group pushing for reform within the International. They were protected from the anti-communist purges that swept other US unions by Pulp Sulphite's venerable president John "Paddy" Burke, who had led the union since 1916.

Just before the union's 1962 international convention in Detroit, however, with the seventy-eight-year-old Burke about to retire, US immigration officials barred Macphee and Braaten from entering the country, citing their recent visits to Cuba. BC delegates who did make it to Detroit often had their microphones turned off when they attempted to speak. Not even a motion to allow Canadian locals to affiliate with the NDP passed muster. Al Smith from the Woodfibre local remembered, "As I left the convention hall, I felt dirty, depressed and a bit dazed. I crossed back into Canada and took a bath."

For Macphee, Braaten and several others, the Detroit convention was the last straw. Feeling there was now no chance of reforming their international union, they decided to establish an independent Canadian union for pulp and paper workers. Although radical at the time, the idea quickly found favour. The founding convention of the fledgling Pulp and Paperworkers of Canada (PPWC) took place just four months later, in early January of 1963. Five of the province's eleven pulp mills were represented. And the breakaways began.

Crofton was the first mill to go. Under the local leadership of Bill Cox, workers voted 94.6 percent to join the PPWC, once the union's name on the ballot had been corrected from the "Pulp and Paperworkers of America." The International fought back, imposing new leadership, sending in vice-president Henri Lorrain from Montreal to try to reason with the members and putting the local under trusteeship. But Cox had planned well, securing the local's assets and making sure all legal requirements were followed. More than 85 percent of the three hundred Crofton mill workers subsequently signed PPWC cards, and on June 26, the new local was officially certified.

Yet Crofton was not the first PPWC local. That distinction belonged to workers at the Castlegar pulp mill. The previous year, before any talk of the PPWC, they had bolted from another international pulp union, the smaller United Paper Makers and Paper Workers Union. They were the first group of Canadian pulp and paper workers to negotiate their own agreement, independent of a parent organization. A few weeks before the Crofton mill formally joined, Castlegar mill workers decided to cast their lot with the PPWC as Local 1 of the new union. Angus Macphee's mill in Prince Rupert and Woodfibre soon followed. By the end of the year, with the addition of certifications in a new Vancouver local, the PPWC had five locals and two thousand members.

At the beginning, with strong local leadership, workers needed little convincing to opt for the PPWC, which soon changed its name to the Pulp, Paper and Woodworkers of Canada. They responded to the union's prominent nationalism, leading critics to mock the PPWC as "flag-wavers." Each local was autonomous, officers were elected

Angus Macphee (left), one of the founders of the independent Pulp, Paper and Woodworkers of Canada union, stands tall at a membership meeting of his PPWC local in Prince Rupert. *Courtesy PPWC Archives.*

Nationalism was a big part of the drive by independent Canadian unions to encourage BC workers to leave their international unions. The Canadian Association of Industrial, Mechanical and Allied Workers unveiled this large sign on voting day to rally support for its raid on a local of the United Steelworkers of America.

UBC Rare Books and Special Collections, BC1902–6–74.

annually by referendum, conventions were held every year, and none of its few full-time business agents and leaders could earn more than the highest rate in the mill. As well, unique among unions in Canada, after five years working for the union, officers had to rejoin the workforce for at least one year.

Stan Shewaga, perhaps the most well-known PPWC leader over the years, said he didn't mind going back into the mill to resume his trade as a millwright. "It's good for you, and it's good for the membership," he reflected. "When you go back to work, it makes the guys feel good. 'He's one of us.'" Shewaga added with a chuckle, "And you end up making more money than you did as a porkchopper." ("Porkchopper" is a colloquialism for a full-time employee of a union, sometimes used derisively, sometimes humorously.)

Dissatisfaction with Pulp Sulphite was not confined to British Columbia. After one more failed convention attempt to push through reforms, twenty-eight thousand union members in Washington and Oregon also left in favour of a new independent union. But the battle for worker allegiance continued to grow in British Columbia, fought out at a number of other pulp mills. The PPWC also

made forays at some IWA sawmills and a bold but unsuccessful effort to represent workers at the large Alcan smelter in Kitimat who had become increasingly unhappy with their union, the United Steelworkers of America.

Raiding is loathed by many in the trade union movement. They believe it deflects focus and resources away from fighting the boss. Some also consider it immoral to pick off already unionized bargaining units rather than organizing the unorganized. The CLC has strong rules against inter-union raiding. (The BC Nurses' Union has been suspended from the CLC since 2009 for raiding other health-care workers.) On the other hand, the right of workers to change unions is guaranteed under the Labour Code, providing a vehicle for them to leave a union they feel no longer adequately represents them. But there is no softening the animosity a raid evokes. Like a civil war, it strikes at the heart of solidarity, pitting union brothers and sisters against one another.

Raids were plentiful in BC in the 1960s and 1970s, most of them clashes between American-based unions and independent Canadian unions seeking to supplant them. Although the independent unions—grouped

152

together after 1969 into the Confederation of Canadian Unions—did by no means sweep the BC labour movement, unions such as the PPWC, the Canadian Association of Industrial, Mechanical and Allied Workers (CAIMAW), the Canadian Association of Smelter and Allied Workers (CASAW) and the Independent Canadian Transit Union (ICTU) made notable inroads into the province's labour movement.

The PPWC's early successes led to the infamous "bugging caper," one of the most bizarre events in BC labour history. It was engineered by one of labour's most colourful and controversial figures, the unique Pat O'Neal. Unquestionably talented, O'Neal had been lured from his post as secretary-treasurer of the BC Federation of Labour to return to his old union, Pulp Sulphite, specifically to stop the bleeding of members to the PPWC. His murky background, which emerged only after he ended his eight years in the Fed's top job, became a legend in labour circles. Not Pat O'Neal at all, he was really Tommy Joe Casey, a native of Ireland's Mayo County. In 1947, he abandoned his British merchant vessel, the *Samadang*, on its arrival in Victoria. The brash ship jumper took the name of an American uncle, Edward Patrick O'Neal.

O'Neal wound up in Prince Rupert, where he worked in a fish cannery before getting a job at the pulp mill. By 1952, he was president of the Pulp Sulphite local. Two years later, the Irishman was on the BC Federation of Labour's executive council. In 1956, he ran successfully against the reunited Fed's official slate to become a vice-president, and in 1958, he completed his remarkable rise with election to the organization's full-time position of secretary-treasurer. During his time there, O'Neal boosted the Fed's public profile and forged a credible fightback capacity for an organization that, when he took over, had only recently shed its divisive past.

But he chucked his job at the Federation to anchor Pulp Sulphite's increasingly desperate struggle to retain its BC membership. At the time, Harmac in Nanaimo, Elk Falls in Campbell River, and Prince George had strong PPWC certification applications pending at the Labour Relations Board. Nor was the cause helped when Pulp Sulphite's international vice-president Joseph Tonelli showed up at a packed union meeting of Harmac workers and began by referring to them as "You boys from Heymac here ..."

But the LRB handed O'Neal and the International a huge reprieve by rejecting all three PPWC applications on the grounds that the Canadian organization was not a bona fide union under provincial labour legislation—notwithstanding its existing five certifications and collective agreements. There were strong protests in all three communities, but O'Neal drew heart from the ruling, embarking on a province-wide tour of pulp mill locals to boost the International's standing with the help of paid-for radio show appearances.

What followed could have come from *Ripley's Believe It or Not!* In early November 1966, PPWC executives gathered at Vancouver's Ritz Hotel to prepare for their fourth annual convention. When Angus Macphee awoke the morning of November 5, he found his roommate, national president Lloyd Craig of Castlegar, dead on the floor, victim of a heart attack. Still in shock, PPWC officials decided to rearrange the room for another use. As they moved some furniture, a small object fell from the top of a wardrobe. No one knew what it was. Not long after that, a hotel switchboard operator who was friendly with one of the PPWC delegates passed along some startling information. She had noticed a large number of calls from Room 309 directly above the PPWC rooms to an unlisted number in Vancouver, which was traced to the residence of Pat O'Neal. When she listened in on one of the calls, she heard someone giving a precise account of what PPWC representatives were saying.

The light bulb went off. They were being bugged. In full *film noir* mode, the union called in Ace Investigations. The detective agency found three more listening devices. When police burst into Room 309, they found a chagrined private detective named Bud Graham and $700 worth of electronic equipment. The plot thickened when Graham confessed on air to radio hotliner Jack Webster that O'Neal had given him $250 for his services. After first denying any knowledge of the bugging, O'Neal 'fessed up, insisting the action was not illegal, which indeed it was not. But news of the bugging caused a public uproar, prompting Premier Bennett to appoint a Royal Commission into the matter.

Commissioner R.A. Sargeant, seemingly charmed by O'Neal's blarney on the witness stand, exonerated the bugger and punished the buggee. Who should wind up in jail but the PPWC's Orville Braaten, sent there by Commissioner Sargeant for contempt

of court after refusing to answer questions about his political past. A BC Supreme Court justice quashed the decision.

Many trade unionists, particularly in the IWA, were outraged by the bugging. Weldon Jubenville, head of the IWA's Duncan local, said labour should dissociate itself from anyone who would "hire private eyes to spy on his fellow workers." Vancouver IWA president Syd Thompson called O'Neal's actions "harmful and detrimental to the entire labour movement and [especially] international unions." He demanded O'Neal's removal from the Fed's executive council.

O'Neal agreed to resign, but far from chastened, he and the International resumed playing hardball against their rivals. They demanded Harmac fire nearly eight hundred of its pulp mill workers for paying dues to the PPWC instead of Pulp Sulphite, which was still the union of record. The LRB averted a showdown by certifying the PPWC at the Nanaimo mill without a vote, citing the union's overwhelming membership support.

But at Prince George Pulp and Paper, at the behest of O'Neal, the company fired five leading PPWC activists for refusing to pay dues to Pulp Sulphite. The group maintained a lonely picket protest through the frigid Prince George winter before the LRB ordered a vote at the mill. The PPWC prevailed 344 to 129, and the fired employees were quickly rehired. Before the decade was done, the independent Canadian union picked off three more mills. Still, O'Neal managed to head off other potential breakaways and keep a majority of the province's expanding pulp mills within the international union.

Few would deny the impact of the PPWC's grassroots trade unionism. Rocked by defections in BC and the western United States, Pulp Sulphite merged with the United Paper Makers to form the United Paperworkers International Union (UPIU). In 1974, Canadian members peacefully left the UPIU to establish their own Canadian Paperworkers Union (CPU), an entirely Canadian union with no ties to its former international

The 1966 union bugging caper was front page news in the *Vancouver Sun,* complete with pictures of the listening devices and description of how Pat O'Neal of the International Pulp Sulphite Union had hired a detective to listen in on convention deliberations of the rival PPWC.

Vancouver Sun, Nov. 8, 1966, p. 1.

unions. This historic decision was the first of a number of other voluntary separations that took place between Canadian and American sections of international unions in the years ahead, as workers felt increasingly comfortable belonging to a Canadian union free of international ties.

Much to the surprise of those who had booted it out of the CLC, the left-wing Mine, Mill and Smelter Workers' Union survived into the 1960s as the province's chief mining union. Members stuck with the lone-wolf union during the worst of the "Red scare," appreciative of its leaders and the job they did representing them. As battles accelerated, Mine Mill hired several committed young organizers including Vince Ready, a non-communist who went on to become the most accomplished mediator in Canada. Ready barely missed death in 1965 when a thunderous avalanche swept over the camp at the new Granduc copper mine near Alaska. Twenty-eight miners lost their lives, and the main bunkhouse was split in two. Ready, who had taken a job to help keep the mine in Mine Mill hands, happened to be sleeping in the far end of the bunkhouse. The rest of the building was demolished.

The union continued to wage strikes, most notably at the Britannia copper mine on Howe Sound north of Vancouver. The multi-month dispute, lasting into 1965, inspired a song by a mine employee that was resurrected fifty years later by folk singer Sarah Jane Scouten. Referring to the company's threat to close the mine, one verse went: "My son, I worked the miner's trade with dignity and pride,/ Until they forced us out on strike, with Mine Mill on our side/ They tried to break our union, a lesson to us teach,/ And that's the cruel reason they closed down Britannia Beach."

Strikers and their families rally at the base of the Anaconda copper mine at Britannia Beach north of Vancouver, fighting to keep the American–owned mine open. They won the strike and the mine continued to operate until 1974.
George Legebokoff photo, courtesy The Fisherman.

Yet raids on Mine Mill locals did not let up. Although the union retained almost all its BC certifications, the constant warfare was wearying. Back east, the union had finally lost its huge Inco local in Sudbury to the relentless United Steelworkers of America by fifteen votes. Mine Mill leaders made the difficult decision to seek a merger with their bitter foes, the Steelworkers. "Mine Mill was broke," said Trail local president Al King. "There was fear we'd end up without any union." The merger, effective on Canada's one hundredth birthday, July 1, 1967, guaranteed jobs for Mine Mill leaders, among them Harvey Murphy, who had poured his heart and soul into the union for more than twenty-five years. Members voted strongly in favour, including those at Trail, who had resisted so many forays by the international union. But there was no denying the emotional residue from one of labour's most long-lasting inter-union conflicts. "I swallowed my pride and voted for the goddamned thing, because in my mind, there was no alternative," said King. The most radical, tenacious mining union the province had ever seen, from its beginning as the Western Federation of Miners, faded into the sunset, still beloved by its loyal, diehard supporters.

While most BC members were content with their US-based unions, international interference in some locals continued to cause problems. One of the most contentious examples took place at Lenkurt Electric, a telecommunications equipment manufacturing plant in Burnaby. The Lenkurt workers were represented by Local 213 of the International Brotherhood of Electrical Workers (IBEW), with a long, progressive history in BC. Granted IBEW's first charter in Western Canada in 1901, the local followed up its organization of early telephone linemen by signing up women telephone operators at the Vancouver phone company, which eventually became BC Tel and later Telus.

Organized into an auxiliary local, the women held their own meetings and elected their own officers. Both 213 units took part in the month-long general strike in Vancouver to back the Winnipeg General Strike. This led to its first run-in with the IBEW's international leadership. Disliking the strike's ties with the radical, all-Canadian One Big Union, the International suspended Local 213's charter until it was restored a year later by a court order. Differences endured over the years as Local 213 continued to wage aggressive strikes and the International expelled elected business agent George Gee for his communist sympathies in 1955.

This cauldron of dissent and tension boiled over at Lenkurt Electric in 1966, Already upset by the International's firing of assistant business agent John Morrison, Lenkurt's mostly women employees elected a tougher new shop steward committee headed by George Brown. During difficult contract negotiations, members voted to impose a ban on overtime at the plant. Local management agreed to the ban, but Lenkurt higher-ups nixed it. Angered by the company's turnabout, a majority of employees walked off the job April 27 on a wildcat strike. The company responded by firing all 257 strikers, and the battle was on.

The dispute turned into a *cause célèbre*. Much of the labour movement joined with the fired employees in defying a quickly obtained court injunction against picketing. Crowds surrounded the plant, trying to keep out employees willing to work, some of whom were newcomers who'd responded to company hiring ads. There were regular scuffles with police, on hand in great numbers to clear a path into the besieged workplace. But the real trouble erupted after employees overwhelmingly rejected a settlement arranged on May 9 by the International's representative Jack Ross and Local 213 president Angus MacDonald.

Under the proposal, fired workers could reapply for their jobs without reprisal, but they would lose their seniority and there was no guarantee how many would be taken back. The BC Federation of Labour and the Vancouver and District Labour Council (VDLC) also denounced the deal. When Local 213 business agent Art O'Keeffe refused to implement it, he was fired by the Canadian vice-president of the union, William Ladyman of Toronto. The firing of O'Keeffe brought trade unionists and labour leaders from everywhere into the fray.

On May 10, the first day of all-out picketing, a mass coughing fit drowned out a sheriff as he tried to read terms of the court injunction to the crowd. Vancouver and District Labour Council secretary Paddy Neale told reporters, "Our intention is to shut down the plant. If necessary, we'll have another picket line here tomorrow, a bigger one." The next day, more than three hundred people showed up on the line. Ferocious clashes broke out as dozens of police struggled to guide non-strikers into the plant. More than two dozen picketers were arrested. That night, some angry strikers burst into a Local 213 executive meeting, physically ejected local president Angus MacDonald onto the street, demanded strike pay and began an occupation of the union's premises. "This is our hall," they told a *Vancouver Sun* reporter. O'Keeffe continued to report for work.

On May 16 a high-powered group of labour leaders, including Syd Thompson of the VDLC, BC Fed vice-president Jack Moore and Jack Ross of the IBEW, met with Lenkurt executives to try to resolve the volatile dispute, but the company refused to budge from the May 9 deal. "We pointed out the labour movement would never tolerate those terms," Thompson said after the meeting. "[But] they're a hard-nosed outfit." Ladyman ripped the BC Federation of Labour for interfering in IBEW matters. "The International has not asked for help from the Federation," he said. "We are quite big enough to settle this for ourselves."

With the company standing firm, court injunctions still in place and IBEW brass opposed to the strike, the fired workers were up against it. On May 28 they voted to return to work under the pact they had earlier rejected. There was a price to pay: more than

seventy-five workers were not rehired, including all members of the shop steward committee, while returnees lost their seniority.

Then the IBEW handed out its own discipline. For defying the International, O'Keeffe was suspended for fifteen years and Tom Constable, a future mayor of Burnaby, was fired as assistant business manager of the local and suspended for three years. Rank-and-file firebrands Les McDonald, Jess Succamore and George Brown were suspended from the union for thirty, twenty-five and fifteen years respectively.

After that, the courts had their turn.

Picketers during the highly charged wildcat strike at Lenkurt Electric in Burnaby in the spring of 1966 were in no mood to respect court injunctions. These copies are being burned.
UBC Rare Books and Special Collections, BC11532–296–1.

Supporters mill outside the BC Supreme Court in downtown Vancouver as trade union leaders Paddy Neale, Art O'Keeffe and Jeff Power are sentenced to jail for disobeying a court injunction, an increasingly common occurrence in the 1960s.
UBC Rare Books and Special Collections, BC1532–7–2.

Trade unionists Paddy Neale (front passenger), Art O'Keeffe and Jeff Power (right) appear relaxed as they are driven to court by a smiling Syd Thompson, president of the IWA's Vancouver local. The three expected to be jailed for defying a court injunction during the Lenkurt dispute, and they were.
UBC Rare Books and Special Collections, BC1532–8–9.

Fifteen workers were fined a total of $3,100 for contempt of court. BC Supreme Court Justice James MacDonald then targeted Paddy Neale, IWA local vice-president Tom Clarke, Boilermakers leader Jeff Power and Art O'Keeffe for jail time. Neale and Clarke got six months, O'Keeffe four months and Powers three months. Newspaper photos showed Neale and Clarke being led off together to prison, ruefully holding up their handcuffs for photographers.

The bitter Lenkurt dispute, ending in such dispiriting defeat, was a turning point for those dissatisfied with the lack of Canadian autonomy in some international unions. More union activists became convinced, like those in the PPWC, that something had to be done to wrest Canadian control from international unions in the country. Shortly after the IBEW announced its suspensions, those suspended or not rehired held a meeting at the Boilermakers Hall that was also attended by officers of the BC Federation of Labour. They expressed sympathy and disappointment that their just cause had not prevailed.

After they left, stirred by their sentiment, Les McDonald stood up and proclaimed, "What we need is a new Canadian electrical workers' union!" The meeting enthusiastically embraced his idea. On November 6, 1966, seventeen trade unionists gathered to form the Canadian Electrical Workers, with George Brown and Jess Succamore taking leading roles. Like the PPWC, the CEW adopted a constitution emphasizing rank-and-file control, paying no full-time officer more than the top rate earned by members of the union and hanging its hat on Canadian nationalism. "[This was] made in Canada by Canadians and only Canadian workers can change it," its founding document stated.

Kept alive financially by secretive membership dues from dissatisfied IBEW members, the CEW launched its first raid against the International early the next year, signing up a majority of workers at Phillips Cable. After spending months scrutinizing the application, the Labour Relations Board ordered a vote. The CEW's narrow 57–50 victory was the beginning of a long presence in BC by the independent Canadian union, which soon aligned with the Winnipeg-based Canadian Association of Industrial, Mechanical and Allied Workers (CAIMAW). CAIMAW was particularly prominent in the 1970s and 1980s, waging a number of long, hard-fought strikes at BC mines amid a series of acrimonious, often successful raids against locals represented by the United Steelworkers of America. The union proved a catalyst in the drive for more Canadian autonomy within international unions and the eventual, uncontested severing of Canadian members from some of the country's leading international unions.

There was no such trouble within the IWA, a model of how an international union should work, at least once its communist leaders had been rooted out. While divisions remained over the union's new moderate leadership, wages, benefits and membership continued a steady rise, though not equally. IWA mills in the Kootenays and Okanagan consistently fell short of gains won by the union's more powerful coastal locals, who liked to kid their Interior cousins by calling them "jack pine savages." By the end of a poor three-year contract that ran out in 1967, the IWA's five thousand members in the southern Interior were earning fifty cents an hour less than their counterparts on the coast for doing the same job. Their bargaining clout was hamstrung by a contract that expired two and a half months after the coastal master agreement. Members decided enough was enough. They determined not to accept any agreement minus wage parity with the coast and a common expiry date.

When the mill owners refused all entreaties by the union's negotiating committee, workers walked out in the fall of 1967. The strike turned into one of the IWA's most epic battles, lasting 224 days and catapulting a tall, outspoken tradesman into the beginning of a high-profile union career that made him

one of the most recognizable individuals in the province for more than thirty years. Jack Munro was then thirty-six; he had grown up in poverty in Alberta and drifted to the BC Interior, where he worked on the railroad and as a welder at Kootenay Forest Products in Nelson. In a few years, Munro's leadership abilities, his passion to represent those on the job, and his penchant for reaming out management in the same salty, oath-laced language that prevailed in the bar and in the workforce had made him job steward, plant chairman and then a full-time local business agent for IWA Local 1-405.

The local was soon awash in a flood of injunctions, ordering picketers to stop building fires on logging roads to halt log deliveries. The IWA responded by picketing a mill represented by another union. When their members crossed the picket line, Munro unleashed a torrent of abusive language on them. As affidavit evidence for their injunction, company officials wrote down what he said. Feeling the language was too blue for a public courtroom, the judge reviewed the evidence in his private chambers. At one point, as recounted by Munro in his vivid memoir *Union Jack*, he burst out to the chastened woodworker, "Jesus Christ, Munro, this is unbelievable."

It was a hard slog for the strikers and their families. To help them through the winter, the union brought in truckloads of potatoes. Afterward, Munro paid tribute to the "guts and determination" of the women involved, both in the home and on the line, to help maintain the strike. At one mill, where there were rumours of trouble, women picketers locked arms outside the plant gate. Inside their purses were rocks and cans of hairspray, just in case.

Exasperated by the union's determination to stay the course, Kootenay Forest Products announced its intention to resume production by advertising in the local *Nelson Daily News* for strikebreakers. Munro opted for a show of union force down the main street of Nelson. A famous photo of the ensuing

After seven months, the companies began to buckle. They offered the IWA close to wage parity, although no change in the contract expiry date. When union negotiators rejected the offer, the government ordered the IWA to put it to the membership for a secret ballot vote. Despite the breakthrough on wage parity, hardened union members gave a resounding thumbs-down to the company proposal. The margin was even larger than their original strike vote.

"That incredible 'no' vote won the strike for us," Munro remembered. "The employers knew we were serious." Shortly afterward, the union had a deal, getting to within fourteen cents an hour of parity with the coast and an expiry date of June 30 a mere sixteen days shy of the coastal contract. After one of the longest strikes in its history, and forking out more than $3 million in strike pay, the IWA had won a clear victory. No one was affected more than Jack Munro himself. He learned the responsibility of leadership.

"That strike completely changed me," Munro said in *Union Jack*. "I had five thousand people really dependent on my decisions. They were giving up everything because of the decisions I was making." In a candid revelation, Munro said he had to work "really really hard at not screwing up, because it wasn't just me I'd be screwing up, but a whole lot of other people." After that, Munro was ambitious for advancement. "I didn't see myself going back to chasing burnt-out yard lights or settling small grievances," he said of life as a business agent. The next year, he moved to Vancouver as third vice-president of the union, and in 1973 Munro was elected head of the fifty-thousand-member organization, drawing a salary of $18,000 a year.

Business agent Jack Munro, in jacket and tie, leads hundreds of IWA members down the main street of Nelson on March 18, 1968. Munro called the march to warn a local mill not to hire strikebreakers during the union's storied seven–month strike in the BC Interior for wage parity with coastal forest workers. *Touchstones Nelson, Museum of Art and History, 1250.*

march shows a lean, almost-boyish Munro in his trademark jacket and tie, leading hundreds of workers toward City Hall. There, he warned the mayor to see that no scabs were hired, or else. The company got the message, and the mill stayed shut. The bold march was a masterstroke. Not only did it head off the use of strikebreakers, it boosted morale and gave the strikers renewed purpose. Through the winter and into the spring, the five thousand strikers remained strong, supported by $100,000 a week in IWA strike pay. Backing from the public was solid too. The beer parlour at the Lord Nelson Hotel became a union hangout at night, where locals were always ready to buy strikers a round.

JAILINGS, A FIRED-UP FED AND PUBLIC-SECTOR FIGHTBACK 14

I N ADDITION TO SERVING AS A REMINDER THAT BC trade unionists could not be relied on to always follow the dictates of their leaders, the Lenkurt dispute was also a key event in labour's growing resentment over the use of court injunctions to stifle union struggles. Seeing top Vancouver labour leader Paddy Neale carted off to jail in handcuffs for six months turned the fight against injunctions into an all-out campaign.

Injunctions had multiplied after the enactment of Bill 43 in 1959. The Social Credit government's new **Trade Unions** Act was a direct affront to the rights of free speech and freedom of assembly. Banned were not only information and secondary picketing, in which striking unions picket companies doing business with their struck employer, but pamphlets or newspaper ads simply suggesting the public might not want to patronize certain anti-union employers were prohibited as well. Labour leaders never tired of pointing out that long-haired hippies could legally demonstrate outside a restaurant that denied them service, but a union was not allowed to protest outside a workplace that was unfair to its own employees.

Companies wasted little time in taking advantage of the new legislation. Even as strikes declined, the number of court injunctions curtailing union activity shot up nearly 50 percent over the next five years. Eighty percent were issued *ex parte*, without a formal hearing. So many were coming down the pipe that the Fed's Pat O'Neal garnered a wave of publicity by wallpapering his office with copies of injunctions and calling in photographers.

The campaign against injunctions became a personal mission for Ray Haynes, who replaced O'Neal as secretary-treasurer of the BC Federation of Labour in 1966. Son of a Vancouver cop, he first became a union man in the late 1940s while working on the green chain at the unionized Canadian White Pine sawmill. After drifting around a bit, he wound up in the wholesale division of the Hudson's Bay Company. Unhappy with the low wages and poor working conditions, he helped organize a union there, eventually parlaying his abilities into a job with the Retail Wholesale and Department Store Union.

During his dozen years with the union as a robust organizer and international representative, Haynes excelled at the rough and tumble of organizing small bargaining units and getting them contracts against resistant employers. He came to realize the value of assistance from a centralized organization like the BC Federation of Labour in winning disputes without the resources and might of large industrial unions. The Fed's only full-time leader for the next seven years, Haynes's passionate push for labour unity and militancy helped propel the organization into becoming a major combatant in BC's labour wars. A cartoonist's delight with his black-framed glasses and prominent features, the pugnacious, poker-playing Haynes became one of the most recognizable individuals in the province, scourge of employers, governments and newspaper editorial writers.

Appointed to the position on his thirty-eighth birthday and already infuriated by the Lenkurt charges, Haynes soon had more cause to be upset. "I'd been on the job one day, and already ten more people were in jail for contempt of court," he remembered. For two years, the International Longshoremen's and Warehousemen's Union (ILWU) had tried unsuccessfully to get maritime employers to recognize statutory holidays included in a rejigged Canada Labour Code. In a bid to bring the issue to a head, the union advised members to ignore a call to work on Good Friday. They did. This sent the employers to court. There, they obtained an injunction prohibiting the union from calling for a similar work stoppage on the next holiday. Union officers paid no attention to the order, and on

IWA members at the Canadian White Pine Company just north of the Fraser River in Vancouver, November 1948. Standing second from left is a young Ray Haynes, who went on to lead the BC Federation of Labour from 1966 to 1973.
Tom Christopherson photo, Vancouver Public Library, 80727.

Victoria Day the waterfront fell silent once again. A few days later, Canadian area president Roy Smith and nine local presidents were cited for contempt of court.

In a ringing courtroom defence, Smith justified defiance of the court's order. "We cannot and we will not allow ourselves to be bullied by the employers into doing something which will take away the rights of the membership," he declared. Unmoved, the court fined Smith $500 and the others $400 each, with the option of three months in jail. All chose prison. "To pay our fines would be an encouragement to the employers' tactics of seeking injunctions and fines as means of harassing our union and draining its financial resources," the group said in a collective statement.

Off they went to the provincial prison camp in Chilliwack. The fact that ten men were in jail for trying to force companies to comply with the Canada Labour Code roused the dozing federal government to action. Labour minister Jack Nicholson promised to strengthen the code's holiday provisions to ensure they applied to dock workers. The ILWU got the holidays. But the fact that employers were able to use the courts to undermine such a legitimate cause reinforced labour's determination to erase injunctions from the field of struggle. "This one item has caused more bitterness and unrest than any other issue in this province," said Haynes. "It has no place in twentieth-century industrial relations."

On the other side of the judicial bar, the courts were also getting edgy, frustrated that their orders were being regularly defied by labour leaders willing to accept time in jail. Instead of concluding that something was inherently wrong with the system, judges opted for even stronger sentences. The first figure to be hit by this "tough on crime" approach was the forceful head of the United Fishermen and Allied Workers' Union, Homer Stevens.

In 1967, the colourful Stevens was already something of a legend in BC for his commit-

Roy Smith, the Canadian area president of the International Longshoremen's and Warehousemen's Union, leaves the courthouse for jail, after being sentenced to three months in prison for defying a court injunction in 1966.
UBC Rare Books and Special Collections, BC1532–6–27.

ted representation of commercial fishermen and fish-plant workers. Of mixed Indigenous and immigrant ancestry, Stevens had been dominant within the UFAWU since his election as the union's full-time secretary-treasurer in 1948 at the age of twenty-five. A big man, his slow, deliberate nature belied an iron determination and vast knowledge of all the many aspects of the complicated, multi-geared fishing industry. His hide and those of others in the union had been toughened over the years by fighting off concerted McCarthyist attacks on the union's communist leadership.

Forced to operate as an independent union after being exiled from the house of labour for its political leanings, the UFAWU had thwarted attempts to break the union by both the thuggish SIU and federal combines investigators, who alleged that bargaining for fish prices was illegal price-fixing. Further complicating union efforts was the legal status of fishermen as independent businessmen rather than workers dependent on the fish companies. Thus excluded from provincial and federal labour codes, the UFAWU held no certifications on the water. Nor was there dues check-off. The union's ability to negotiate with the hard-nosed fish companies depended solely on collective support from individual fishermen, who had to be signed up every year boat by boat.

Negotiating leverage was almost entirely dependent on gauging the size and timing of the peak salmon runs, the same high-stakes showdown that had pitted fishermen against companies since the turn of the century. It was not for the faint of heart. The union had its biggest breakthrough in 1959, shutting down all segments of the coastal salmon industry for the first time in a successful two-week strike that produced large gains.

In 1967, however, the UFAWU launched a difficult strike to bring trawler vessel owners under a union crew-share agreement. With a strong mandate from crew members, the fleet tied up on March 25. A few days later, five trawlers came into Prince Rupert loaded with fish. When the UFAWU declared their catch "hot" and not to be processed, the owners swiftly obtained an *ex parte* injunction against the union. The UFAWU was directed to order its officers and members to allow the fish to be unloaded and processed. Instead, the union's executive board put the issue to a vote by the membership, which voted 89 percent to leave the fish where they were. After going bad, the catch was dumped.

Notwithstanding the vote, some union shore workers at the large Prince Rupert Co-op fish plant began to handle fish caught by non-UFAWU boats. This brought union pickets and plenty of Mounties to the waterfront. At one point, Stevens, business agent Jack Nichol, twenty-one-year-old organizer George Hewison and fisherman Jose Verde were arrested by the RCMP, which had been running interference for non-union boats. The four were held in jail until midnight on charges that were never made public and never pursued. "You almost felt like you were catapulted back into the labour battles of the 1930s," observed Stevens in his autobiography written with Rolf Knight. "It was about as stiff a battle as had ever hit the fishing industry in BC."

Members of the United Fishermen and Allied Workers' Union picket a Prince Rupert trawler for ignoring the union's strike during the UFAWU's difficult dispute in 1967 to win a coast–wide trawler agreement.
UBC Rare Books and Special Collections, BC–1532–329– 124.

Emotions intensified when the "Marching Mothers" began harassing the union. They were led by Iona Campagnolo, who went on to serve in Pierre Trudeau's cabinet and later as lieutenant governor of BC. In those days she was a local school board trustee married to a fisherman and among a number of anti-union women who wanted the UFAWU gone from Prince Rupert. Contending the UFAWU had brought nothing but division to the community, the mothers paraded through the city with banners calling for its decertification at the Co-op and urging the union to get out of town.

The situation was further worsened by the role of the Deep Sea Fishermen's Union, a Prince Rupert–based CLC affiliate that had been signing up boats behind the union's back. A vote to decertify the UFAWU at the Co-op was the last nail in its coffin. In August, after signing several trawl agreements elsewhere on the coast, the UFAWU bitterly called off the strike. By then, the courts had ruled on the decision to submit its order to the membership at the outset of the strike. Noting that despite repeated jailing, unions were continuing to ignore court injunctions, Supreme Court Justice Thomas Dohm said it was time to send a sterner message.

On June 21, in addition to fining the union $25,000, Justice Dohm sentenced Homer Stevens, union president Steve Stavenes and business agent Jack Nichol to a year in jail for contempt of court. "I am sorry for the families of these men," he professed, "but they did what they did here coldly and calculatingly." Justice Dohm warned that those disobeying future injunctions should expect even "more severe" penalties. With that, the trio was whisked from the courtroom to Oakalla, where they languished for ten days until lawyers managed to secure their release, pending an appeal.

Despite the UFAWU's communist leanings and tendency to operate outside the mainstream union movement, the severity of the court's punishment caused an uproar among organized labour. At the Vancouver

and District Labour Council, there was talk of a forty-eight-hour general strike. "If this is equality under the law, we [might as well] move to some fascist country," stormed VDLC president Paddy Neale, who had earned his spurs with his own six-month sentence. "The way injunctions are being issued, in a few years we could be getting thirty years. In ten years, we could be getting life."

The call for a general strike did not get off the ground, but with seventeen trade unionists having been imprisoned in the last year, Ray Haynes announced a massive petition drive to end court injunctions in labour disputes once and for all. Tens of thousands of dollars were raised to help fight the case, including donations from some of the UFAWU's fiercest anti-communist critics within the labour movement. When the BC Court of Appeal upheld the one-year jail terms meted out to Stevens and Stavenes (Nichol's sentence was overturned by a 2–1 decision), the Fed announced a special convention on injunctions for January 1968. "Continually imprisoning trade unionists does nothing to improve the already chaotic labour-management relations in this province," said Haynes.

Fishermen's union president Homer Stevens gives a wave as he heads off to jail to serve a one–year sentence for contempt of court in connection with the Prince Rupert trawler strike in 1967. Behind him is union business agent Jack Nichol, acquitted on a technicality, who went on to lead the union for sixteen years after Stevens retired in 1977. *UBC Rare Books and Special Collections, BC1532–10–1.*

The British American Oil Company was the first of seven "big oil" operations to be hit by members of the Oil, Chemical and Atomic Workers Union, as part of the union's escalating strike over automation. Picket lines went up September 14, 1965. *Dan Scott photo, Vancouver Sun.*

Haynes told delegates. "But Lord help you if you picket some anti-labour sweatshop employer to advise the public that he has no union agreement or that he has fired his employees because they tried to organize a union." He referred to an ongoing strike at Canada Rice Mills in Vancouver. There had been no incidents, no violence, no mass protests, nothing but peaceful picketing. But that hadn't stopped the companies from seeking seven separate injunctions in the previous six weeks. Although it would take five more years before anti-picketing injunctions ended, labour's unrelenting campaign had made the matter a prime area for change.

The BC labour movement had also reached a realization that extraordinary measures were often needed if any disputes were to be won. Led by the Federation of Labour, unions demonstrated a significant uptake in collective solidarity and a willingness to wage industrial-relations warfare on a wide scale for the first time in years. The province had received its first inkling of this combative mood in late 1965, which hinged on the emergence of automation as a worrisome workplace issue. With more and more jobs being lost because of production advances, the labour movement opted to throw its weight behind a challenging strike on that very issue by the Oil, Chemical and Atomic Workers Union (OCAW).

Faced with rapid automation that had cut its membership in half at the province's seven unionized refineries, the OCAW sought protection and/or compensation for future employees sent packing by technology. At the bargaining table, union negotiators demanded eighteen months' written notice of further automation, retraining for displaced workers and generous severance pay.

When the oil companies refused to even address the matter, the OCAW served strike notice at all refineries, electing to walk out first at the British American Oil refinery on September 14, 1965. Due to the very technological change the union was confronting, company supervisors were able to maintain

At the anti-injunction convention in Victoria, Haynes hammered away at the devastating impact Bill 43 and the resulting accumulation of injunctions had had on unions. With the ban on leafleting, protesting outside an anti-union business, or publishing information about working conditions there, organizing had become an exceedingly uphill battle. Labour cited the legislation as a major reason unionization had fallen from its high of 53.9 percent in 1958 to 42.7 percent in 1966.

"You can picket any supermarket your heart desires providing you are protesting prices or the sale of Dow chemical products,"

regular deliveries and production at the plant. When talks continued to go nowhere, the union launched a second strike at Imperial Oil's Ioco refinery on November 5, fuelled by the company's suspension of thirty-five workers. A strike deadline at the other five refineries was set for midnight, November 15. That brought a pumped-up BC Federation of Labour into the action.

This time, there would be more than angry words and demonstrations. Labour leaders began planning the first general strike in BC for close to half a century. Determined to go to bat for the oil workers, who were finding it difficult to pressure the industry, the Fed aimed to shut down much of the province for forty-eight hours in conjunction with the OCAW's own expanded walkouts. To give the Federation more time, the OCAW extended its strike deadline to midnight, November 24. Plans were worked out at a series of large meetings attended by union representatives from across BC.

A general strike would demonstrate "labour's solidarity in support of oil workers battling for protection against automation," the Fed's strike co-ordinator George Johnston told the Vancouver and District Labour Council. "Perhaps we should have done this a long time ago." The plan involved a forty-eight-hour "hot declaration" imposed on all petroleum products, which would essentially shut down unionized industrial workplaces throughout the province. Others untouched by the oil embargo would also walk out.

When the strategy was announced, industry and government seemed to break out in hives. Union leaders have "rocks in their head," raged Socred Attorney General Robert Bonner. Labour minister Leslie Peterson called it an NDP plot. "It's the most idiotic call I've ever heard of." A front-page story in the *Vancouver Sun* explained helpfully to readers that a general strike is "the hydrogen bomb in organized labour's arsenal... and the collective finger of the BC Federation of Labour is now on the button."

Some international union representa-

tives opposed the action. Dave Chapman of the International Association of Machinists advised his union's six thousand BC members to stay on the job. "Like it or lump it, there are laws," Chapman told the *Vancouver Sun*. William Ladyman, Canadian vice-president of the International Brotherhood of Electrical Workers, instructed IBEW members to report for work. In defiance of his directive, and foreshadowing the Lenkurt dispute, they voted overwhelmingly to back the strike.

Amid feverish media coverage, the pressure began to build. With two days to go, the Canadian Manufacturers' Association and its six hundred members in BC warned workers of "serious consequences" if they left their jobs, ranging from a loss of rights and benefits to suspension to outright dismissal. But the oil workers' cause was bolstered from an unexpected source.

The final edition of the November 24, 1965, *Vancouver Sun* emblazoned the breaking news across the top of its front page that BC's first general strike since 1919 had been averted.

BC labour leaders, including Federation of Labour head Ray Haynes (second from left), picket a Safeway supermarket in 1969 in support of the ongoing struggle by the Cesar Chavez–led United Farm Workers to organize California farm workers.

Ray Allan photo, Vancouver Sun.

Ed Lawson, BC leader of the independent Teamsters Union and perpetual thorn in the side of the Federation of Labour, had refused to join the Fed's general strike. To the surprise of his adversaries, however, he said Teamster truck drivers would refuse to "handle or use" any oil products considered "hot," as soon as the oil workers expanded their strike. Once their gas tanks were empty, trucks would be off the road. "You don't have to be a genius to figure out what effect that … will have on the trucking industry in the province," said Lawson. It would be a strike in all but name.

As the hours ticked down, the government grew alarmed at the prospect of mass job action. W.A.C. Bennett blinked. On Wednesday, November 24, with the strike due to begin at midnight, he called both sides to meet with him at the Hotel Vancouver. There, he tabled a proposed settlement and strongly advised the parties to accept it.

Bennett's package included a joint labour-management committee to study the impact of automation. In the meantime, companies would have to provide

six months' notice of layoffs. For displaced workers, there would be retraining and one week's pay for every year of service. The proposals were far beyond anything the industry had offered. The OCAW quickly agreed to the premier's terms. Far from happy, the oil companies waited until a few hours before midnight before they reluctantly said yes too.

It was a significant victory for the union and organized labour in BC. Thanks to the oil workers' breakthrough, automation was now on the bargaining table. Employers could no longer simply dismiss the adverse effects of technological change as the way of the world. Many other industrial unions began to negotiate agreements that also tempered technology's impact on workers. Knowing the issue was won because of the collective solidarity and strength of virtually the entire labour movement made the result that much sweeter. The next day, a triumphant Federation of Labour took out a bold ad in the *Vancouver Sun*. Under the headline "THANK YOU!" in large black letters, the organization acknowledged all those who had pressured the government and big international oil companies into addressing automation, "the foremost of all challenges facing both blue- and white-collar workers."

After years of noisy protests that yielded few concrete results, this was a high-water mark for the revitalized Federation. There was no turning back. Under Ray Haynes, the organization had worked hard to plaster over its cracks to become a unified, centralized force to be reckoned with.

Stormier times were ahead for the Federation and the labour movement, but when he was not in the trenches, Haynes pushed the Fed to take stands on social issues that were not immediate concerns of its 125,000 members. The Federation gave unswerving support to a boycott of non-union-picked California grapes in aid of the courageous organizing crusade of Cesar Chavez and the United Farm Workers union. Chavez made regular appearances at Fed conventions to personally thank the BC labour movement, which he said was the most effective in North America.

In its annual brief to the Social Credit cabinet, the Federation took several positions on the environment, opposing oil drilling in Georgia Strait, flooding the Skagit Valley and logging at Cypress Bowl above West Vancouver. The brief harshly criticized the government's inaction on pollution control while calling for grants to municipalities to fund anti-pollution campaigns. At the 1971 Fed convention, delegates urged affiliates to set up environment committees and negotiate anti-pollution funds into their contracts. An employer contribution of one cent for every hour worked by an employee could raise $3 million a year to help protect the environment, the Fed asserted.

Just before the convention, the Federation made an unprecedented gesture in the campaign for nuclear disarmament. On November 3, to protest a US underground nuclear test on Amchitka Island, Haynes called on union members to stop work for thirty minutes as part of a "Shutdown for Survival"

labour protest against the explosion. Despite little notice, some did. A front-page picture in the *Vancouver Sun* showed a group of hard-hatted construction workers marching against the nuclear test, peace symbols on their placards.

"For the first time in North America," Haynes told protesters outside the US consulate, "workers are downing tools, not over wages, not over working hours, and not over working conditions, but because of a danger to all mankind." At Fraser Mills in New Westminster, local IWA president Gerry Stoney said three hundred workers stood in the canteen during the protest. "If we had a week's notice, we could have almost shut down the industry tight," said Stoney.

Vancouver Sun columnist Bob Hunter, the legendary co-founder of Greenpeace, heaped praise on Haynes and the labour movement for its stand. "Let me take my furry Yippie hat off to organized labour in BC," he wrote the following day. "Never before had labour unions on this continent stopped work over an issue like this one. The stoppages may have been spotty, but some workers did it ... More to the point, their leadership not only endorsed the move but pushed for it. That was a first." The BC labour movement was

Members of the International Brotherhood of Electrical Workers are among scores of construction workers taking a break from work to join protests in front of the US consulate on November 3, 1971, against the imminent Amchitka nuclear test. *George Diack photo, Vancouver Sun.*

also an active participant in the many protest marches against the US war in Vietnam, a marked contrast to the military cheerleading of AFL-CIO president George Meany and other American trade union leaders.

Haynes's last four years with the Federation were dominated by the long, concerted fight against Social Credit's most anti-union legislation yet. Spooked by growing labour unrest in the province and a strike by BC ferry workers, the government introduced the Mediation Commission Act (Bill 33) in early 1968. It provoked all-out war. For the first time in peacetime Canada, a government gave itself powers to settle disputes in both the public and private sector through binding arbitration, a capacity that existed nowhere else in North America.

Strikes and lockouts deemed by the cabinet to be against the public interest or public welfare were to be referred to a three-person Mediation Commission, which could then impose a settlement commissioners decided was "fair and reasonable." Once a designated dispute was before the commission, job action was prohibited, with heavy fines for noncompliance. Bill 33 also banned provincial government employees from going on strike at all.

"Labour is going to put up a fight that's never been put up before," vowed Haynes. Two weeks later, the Federation held a special convention to map its plan of attack. This time, calls for a general strike were deflected. Instead the Federation opted for protracted battle. Union members were asked to donate a day's pay to finance the fight. There were public protest meetings, pamphlets with the slogan "Keep freedom alive—beat Bill 33" and pledges of full support for any union forced into compulsory arbitration.

Bill 33 did not become law until December. By then, the Federation's strategy was in hand. At its annual convention a few weeks earlier, more than six hundred delegates voted unanimously to boycott all hearings by the Mediation Commission. It was a strong policy, and undoubtedly one reason the government avoided an early showdown with the labour movement over the act's draconian powers. When strikes occurred, government mediators continued to work with the parties without involvement from the Mediation Commission.

Officers of the BC Federation of Labour preside over a special conference in 1968 to map a strategy against Bill 33, which gave government the right to mandate compulsory arbitration in labour disputes. At the podium is Fed president Al Staley. On his right is Jack Moore of the IWA, and on his left is secretary–treasurer Ray Haynes, George Johnston of the meatcutters' union and Len Guy of the International Typographical Union.
UBC Rare Books and Special Collections, BC1429–13a.

But labour's boycott was not airtight, as evidenced by a serious spat between the Federation and the OCAW just a few years after organized labour had committed to a general strike to back the same oil workers in their struggle against automation. In May 1969, when the OCAW again struck the oil companies in a more normal dispute over wages, solidarity went out the window. Besides quarrels over the OCAW's picketing and fundraising tactics and a "hot" boycott, there was disagreement over response to a tragedy on the picket line. Two months into the strike, oil worker James Harvey was struck and killed by an oil truck driven by a non-union employee as he walked an early-morning picket line at the Shellburn refinery. To commemorate Harvey, thousands of union construction workers booked off work for half a day. But the OCAW vetoed a Fed plan to shut Shellburn down completely with mass picket lines.

More aggravating was the OCAW's decision to ignore labour's boycott of the Mediation Commission. In a telegram, Haynes warned the union that "any co-operation [with the commission] can only be detrimental to the entire labour movement." The OCAW went anyway, contending the process might lead to a voluntary settlement.

The lengthy strike was eventually settled without the Mediation Commission, but Haynes remained furious that a union that had benefited greatly from the Federation's support in 1965 would so soon turn its back on a key policy. The Fed threatened the OCAW's BC division with expulsion. In turn, the oil workers filed charges with the Canadian Labour Congress, accusing the Federation of "unwarranted interference" in the affairs of an affiliate. Before the feud could play out on the floor of the 1969 Fed convention that November, the two sides patched up their rift during a two-hour closed-door session on day one.

The peace accord wasn't good enough for delegates increasingly rankled by Haynes's tough, hands-on approach to affiliates. One

of them was Vancouver labour leader Paddy Neale, whose jailing for defying an injunction in the Lenkurt dust-up was still fresh. Neale decided to run against Haynes, demanding the organization return to co-ordinating rather than dictating strategy for affiliates embroiled in difficult strikes. Haynes retorted that past conventions had endorsed a strong leadership role for the Federation and he saw no reason to change it. His view prevailed. In a significant vote that confirmed the Federation's brawny activism under Haynes, delegates rejected Neale's bid 299–178.

As labour strife swirled around them, the BC Government Employees' Association gathered in the fall of 1968 for its annual convention. The BCGEA had recently weathered seven years of no dues check-off, after it was abruptly cancelled by W.A.C. Bennett in 1960 over the association's membership in the BC Federation of Labour. "Our whole world seemed to be coming to an end," said BCGEA president Ed O'Connor, looking back. "There's no doubt that it was [Bennett's] way of getting even for the strike in 1959." In full panic mode, the provincial executive voted to suspend affiliation with the Fed in hopes the government would restore payroll dues deductions. There was no response.

The move forced the association to virtually beg employees for their $2 monthly payments. Membership and revenue fell by 40 percent. Thanks to the efforts of hundreds of volunteer collectors like Ike Nelson, however, the association managed to survive until late 1967, when Bennett just as unilaterally restored dues deductions. "We had about eighty members in the Williams Lake branch in those days," remembered Nelson. "I was the guy who would give 'em the gears if they didn't pay their dues. I had to go from unit to unit to pick up the money."

At the 1968 convention the organization debated whether to call itself a union. "Let's be honest. We're working stiffs who aren't earning the money we should be," said liquor store delegate Bob McMaster. "We've got nowhere with the name 'association.' Adopting the name 'union' would make a big difference." But delegates voted 51–48 to remain an "association," still concerned the word "union" would frighten members away.

A heated convention fight over the issue repeated itself in 1969. Again the vote was close, but this time "union" advocates won a narrow victory. When the tally was announced, even those opposed to the change joined in rousing cheers that rocked the convention floor. There was no turning back. "If you walk like a duck and talk like a duck, call yourself a duck," reasoned the organization's bright new thirty-one-year-old general secretary, John Fryer.

The hiring of Fryer, with his degree from the London School of Economics and stints as research director for the CLC and the AFL-CIO, was a clear sign that BC's government employees had embarked on their most determined course yet to win the same collective bargaining rights that their counterparts enjoyed across the country. With a new slogan, "Collective Bargaining Rights Now!" the BCGEU raised its monthly dues, hired a full-time communications director, took on more organizers and began to seriously pressure the government for real negotiations. The way had already been set by the provincial ferry workers' pivotal twelve-day strike the previous year. That resulted in a signed deal, although the government insisted it was merely a "memorandum of agreement," not a formal contract.

For other unions in the public sector, the 1960s was also a time of breakthroughs and expansion. The greatest leap forward took place among municipal workers. Two unions, the fifty-thousand-strong National Union of Public Employees (NUPE), which had a broader reach than civic employees, and the thirty-thousand-member National Union of Public Service Employees (NUPSE), whose roots went back to 1921, concluded seven years of difficult, sometimes testy negotiations with a new national union. The founding convention of the Canadian Union of Public Employees was held at Winnipeg's Fort Garry Hotel on September 24, 1963. Overnight, CUPE became the second-largest union in the CLC, trailing only the United Steelworkers of America.

Most of BC's sixty-nine delegates opposed the merger. They did not like paying extra dues when they felt well served already as members of NUPE. But opposition soon melted away and the new union rapidly began signing up unorganized public employees across the province. For CUPE's three full-time regional reps in BC, it was a daunting chore to both service and organize over such immense distances. Interior rep Pete Driedger liked to say his territory covered "eight hundred miles, three mountain ranges and two time zones." Initially, he operated out of his car, lugging around a homemade plywood box full of files and a red portable typewriter, which he used to type up agreements in his hotel room. His life was not made any easier by independent-minded locals who had always done it their way and by directives from the national office with little understanding of BC geography. "They'd say things like, 'While you're in Prince George, why don't you run over to Prince Rupert and see what's going on there?'" Driedger recalled.

The hard-working union rep left a valued legacy when he negotiated a difficult master agreement for Kelowna municipal workers that contained a solid union security clause. Driedger used language in the Kelowna clause, based on a template devised by CUPE research director Gil Levine, as a negotiating benchmark for other agreements throughout his territory. For the next thirty years, Driedger's contract was used by the union across Canada as a model of what can be achieved for workers at the bargaining table.

Within ten years, CUPE had more than doubled its membership, supplanting the Steelworkers as Canada's largest trade union. The public sector's rapid growth was beginning to change the nature of the trade union movement. It was not long before nearly half the members of the CLC worked for various

levels of government. "Labour in Canada had always been a blue-collar, predominantly male organization," observed labour historian Desmond Morton. "Public-sector unions added hundreds of thousands of members who were women or middle class, or both."

As Morton noted, many of the new recruits were women. But it was telling that among BC delegates to CUPE's founding convention, Verna King, secretary of NUPE's Fraser Valley District Council, was the only woman. She went on to serve several years on the executive board of CUPE's BC division, again as the lone woman. "The union sent me to talk to women in different locals to tell them how it would be good for them to be part of the unions. In those days, women didn't always believe that," King recounted. "Union work is very demanding. But I made a lot of friends through it. They are the finest quality of people you could find. You never forget them."

For Thelma Roberts, secretary at Quamichan Junior High School in Duncan, union-

ization also meant walking a picket line for the first time when her CUPE local went on strike to win better wages for women workers like herself. "I didn't even know how to walk a picket line," she remembered. "I just knew you had to keep moving. Once, [CUPE rep Tom Smith] came up to me and said, 'Thelma, you don't have to walk so fast.'"

In 1966, CUPE beckoned the large Vancouver Civic Employees' Union (VCEU) in from the cold. The union, representing outside workers at City Hall and the Pacific National Exhibition, had been tossed out of the mainstream labour movement during the purge of communist-led unions in the early 1950s. As an independent union that resisted numerous raids from other unions, the VCEU had staged several successful strikes, winning wage increases that raised the bar for all municipal workers. After fourteen years outside the house of labour, the union opted to join CUPE as Local 1004. At first, Cold War forces continued to keep the left-wing Vancouver local out of the Canadian Labour

The Canadian Union of Public Employees holds its founding convention in Winnipeg in the fall of 1963. Resulting from the merger of two existing public–sector unions, CUPE was soon the largest union in Canada.
Courtesy Canadian Union of Public Employees.

There's nothing like a good comfy chair on the picket line. Vancouver civic workers take it easy at the Kerr Road garbage dump during their 1966 strike against the city.
Gordon F. Sedawie photo. Vancouver Public Library, 44757.

Congress. Only when CUPE threatened to withhold its large per-capita payments to the CLC did the congress relent.

Lengthy municipal and school board strikes became less of a rarity as CUPE members increasingly resisted employer attempts to lowball their wages in the face of escalating costs. "Our challenge is to stop governments from thinking of public employees as instruments of fiscal policy," national president Stanley Little told CUPE's annual convention in 1969. "It seems the lower down you are on the economic rung, the more you get stepped on." There were long strikes in Kamloops, Penticton, Trail and once more in Vancouver. Through all the disputes, CUPE followed labour's boycott of the Mediation Commission, sometimes under intense political fire. "We were called down to Victoria and pressured by the minister of labour. But we wouldn't buckle," said Alan Underwood from CUPE's striking Trail local. Public-sector workers were making their mark in BC's seasoned trade union movement.

The Hospital Employees' Union (HEU), representing non-professional health-care workers, had emerged in 1944 when separate male and female unions at Vancouver General Hospital united to fight for better conditions for themselves and their patients. Bill Black, described in his obituary as "a fiery diminutive Scot," became its early

secretary-business agent and was respected enough to become the first elected president of the BC Federation of Labour in 1956. Adopting an industrial union model, the HEU was soon organizing across BC, growing in strength as public health care became the norm in Canada.

The HEU was one of the first locals to join the new Canadian Union of Public Employees in 1963. Five years later, the union won its first province-wide master agreement. The landmark pact standardized rates and working conditions in all of BC's unionized hospitals, setting the tone for the union's ambitious drive to organize long-term care facilities in the private sector.

Elsewhere in the public sector, with vast numbers of new teachers needed to handle baby boomers flooding the classrooms, the ranks of the BC Teachers' Federation grew dramatically, launching the union on a tradition of militant leadership that made it a force to be reckoned with in education. Registered nurses, too, flexed their bargaining muscle, even under the staid labour-relations umbrella of the Registered Nurses Association of BC. Since receiving its first hospital certification in 1947, the RNABC had twice threatened to strike, in 1957 and 1959, when hospitals refused to accept a conciliation board's contract recommendations. Each time, the government came up with extra money.

On the political front, after three election defeats in nearly thirteen years at the top, BC NDP leader Bob Strachan's resignation in 1969 led to a testy battle between Tom Berger and Dave Barrett to replace him. At the leadership convention, union delegates were almost all for Berger. With their support, Berger eked out a slim thirty-six-vote victory. The capable, youthful labour lawyer was seen as "a man of the times," compared to the province's aging premier. NDP election billboards displayed a smartly dressed individual striding toward the legislature, attaché case in hand, with the words "Ready to Govern."

All signs pointed to the end of Social Credit's seventeen years in government. Instead,

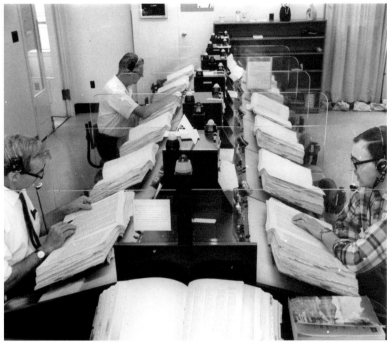

Bennett won his largest majority ever. Bennett's over-the-top accusations that Berger's NDP would put unions in control of the province worked. For added measure, Bennett unleashed the communist bogeyman, conjuring up visions of state-owned collective farms and comparing labour's urging of members to vote NDP to the Soviet Union's suppression of Czechoslovakia. Social Credit's slogan, "Strike Pay with Berger. Take Home Pay with Bennett," struck home. The NDP was reduced to a humiliating twelve seats. Given the extent of labour turmoil that swept over BC during the next few years, a more accurate election prediction would have read, "Strike Pay with Bennett." The province became a forest of picket signs.

There was an indication of what was to come even as Bennett campaigned on keeping unions in their place. BC telephone workers were into the second month of their first strike in fifty years. It was a lively dispute. With supervisors able to maintain telephone service, the Federation of Telephone Workers went after repairs and installation work. Flying picket squads picketed construction sites whenever non-union installers showed up. Coupled with a BC Federation of Labour "hot" declaration against all new telephone wiring, the tactics put a serious crimp in construction activity throughout the Lower Mainland.

On the picket line, stoked by years of resentment against the company's US-style industrial relations, the workers' mood was buoyant. As pressure mounted on both sides, the federal government, which had jurisdiction over the communications industry, stepped in and a tentative two-year agreement was reached, nudging wages up by 2.84 percentage points over the company's pre-strike position. It was not a large amount, but members voted 65 percent to accept. Getting the hard-boiled honchos at BC Tel to move at all was a victory, and a newfound solidarity had emerged among the union's clerical, traffic and plant divisions.

Ever since Social Credit brought in the Mediation Commission, the number of strikes had been going up. The lid came off in 1970, a year that became an industrial relations battleground from beginning to end. Over the course of the year, a record 2.9 million workdays were lost through labour disputes. So much for "Take Home Pay with Bennett."

Above left: With strong union support, Tom Berger (left) was elected leader of the BC NDP in 1969. Shown here talking to Ray Gardiner of the UFAWU while on the campaign trail in Prince Rupert with his wife, Beverley, Berger led the party to a surprising defeat in the election that year and was soon replaced as leader by Dave Barrett. *UBC Rare Books and Special Collections,* BC1532–1434–2.

Above right: BC Tel supervisors awkwardly fill in for unionized telephone operators during a strike by members of the Federation of Telephone Workers in 1969, the first to hit the phone company in fifty years. *Basil King photo, New Westminster Archives,* 72218.

15 THAT SEVENTIES SOCIALISM

THE BC LABOUR MOVEMENT ENTERED THE 1970s in fighting trim. While court injunctions and anti-labour bills had taken a toll, the province's trade unions had proven to be durable combatants, regularly winning respectable wage increases at the bargaining table. At 140,000, membership of the BC Federation of Labour was nearly double that at its founding convention in 1956. Although legislative hurdles and an expanding, unorganized service sector had reduced the rate of unionization to 43 percent of the workforce, BC remained the most unionized province in Canada. Its industrial unions were the country's most consistently militant. Wages in the province's big industries were enough for a young person without a university education to get a union job, buy a home and comfortably raise a family. A greatly expanded public sector was flexing its muscles too, no longer willing to tamely accept government-prescribed wage increases. The sixties had fostered a mood of rebellion in the land. While union members were hardly part of the Love Generation, they were also no fans of the status quo.

Sensing this increased militancy and noting recent union gains, BC employers stole a leaf from labour's solidarity handbook. They themselves began banding together into industry-wide bargaining associations to a degree unmatched in Canada. The new kid on the block was the Construction Labour Relations Association (CLRA), which had managed to unite hundreds of independent-minded contractors into one large bargaining unit. Chuck Connaghan, the CLRA's confrontational head, along with the influential Employers' Council of BC, urged companies to get some backbone and start standing up to unions. Profits were being eroded by union wage increases, complained council president Tony Peskett.

Amid this polarized environment, employers and unions prepared for 1970. Con-

The new bargaining agent for BC contractors, the Construction Labour Relations Association, flexed its muscles by locking out members of the BC building trades for three months in 1971 before a settlement was reached.

UBC Rare Books and Special Collections, BC1532–335.

tracts covering more than one hundred thousand workers in the province's major industries—forestry, mining and construction—were due to expire. There had never been a bargaining year like it. Reporters from across Canada flocked to BC to cover the pending showdowns. The BC Federation of Labour fired the first shot across the bow, bringing leaders of leading unions together for a closed-door strategy session to plan a first-of-its-kind attempt to co-ordinate bargaining during the coming year. Attendees included the IWA, Pulp Sulphite, the United Steelworkers of America, the building trades and CUPE. As meetings continued, the Fed's Ray Haynes told *The Globe and Mail*, "The major purpose is to keep the employers from forcing a settlement on a weaker group. No group is going to settle unless the other group settles."

To underscore the strategy, Haynes and Pulp Sulphite leader Pat O'Neal accompanied IWA negotiators to their first bargaining session with the forest industry. The companies walked out. When Haynes and someone from the pulp union again showed up for the parties' second meeting, company negotiators stayed but refused to talk to the IWA. The two sides sat across the table staring at each other, reading newspapers and talking among themselves. Afterward, John Billings, president of the companies' bargaining arm, Forest Industrial Relations (FIR), said there would be no talks with the IWA "in front of people who are not the direct representatives of the industry or its employees."

Labour soon had a real fight on its hands. In its initial set-to with the rugged building trades, the CLRA was determined to apply a province-wide settlement to stop a bargaining practice known as whipsawing, in which weaker segments are targeted for union pressure. Those deals are then used to strike equivalent or better terms with the rest of the industry. Partly as a result, BC construction rates were the highest in Canada. After a sprinkling of job action, the CLRA locked out nine of the construction unions across the province, idling twenty thousand construction workers. Others were laid off when many building sites closed down completely. Unions should expect more tough bargaining, vowed Peskett of the Employers' Council. Companies had been giving in to union demands for too long, he said.

But coverage of all labour stories that spring was missing from the pages of the *Vancouver Sun* and *Province*. Union employees at both papers had their own strike. Vancouverites could still read what was happening in a new newspaper on city streets, *The Express*. The paper was published three times a week by striking members of the American Newspaper Guild. Keeping to the straight-and-narrow approach of mainstream newspapers, *The Express* proved a resounding success, packed with ads and gobbled up by a public starved for news. Revenue from the paper boosted strike pay and helped pressure the publishers to settle the dispute. A new contract was reached with the assistance of mediators from the Mediation Commission, accepted voluntarily by both sides. The deal confirmed labour's position, said Ray Haynes, that skilled mediation rather than compulsion was the way to settle difficult strikes.

In the public sector, the BCGEU's new general secretary John Fryer irritated the Bennett government to no end. With admirable cheek, he began sending out the government's mandated wage increase to the membership for ratification, even though the terms were fixed. Protests multiplied. On one memorable occasion in the fall of 1969 that made news across Canada, the union hired a Cessna airplane to fly over the legislature towing a banner reading "Drop us a line, Mr. Black. —BCGEU." The message referred to Wesley Black, cabinet minister for the public service, who continued to ignore all missives from the union.

The government's long mean-spirited treatment of its employees had welded them into a strong union, far removed from the cap-in-hand association of the past. *Victoria Times* labour reporter Roger Stonebanks noticed the difference at the union's 1971 convention. "[The 1965 convention] seemed a cross between a social club and a debating society, held together as much by char-

ter flights to the Old Country as anything," Stonebanks wrote. "[Now] the actions of the delegates are stronger. Speakers urge a militant stance." Their day was coming.

Soon more labour turmoil surfaced from an unexpected source. The Canadian Merchant Service Guild (CMSG), representing about a thousand officers and engineers on BC towboats, struck for the first time in years in a dispute over staffing requirements and safety conditions. When the towboat companies began running tugs operated by supervisors, the CMSG expanded its picket lines to a number of IWA sawmills and several pulp mills using logs and wood chips transported by non-union tugs. The forest companies went to court, emerging with fistfuls of injunctions against the guild's broadened picketing. Proclaiming that safety was too important to be decided by the courts, the union defied the injunctions.

"We will not drown one more man or maim one more person because of unsafe conditions," declared an emotional CMSG president Captain Cecil Rhodes, pointing to the deaths of fifty union members in towboat accidents over the previous ten years. "Make no mistake about it. There's a lot of us going to jail to change the laws." The secondary picketing put fourteen thousand IWA members and nearly five thousand pulp workers off the job. With the wide net cast by CMSG pickets, the construction lockout, and a simultaneous strike by staff at hotel beer parlours, BC was a sea of labour trouble.

Emotions were cranked up by large union rallies to support leaders of the Merchant Service Guild as they awaited contempt-of-court convictions. Ray Haynes endorsed their civil disobedience, pointing out that restricting CMSG pickets to company offices would doom their strike. Ed Lawson of the BC Teamsters Union, while not condoning the union's defiance, said he understood it. "When the courts are abused, when injunctions are used as a bargaining lever by employers, they almost forfeit the right to responsibility from the other side," Law-

Towboat crew members Hugh Gwynn and Jim Hutton maintain a watery picket line to support their union's 1970 strike for improved safety regulations aboard BC towboats.

City of Vancouver Archives, Pugstream Publications, 134–175.

son told the *Vancouver Sun.* The IWA's Syd Thompson said his members accepted losing work because of guild pickets. "When you're at war with the boss, there can be no division and no differences of opinion in the labour movement," he thundered at a boisterous, two-thousand-strong protest outside Mac-Millan Bloedel headquarters in Vancouver.

As tension grew, Ottawa sent in its top mediator, Bill Kelly. With his assistance, the towboat dispute was settled. But there was a huge price to pay. Supreme Court Justice Thomas Dohm, who had sent Homer Stevens to jail for a year, sentenced the chief union negotiator, Captain Arnie Davis, to six months behind bars. Even more onerous, he fined the virtually penniless CMSG $75,000, the largest fine ever imposed on a union. There were also steep legal costs. Labour leaders were enraged, pointing out that the strike was not over wages but the lives and safety of towboat workers, matters that should have been federally regulated. Even Jack Moore, the moderate president of the IWA, called the courts' treatment of the CMSG "an orgy of revenge." Others branded employers' use of the courts "a campaign of terror." When the punishment was upheld, labour banded together to pay the record fine on behalf of the guild. The Federation of Labour

pledged its East Broadway headquarters as security.

Meanwhile, confronted with a three-month shutdown of the construction industry, the provincial government invoked the **Mediation Commission Act** in a major dispute for the first time. After a round of fruitless talks in Victoria, BC labour minister Leslie Peterson used his powers under the act to issue a back-to-work order and proclaim compulsory arbitration. When contractors accordingly lifted their lockout, only three

Workers are protesting the jailing of Captain Arnie Davis, chief negotiator for the Canadian Merchant Service, who was sentenced to six months for defying a court injunction during the guild's bitter towboat strike in 1970.

UBC Rare Books and Special Collections, BC1532–336–2.

The first six months of 1972 featured an all–out battle by BC construction unions against the province's contractors, the twenty–year government of W.A.C. Bennett and the loathed Mediation Commission, with its power to impose compulsory arbitration. This demonstration took place in June at Pacific Centre in downtown Vancouver.
Deni Eagland photo, Vancouver Sun.

of the locked-out unions went back to work. Six building trades thumbed their noses at the back-to-work order, risking heavy fines by maintaining labour's two-year boycott of the Mediation Commission.

At a special mass meeting, the Federation of Labour pledged total support for the construction workers. As a showdown loomed, the government drew back. Instead of cracking down on the unions' now illegal strike and putting the matter to binding arbitration by the Mediation Commission, Peterson parachuted himself into a critical round of further negotiations at the Empress Hotel. After eight hours of tense talks, the parties reached an agreement. Striking construction unions would go back to work and the dispute would be put in the hands of an independent mediator. The Mediation Commission was sidelined. In its first big test over the act, labour had prevailed. "We have really ended Bill 33," exulted Ray Haynes.

The long, hot summer continued. The Pulp, Paper and Woodworkers of Canada had been negotiating at the same time as

their Pulp Sulphite adversaries. With talks going nowhere and fearing an IWA settlement would set a wage pattern they didn't like, close to five thousand PPWC members at the union's BC pulp mills walked off the job just as the building trades shutdown ended. Even after both the IWA and Pulp Sulphite settled, PPWC members stayed out for eight more weeks, determined to win a better deal than the three-year contract accepted by other pulp and paper workers. Not surprisingly, the industry refused to sweeten its offer, and PPWC members eventually voted to return to work. The failure of their strike did a lot to convince the PPWC that joint negotiations with their rivals seemed the only realistic way to take on the pulp and paper industry at the bargaining table.

Also in 1970, an exceptionally bitter strike by eighteen hundred members of the United Steelworkers of America shut down Alcan's vast smelter in Kitimat for three months. Some of the bitterness was directed at the union's handling of negotiations and a hotly contested return to work with no apprecia-

ble increase. The Steelworkers eventually lost their certification to an upstart plant union, the Canadian Association of Smelter and Allied Workers, another of the independent Canadian unions making their mark in the province. Smaller but prolonged strikes dotted the labour landscape as well, including a five-month strike by municipal workers in Penticton and, little noticed at the time, a walkout by women employees at the private Sandringham Hospital in Victoria that turned into the longest strike in Canadian labour history.

Throughout the strife, the BC Federation of Labour was a constant factor: rallying the troops, pressuring employers and government, and ensuring respect for its policies. Intrigued by the extent of union ferment, *The Globe and Mail* sent its veteran labour reporter Wilf List to take a look. List told his readers there was no labour climate like it. "The reputation of BC labour for militant action has spread far beyond the boundaries of the province," he wrote. "There is more co-operation among unions than anywhere else in Canada and perhaps North America." List pointed to the sanctity of the picket line and the effectiveness of "hot" declarations in BC, unmatched, he said, anywhere in Canada.

The war continued in 1971. Teachers got into the act, with the first province-wide strike in their organization's fifty-four-year history: a one-day action to press demands for better pensions, not for themselves but for teachers already retired. Underlying their action was anger over restrictive policies that capped wage increases while leaving them with class sizes among the largest in Canada. As it had done ten years earlier to the BC Government Employees' Association for its brief strike, the Bennett government punished the BC Teachers' Federation. A long-standing clause in the **Public School Act** assuring compulsory BCTF membership was simply removed, leaving the organization vulnerable to any number of withdrawals. In a raspberry to the government and an impressive show of support for its organization, only sixty-nine of the BCTF's twenty-two thousand members took the opportunity to opt out.

Accompanied by Bennett tirades that regularly excoriated labour leaders, Social Credit's record of anti-union legislation was unrivalled in the history of BC. By the time of the 1972 election, the province's unions were in a virtual state of war against Bennett, his government and BC employers. That year, labour disruptions topped even those in

Above left: The first province–wide strike by the BC Teachers' Federation was a one–day walkout in 1971 to demand better pensions for retired teachers, some of whom brought their protest to the steps of the legislature in Victoria.
Courtesy BCTF Archives.

Above right: On June 21, 1972, RCMP officers swooped on construction union offices across BC, seizing stacks of documents, including these from the Plumbers' Union in Vancouver. A dozen union leaders were subsequently charged with counselling defiance of a back–to–work order by the Mediation Commission. The new NDP government quashed the charges.
Glen Baglo photo, Vancouver Sun.

1970, accounting for the loss of an incredible two and a half million workdays among a workforce of fewer than a million employees. "That is a ratio I have never known to be attained anywhere," said labour law academic Paul Weiler.

Unions were determined as never before to finally put an end to Social Credit rule. The premier got a taste of what was to come during his annual cabinet tour of the province that spring. Locked-out/striking construction workers, furious at another back-to-work order issued by the Mediation Commission, showed up to vent their anger at many of Bennett's campaign-like stops. In Kamloops, they drowned out the opening of a new vocational school with a cascade of boos and catcalls. As Bennett left the event, surrounded by police and protesters, his famous smile frozen in place, one construction worker jeered loudly, "Keep smiling, Wacky!"

The melee was far worse at the Royal Towers Hotel in New Westminster, where the tour wound up. Hundreds of fired-up building trades members gathered outside. Many carried protest signs nailed on two-by-fours. Bennett was escorted in by a back entrance, but cabinet ministers had to make their way through an intimidating gauntlet of placards. Several ministers were hit on the head. Agriculture minister Cyril Shelford suffered a broken collarbone when he tried to deflect a placard aimed at cabinet minister Isabel Dawson. Amid cries of "*Seig Heil!*" and "Get that Mussolini!" protesters pounded the car of high-profile minister "Flyin' Phil" Gaglardi.

It was an ugly scene. But two decades of attacks from government, the courts and anti-union business hawks had left labour tempers short and civility on hold. The Mediation Commission's arbitrary interference in the ongoing construction industry dispute was the last straw. Shortly after the New Westminster dust-up, the RCMP raided a number of construction union offices for evidence that leaders had counselled defiance of the commission's back-to-work order. The raid prompted BC Fed secretary-treasurer Ray Haynes's cutting comment, "There is no way you can build skyscrapers with search warrants." Criminal charges were soon laid against a dozen leaders of the building trades.

Fresh from its one-day strike over pensions, the BCTF set up a cash-flush Political Action Committee to oust Social Credit. Friendly with Bennett in the past and no friend of the Federation of Labour, BC Teamsters Union leader Ed Lawson had nonetheless seen his union burned by the Mediation Commission as well. "In every case, our membership wound up being penalized [by the commission]. Stabbed in the back might be a better explanation," said Lawson. He too pledged an all-out effort to get rid of the Socreds.

The labour movement unleashed hundreds of volunteers in ridings across the province, flooding NDP coffers with cash. Yet party strategists were spooked by Bennett's past success in linking them with "big labour." Dave Barrett, who had taken over as leader following the Berger election debacle in 1969, persuaded Ray Haynes to withdraw as the party's prospective candidate in Vancouver Burrard. Trade unionists were urged to keep a low profile. Many top union organizers found themselves shunted to the seemingly hopeless North Vancouver campaign of the BC Fed's political action director, Colin Gabelmann. "We had twenty-five union types working for me full-time. They were bumping into each other," Gabelmann recounted, laughing at the memory. "I had one guy who did nothing but make sure I got fed, my shoes were shined and my shirts ironed and clean. These were people not welcome anywhere else. And some were pissed that Ray Haynes had been shut out [in Burrard]."

But Barrett ran a masterful campaign. He hammered home his ringing cry, "Enough is enough!" with gusto and humour at every stop. The seventy-one-year-old Bennett seemed hesitant and out of touch, his fire gone. When the ballots were counted that unforgettable night of August 30, 1972, Social Credit was out, reduced after twenty years in power to just ten seats, done in by a

5.7 percent increase in the NDP's popular vote and large numbers of British Columbians who split the "free enterprise" vote by switching to Liberal and Conservative candidates. Barrett and the NDP swept to power, taking thirty-eight of the fifty-five available seats. Even Colin Gabelmann won. The province had its first socialist government.

After weathering so many bitter electoral losses and government attacks, the labour movement saw its party in power at last. Amid joyous scenes at the NDP's frenzied election headquarters in Coquitlam, Rudy Krickan of the Retail Clerks' Union, a veteran of party campaigns since the 1930s, spoke for many when he told a reporter, "This is the greatest day of my life." Despite a difficult relationship with Barrett, who was uncomfortable with labour's ties to the NDP, union leaders felt their time had come. They looked forward to not only the overturning of Social Credit legislation but to laws that would allow unions and their members to expand and prosper. "For the first time I had the feeling we had a government we could work with," said Haynes years later. "I felt we could bury the hatchet."

Matters began well. During a quickie ses-

sion that fall, the hated Mediation Commission and its compulsory arbitration powers were axed. The minimum wage was raised from $1.50 an hour to $2.00, with a commitment to $2.50 in 1974. Wage caps on teachers were eliminated and compulsory BCTF membership restored. And all charges against construction union leaders for defying the Mediation Commission's back-to-work order were dropped.

Then the bombshell hit. Bill King, the

Above: The NDP's Bill King shakes hands at the Arrow Lakes Hospital in Nakusp during the 1972 provincial election campaign, while leader Dave Barrett looks on. When the NDP won the election, King, a trade unionist and former railway engineer, was named labour minister. *Image 2014–018–1473, Arrow Lakes Historical Society.*

Left: Early on in his term, populist NDP premier Dave Barrett (right) experimented with briefly trying his hand at various jobs as a way of experiencing the working life, a venture some media critics described as "quasi–Maoism." He spent part of a day on a fishboat. His first words on going aboard: "When do we eat?" *Steve Bosch,* Vancouver Sun.

new minister of labour, announced the appointment of a three-person commission to propose major revisions to the province's outmoded labour code. None of the "three wise men," as they were soon labelled, came from organized labour. Instead of the pivotal role they anticipated, unions were told they could present their views at public meetings like everyone else. For a process that would have such a profound effect on their members, this was a blow. "You help get the government elected. You think you're partners," explained Ron Johnson, who worked for the Fed in those days. "Then the three wise men are appointed. There was huge friction, right off the top."

But this friction was not initially apparent when King introduced the NDP's labour code in October 1973. It was a breathtaking document, detailing the most progressive industrial relations system in North America. For the first time anywhere, jurisdiction over picketing was taken from the courts and given to a newly powerful Labour Relations Board. There would be no more speedy *ex parte* injunctions that had stymied so many strikes and sent union leaders to jail. New

rules facilitated union organizing. Employer hands were now tied during sign-up campaigns, and unions would be granted automatic certification without a vote if a majority of the workforce inked membership cards.

Police, firefighters and hospital workers were given the right to strike, with an option of binding arbitration without employer consent. Companies could be denied relief over a wildcat strike if the LRB determined they did not have "clean hands." Professional strikebreakers were outlawed, while an innovative section on technological change gave unions the right to appeal to the LRB if significant mid-contract changes to existing work practices took place. After the dark decades of Social Credit, the sun seemed to be shining on organized labour in BC.

But among all the advances that were the envy of other unions across Canada, there were initiatives that labour leaders resented and fastened on. Many opposed a clause allowing union members to opt out for religious reasons. "Anti-union!" stormed Marine Workers' head William Stewart in his thick Scottish burr. "We are now going to be asked to subsidize some other form of organiza-

Workers, mostly women, at the private Sandringham Hospital in Victoria were into the second year of their strike for a first contract in 1971. They would not reach a settlement for another two years, making their determined walkout against the hospital's recalcitrant owners one of the longest in Canadian labour history. *UBC Rare Books and Special Collections, BC1532–339–1.*

tion, whether it's the Christian Labour Association or those funnily dressed people [Hare Krishnas] who make strange noises outside the Bay." Nor did labour embrace an intriguing section allowing unions to seek binding arbitration to settle first contract disputes. That arose from Bill King's frustration over his inability to settle the ongoing strike at Victoria's private Sandringham Hospital, then into its fourth year. CUPE had managed to organize the mostly female workforce, but could not get the millionaire owner to negotiate an agreement. "It was tragic, totally unfair," King reflected. With the code looming, the strike was finally settled after the twenty-eight strikers had spent a record thirty-nine months on the picket line. No matter how worthy its intention, however, organized labour refused to condone any use of binding arbitration.

But the biggest concern was picketing. Most union leaders preferred fighting in the trenches of industrial warfare without restraint. To their dismay, the code restricted their right to set up secondary pickets wherever they felt they were justified. Jurisdiction over secondary picketing was given to the LRB, and it was not wide open. "They were really heartbroken, because the one thing they wanted was the right to secondary picket," said Ron Johnson. Several hundred union representatives journeyed to Victoria to lobby the government to change the code, but Bill King held firm.

"The BC Fed took the position that they had supported our party for years, which was true," said King in 2008. "And labour had suffered from inequality and unfair treatment under a pro-management government. I was sympathetic to that argument, but I wanted to strike a balance." Three NDP backbenchers—Gabelmann, Harold Steves and Rosemary Brown—voted against various sections of the code, but it sailed through the legislature after a remarkably rancour-free debate.

Despite the Fed's unhappiness, organizing boomed under the code. Unionization rose to 44.9 percent of the workforce. The NDP also passed a fair-wages act, ensuring that union rates were paid on all public contracts. And although the Federation was skeptical about the new Labour Relations Board and its powers, the choice of Ontario legal professor Paul Weiler to chair the landmark tribunal turned out better than anyone could have foreseen. His measured decisions and judicious use of the board's mediation powers gave unions the fairest treatment they had ever received. Under Weiler, the board specialized in practical judgments based on the nuances of a specific problem, a huge advance over "letter of the law" rulings from the courts.

There were also momentous changes to workers' compensation and workplace health and safety. For the first time in Canada, independent boards of review were established to rule on Workmen's Compensation Board appeals, ending years of having them decided by the compensation board's own officials. The boards of review also published their decisions, as did the WCB, another Canadian first. Disability and widows' pensions were hiked to fairly reflect loss of earnings and cost-of-living increases. Compensation for injured workers was raised too.

The ridiculous practice of giving companies notice of WCB inspections was ended. Worker representatives were allowed to accompany inspectors on their tours. More inspectors strengthened enforcement of WCB orders. The cost of noncompliance with safety measures skyrocketed. Premiums went up for industries found to be consistently hazardous. The definition of occupational disease was broadened. Toxicologists and hearing specialists were hired as part of unprecedented attention given to the complexities of industrial disease. Tougher contamination levels were set in many industries, and safety regulations extended to agricultural workers and fishermen. As a capper, the WCB's name was changed to the non-sexist Workers' Compensation Board, reflecting the large number of women in the workforce. Presiding over this sea change was Canada's leading academic authority on workers' compensation and health and safety, Terry Ison from Queen's University in Ontario.

Labour welcomed these far-reaching measures but remained dissatisfied over the labour code. After Ray Haynes surprised everyone by quitting as secretary-treasurer in the fall of 1973 to run a resort on Quadra Island, the fight was aggressively taken on by his replacement, a blunt, tough-talking printer and air force vet named Len Guy. For the next two years, Guy and Bill King, a railway engineer and no pushover himself, locked horns in an ongoing confrontation over NDP labour policies. Guy was a class warrior. "Anybody who tells you he can shake hands and have a drink with the employer is screwing his membership," he told Marcus Gee of the *Province*. For his part, as labour minister, King also wanted a good deal for workers. "But I think you have to be viewed as even-handed by the parties," he later explained. "If you lose that, you've lost your effectiveness." At times it became personal. Once, according to King, the two came close to blows during a private hotel meeting. Neither liked to back down.

The rupture became complete in 1974 when the NDP introduced a series of seemingly innocuous labour code amendments that solidified the LRB's jurisdiction while strengthening its hand on arbitration matters. To Guy and a majority of Federation officers, the amendments confirmed that the government had no interest in addressing their concerns. After the amendments passed, Guy and president George Johnston told reporters that the BC Federation of Labour had lost confidence in Bill King as labour minister. They called on him to resign or be fired. After a mere two years of government by "labour's party," it was a shocking declaration.

A much worse confrontation erupted during the long, hot summer of 1975. Sky-high inflation had driven unions to negotiate unheard-of wage increases. Settlements were coming in with annual increases of close to 20 percent. Employers who resisted

were struck. Members of the BC Employers' Council decided the upward wage spiral had to be squelched. They began with the province's dominant forest industry. Contracts of both pulp unions and the coastal IWA, covering more than forty thousand workers, expired within two weeks of each other. To harness their bargaining power, leaders of the Canadian Paperworkers Union and the Pulp, Paper and Woodworkers of Canada put aside their deep-rooted enmity to form a common front for the first time. Jack Munro and the IWA, though no fans of the pulp unions, agreed to keep communication channels open.

Far from cowed, the companies welcomed a showdown. In the face of double-digit pay hikes sweeping the province, the industry offered its workers a one-year contract extension with no wage increase at all except for a cost-of-living adjustment (COLA) at the end. It was a convenient time to take on the unions. With a worldwide glut of pulp and thousands of IWA members laid off by a softening lumber market, the bottom seemed to have fallen out of the industry. How much could a strike hurt?

Yet nothing slowed the pulp unions. Outraged by the companies' provocative offer, brushing aside pleas from the government to give mediator Henry Hutcheon a chance, thirteen thousand workers walked out at all twenty BC pulp mills on July 16. The IWA stayed at the bargaining table. But a month later, sixteen thousand of its members were off the job anyway, idled by the ongoing industry slowdown and fallout from the pulp strike.

Hutcheon's report to settle the dispute exacerbated the growing divide. The BC Supreme Court judge recommended a two-year total wage boost of $1.55/hour, plus a modest COLA clause. A healthy 28 percent increase on the base rate, it was still below recent BC settlements. The pulp unions rejected it without a vote. CPU leader Art Gruntman scorned the package as "not within a whisker" of the $3.00 an hour over two years they were seeking. The forest companies reluctantly accepted Hutcheon's recommendations. The IWA was split. Its membership rejected the package by a slender 51.2 percent. Nevertheless, Jack Munro, who had urged a "yes" vote, opted to keep negotiating rather than joining a strike he felt was doomed.

When hard-pressed pulp workers decided to escalate their picketing to IWA operations, festering tensions among the three unions exploded. Munro blasted "super [pulp] militants" for "spreading their mess around" at a time when his union was anxious to keep as many of its members working as possible. Picket signs were ripped up at one mill, and verbal clashes took place at a Federation "unity" gathering. The pulp unions responded by slagging the IWA's alleged lack of militancy and union solidarity.

The shutdown continued into a third month. In the mill towns of BC, hundreds of pulp workers began applying for welfare to feed their families. The prolonged dispute was also a major financial headache for the NDP government, which relied on the $3-billion-a-year industry for a large chunk of its revenue. Other strikes added to the malaise. Bakers, meat cutters and members of the Retail Clerks' Union at 125 Lower Mainland supermarkets walked out at the beginning of September 1975, demanding annual wage increases of up to 50 percent. BC Rail was beset by rotating strikes, and a comparatively minor strike by 180 propane truck drivers was starting to disrupt the supply of heat to seniors' homes on Vancouver Island. As September rolled along, the entire province appeared to be behind picket lines.

In Victoria Bill King, who had spent many frustrating hours to get the warring forestry parties to talk peace, was running out of patience. So was the premier. The government summoned the legislature in early October, ostensibly to order striking propane drivers back to work. Instead, they did the unthinkable. In one stunning swoop, they legislated everyone back to work. Pulp workers, supermarket workers, BC Rail workers and

yes, the propane drivers, were given forty-eight hours to put down their picket signs and report for duty. The IWA was lumped in too. In all, Bill 146 covered more than fifty thousand union members, the most sweeping back-to-work edict ever made in the country's private sector.

Labour leaders were aghast. "My first reaction is one of disbelief," said Len Guy. "It's utter strikebreaking," stormed embittered pulp union leader Art Gruntman. PPWC negotiator Stan Shewaga said members were tearing up their NDP cards. He predicted "total warfare" in the mills. Plans were made to resist. "Rarely in modern times has a government in Canada interfered so brutally in free collective bargaining," declared Guy. "It's a complete betrayal of the principles and policies of the NDP and a complete betrayal of the working people who helped elect this government." He pledged Federation support for any union choosing to disobey the back-to-work order.

There were no takers. Although CPU leaders recommended defiance, union delegates voted 51 percent to comply. Despite the tough talk and leadership outrage, there was not a lot of fight left on the ground. Seeing no point continuing a struggle they felt likely to lose, many rank-and-file workers began heading back to their jobs even before the forty-eight-hour deadline. Supermarket employees were not far behind. The government's bold action had succeeded, and one of the province's largest waves of labour conflict was over. But it was a distressing culmination of the strained relationship between the Barrett government and a significant portion of organized labour that had wanted something different from an NDP administration, even though—to outsiders, at least—it seemed the most labour-friendly government BC had ever had.

No such rancour existed in the public sector. Having achieved full collective bargaining rights for the first time, the BCGEU negotiated the largest ever pay increases for government employees, along with a thirty-five-hour workweek. And a spontaneous one-day strike by one thousand Surrey teachers in February 1974, led to a lower pupil-teacher ratio that added close to four thousand teaching jobs over the next five years. The deal resulted from an impromptu meeting between BCTF president Jim MacFarlan and Barrett, who asked what it would take to get protesting teachers off the legislature lawn. An annual two-point drop in the pupil-teacher ratio, responded MacFarlan. Barrett offered a one-point drop. MacFarlan suggested 1.5, and the deal was struck. Such was policy-making in the early days of the freewheeling NDP government.

Three weeks after his back-to-work shocker, Dave Barrett called a snap election. Coincidentally, the BC Federation of Labour's annual convention took place a few days afterward. When Barrett spoke to the convention, CPU delegates walked out. Others remained seated during several standing ovations the NDP leader received. There was further discord during the convention. Munro harangued the pulp unions for their "useless strike" and the Federation for supporting their "picketing mistakes." Guy strode to the microphone to defend the Fed. "Put labour first and party second," he said. "No government could have done what this government did if we had been united." Local IWA president Gerry Stoney put the best possible face on the acrimony. "The labour-NDP relationship [is still strong]. Bill 146 was labour's night on the couch."

A recommendation to continue labour's support for the NDP was approved almost unanimously. "It was a family fight," Guy told reporters. "We had a good one, but there's [no way] we would support anyone else." Gruntman was a holdout. "I can't do it," he said. "I have to put my members' welfare number one." But most delegates seemed to agree with IWA delegate Lyle Kristiansen, who reminded them, "Barrett is not the devil incarnate. The only question is: which side are *you* on?"

After one of the nastiest election campaigns in BC's tempestuous political history, the NDP retained its share of the popular vote, but a united right returned a reborn Social Credit to power. While the Barrett government was far from perfect, its brief thirty-nine months in office left behind an unsurpassed legacy of progressivism in almost every ministry, including the Agricultural Land Reserve, publicly owned auto insurance, Pharmacare, rent controls and the purchase of two pulp mills and several other enterprises to preserve jobs. The new premier was W.A.C. Bennett's son Bill, who authored the solidarity of right-wing voters desperate to get rid of the NDP.

New labour minister Allan Williams's first act was to fire Terry Ison as head of the WCB. On the other side, skilled poker player that he was, Len Guy knew when to hold 'em and when to fold 'em. The game had changed. His first move was to warn Williams not to touch the same labour code that the Fed had criticized so heavily under the NDP.

INFLATION FOR THE NATION 16

————————

AS THEY AWAITED THEIR FATE UNDER Social Credit, BC unions had more pressing concerns. On Thanksgiving, October 14, 1975, fretting over cascading inflation and soaring wage increases, Prime Minister Pierre Trudeau announced Canada's first peacetime wage controls. Although prices were also to be controlled, wages were the chief target. Over the next three years, pay raises were to be limited to 8, 6 and 4 percent, with an annual upward adjustment of 2 percent allowed for productivity and catch-up. After two years of generous increases, workers were now handcuffed to a third-party tribunal, the Anti-Inflation Board (AIB). The heaviest government intervention in the economy since the end of World War II, controls were aimed directly at unions and their members. It was far easier to limit wage increases than prices. Adding to the sense of betrayal was Trudeau's strong opposition during the 1974 election to the very wage controls he was now imposing. His anti-wage-control stance had drawn working-class NDP votes from across the country and catapulted the Liberals into a majority.

In BC, the program had an immediate impact on workers hit by the NDP's back-to-work legislation. The IWA had escaped controls by the skin of their teeth, accepting the $1.55/hour wage increase already on the table, plus a few modest improvements, just days before the program was announced. But the pulp unions were trapped. In an ironic twist of fate, however, after scorning the IWA throughout the summer's troubles, they were saved by its fortuitous settlement. The AIB exempted the two pulp unions from controls based on their historic wage relationship with the IWA. They were thus able to secure the same increase as the IWA, amounting to 28 percent over two years, well over wage guidelines. Supermarket workers were not so lucky. Wage controls forced them to accept a settlement that was significantly less than what they had been offered before they went on strike.

When federal labour minister John Munro spoke to the BC Federation of Labour convention in 1975, just after the Liberal government announced its wage control program, he was greeted with a forest of protest signs.
Sean Griffin photo, Image MSC160–171–07, Pacific Tribune Photo Collection, Simon Fraser University Library.

Millions of WHY ME? buttons were distributed during labour's 1976 campaign against federal wage controls.

Union leaders were livid at the program. Even Joe Morris, the mild-mannered president of the Canadian Labour Congress, was roused to fury. At a meeting with NDP premiers Allan Blakeney of Saskatchewan and Ed Schreyer of Manitoba, who signed on to the federal program, Morris became so upset that he "literally chased them from the room, prepared to physically assault them," former CLC research and legislative director Ron Lang disclosed in 2010. "I have never seen him so angry." On another occasion, Morris was heard shouting behind closed doors, "This is one goddamned law I am prepared to disobey no matter what the costs!" His outrage was widely shared. A labour war chest of close to half a million dollars was quickly raised to fight controls, *Why Me?* buttons were ubiquitous and information seminars were held across the country. Unions were advised to negotiate as if controls did not exist. At the CLC convention in May of 1976, delegates voted overwhelmingly to endorse a plan of

action that included a first in the arsenal of the national labour movement: a general strike or strikes "when and if necessary."

In spite of all the fist-pumping vows from union leaders to defy controls, the major confrontation took place far from their podiums in the isolated community of Kitimat, home of the giant Alcan smelter in northwest BC. Although company towns had been part of BC's resource-based economy since Robert Dunsmuir stumbled on the rich Wellington coal seam in 1869, none was quite like Kitimat. Hacked out of the rugged wilderness in the traditional territory of the Haisla, it was where Alcan had masterminded what was then North America's largest private construction project. When Prince Philip poured the first ingot in 1953, thousands of construction workers, many of them Portuguese newcomers to Canada, had built a huge hydro dam, a power plant, a lengthy network of transmission towers, a deep-sea terminal, the world's second-largest aluminum smelter and a townsite. For their instant town, Alcan hired a renowned urban designer to create a model community of happy, contented workers.

Twenty-three years later, those high hopes were in disarray. In the words of newspaper columnist Allan Fotheringham, Kitimat had become "a blueprint without a heart." Unhappiness had been rife for some time. Fed up with their unsuccessful three-month strike in 1970 and union discipline meted out to some members by the United Steelworkers of America, smelter workers bolted from Steel to form their own union. The vote in favour of the Canadian Association of Smelter and Allied Workers was an overwhelming 1,112–305. On-the-job dissatisfaction, punctuated by class division, was also on the rise. Workers complained of arrogant treatment from company managers, many of whom lived in a more exclusive part of town. Their mood was further soured by the Anti-Inflation Board's decision to hold their recent two-year contract to federal wage guidelines, saddling them with a wage increase of 15.4 percent while other workers won exemptions—most notably those at the nearby Eurocan pulp mill with their 28 percent pay hike.

On June 3, 1976, simmering discontent erupted into a full-scale revolt. When union electricians and welders walked off the job in a grievance dispute, they were soon joined by almost all of the union's eighteen hundred members. It was the beginning of an intense wildcat strike that echoed across the country. At a heated meeting that night, union members voted 60 percent to continue their strike, rejecting an executive recommendation to return to work. They rallied behind a demand to reopen their contract. CASAW president Peter Burton spelled it out. The main cause of the wildcat strike, he said, was "Prime Minister Pierre Elliott Trudeau … and his rotten Anti-Inflation Board." It was a fight against wage controls.

The strike became an all-out siege of the smelter. Workers barricaded the only road

Workers blockaded the road to the Alcan aluminum smelter in Kitimat for nine days during their rambunctious 1976 wildcat strike to pressure the company to reopen a contract that complied with federal wage controls. *Courtesy Unifor Local 2301.*

to the plant with boulders, logs and a high plywood fence. Hemmed inside were four hundred non-union personnel, struggling to keep the pot lines operating to avoid a multi-million-dollar restart if they went cold. In sweltering conditions, they toiled six hours on and six hours off, sleeping where they could on couches and rubber mats. Food and supplies arrived by helicopter and seaplane. After three difficult days, Alcan flew in two hundred supervisory reinforcements from the company's smelter in Arvida, Quebec, which had been shut down by a legal strike.

The Alcan workers ignored a cease-and-desist order by the BC Labour Relations Board. On June 8, the board upped the ante by filing its order with the BC Supreme Court. This made strikers liable to contempt-of-court charges, carrying the possibility of large fines and even imprisonment for staying out. On the picket line, amid a festive air of feasting, footballs and Frisbees, the mood remained defiant. "We just want what's ours," said one worker. An older employee said company attitudes had hardened. "In the past, it was a pleasure to work. Now, we're just like a number and a dollar sign." CASAW repeated its call for Alcan to reopen their collective agreement and support an application to the AIB for a wage adjustment. That, Alcan reaffirmed, was a non-starter.

That evening, at a massive steam bath of a union meeting, the contempt-of-court threat only toughened resistance. More than 60 percent opposed another "strong" executive recommendation to return to work, the highest percentage so far. Earlier that afternoon, meanwhile, sombre news had come from inside the smelter. Kevin Rooney, a thirty-five-year-old reduction development engineer, father of two and unused to pot line work, died of a heart attack after completing his six-hour shift.

By then the RCMP had sent in superintendent Gordon Dalton to oversee restoration of law and order. Tension swept the community, heightened by throngs of media waiting for what seemed an inevitable showdown between workers and police. But Dalton was cut from different timber than the Mounties who had busted so many picket lines in the past. He stayed his hand, hoping to get the two sides to resolve matters voluntarily. On a visit to the picket line, he warned strikers they were forcing an "extremely dangerous" confrontation. Careful not to choose sides, Dalton said he wasn't concerned by defiance of the courts, but by their blockade of the highway. That was a criminal offence and a matter for police. "This is going to create many problems," he told them. "You are going to be the loser, the plant is going to be the loser and the community is going to be the loser."

Neither side moved. Burton said union members understood the consequences of their ongoing resistance. "But they have stated five times in the last eight days that they don't feel they are getting justice under the regime of Alcan and [AIB chair] Jean-Luc Pepin." When picketers refused to allow company personnel returning from Kevin Rooney's funeral back into the smelter, police action seemed inevitable. That Friday night, hundreds of workers congregated along the road leading to the barricade. Portuguese strikers turned the occasion into a community gathering. They picnicked, drank wine, sang and waited to be arrested. Scores of vehicles were parked helter-skelter in the middle of the highway to make police manoeuvres as difficult as possible. By midnight, with no sign of the cops, almost everyone had packed up and gone home.

The raid came at dawn, signalled by a stream of headlights cutting through the morning mist. In a long line of cars and buses, the police arrived in force. Wearing visored helmets, beating a steady tattoo with their long riot sticks, 150 Mounties advanced toward the union line. About thirty groggy picketers waited for them. When Superintendent Dalton asked the group to come forward to be arrested "or we will come to you," they quietly complied. In short order the strikers, including Burton and national union president Bob Feltis, were bundled onto a bus and driven off to jail. A company front-end loader shunted aside the logs, boulders and plywood barrier that had blocked the road for the past ten days. The siege of the smelter was over.

But that was not the end of the strike. Three hours after the blockade came down, eight workers from Alcan's strikebound Arvida smelter in Quebec set up their own picket line. CASAW members refused to cross, while news of the arrests aroused an outburst of pent-up emotion. Hundreds surged onto the smelter highway. A car that tried to get through was jostled and turned back. The head of the Kitimat RCMP detachment was pushed into a ditch by the wife of one of the strikers, who told him, "Now, you will remember a Portuguese woman." Speaking from the back of a pickup truck, union executive member Wiho Papenbrock managed to calm the crowd, but hard feelings persisted, particularly toward members who had returned to work; there were fist fights, slashed tires, parking lot confrontations and threats.

Still, the strike lost much of its oomph. Now that Alcan controlled the road, more members began going to work. On Friday, June 18, the LRB ruled the Arvida picket line

When a dawn raid by 150 police dismantled the Kitimat smelter workers' road blockade on June 12, 1976, a contingent of strikers from Alcan's Arvida smelter in Quebec set up their own picket line, and the wildcat strike continued for another eight days.
Courtesy Unifor Local 2301.

was also illegal, and it came down. Later that night, trouble flared anew on the road to the smelter. CASAW leaders were told to stay away. Short-lived barricades went up, bottles were thrown and a foreman's windshield was smashed. Police convoys patrolled the road all night to maintain an uneasy peace. But it was a last gasp. Two days later, a quiet crowd voted on ending the strike. With no further options, half still opted to keep fighting. The count was tied, 374–374. As chair of the meeting, Peter Burton cast the deciding vote to return, after seventeen days of the most determined challenge in the land to the federal government's wage controls.

Alcan moved swiftly to punish the strikers. Thirty were fired, seventy-four suspended from one to twelve weeks. However, in a ruling that confounded Alcan officials, the firings were subsequently overturned and suspensions reduced by LRB vice-chairman John Baigent. Not only did the company not have "clean hands" in the dispute, Baigent concluded that a discharge or lengthy sus-

pension in a community like Kitimat, with little other viable employment, was "qualitatively different from that same discipline in another setting. In company towns, a job is more a way of life than it is in the more populous southern part of the province."

The company also failed in its attempt to charge a dozen of the strike ringleaders with contempt of court. BC Supreme Court Justice Henry Hutcheon dismissed the case on the grounds that by the time Alcan filed the charges, the strike had ended and the back-to-work order was immaterial. "The courts should not be used as a means of punishing those who disobey orders of the Labour Relations Board," Justice Hutcheon said. His judgment showed just how far industrial relations had travelled in the three years since the NDP ended *ex parte* court injunctions, which regularly put union leaders in jail. Even the thirty workers arrested on the picket line got off, after the presiding judge threw out the first case against Peter Burton for lack of evidence on his public mischief charge. Only in the company's suit for damages was a price exacted, although CASAW managed to negotiate Alcan's original $1.3 million claim down to a still onerous $135,000.

Years later in a union history, smelter worker Brent Morrison looked back on CASAW's stand with pride. "It's quite a big deal when you go on a wildcat strike for three and a half weeks with one of the largest corporations in the world," he said. "They don't like you going on strike in the best of times, the little working man being able to head out and just stop a big company's production. You can imagine how big a deal it was for a wildcat strike."

Beyond statements of public support and donations from some individual unions, the mainstream labour movement did not rally behind the Alcan workers' wage-control fight. CASAW was an independent Canadian union that had broken away from a house of labour affiliate. Instead, the CLC and BC Federation of Labour geared up for their own protest. Plans were set in motion for a one-day general strike on the first anniversary of wage controls: October 14, 1976.

This was new territory for the labour movement and for Canada. Editorial writers, business leaders and most politicians reacted with predictable hysteria. Outspoken Vancouver Liberal MP Simma Holt topped them all, suggesting the proposed strike was tantamount to treason. Opinion polls found most Canadians felt the CLC was acting irresponsibly. Many predicted the protest would be a flop. Undeterred, labour leaders continued to organize and plan for their wage-control D-Day. In BC, labour got a big boost on the eve of the strike when LRB chairman Paul Weiler sent shockwaves through government and the employer community by rejecting their application to have the walkout declared illegal. Weiler concluded that the planned action was political and not designed to improve wages and working conditions. Therefore, it did not meet the definition of a strike under the province's labour code.

As October 14 dawned west of the Rockies, wheels of production in the province ground to a halt. The public sector was quiet too. Nearly two hundred thousand BC workers answered the call to strike. The forest industry went down. So did the mines and the waterfront. Buses and ferries didn't

OUT TO FIGHT CONTROLS bumper stickers were affixed to vehicles across Canada as part of the buildup to labour's general strike against wage controls on Oct. 14, 1976. *Courtesy CLC Archives.*

run. Garbage piled up for a day, and phones went unanswered in government offices. Normally humming construction sites were silent. No presses printed the *Vancouver Sun* and *Province*, though the Fed granted dispensation to their reporters so the day would not be covered by non-union employees. Downtown Vancouver streets had never been so deserted on a weekday. The walk-out was capped by a march and boisterous downtown rally attended by more than six thousand good-humoured workers.

Overall, an estimated million workers took the day off to protest, with BC reporting the highest participation rate in the country. To the surprise of many, the twenty-four-hour national general strike—the first in Canadian history—was a resounding success from Victoria to St. John's. Although labour leaders vowed to continue the struggle, this was the last arrow in their quiver. If anything, the strike's impressive show of strength had served as an outlet for labour anger. Once it was over, spirit to keep fighting ebbed. After running its three-year course, wage controls died a quiet, natural death.

BC unions were also grappling with the return of Social Credit. But first they had to go through a bruising internal brawl over the direction of the BC Federation of Labour. Len Guy's leadership and harsh criticism of the NDP government had divided the Fed. Moderate leaders like IWA leader Jack Munro blamed Guy for contributing to the NDP's defeat. They wanted closer ties with the party, whereas Guy and his supporters embraced what they referred to as "the trade union position." That meant functioning independently of the NDP, putting union interests ahead of party interests. In the background was Munro's continued anger over the 1975 pulp unions' strike and their decision to picket IWA sawmills. Both actions had been backed by Guy and the Fed. The duel played out on the floor of the Federation's annual convention in November 1976.

On one side were large unions such as the IWA, BCGEU, CUPE and the Steelworkers.

On the other side, supporting Len Guy, were the building trades and most of the Federation's many mid-sized and smaller affiliates that didn't have the clout of big unions and were more reliant on the Fed. Guy had fired the first public shot at a CUPE convention that summer. Without naming Munro or his union, Guy attacked "some unions and union leaders" for weakening labour by "siding with politicians against the trade union movement. They insist we should try to resist attack only with kid gloves behind closed doors."

The factions fought it out with gusto at the convention. Anti-Guy forces threw their weight behind Art Kube, the CLC's effective but relatively low-profile BC education director, who challenged Guy for the Federation's top job. Most unions sent a full contingent of eligible delegates, cramming the vast convention floor to the hilt. Exchanges were hot and heavy. At one point, Munro complained that Guy was following him from microphone to microphone to respond to every criticism. "I feel like I'm pissing into the wind," the caustic Munro raged. "Sometimes you need to do it, but you know some of it is

The fight against wage controls culminated in the largest protest in Canadian history as a million union members across the country stayed out to fight controls on Oct. 14, 1976. In Vancouver, six thousand workers marched to the Queen Elizabeth Plaza for a spirited rally to mark the one-day general strike. *Sean Griffin photo, Image* MSC160–256–06, *Pacific Tribune Photo Collection, Simon Fraser University Library.*

going to blow back on you." President George Johnston brought the house down when he responded, "Piss away, Brother Munro. Piss away." Even Munro had to laugh.

But the rift could not be papered over with humour. Matters came to a head over the executive report endorsing a Federation independent of the NDP. After an emotional debate, the report was narrowly approved. Gerry Stoney of the IWA immediately called for a roll-call vote, a lengthy, arcane procedure in which each delegate comes to the microphone to announce his or her vote individually. The laborious process took a full day. Although the gap narrowed slightly, the Fed position still prevailed. After that, it was clear Guy would continue as secretary-treasurer, preserving the Federation as a labour organization prepared to take on all governments no matter what their political stripe.

Surprising to those in the labour movement who feared the worst, Bill Bennett's first years as premier did not provoke a full-blown confrontation. Changes to the labour code, while significant, were not as draconian as expected. The definition of essential services was expanded, but for the moment the core of the code remained intact. Not so at the WCB. When Terry Ison was fired, to the joy of BC

employers, workers lost a passionate advocate for their right to work in safety, coupled with a willingness to crack down on hazardous conditions. Just before his firing, Ison imposed a stiff financial penalty on Cominco for excessive lead levels at its Trail smelter. With him gone, the WCB returned $1 million in fines to the company in expectation they would use the money to clean up the smelter. They did, eventually, but on Cominco's timetable rather than the WCB's.

Ison's hands-on approach to workers' health and safety had also targeted the fishing industry. Harvested almost to extinction, herring had begun to return to BC coastal waters in a big way in the early 1970s. With insatiable demand for the herring's roe in Japan, where it sold as a high-price luxury product, astronomical prices were to be had. The fishery turned into a wild, gold-rush-like pursuit of the lucrative roe. Skirting lax federal inspections, a number of boats took to the seas in risky shape. During the spring opening in 1975, two seiners and a gillnetter went down, claiming thirteen lives.

Ignoring federal jurisdiction, Ison flew to Prince Rupert and ordered WCB teams to begin checking fishboats in time for the final opening. The *Fisherman* newspaper hailed his bold action as "the first time in history inspectors were out in the field to protect fishermen." Inspectors ordered several boats tied up, cited as a danger to their crews. Others were found lacking in proper equipment. The WCB continued its fishboat inspections through the 1976 spring herring fishery. But gradually, the federal Ministry of Transport (MOT) reasserted its jurisdiction. With no protest from the Social Credit government and a weaker board, fishboat inspections by the WCB ended in July. All told, their inspectors had written 4,866 orders on 585 vessels. It was back to MOT policy: no inspections of the small boat fleet and once every four years for vessels over fifteen tons.

Elsewhere at the board, cost cutting resulted in serious delays processing worker appeals, while the trio of commissioners who replaced Ison declined to implement board-of-review rulings that overturned WCB decisions. In November 1976, board secretary Connie Sun was fired for resisting this policy. The brief existence of a compensation board that gave workers the benefit of the doubt was now but a memory.

Labour minister Allan Williams was an austere, white-haired lawyer who had played a key role in Bennett's victory with his late switch from the Liberals to Social Credit. No ideologue, Williams fought off attempts within Social Credit to advance anti-union right-to-work measures similar to those in the southern United States. But he had little understanding of labour relations. Williams allowed education minister Pat McGeer, a fellow former Liberal, to push through legislation barring university faculty associations from unionization. The Labour Relations Board found McGeer guilty of an unfair labour practice for interfering with faculty bargaining rights at the decommissioned Notre Dame University in Nelson. Human resources minister Bill Vander Zalm won his anti-union spurs by not only wiping out the much-loved Vancouver Resources Board, but decertifying its fourteen hundred unionized employees ahead of the chop.

The day after Labour Day, 1977, Williams did his part by announcing changes to quell union organizing. Certification votes would now have to be won by 55 percent rather than a simple majority. That evoked such ridicule Williams soon withdrew it, with the humiliating admission he hadn't read the drafted bill closely enough. "It was all a mistake." There were no errors in other amendments. Employers would no longer have to provide employees' names, addresses and phone numbers to prospective organizers, and they were now allowed to convey their views to employees during an organizing drive. After the flood of new certifications under the NDP's organizing rules, it was back to the same old ball game. "This removes [our] shackles," said pleased Employers' Council president Bill Hamilton. The new measures were rammed through the legislature in such haste that Dave Barrett wondered if Williams feared "a conspiracy among working women to join a union in the next few hours and overthrow their bosses."

It was a difficult time for labour. With wage controls in place, strikes were rare. Average annual contract increases plummeted

Workers picket the Workers' Compensation Board in 1979 to call attention to a disastrous cutback in benefits and outright denial of compensation to many workers since Social Credit replaced the NDP as government in 1975. *Sean Griffin photo, Image MSC160–453–17, Pacific Tribune Photo Collection, Simon Fraser University Library.*

in a single year by more than a third, from 11.9 percent to 7.4. "We're in relatively poor shape," confessed Len Guy. A month after the labour code amendments, workers on the expanding BC ferry fleet bucked the ebbing fightback tide, taking on the government in the biggest scrap of Bill Bennett's first term as premier. When Williams moved to head off a union strike by imposing a ninety-day cooling-off period, the twenty-four hundred members of the newly formed BC Ferry and Marine Workers Union walked out anyway. On Friday, October 7, at a series of charged union meetings up and down the coast, ferry workers voted unanimously to keep the big boats tied up, in defiance of the government's order. The next day, the LRB issued its own back-to-work edict. Still angered by a host of layoffs the previous year and fighting off attempts to gut their contract, ferry workers maintained their illegal shutdown through the Thanksgiving weekend.

Heading the strike was terminal attendant and rookie union president Shirley Mathieson. Just twenty-eight years old, Mathieson proved cool as the proverbial cucumber in the face of a fuming government and frothing media. An "adolescent, power-intoxicated [union is] trampling on the helpless and innocent travelling public,"

encouraged by "revolutionary screaming from the BC Fed," seethed the *Vancouver Province*. Looking back, Mathieson said she was neither overwhelmed nor frightened by possible legal consequences of the strike. "I didn't know how it would play out, but it was the will of the membership," she recalled. "It was quite exhilarating."

On October 11, a frustrated Williams

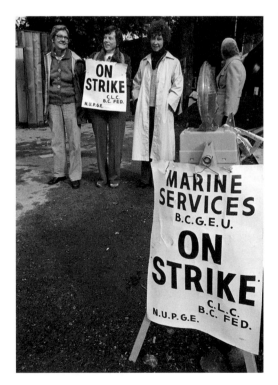

reinserted mediator Clive McKee into the conflict. A day later the union agreed to go back to work while negotiations continued. In return, LRB chairman Paul Weiler signed an undertaking that no legal action would be taken against the union or any of the strikers. Ferries resumed running on October 14. Their employees had stared down the Social Credit government, the Labour Relations Board, the BC Ferry Corporation and the *Province* editorial board for an entire week without blinking. Several months later, both sides accepted Clive McKee's recommendations to settle the dispute. Takeaways demanded by the ferry corporation were gone.

Over in Victoria, Bill Bennett hated every minute the ferry workers thumbed their nose at Allan Williams's ineffectual ninety-day cooling-off period. The moment ferry service returned, he announced a major expansion of essential services legislation—previously restricted to police, firefighter and healthcare unions—to include any union whose job action the labour minister ordained was "an immediate and substantial threat to the economy and welfare" of BC and its citizens. How that exceedingly broadened definition might be applied was uncertain.

But the NDP's measured approach to essential services strikes was clearly over. The Barrett government pioneered the designation of specific services to be maintained by striking employees. That received its trial by fire during a hospital strike by the Hospital Employees' Union in 1976. LRB chairman Paul Weiler said that deciding which employees had to remain at work, without easing pressure on the employer or endangering patients, was "the tensest, most difficult thing I've ever done." But it worked, and the HEU won the strike.

Not all labour happenings concerned the provincial government. One day in June 1977, bank worker Dodie Zerr was in the large vault of the Canadian Imperial Bank of Commerce's branch on Vancouver's Victory Square. She was about to hand over great dollops of cash to a couple of gun-toting

guys from Loomis when ledger-keeper Jackie Ainsworth came dashing into the vault. "We won!" she yelled at Zerr. "It's branch by branch!" Their downtown workplace had just made labour history. According to a Canada Labour Relations Board (CLRB) decision released moments earlier, bank workers could now be organized by individual branches. No longer would they have to wait for a union to achieve the impossible task of signing up a majority of all branch employees across the country in one mammoth national bargaining unit. With their legions of poorly paid women employees, the country's powerful chartered banks were effectively open to unionization for the first time.

The historic breakthrough was made by the most unlikely of unions. The Service, Office and Retail Workers' Union of Canada was everything the mainstream union movement was not. It was small, grassroots-based, staunchly political and overtly feminist, with the goal of "organizing the unorganized." In

It was big news on June 15, 1977, when the Service, Office and Retail Workers Union of Canada won the right to organize banks, branch by branch. Officers Jackie Ainsworth, Elizabeth Godley and Charlotte Johnson told the media that the small feminist union would now launch a major drive to organize long-underpaid employees of Canada's chartered banks. *Sean Griffin photo, Image* MSC160–304–09, *Pacific Tribune Photo Collection, Simon Fraser University Library.*

the words of a labour relations officer, SOR-WUC saw itself as "an instrument of social reform rather than a bread-and-butter union." Its specific targets were women in service occupations at the bottom of the wage ladder who tended to be bypassed by established unions as too tough to organize: restaurants, bars, fast-food outlets—and banks. Founded by several dozen women in the fall of 1972, SORWUC's constitution stressed membership empowerment rather than top-down leadership. In its first few years, the union won a mere scattering of diverse certifications with few workers: day-cares, social services units, offices, pubs and a tuxedo rental store.

With no paid staff, one typewriter, one phone, a donated mimeograph machine, a working/meeting space in a member's basement and a band of dedicated volunteers, SORWUC decided on an audacious campaign to break into Canada's five chartered banks. Employees deserved a greater share of the banks' $120 billion in total assets, the union asserted. Mostly women, their starting pay hovered around $600 a month, far below the national average wage. Merit increases were arbitrary. Working conditions could be onerous, with tellers often forced to make up balance shortfalls from their own meagre earnings and unpaid overtime considered part of the job.

In fact, it was unhappiness over over-time at CIBC's Victory Square branch that started everything. Fed up having to stay late without compensation, employees met one night at the nearby Railway Club bar. Ainsworth, an early SORWUC supporter who had entered the banking business with union thoughts dancing in her head, suggested they approach the union. The next morning SOR-WUC volunteers were outside the branch, handing out pamphlets extolling the virtues of unionization. Within a month, nine of the bank's twenty employees had signed union cards. Under the federal labour code, that was enough to apply for certification.

On August 16, 1976, SORWUC submitted its application for certification to the CLRB, the first such application in seventeen years. The news lit a fire in the industry. Tiny SOR-WUC was soon swamped by requests from bank workers across BC. By March 1977, the union had applied to represent employees at twenty-two branches. The banks argued vociferously that single branch certifications would lead to banking chaos, but the board opted for SORWUC's view, ably argued by lawyer Ian Donald. The union was granted five automatic certifications. Votes were ordered at seventeen other branches. It was truly a milestone decision.

The union office was "nutso," said one member. "Phones rang all day long. We'd done what everyone said was impossible." For the moment, the little union that could had triumphed. Although SORWUC won only three of the first seventeen certification votes, employees continued their clamour to be organized. Within a year, SORWUC had amassed twenty-four official certifications. The union's ambitious bargaining proposals, set by employees themselves, called for an 80 percent increase in the starting wage, based on the salary needs of a single mother with one child. They also sought a thirty-five-hour week, seniority rights, double pay for overtime, involvement in shift schedules and a paid holiday on International Women's Day.

Talks did not go well. However much they detested the pesky little union fly buzzing around them, the powerful banks were far from beaten. When SORWUC asked for centralized bargaining in order to facilitate contract talks, the banks, which had argued so strongly against branch-by-branch certifications, now insisted on negotiating by individual branch, knowing that would stretch the union's thin resources. As often as not, this led to young female employees preparing for talks in a nearby coffee shop, then sitting across from top executives in a fancy hotel meeting room. As described by bank worker Sheree Butt, "Right on time, in walked five men, all dressed in three-piece business suits, each carrying a briefcase. They sat

INDIGENOUS WORKERS WALK OUT

In Vancouver, the opening of the Muckamuck Restaurant in 1971 was a revelation. Amid cedar and First Nations decor, it featured an appetizing melange of West Coast seafood with such trappings as edible seaweed and ferns, herring roe, soapberries and bannock. The owners made a point of hiring a number of Indigenous men and women to cook and serve the food. The restaurant became a magnet for residents and tourists alike.

Behind the scenes, however, all was not well. Many staff felt exploited by low wages and their treatment by owners, including fines for on-the-job mistakes. In early 1978, eighteen of Muckamuck's twenty-one employees joined the independent, feminist Service, Office and Retail Workers Union of Canada (SORWUC). As soon as certification was granted, several pro-union employees were fired, and the battle was on. Picket lines went up June 1. On the eve of the strike, a manager rejected charges the restaurant had exploited First Nations culture. "If there has been any discrimination," he told the *Vancouver Sun*, "it has been against the highly qualified whites we've passed over to hire untrained Native people."

The strike was a rare example of Indigenous workers turning to a union to redress workplace and cul-

Indigenous employees in the early days of their strike against the Muckamuck Restaurant on Davie Street in Vancouver. *Sean Griffin photo, Image MSC160–380–2A Pacific Tribune Photo Collection, Simon Fraser University Library.*

tural grievances. In an article for *The Indian Voice*, employee Ethel Gardner detailed many affronts endured by Muckamuck staff, then wrote, "We are doing our part to add to the renewed struggle by Native people to gain the rights and respect denied to us since Captain Cook landed here." On day one, Indigenous drummers pounded out a throbbing beat for employees, some in traditional dress, walking the line.

It became a bitter and at times nasty dispute. Some Indigenous employees continued to work as the owners struggled to stay open. Finally after three years, the doors shut for good. Two years later, the Labour Relations Board ordered Muckamuck to pay SORWUC $10,000 in damages for its anti-union conduct. It was a hollow victory. The owners were long gone to the United States, and the award fell far short of the union's estimated financial hit. As a SORWUC organizer observed acidly, "We would rather not collect $100,000 than not collect $10,000."

down and proceeded to pull mounds of paper out of their briefcases. This went on for about five minutes before the meeting could begin." All five chartered banks used similar tactics: stall, agree to almost nothing, exhaust employee negotiators who were still working full-time and demonstrate to non-union employees there was no advantage to joining a union.

Beyond these strategies, there was also a wage freeze. While employees at non-union branches received pay raises of 5 percent, those at union branches had their wages frozen until they secured a contract. The impact was devastating. Organizing ground to a halt. Membership dwindled to a third of its former level. "Bank workers obviously felt that a wage increase in hand was worth more than [possible] improvements that unionization promised," wrote Elizabeth J. Shilton Lennon in a study of bank organizing. Workplace intimidation also sapped momentum, as the union became mired in fighting a slew of unfair labour practices at the CLRB. The banking sector accounted for more than a third of all complaints brought to the board in 1977 and 1978, prompting board chair Marc Lapointe to admonish banks for their seemingly deliberate campaign "to discourage employees from exercising their rights under the [Labour] Code."

SORWUC struggled forward, but the writing was on the wall. Bereft of funds, turned down by the Canadian Labour Congress in its request for assistance, stymied by the banks' refusal to negotiate any kind of decent agreement, hampered by the smallness of individual branches, the union was running on empty. Unwilling to sign contracts containing conditions no better than those already in effect at non-union branches, and believing there was no way to win a strike against the billionaire banks, SORWUC threw in the towel. At an emotional meeting in late July 1978, members voted to take the unprecedented step of withdrawing all twenty-four of its bank certifications in BC. The banks had won. Decades later, Jackie Ainsworth remembered the acute anguish of the decision. "It was horrible. We kept going round and round," she said. Ainsworth stayed in banking and worked her way up to become a vice-president at US Bank in Seattle. "But we knew we just couldn't bargain a good contract. It broke our hearts."

There were several postscripts to the union's banking saga. After SORWUC's breakthrough, the CLC rushed to form its own bank workers' union. The Union of Bank Employees acquired a number of certifications across the country. Unlike SORWUC, the CLC union opted to sign status quo agreements when they could get them, providing wages and conditions similar to those of non-union employees but with an actual contract and union security in place. Over time however, despite the CLC's clout and finances, most of their branches decertified as members questioned paying union dues for little benefit.

Yet the threat of unionization changed conditions for all bank workers. When SORWUC threatened to take the banks to small claims court over forcing employees to personally balance shortfalls, the practice ended. SORWUC also fought successfully against the banks' use of lie detector tests. Best of all, when federal wage controls ended, bank workers received healthy pay raises. They also got a dental plan, regular coffee breaks, daily payment for overtime and improved vacations and job postings. (Once worries over unionization eased, however, banks went back to some of their old ways. In 2016, a class-action lawsuit led to a court-approved settlement awarding $20.6 million to sixteen hundred Scotiabank employees for years of unpaid overtime.)

Brief though it was, SORWUC's success among unorganized bank workers, considered just about the toughest of union nuts to crack, was a singular chapter in the long fight of women workers to achieve respect and decent compensation from their employers. The idealism and grassroots lure of SORWUC, for all its shortcomings and ultimate failure, attracted bank workers to its fold in a way no

KATE BRAID, CARPENTER

In 1977, Kate Braid was thirty years old, living happily on a Gulf Island. Becoming a pioneer for her gender in the building trades was the last thing she expected. But through a combination of circumstances, fuelled by bar talk, she applied for a labourer's job at a new school being built and was hired. To her surprise, she became hooked, loving the physical work and the permanence of construction. After three tough weeks on the job, she wrote, "My knees ache when I walk, my shoulders are twisted cables and I am serenely happy." Braving ostracism, resentful work partners, constant scrutiny for mistakes and verbal hazing, she worked her way up the trades ladder. Thankfully, there were supportive and helpful workmates too, and she was taken on as the first woman apprentice with Local 452 of the United Brotherhood of Carpenters and Joiners.

Once Braid became part of a union, things changed. "Sister," a veteran dispatcher told her, "in this union, if you have any trouble, we're all behind you." Her first union pay cheque was notably higher. Braid mused, "I really feel I'm worth the huge amount of money I've just been given—like all the men around me." She enjoyed calling herself "a sister in the Brotherhood" and was particularly proud of a sign posted at one site: CAUTION: MEN AND WOMEN WORKING ABOVE. Yet the wear of regularly being the only woman on the job led Braid to a support organization called Women in Trades. "We went round the table, with these women saying, 'I'm a carpenter. I'm a welder. I'm an electronics technician.' It was heart-stopping."

By writing about her experiences as a "journeyman" carpenter, Kate Braid shone a light on the ups and downs of life as a woman in the building trades. *Dan Scott photo,* Vancouver Sun.

Despite the pioneering of Braid, who left construction to write, and other tradeswomen, the percentage of women in construction has stalled, at about 4 percent of the workforce. Although electrician Lisa Langevin's local is relatively proactive on the matter, too many problems remain on male-dominated worksites, Langevin told interviewer Jan Nichol. "Women love the work, but they are not staying. We need to change the culture." Anna Lary, an electrical trades instructor at the BC Institute of Technology, agreed. "It's just not set up for women," Lary said in an interview. "When you consider how much money you can make, it's telling that their participation is very static." With government and union support, the industry has recently renewed efforts to bring more women into construction.

other union managed, although unions such as the BCGEU and the United Steelworkers have made inroads in the province's many credit unions. (SORWUC continued as a one-of-a-kind feminist union but never with anything near the impact it had had on the banks. Its last bargaining unit, representing fifty-seven home-care workers, merged with Local 1518 of the United Food and Commercial Workers in 1987.)

SORWUC's bank endeavour was not the first advance by an overtly feminist union. Two years earlier, the brand new Association of University and College Employees (AUCE), formed by some of the same people who went on to prominence with SORWUC, won a thumping certification vote to represent twelve hundred underpaid, underappreciated and previously unorganized library and clerical workers at the University of British

Unions at work. Women shoreworkers show their support for the next stage in contract negotiations at the Canadian Fish Company plant on the Vancouver waterfront in the early 1980s. *Geoff Meggs photo, Fisherman Publishing Society, SFU Special Collections, MSC179–31632.*

Columbia. The core of the union's message was feminism: that women workers deserved to be treated and paid equally. AUCE carried that message to the bargaining table.

The result was a pioneering collective agreement that provided an across-the-board wage increase of $225 a month over eighteen months, amounting to an average pay hike of 54 percent. There were also clauses proscribing dress codes and making coffee for the boss, plus a landmark commitment to top up unemployment benefits received by women on maternity leave, so they would suffer no loss of income. This boon to working women was a BC first and soon a part of other contracts covering large numbers of women members. After this triumph, the union became a driving force on the province's campuses, as support staff at other post-secondary institutions, including a large bargaining unit at Simon Fraser University, rallied to join.

Exploited for years, women were simply no longer willing to take it anymore. This hardening attitude, reflective of the changing times, paved the way for the ultimate goal: equal pay for work of equal value, or pay equity. That would eventually be won

by larger unions such as the BCGEU, CUPE and health-care unions within the house of labour. Membership-driven unions like AUCE were absorbed over time into more established unions, offering greater security and financial support. Although AUCE disappeared, it left behind a trailblazing legacy for the victories to come.

Women were changing the labour movement. Between 1965 and 1981 the number of women in trade unions, particularly in the public sector, more than tripled. New issues emerged at the bargaining table: decently paid maternity leave, family and sick leave, and of course, pay equity.

Male trade unionists sometimes had to be educated on the changing landscape. After winning collective bargaining rights, the BCGEU launched a campaign to eliminate sexism both on the job and within its own union. Alice West, the wartime plywood plant worker, worked her way up to national director for BC in the Public Service Alliance of Canada (PSAC) representing federal civil servants, only to find she was not taken seriously by male union leaders. "It took a while to get 'the suits,' as I call them, to listen to us," West recalled. "When women began speaking up, they weren't used to it." She and other PSAC women negotiators took on the issue of paid maternity leave. When they finally achieved it they were thrilled, only to be subjected to a backlash from many PSAC men and some older women who resented a benefit they couldn't use. The historic breakthrough turned bittersweet, said West. "We hadn't done a good enough job explaining the issue to our members."

In 1973, women shore workers in the fishing industry finally won parity with male plant workers after years of wage discrimination, boosting their rates by 35 to 75 percent. About the same time, the Hospital Employees' Union launched its long, ultimately successful campaign for pay equity in the province's hospitals. There was no going back.

NEW TACTICS AND WORKPLACE TRAGEDIES 17

M UCH TO BILL BENNETT'S SURPRISE, Social Credit almost lost the 1979 election. A rewarming of voters toward Barrett and the NDP and a lacklustre campaign left the Socreds with only a narrow, five-seat majority. Bennett cleaned house, turfing party veterans in favour of young, smart, talented political operatives, many from Premier Bill Davis's "Big Blue Machine" in Ontario. They brought with them a neo-conservative gospel of reduced government and a free market unrestricted by such inconveniences as unions. The years that followed would be defined by almost constant warfare between a strong-willed Bennett and an equally resolute trade union movement, culminating in the most heartfelt and concerted protest movement in the province's history.

Decades later, the uprising known as Operation Solidarity remains as a distinctly astounding event that brought hundreds of thousands of British Columbians into the streets in a never-to-be-forgotten crusade for social justice and basic union rights. On the other side, the war was fought under the all-encompassing umbrella of "restraint," Bennett's term for everything his government did to combat the province's worst economic downturn since the Great Depression. But much of what was unleashed had more to do with ideological conviction than any prescription for the economy.

Fittingly, the 1980s kicked off with an inspiring struggle against an employer whose aggressive anti-union approach unsettled even the Employers' Council. The US-owned BC Telephone Company had put the Telecommunications Workers Union (TWU) through a difficult three-month lockout in 1977–78. The union entered the next round of talks in 1980 determined to pressure the company without triggering another lockout. The head-butting began after BC Tel rejected proposals by conciliation commissioner Ed Peck as too generous and too restrictive for its workplace authority. A one-time company negotiator himself with the towboat industry, Peck noted that BC Tel had "an exaggerated notion of management rights." When TWU members voted 81 percent to accept Peck's proposals, the die was cast.

The union launched its action plan on September 22, 1980. Five hundred and thirty craft employees—who repaired business switchboards, did wiring work on new buildings and installed new telephone systems—refused all work but emergency repairs. The TWU aimed to cut off these money-making areas while keeping most members on the job. Idled craft workers spent their time playing parking-lot volleyball, endless games of Monopoly, cards, chess and checkers. Those remaining at work contributed $13 a week to provide them with 70 percent of their regular salaries.

As unfilled orders piled up, BC Tel began dispatching supervisors to do the work. Mobile pickets tailed the supervisors wherever they went. Management drivers ran amber lights, dashed the wrong way up one-way streets, dodged in and out of traffic, but were rarely able to shake the tenacious picket squads. As in the past, members of the building trades walked out whenever TWU picketers showed up at a construction site.

In December the company began to squeeze the union. A thousand employees were temporarily sent home for wearing buttons proclaiming the union's desire for a "Crown Corporation Now." Cars bearing the same message on bumper stickers were banned from company parking lots. Early in 1981, BC Tel started suspending workers for "low productivity." At the end of January, more than a thousand employees were on permanent suspension. TWU strategists knew something bold was needed to head off another lockout. What if, someone suggested, workers simply refused to leave in the event of a lockout and took over operation of the phone company?

The spark was lit on Vancouver Island. On February 3, twenty-one maintenance workers in Nanaimo were suspended for "going slow." Employees gathered in the main lunchroom and, just like that, they began to occupy the building. Workers took control of the switching equipment and switchboards. Shop stewards drew up round-the-clock shift schedules. During the evening, replacements arrived with sleeping bags and provisions. A banner hanging from the company's microwave tower declared, UNDER NEW MANAGEMENT. "We're just your common switchmen," suspended employee Alf McGuire told reporters. "When ordinary people get desperate enough to take over a building, things are getting pretty desperate." With no supervisors, the mood was jubilant.

On the morning of February 5 in the supply depot at BC Tel's high-rise "boot" in Burnaby, shop steward Lila Wing was told to leave and change her anti-company T-shirt before returning to work. When Wing asked the union for direction, the TWU called on workers to take over the building. Similar instructions were issued to employees at fourteen additional company exchanges throughout the province. By the time the clock struck twelve, the deed was done. TWU president Bill Clark told the public that union members would be staying at their posts, providing basic telephone service twenty-four hours a day.

Switchboard operators were soon answering information calls with "TWU directory assistance" or "BC Tel, under workers' control." There was a new feeling of co-operation and solidarity among union members, who mingled in areas they had never visited before, learning and appreciating what their co-workers did. The media, police and company managers were invited to tour the occupied facilities to observe the lack of damage to equipment. With its incessant rate increases, seen by many as gouging, and its rejection of the Peck report, BC Tel had few admirers. The union's unlikely seizure of BC Tel premises captured the imagination of the public. While BC Tel railed about "anarchy," papers like the *Daily Times* in Nanaimo saluted union members for "pulling off a diplomatic coup."

The situation energized the BC Federation of Labour and its steely president Jim Kinnaird. A former head of the BC building trades who also spent time as deputy labour minister under the NDP, the forty-eight-year-old Kinnaird had taken over the Fed from Len Guy in 1978 and managed to soothe its divisions. Normally soft-spoken and low-key, he could be hard as nails when riled. Noting other ongoing labour disputes in the province, Kinnaird accused BC employers of thwarting labour's legitimate aspirations with injunctions, drawn-out wrangles at the LRB and inflexibility at the bargaining table. In a fiery speech at a public rally in support of the telephone workers, Kinnaird declared "industrial relations war" on the employers of British Columbia. Evoking Tom Joad's spellbinding farewell vow of commitment to his mother in *The Grapes of Wrath*, Kinnaird told the crowd that wherever workers were on the line, the BC Federation of Labour would be there, and wherever workers were punished for taking a stand, the BC Federation of Labour would be there. "Tonight I am telling you, we are going back, back to the old, bare-knuckled ways of fighting labour disputes," declared Kinnaird in his distinctive Scottish accent. "The gloves are off." He announced a series of regional general strikes to begin within a week.

Police made no move to end the occupation. They waited for the courts to deliver their verdict. That came on day five. The BC Supreme Court found the TWU guilty of criminal contempt of court for ignoring an injunction against occupying BC Tel property, fining the union an indeterminate amount to be increased each day the occupation continued. The prospect of losing all its assets left the union with little choice. The executive ordered its members onto the streets to begin a full-scale strike.

The last building to empty was the

The street and parking garage opposite BC Tel's main building in downtown Vancouver are packed with cheering union supporters as members of the Telecommunications Workers Union end their five-day occupation of the premises and launch an all-out strike in mid-February 1981. Wearing a picket sign, TWU president Bill Clark applauds their exit. *Sean Griffin photo, Image* MSC160-589-15A, *Pacific Tribune Photo Collection, Simon Fraser University Library.*

company's twelve-storey "nerve centre" in downtown Vancouver. At noon the next day, hundreds of workers poured from the building in a lengthy, spirited procession led by a union bagpiper. They were joined by hordes of noon-hour construction workers and other supporters who filled the street and crowded all four levels of a parking garage overlooking the building. Speeches of support were delivered by Jim Kinnaird and Jack Munro, who ended the rally with the worst rendition of "Solidarity Forever" ever heard at a union gathering. "I've got to admit, I'm the worst singer in the goddamn crowd," laughed Munro. More seriously, Bill Clark told TWU members to report to their picket captains. "Let's get to it."

Although the first workers' occupation of its kind in BC was over, morale among the strikers was through the roof. The federal government and even other employers began to fret about BC Tel's attitude. Observing that the company was "perhaps not as sensitive to the situation in British Columbia as might be desired," federal labour minister Gerald Regan sent in troubleshooter Bill Kelly. Over the years, the veteran red-haired mediator had helped resolve some of the country's most difficult labour disputes. He had seen just about everything. Nothing prepared him for BC Tel. In a move that the *Province* newspaper said could come "only from someone dwelling in Never-Never-Land," the company insisted it could not improve its wage offer without yet another rate increase from the CRTC. "That's a new experience in any mediation I've been involved in," Kelly said. He returned to Ottawa.

Private pressure from a worried employer community and a wave of negative public opinion finally forced BC Tel back to negotiations. On March 2, 1981, the parties reached a tentative deal, embracing Ed Peck's wage package of long ago, plus more accumulated time off and a compromise on jurisdiction and scheduling. But that did not end the strike. BC Tel refused to take back twenty-four workers fired during the strike. The union would not return without them. The one-day regional strikes vowed by Jim Kinnaird were back on. Nanaimo, scene of the first TWU occupation, was chosen for walk-out number one.

On March 6, a makeshift sign posted at the entrance to the Vancouver Island city announced in large letters, NANAIMO

CLOSED. It was. Thousands of private- and public-sector union members took the day off. PPWC members at the large Harmac pulp mill put aside their differences with Fed affiliates to walk out too. "We are with the Telecommunications Union 100 percent," said Harmac local president Bill Bryant. From dawn to midnight, almost every union work site in the area was shut tight as a drum: ferries, supermarkets, liquor stores, government offices, the post office, construction sites, buses, sawmills, the docks. It was a prime example of union solidarity. The next strike, Kinnaird said, would take place in the Kootenays, halting production at the giant Cominco smelter, a number of mines and a wealth of sawmills.

BC employers became increasingly nervous that this union muscle-flexing would spill over into their own negotiations. In private, they increased heat on the telephone company to settle the dispute once and for all. The upshot was an agreement to submit the twenty-four firings to Prince George arbitrator Allan Hope for a quick decision before a return to work on March 23. Fifteen months after their old contract had expired, after a rousing six-week strike, the TWU's ten thousand members voted to ratify their new agreement.

They returned to work in triumph, having wrestled the most obstinate employer in the province to the ground. There was one further bonus. Arbitrator Hope rescinded the firings of all twenty-four employees. Stunned, the company appealed to the BC Supreme Court, which overturned Hope's decision. But by then BC Tel no longer had the will to evoke more bitterness. The fired employees stayed at work.

There was no such victory in the field of health and safety. The tough sledding of the latter 1970s continued into the 1980s. The labour movement was in perpetual conflict with a Workers' Compensation Board that was underfunded, poorly run and tilted toward employers. Workers continued to be maimed, injured and killed on the job in distressing numbers, guilty of nothing more than going to work. There was little publicity for most of those who perished, their deaths noted only by grieving families and mourning workmates.

But what happened January 7, 1981, in downtown Vancouver was different. It would continue to resonate for decades after three journeymen carpenters and one apprentice ventured that sunny afternoon onto the outer edge of a construction work platform known as a fly form on the thirty-sixth and final floor of Bentall Tower IV. The building was close to completion as the highest of a multi-tower development on Burrard Street. Without warning, the fly form toppled over the edge, hurling the four men to gruesome deaths on the concrete plaza far below. "I heard a noise. I turned around and the panel was gone," said co-worker Dieter Goeldner.

Killed were Brian Stevenson, twenty-one; Donald Davis, thirty-four; Yrjo Mitrunen, forty-six; and Gunther Couvreux, forty-nine. Their deaths shook everyone in the construction industry and beyond. In an emotional statement at the coroner's inquest, read for her after she broke down in sobs, widow Carol Davis said that her husband had walked out onto the platform "convinced in his own mind, absolutely, that he was safe."

BC Federation of Labour president Jim Kinnaird, a unifying leader whose low-key, public demeanour belied an inner toughness, presides over the last day of the Fed convention, Dec. 4, 1981. Kinnaird's sudden death in early 1983 at the age of fifty, after barely four years in the job, rocked the labour movement.
Sean Griffin photo, Image MSC160-653-04A, Pacific Tribune Photo Collection, Simon Fraser University Library.

BC and Yukon Building Trades president Roy Gautier presides over a sombre memorial in downtown Vancouver on Jan. 12, 1981, commemorating four construction workers who plunged to their deaths five days earlier from the thirty–sixth floor of Bentall Tower IV in a terrible workplace accident.
Pacific Tribune Photo Collection, Simon Fraser University Library.

The inquest was thorough. After eight days of intense testimony from workers, contractor representatives, independent experts and relatives of the dead men, the culprit was clear. The fatal fly form used in the floor-by-floor pouring of concrete had been "grossly under-designed" by its supplier, Anthes Equipment Supply of Toronto. Dominion Construction was also faulted for paying insufficient attention to the fly-form drawings and its assemblage. And the WCB was singled out for irregular inspection of the site and a failure to enforce existing industrial health and safety regulations.

Jury members worked past midnight to craft a series of recommendations to ensure such a tragedy would not happen again. They were undoubtedly affected by words at the inquest earlier that day from Kit White, mother of Gunther Couvreux. "What a terrible way for five women to become friends," said White, referring to the sad bond formed by survivors of the victims. "Four men are dead. Four children ages six to thirteen are fatherless. Who cares? Who will look after them? ... Life seems cheap in the construc-

tion industry. How many more will die before changes are made?" Her five-minute statement left many of those present sniffling and blinking back tears. An official termed it one of the most moving scenes he had witnessed in twenty years of attending inquests.

In addition to tightening the design, construction and professional scrutiny of construction fly forms, the jury demanded more on-site inspections by the Workers' Compensation Board, clearer written regulations, increased on-the-job safety education and diligent compliance with safety standards. Finally, the jury—two carpenters, two engineers and a construction labourer—called on labour minister Jack Heinrich to strike a comprehensive inquiry into all aspects of safety in the BC construction industry.

A month later Heinrich appointed the Construction Industry Safety Inquiry, the first in-depth look at construction safety practices in years. With a panel of union, company and engineering representatives, the inquiry spent a year touring the province, holding public meetings, visiting construction sites and determining what needed to be done. By December, a special group had prepared a meticulous list of regulatory changes to address the urgent matter of fly-form safety. The most advanced in North America, they were quickly put in place. There has not been a fly-form fatality since.

The final report contained sixty recommendations to address carnage in the construction industry. The panel found a direct link between fewer WCB inspections and a higher accident rate. After initial resistance, the WCB accepted the need to hire more construction inspectors and visit all sites at least once a month. Another offshoot of the report was the Construction Safety Advisory Council, a permanent, multipartite body to oversee workplace safety in the industry. Small consolation as it may have been to their surviving families, the four workers did not die in vain. Improved practices live on after them. Each year on the anniversary of their deaths, a memorial gathering takes place at a small pocket park in the shadow of Bentall Tower IV to remember them and renew the commitment to safety on the job.

Not that far from the Bentall Tower and other gleaming office towers, away from the view of most Lower Mainlanders, conditions akin to the Third World prevailed on many farms in the Fraser Valley. Thousands of mostly South Asian immigrants toiled long hours in the summer heat, under the heel of labour contractors who skimmed their low wages and farm owners who relegated them to abysmal living quarters. Young immigrant Raj Chouhan was shocked by what he found when he sought work on a few farms. "There was no running water, no toilets, absolutely no facilities," Chouhan told a *Burnaby Now* reporter years later. Employees often lived in converted barns, six to a cubicle, their kids among them. "I was expecting, in a country like Canada, there would be something better than that," said Chouhan. When he asked questions, he was fired, and the young immigrant had a cause.

Stretching into the 1980s, along with Sarwan Boal, Judy Cavanaugh, Charan Gill and

the IWA's Harinder Mahil, aided by scores of volunteers and supporters, Chouhan led a valiant effort to organize Fraser Valley farm workers, publicize their plight and secure decent working conditions. Against the farm workers were an indifferent Social Credit government that purposely excluded them from regulations and labour standards covering other BC workers, a recalcitrant WCB, intimidation and violence. Yet they persevered, winning certifications and shining a spotlight on the dark corner where farm workers had been shunted by government and an unaware public.

Most farm workers spoke no English. Two-thirds were women. New to Canada, they were fearful of their fate if they complained. But privately, many detailed their grim situation to Chouhan and others in the community. On February 28, 1979, a small group gathered in a room at the New Westminster library to form the Farm Workers Organizing Committee (FWOC). It did not take long to have an impact. That summer, Mukhtiar Growers was beset by picket lines and walkouts until the owner forked over $80,000 he owed in back wages. On another occasion, a three-mile organizing march by more than a hundred FWOC supporters along farm-lined Huntington Road in Abbotsford drew farm workers out of the fields to join them. "Our purpose is to show the farmers and contractors that we will not be intimidated," Chouhan declared at a wind-up rally in front of their ramshackle living quarters.

On April 6, 1980, to the rousing cry of "*Zindabad!*" (long live!), the FWOC upgraded itself into a union. Despite strong pledges of financial support from BC unions and the Canadian Labour Congress, organizing proved daunting. Ten days after formation of the Canadian Farmworkers' Union (CFU), bat-wielding thugs attacked the home of vice-president Jawala Singh Grewal, smashing windows and trashing his pickup truck. On his way home from a banquet celebrating the union's first certification at Jensen Mushroom Farm in July, Sarwan Boal was savagely

Canadian Farmworkers' Union executive member Pritam Kaur and other farm workers protest the Social Credit government's reneging on its commitment to include farm workers in provincial health and safety regulation, April 1983.

Craig Berggold photo.

beaten. It would take two years and a long, difficult strike before the CFU was able to win a first contract at Jensen's Langley farm.

In the meantime, tragedy swept the growing fields. Sukhdeep Madhar, a seven-month-old baby, drowned when she rolled off a small bunkbed into a large bucket of drinking water in the converted horse stall used to accommodate her family. The farm owner, whose mansion, Cadillac, Mercedes-Benz and tennis courts were close by, had provided no running water. Barely a week later, three young boys, left to play by themselves while their parents picked berries, drowned in a nearby abandoned gravel pit. The deaths shocked British Columbians. Decrying the "horror" of living conditions on the farm, a coroner's inquest into the infant death called for immediate inspections of all agricultural accommodation in the province. For the families of the three drowned boys, the CFU helped win $30,000 in damages from the gravel-pit owner.

The union pressed forward with demonstrations, public meetings and well-researched briefs, backed by a supportive media and public. Under pressure, the government announced WCB coverage would be extended to agricultural workers effective April 4, 1983, only to renege on its commitment just before that spring's election campaign. Raj Chouhan lambasted the turnabout as Social Credit's "most dishonest betrayal."

Then there was another death. With no comprehensive regulations or mandatory training in place, nineteen-year-old farm worker Jarnail Singh Deol died of pesticide poisoning. "Jarnail's death stands as a monument to government inaction," raged the usually even-tempered Chouhan. "To those who demand patience, to those who are tired of our voices shouting for equality, we say, 'No more deaths! No more watching our young people die!'" Finding Deol's death "a preventable homicide," an inquest jury recommended effective pesticide regulations and strict enforcement to prevent similar fatalities in the fields. The WCB began the process, but once again failed to follow through. Farm workers would have to wait until 1993 before they were brought under the same health and safety umbrella as other BC workers.

On the organizing front, inspired by the example of California's brave organizer Cesar Chavez, who came up several times to lend his voice to the struggle, the CFU fought hard to bring farm workers the protection of a union contract. Bell Farms in Richmond was one of the few growers to accept the union. Covering ten full-time and thirty seasonal employees, the CFU contract at Bell Farms prescribed a forty-hour week, benefits and improved wages. A union hiring hall replaced the use of labour contractors.

Most growers fought the union every step of the way, mounting costly legal challenges, discriminating against union supporters, and intimidating workers with threats and firings. A gruelling strike at Jensen Mushrooms ended with good raises, benefits and April 6 as a holiday for Farmworkers' Day. But the farm rehired few of the original workers. Four months later, the union lost a close vote to decertify. A long strike against Country

Farms Natural Foods, which included picketing of the owner's popular Naam vegetarian restaurant in Vancouver, was never resolved.

Organizing drives at Choi Mushrooms and Hoss Farm typified the uphill battle. In both cases, workers who joined the union were fired. To get their reinstatement and back wages, the union had to fight long and hard at the labour board and in the courts. It took nearly four years and a Supreme Court order to force Choi's single-minded owner to pay out the $35,000 he owed his illegally fired workers.

At Hoss Farm, the fired women began picketing the next day. "I feel good about the picket line, because we are fighting," said Jasweer Kaur Brar. But it took an all-out campaign by church groups, social organizations and the labour movement, including a "hot" declaration against Money's Mushrooms, which used Hoss as a supplier, before the owner agreed to take back seven of the eleven fired women. Although certified at each location, the union was unable to reach a collective agreement at either farm.

The exhausting slog needed for the most minimal advances eventually wore down the union's leaders, dogged by burnout and years of meagre incomes. They left to take other jobs, and the Canadian Farmworkers' Union began to fade. Yet there was a strong sense its success could not be measured solely in certifications. The CFU was as much a social movement as a traditional trade union. With the help of the BCTF and Frontier College, the union had launched a successful "ESL Crusade" to teach Punjabi-speaking farm workers basic English. Instructional videos were pro-

duced on the safe use of pesticides and other health and safety practices. The union's high-profile campaign on behalf of immigrants at the bottom of the wage scale and victims of abominable working conditions represented a social activism that began to hammer cracks in the Social Credit dynasty through the rest of the 1980s.

Sakhdarshanpar Machi, Jasbir Kaur Sagoo and Jasweer Kaur Brar (left to right) picket the lonely country road leading to the Hoss mushroom farm in the Fraser Valley on May 29, 1984, the day after they were fired for joining the Canadian Farmworkers' Union. *Craig Berggold photo.*

18 OPERATION SOLIDARITY

CANADA'S LONG RUN OF POSTWAR ABUNDANCE came to an end in the early 1980s. The country found itself mired in the worst economic downturn since the Depression. The malaise was particularly hard on resource-dependent British Columbia. In 1982, the province's real GDP fell an improbable 6.1 percent, unemployment climbed significantly above the national average and galloping inflation was putting pressure on both government spending and unions trying to keep pace at a time when resource revenue had been cut in half. Far from downhearted, however, Bill Bennett and his advisers also saw the recession as an opportunity to slash the public sector and curb the power of their unions. On February 18, 1982, the premier announced the province's first public-sector wage-control program. It was the opening shot in what became a consuming crusade to force workers to accept what Bennett called "the new economic reality."

Wage limits under the Compensation Stabilization Program (CSP) were initially rather generous, reflecting an inflation rate of 12.9 percent and average settlements of 15 percent in the private sector. Affecting two hundred thousand public employees, annual wage increases were to be held between 8 and 14 percent. But labour was outraged by the interference in free collective bargaining. "To hell with him," burst out BC Fed president Jim Kinnaird, moments after Bennett's announcement. "We'll give him a confrontation on this one."

Ignoring Kinnaird's hawkish response, the government moved in short order to further restrict wage limits to public employers' "ability to pay"—whatever that meant. The program was to last two years. Former LRB vice-chair Ed Peck was appointed as "wage czar," with the power to roll back settlements not within the CSP's vague and shifting guidelines, dubbed "the Rubber Room" by some wags in the media.

The forty-thousand-member BC Government Employees' Union led off negotiations in the new environment. Coming off a three-year contract that had been surpassed by other agreements and eroded by inflation, the BCGEU was seeking major gains in a one-year deal. Under the slogan "Catch Up, Keep Up," the union demanded a 14 percent wage increase, two cost-of-living adjustments and a reduction in the ten thousand auxiliaries that allowed the government to avoid hiring full-time employees.

When talks went nowhere, a number of labour firsts soon followed. The largest strike vote in BC history, involving 488 polling stations in 192 communities and 86 Labour Relations Board monitors, produced an overwhelming 89.6 percent vote in favour of a strike. At a minute past midnight on August 6, BCGEU members hit the bricks. It was the union's first all-out strike. The government had offered 6.5 and 5 percent increases over two years, contingent on a 4 percent boost in productivity. When Bennett claimed rank-and-file members favoured the package, BCGEU general secretary John Fryer put it to a vote. The result was 93 percent "no."

In keeping with the strike's historic nature, Fryer employed some unusual manoeuvres that had veteran union observers shaking their heads. First, "as a show of good faith," the union went back to work on August 12 to facilitate a resumption of negotiations. When talks stalled once more, a second full-scale strike resumed August 31, only to end after twenty-four hours in favour of rotating strikes. Finally, on Jack Webster's widely watched TV show, pressed by Webster to justify BCGEU demands amid high unemployment and a stumbling economy, Fryer said the union would lower its demands if the money saved by the government went into job creation. The proposal was entirely Fryer's own, with no notice to a less-than-pleased bargaining committee.

But Fryer's off-the-cuff gambit sparked interest from the government. Contract talks resumed. The quirky TV proposal was quickly forgotten, and the two sides hammered out a new deal. The government stuck to its 6.5 and 5 percent wage offer but over fifteen months rather than two years, and fifteen hundred auxiliaries were given full-time status. Although short of union expectations, it was enough of a victory to whet the appetite for fiercer struggles ahead.

In the meantime, the modernized Social Credit machine had tested its new "high-tech" political machinery in a 1982 Kamloops by-election that all pundits had ceded to the NDP. Relying on sophisticated polling, phone banks, hundreds of volunteers and skillful presentation of Bill Bennett's unwavering restraint message, the party's efforts sent local Rube Band trumpeter Claude Richmond into the legislature. The same machine was oiled and primed for action when Bennett called a provincial election the next spring. The theme would be restraint: Bill Bennett staring down the recession, determined to cut spending and rein in the unions.

Yet early on, little went right for Bennett, while Dave Barrett was greeted with enthusiastic crowds wherever he went. With two weeks to go, the NDP seemed on a roll to victory. Then Barrett's blunder on a union issue turned the election around. The NDP leader promised, if elected, to scrap the government's wage-control program as quickly as possible rather than let it run its course. It was a huge political gaffe. Not only was the program popular with hard-hit British Columbians, ending it in the middle would be unfair to unions already affected. Barrett scrambled to clarify his position, but it was too late. A revived Bennett had his restraint message back on track. Social Credit cruised home with a satisfying majority.

No one could have guessed what was coming next. Sensing this term would be his last, Bennett prepared to unleash a full-frontal assault on unions and government itself. At a cabinet retreat, egged on by the right-wing Fraser Institute, the premier urged ministers to be bold in slashing government. When labour minister Bob McClelland tentatively gave voice to his long-held distaste for the Human Rights Commission, he was encouraged to go after it. Heartened by the response, ministers began happily hacking away at other elements of government they detested. Their efforts were unveiled to a stunned population on budget day, July 7, 1983.

There had been no sense of the storm to come during the traditional budget lockup for the media. Reporters trooped back to the legislature, their stories written in advance, waiting for finance minister Hugh Curtis to begin his budget address before sending them on their way. But once Curtis stopped speaking, all hell broke loose. One by one, ministers rose in the legislature to introduce a new bill. When they were finished, no less than twenty-six pieces of legislation had been put forward, representing a premeditated strike on all those elements of society the Socreds had never really liked: social justice, community activists, rights of the disadvantaged and above all, public employees and their unions.

The Human Rights Branch and the Human Rights Commission were axed, commissioners and staff fired on the spot and told to turn in their keys before the day was out. The rentalsman, established under the NDP to safeguard tenant rights, was abolished, along with rent controls. Landlords were given the right to evict tenants at will. Gone too were the Employment Standards Board, the Alcohol and Drug Commission, vehicle testing stations, the BC Harbours Board and legislative scrutiny over Crown corporations. The government also strengthened its hand in education, assuming power to oversee school district budgets and fire elected boards unwilling to co-operate.

The most jaw-dropping measures were aimed at public-sector unions. Wage controls were extended indefinitely. Bill 2, the **Public Sector Labour Relations Act**, pretty much gutted the BCGEU's contract of all employee rights beyond wages and benefits. But the *pièce de resistance* was Bill 3, the Public Sector Restraint Act. In blunt language

that provoked gasps of disbelief, the bill gave all public-sector employers in the province, including the government, the power to fire employees without cause. No province in Canada had mounted such a multi-pronged, single-day assault on so many existing rights—rights most British Columbians had taken for granted. Not a word of it had been mentioned during the election campaign, a tactic praised by none other than Milton Friedman, economic guru of neoliberalism, who loved what Bennett was doing.

The timing could not have been better. Dave Barrett had announced his intention to quit. The BC Federation had also lost its main man when Jim Kinnaird died suddenly of a heart attack in February. His replacement was Art Kube, the CLC's stolid regional education director, who had been on the job for only two months. Like everyone, Kube was caught off guard by the Social Credit onslaught. He issued a rote response and not much else. But that was not a sign of what lay ahead.

Within days, George Hewison of the UFAWU, head of the labour council's unemployment committee, called a meeting at the Fishermen's Hall. More than a hundred people showed up, spilling out of the meeting room. They agreed to hold a demonstration on Saturday, July 23. Community activists, horrified at what was happening to basic rights and social services in the province, were just as fast off the mark. The day after Hewison's meeting, hundreds came to a forum addressed by fired members of the Human Rights Commission. The next day, Women Against the Budget was formed, a broad-based umbrella organization of activist women that was a force throughout the next four months. Small gatherings, large gatherings, discussion groups, planning meetings and action caucuses seemed to be everywhere.

Getting up to speed, Kube announced that the Fed would be leading a major campaign to oppose the budget. Not even Art Kube knew just how "major" it would become. On

Friday, July 15, he convened a historic one-day convention of all labour organizations in British Columbia. For the first time, independent Canadian union delegates sat in the same hall as the Federation's international union affiliates, their animosities set aside for a common purpose. Teachers were there, nurses, university professors, even doctors, who had also been singled out by the budget. A ten-point action program emerged from the convention, plus an initial $1 million war chest and the Polish-born Kube's brilliant branding of the swelling protest as "Operation Solidarity," derived from the Solidarnosc union protests in Poland. With its distinctive red and white banner, Operation Solidarity was soon a household name and galvanizing force across BC.

The meeting at the large Operating Engineers Hall in Burnaby was the start of Art Kube's emergence from the shadows of union backrooms into the public spotlight. For the next four months, he became as well known as the premier, leading a mass movement that rallied hundreds of thousands of British Columbians, many of whom had never protested anything before. It was the cause of his life, and the heavyset former union fixer, who had survived a harrowing wartime childhood fleeing the Nazis through a bombed-out Germany before landing in Canada on a whim, rose to the occasion with a drive and commitment few could have foreseen.

The first major action under the Operation Solidarity banner took place in Kamloops at the sprawling Tranquille residential complex for people with developmental disabilities. On July 19, union rep Gary Steeves was called to a meeting by senior government officials in Vancouver and told Tranquille was going to close. All six hundred BCGEU members would be laid off with no regard for their contract rights. It was as if Bills 2 and 3 were already law. Steeves left the meeting so dumbfounded and lost in thought that he ran a stop sign and caused a minor accident. He quickly boarded a flight to Kamloops for a mass membership meeting at Tranquille that night. When workers heard about the pending closure, with no apparent plan for

Members of the BC Government Employees' Union are on duty to ensure bosses are kept away from their offices during the union's occupation of the Tranquille institution in Kamloops in July 1983. This was the first action under the auspices of Operation Solidarity, the anti–government protest movement that swept the province that summer and fall.
BCGEU.

the 325 residents or their own future, they eagerly embraced the idea of taking over the facility themselves.

Much in the manner of the stirring TWU occupation of BC Tel three years earlier, Tranquille employees evicted managers from their offices, changed the locks and put up signs reading, "Under New Management." At a special courtyard ceremony, they replaced the BC flag with a makeshift BCGEU/Tranquille standard fashioned from a pale blue bedsheet. The occupation lasted twenty-two days.

The general manager, holed up in an outbuilding with other bosses, dutifully signed off on expenses, including workers' salaries. When the creaking rooftop air conditioner in the cerebral palsy ward gave out in the baking summer heat, Steeves was able to persuade the manager to approve a $350,000 replacement. "That was the only time I was frankly nervous," said Steeves of the large purchase, "but we had to have something for the residents."

The occupation received wide coverage, but the BCGEU knew it could not last forever. After three weeks, the union agreed to return Tranquille to its overseers. In return, the layoff issue was shunted to negotiations about to begin in Vancouver and the union extracted a promise of no reprisals. On the pressing matter of the residents' future, the government gave a first-of-its-kind commitment to work with community care advocates to prepare an individual placement plan for each one. "That was unheard of," said Steeves, who camped out in a boardroom throughout the occupation. "We did stuff that had never been done before." The union flag came down on August 10. Government employees from all over the city attended a celebratory downtown rally, hailing retention of the workers' seniority and bumping rights. When Tranquille finally did close, many found government jobs elsewhere.

In Vancouver, Kube's request to delay the hastily called July 23 protest to ensure a better turnout was rebuffed. The march went ahead. More than twenty thousand boisterous demonstrators took to the streets on a beautiful, sunny afternoon, twice the number expected. Four days later, an estimated twenty-five thousand people amassed on the lawn of the legislature and surrounding streets for the largest-ever protest in Victoria. Many were government employees who had walked off their jobs to attend the ninety-minute rally. Also taking time off were hospital employees, bus drivers, municipal workers and at least one private-sector group—four hundred BC Tel employees. Local transit was shut for three hours. All liquor stores from Nanaimo south were closed. "This is bigger than the Queen," said an impressed police officer.

Among the sea of signs were many referring to BC as "Canada's Poland," where the communist government had crushed the labour movement. There were podium warnings of a long, intensive campaign against the twenty-six bills, industrial relations chaos and civil disobedience. That prospect was raised by CUPE president Grace Hartman. "We may end up in a position where we might have to resort to [it]," professed Hartman, the first woman to head a large national union, who at sixty-two had spent thirty days behind bars for defying a court injunction. "We cannot be afraid." Her pronouncement drew a roar of approval.

"Black Thursday" sparked a summer of protests, rallies, meetings and feverish community organizing, the likes of which had never been seen in BC. In Social Credit strongholds far from Vancouver, they marched—four thousand in Kamloops, four thousand in Kelowna, two thousand each in the dusty, spirited Cariboo communities of Williams Lake and Quesnel. Even Fort St. John and Dawson Creek, the heart of free-enterprise thinking in BC, held substantial protests, ignoring catcalls from locals in passing pickup trucks. "It took a lot of courage in that environment," said Steve Koerner, a representative of the Hospital Employees' Union. "But we had no choice but to fight the legislation. We had done nothing to deserve it." Dozens of brief wildcat strikes

On July 27, three weeks after Social Credit's all-out legislative assault against long-standing union rights and social programs, twenty-five thousand protesters, many of whom booked off work for the day, amassed in front of the BC legislature. Operation Solidarity leader Art Kube vowed to keep up the protests until all twenty-six bills were withdrawn. *Sean Griffin photo, Image* MSC160–865–28, *Pacific Tribune Photo Collection, Simon Fraser University Library.*

The massive Victoria protest was symptomatic of what was to come. The government's so-called restraint budget stripped away so many rights it united a vast sea of diverse groups into a united, angry protest movement. *Sean Griffin photo, Image* MSC160–866–17, *Pacific Tribune Photo Collection, Simon Fraser University Library.*

by BCGEU members also took place across the province as closures, cutbacks and government layoffs accumulated.

In the midst of it all, the otherwise unflinching Bill Bennett gave an inch. Perhaps he was shaken by a dramatic newspaper ad showing the black silhouette of a police officer complete with cap, gun and holster. In the middle of the silhouette were the words, "How will I investigate criminal allegations against politicians when I can be fired without cause? Think about Bill 3." The ad was paid for by the BC Federation of Police Officers. Responding to universal criticism over giving employers the right to fire anyone without cause, the government removed the problematic phrase from Bill 3, clarifying that the bill was to govern layoffs, not firings. This was scant comfort, however,

to the sixteen hundred BCGEU members who had already been singled out for dismissal the moment their contract expired on November 1. Under Bill 3, they would have no seniority or bumping rights.

The long, hot summer hit its peak on August 10 at Empire Stadium in Vancouver. Public-sector workers across the city booked off to attend the gigantic, festive gathering. Buses were corralled from wherever they could be scrounged to transport trade unionists to the site. Non-union members of the public and activists also streamed to the stadium to celebrate their solidarity and vent their rage against the government. Much of the city, including public transit and liquor stores, was shut for the afternoon. An estimated forty thousand people crammed every nook and cranny of the creaking old

Below left: Ahead of joining the general strike, CUPE members ordered up placards for their turn on the picket line.
Brian Kent photo,
Vancouver Sun.

Below right: The BC Federation of Police Officers placed this dramatic, hard–hitting ad in the *Vancouver Sun* shortly before the big Operation Solidarity rally at Empire Stadium, indicating how many boundaries opposition to Bill 3 had crossed.
Courtesy Rod Mickleburgh.

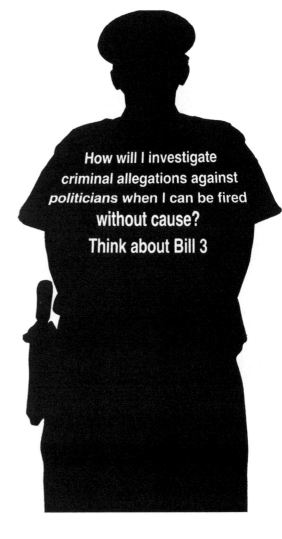

The wave of summer protests peaked on Aug. 10 as forty thousand activists and public–sector union members, who also left work to attend, packed Empire Stadium in Vancouver. When the firefighters' band entered the stadium, followed by other firefighters, uniformed bus drivers and outside municipal workers, there wasn't a dry eye in the house. But the tears were of joy.
Craig Berggold photo.

The infectious fighting spirit of the Operation Solidarity rally at Empire Stadium, on a beautiful August day, buoyed the whole movement in its determination to force the repeal of all twenty–six bills, which included the right to fire workers without cause, the right to evict tenants without notice and an end to the Human Rights Commission.
Dan Keeton photo, Image MSC160–869–17, *Pacific Tribune Photo Collection, Simon Fraser University Library.*

stadium and onto the field—far more than The Beatles had drawn in 1964.

Just when it appeared the stadium could not hold one more person, in marched several hundred uniformed firefighters, led by their rousing brass band, followed by hundreds of bus drivers, also in uniform, and a thousand CUPE outside workers. As the band played on, people were crying with joy and cheering their hearts out. Ovations reverberated through the stadium in great ascending waves as the procession wound its way around the infield track. For many, it was the emotional highlight of the entire

Operation Solidarity movement, a moment when anything seemed possible.

Much of the energy and momentum came from outside trade union ranks. A key element in Kube's strategy was to harness community and social justice advocates to the movement by concentrating on all twenty-six bills rather than just those affecting unions. Kube enlisted one of the fired human rights commissioners, Renate Shearer, as his main contact with those fighting against the budget's erosion of basic rights and social services. In mid-July, 450 activists had crowded into a Vancouver

meeting hall to form the Lower Mainland Budget Coalition, while the militant Women Against the Budget continued its aggressive organizing. No community of any size was without some form of anti-budget group. On August 3, Kube, Shearer and a few others drew together all the diverse strands for a large conference at the same Operating Engineers Hall where Operation Solidarity had been born.

What emerged was a separate, BC-wide organization called the Solidarity Coalition. Operation Solidarity was now the union arm of the protests, while the coalition, assisted by labour, carried the fight on social issues. Its three co-chairs were Kube, Shearer and Father Jim Roberts, a liberal theologian who taught religious studies at Langara College. The coalition received $20,000 a month from the labour movement, enough for staff and office space plus three full-time organizers: anti-poverty fighter Jean Swanson from the Hospital Employees' Union; Clay Perry, legislative director for the Canadian arm of the IWA; and BC Fed staffer Gerry Scott. The alliance between Operation Solidarity and the Solidarity Coalition represented an unprecedented partnership between trade unionists and community activists.

However, after the high of Empire Stadium, Operation Solidarity appeared to disappear from view. Information meetings, an advertising campaign and a province-wide petition drive that sucked up a lot of effort with little reward created a lull after all the fireworks. The government took heart during the letup, dismissing the protesters as disgruntled British Columbians refighting the last election. After weathering Operation Solidarity's summer-long barrage, Social Credit was ready to move ahead with a full-court press to ram its budget bills through the legislature. Beginning September 19, the government imposed a punishing agenda of twenty-four-hour sittings and closures to get its way. Tempers frayed during the Socreds' all-out offensive against legislative niceties. At one point, Dave Barrett was dragged from

222

A two–month lull followed Empire Stadium. Then, on Saturday, Oct. 15, with Social Credit ramming bills through the legislature, the biggest protest of all took place. More than sixty thousand people paraded through the streets of Vancouver, chanting "Socreds Out!" as they passed the Hotel Vancouver, where Social Credit's annual convention was taking place. A general strike was getting close.
Les Bazso photo, Vancouver Sun.

the legislature for resisting an order from rookie speaker John Parks to leave and was dumped, rump first, on the corridor's hard floor. Many of the bills were passed in the pre-dawn hours between 3 and 6 a.m.

By then, attention was beginning to shift for the first time to actual negotiations. Contract talks between the government and the BCGEU began October 3. Staring both sides in the face was midnight, October 31—Hallowe'en. That's when the union's master agreement expired, and pink slips previously handed to sixteen hundred government employees would take effect. Armed with an 87 percent strike vote, it was also the BCGEU's strike deadline. The union was adamant: there would be no new agreement without an end to Bills 2 and 3.

As talks continued, plans were underway for Operation Solidarity's biggest gamble. More than a month after anti-government dissent had soared to rare heights, leaders seemed uncertain of their next move. Frustrated, members of the Solidarity Coalition managed to convince a reluctant Kube and other Solidarity leaders to jointly sponsor a public protest in the streets of Vancouver

on October 15. That would coincide with the Socreds' annual convention at the Hotel Vancouver. Privately, Kube worried the protest might be a flop, which would be fatal to the movement's credibility. Three months after Social Credit's July budget bombshell, how much fight remained?

He need not have worried. In yet another example of the depth of people's commitment, a mind-boggling sixty thousand people wound their way through downtown Vancouver, the largest anti-government protest in the history of a city that had seen so many over the years. As they wound in unending waves past the Hotel Vancouver, where Social Credit delegates and an occasional cabinet minister ventured out from the lobby to take in the view, the marchers chanted, "Socreds Out! Socreds Out!" The size of the turnout changed the game. Clearly, Operation Solidarity and the Solidarity Coalition were still in business. High-level strategy sessions to take the struggle to another level were soon in motion. There were simply too many signs reading "Prepare the General Strike" to be ignored. Operation Solidarity's steering committee began

Social and community groups were represented in Operation Solidarity by a disparate, separate organization called the Solidarity Coalition. Five days after the Oct. 15 protest, coalition leaders (left to right) Father Jim Roberts, Art Kube and Renate Shearer vowed social issues would not be forgotten as labour prepared to go to the wall over the government's anti–union legislation.
Sean Griffin photo, Image MSC160–896–4A, *Pacific Tribune Photo Collection, Simon Fraser University Library.*

holding daily breakfast meetings at the Villa Hotel in Burnaby.

Three days after the march, BCGEU contract talks broke down in acrimony. Sensing the situation was becoming a tad too unpredictable, Premier Bennett took free time on BCTV to try to calm things down. Just six days after his defiant declaration to cheering Social Credit delegates that "we will never turn back," Bennett announced an adjournment of debate in the house "to let tempers cool off." He suggested the pending layoffs might be delayed if there were progress at the bargaining table. Negotiated exemptions from odious sections of Bill 3 might be possible. The new message from the normally combative premier was now consultation over confrontation. Sort of. "You can't picket your way to prosperity," he admonished the forces arrayed against his government.

Negotiations resumed the next day at the Labour Relations Board in Vancouver. Bennett's deputy minister Norman Spector joined the talks. It was a sign the government was playing for keeps, but also a sign that Bennett wanted a deal. Just days before the union's strike deadline, former Mine, Mill and Smelter Workers' Union representative Vince Ready took up the challenge to act as mediator. Still, not much moved.

Meanwhile, several hundred Solidar-

ity Coalition delegates had held their first province-wide conference. They passed a resolution calling for job action "up to and including a general strike" to force the government to withdraw all twenty-six bills. This irritated many private-sector union leaders, notably Jack Munro of the IWA, who felt non-trade unionists had no business demanding their members take on the struggle. But the militant mood at the gathering was infectious, buoyed no doubt by the Vancouver protest a week earlier. When Kube reminded delegates that any action by the labour movement would be primarily aimed at Bills 2 and 3, not the entire package of Social Credit legislation, some responded with anger.

With a BCGEU strike looking increasingly likely, Operation Solidarity stepped into the breach. After weeks of closed-door deliberations and countless revisions as the timetable for affected unions bounced around, Kube revealed the organization's final "program of action" to support the BCGEU and the quest to kill Bills 2 and 3. Province-wide walkouts were at the heart of the action plan. They would be triggered November 8, if BCGEU members were still on strike. Rather than a big bang by all public-sector unions, Operation Solidarity opted for an escalating series of strikes.

The education sector, including thirty thousand teachers, would be the first group out. On November 10, unionized employees at the province's many Crown corporations would leave their jobs. Week two would be even more dramatic. On Monday, November 14, BC's ferry workers, municipal employees and other related groups were scheduled to walk out; and the day after that, all public transit in the Lower Mainland was due to be shut down. Finally, at the end of the week, the province's large public-health sector would be targeted, with hospital workers pouring off the job. By then, a total of two hundred thousand public employees in the province would be on the street, as close to an all-out general strike as BC had ever come. Private-sector unions pledged to join the fray

should any public-sector worker be punished for joining the protest strike.

What had begun in the early days of summer was nearing its climax in grim, rainy November. Mike Kramer, the BC Federation of Labour's blustery secretary-treasurer, publicly warned the price of poker would go up once the Operation Solidarity walkouts were launched. All twenty-six bills would be back on the table. The BCGEU rebuffed last-minute entreaties from Bill Bennett to put off its strike. Picket lines went up on the stroke of midnight, October 31. Spirits were high. After so much talk, there was a real strike at last, by the province's largest union.

Unions pinpointed by Operation Solidarity for job action had been holding their own strike votes. It was not always easy. Hesitant about leaving their jobs for uncertain goals, BC teachers voted just 59 percent in favour of a strike. The teachers' low vote undoubtedly caused a government sigh of relief. Privately,

Operation Solidarity leaders blanched too. If the teachers' November 8 walkout turned into a fiasco, with significant numbers going to work, it was difficult to see any future for labour's action program.

Operation Solidarity leaders desperately sought some sort of settlement that would avoid their pending date with destiny. As November 8 neared, Kube thought he had a deal. Private negotiations involving many of the main players had produced an agreement between the North Vancouver School Board and the BCTF's North Vancouver local that would exempt teachers from the draconian layoff provisions of Bill 3. The idea was to use it as a template for similar Bill 3 exemptions for all other public-sector bargaining units in the province.

It seemed incongruous that a single side-deal in North Vancouver would be enough to end the most concerted citizen resistance in the province's history. But Kube and other

At the stroke of twelve on Halloween night, forty thousand members of the BCGEU hit picket lines across BC to fight for a new contract and an end to the government bills attacking their union rights. For the first time since Social Credit's infamous July 7 budget, there was now sustained union job action.
BCGEU.

union leaders, with their focus on Bill 3 over all other bills, were convinced this strategy would fly. Instead, Bill Bennett the street fighter called Operation Solidarity's bluff. Sensing its eagerness to avoid a confrontation and taking sustenance from the teachers' low strike vote, the government scuttled the North Vancouver agreement. Bennett reasoned the movement would collapse on its own.

Crushed, an ashen Kube summoned reporters late on Monday afternoon, November 7. In a sombre voice he announced that "unfortunately" Operation Solidarity's strike agenda would begin as scheduled the next morning. There were no ringing words of defiance. At a meeting in New Westminster that evening, Kube broke down in tears. Emotionally and physically exhausted after 120 days of long hours and countless meetings, under almost unbearable pressure, the indomitable labour leader was spent. He was diagnosed with pneumonia and ordered to bed.

Everything hinged on the teachers' response. They had never had more than a one-day province-wide strike before. More than 40 percent of the BCTF membership had voted against it. The situation became even more problematic when the Vancouver School Board obtained a late injunction banning the BCTF's largest local from picketing, making it easier for reluctant teachers to report for work. "We're going to kick their ass," crowed school trustee (later prime minister) Kim Campbell.

But something remarkable happened. In the early hours of Tuesday morning, phones began ringing across the city, rousing Solidarity Coalition activists from their sleep. The word went out: "You're needed on the line at every public school in Vancouver." Before dawn, groups of mostly women activists huddled in the miserable, steady rain, ready to go. Hastily worded picket signs were handed out. When teachers and other school employees arrived that morning, they found their schools ringed with pickets. Almost no one crossed.

Similar support for the walkout reverberated at schools across BC. The teachers stayed out; they had delivered in a way few had foreseen. Thousands of other education workers, including college faculty, university clerical staff and public school maintenance employees were also off the job. On Thursday, the strike was joined by several thousand Crown corporation employees, including those at the Insurance Corporation of British Columbia (ICBC). Euphoria reigned. If the planned ferry shutdown took place on the Monday, followed by public transit workers on Tuesday and hospital employees at the end of the week, who knew what might happen?

It was crunch time, and all of Canada was watching. At the Labour Relations Board, tense and at times vitriolic negotiations to hammer out a new BCGEU contract had left everyone bleary-eyed and punch drunk, as mediator Vince Ready hounded the parties to get it done. The board's large reception area was packed with lights, cameras, microphones and scores of reporters thirsty for any scrap of news. Whenever someone emerged from behind closed doors, even if only for a bathroom break, the throngs followed like a large, twisting snake. At the same time, unbeknownst to all but a few, secret discussions were going on in the upper-floor office of board chair Stephen Kelleher. The government now accepted that something had to be done beyond settling with the BCGEU in order to satisfy Operation Solidarity and put a halt to its escalating job action.

With Kube sidelined, Operation Solidarity was represented by Mike Kramer and a worried Jack Munro, increasingly nervous that the union movement was headed over a cliff and angry that social activists were expecting their battles to be fought on the backs of unions. The government side was mostly Norman Spector, who shuttled back and forth between BCGEU talks and those with Munro and Kramer upstairs. From its original lofty demand that all twenty-six bills be withdrawn, by Friday Operation Solidarity appeared ready to accept a deal that included the killing of Bill 2, exemptions to Bill 3's layoff measures, a government commitment to keep salary savings from the teachers' walkout in the education system, and promises of consultation on the bills covering tenant and human rights. It was also agreed that once the government employees had an agreement, Jack Munro would head to Kelowna to meet Premier Bennett to confirm details of the package.

Down on the first floor with the BCGEU, momentum was building for a settlement. An experienced mediator, Ready could sniff when parties were ready to deal, and his well-worn practice was to keep them at the table until it was done. As the two bargaining committees went at each other for one last round-the-clock session, their large negotiating room reeked of stale pizza, too many cigarettes and too few showers. At last on Sunday afternoon, November 13, Spector and the BCGEU's Cliff Andstein wearily announced the two sides had reached a tentative agreement. The money wasn't much, but it was better than previous government offers. More importantly, the government agreed to let Bill 2 die on the order paper while providing an exemption to Bill 3 that ensured layoffs would proceed according to seniority and the right of laid-off employees to transfer to available jobs across the entire workforce. Firing without cause and without regard to seniority was dead and buried.

Munro swung into action. Taking the Fed's Gerry Scott with him, the imposing IWA leader boarded a government jet along with Spector and flew to Kelowna to meet Bill Bennett that evening in his living room. Given the previous understanding with Spector, Munro expected a relatively easy time of it. But things had changed. On Saturday, the *Vancouver Sun* disclosed the secret talks between Operation Solidarity and the government, along with details of a possible package to end the walkout. Bennett's phone began ringing. Some cabinet ministers and Social Credit caucus members were furious to learn the government was talking without their knowledge to people they considered rabble-rousers and lawbreakers. The calls reinforced Bennett's own instinct to give virtually nothing to Solidarity, still sensing they wanted out of the imminent escalation more than he did.

In the glare of TV lights, Bennett greeted Munro on the porch. For the next three hours, the province held its breath, unsure whether there would be peace on Monday morning or another major step toward a general strike. Behind the closed drapes of Bennett's living room, Munro found himself in a tough position. There were a few nods on consultation and an apparent willingness to keep strike savings in the education system, but Bennett would agree to put nothing in writing. Using the upstairs phone in the Bennetts' bedroom, staring at the premier's dressing gown and slippers in the closet, Munro consulted BC Fed leaders back in Vancouver. He also phoned the ailing Art Kube. Kube advised him to "get the hell out of there," as did Gerry Scott, but the other BC Fed officials told Munro to get what he could.

While Munro and Bennett dickered, there was a celebratory mood out at BCGEU headquarters in Burnaby. Although Cliff Andstein had made it clear that union picket lines would not come down until there was a settlement with Operation Solidarity, government employees had already won their battle. Someone brought champagne and the party was on, to the disgust of some members of the Solidarity Coalition on hand who felt their issues slipping away. Back in Kelowna as the clock ticked toward 10 p.m., Munro made one more report to the BC Fed's steering committee on what he had achieved. On behalf of Operation Solidarity, the committee voted to accept, though the decision was not unanimous. Shortly before 10:30, Munro and Bennett appeared on the premier's darkened porch, lit up by camera lights, and announced a settlement of sorts. Bennett called it "an avenue for resolving the difficulties." Details of what became known as the Kelowna Accord were sketchy. But crystal clear was that Operation Solidarity's mass protest movement was over. The picket signs were coming down.

It was a tough moment for leaders of the Solidarity Coalition, who had poured so much into the four-month struggle. They were not consulted, nor were they privy to any of the high-level talks aimed at ending the looming general strike, which had been sold to the public as being about more than trade union issues. Renate Shearer, along with union representatives Leif Hansen and Joy Langan, arrived at the coalition's downtown office to provide what details there were. "It was a terrible night," said Shearer afterward. "People believed and they cared and they were desperate, and everything we had come together for was still up in the air." At a Lower Mainland Solidarity Coalition meeting at the Fishermen's Hall the next evening, a recovered Kube and Mike Kramer were booed, denounced and accused of selling out. The two labour leaders left.

Beyond the demise of Bill 2 and an agreed process to negotiate exemptions from the worst of Bill 3, the Kelowna Accord included a commitment to use some of the salary savings from the teachers' strike on education programs, and unwritten promises of consultation or advisory committees on human and tenants' rights, the next provincial budget and any changes to the labour code. With nothing on paper or recorded, however, it was easy for the government to renege on even these minimal terms, which by and large they did. The resulting ill will surfaced at the next convention of the BC Federation of Labour. Munro, whose role in the Kelowna Accord and intemperate remarks about coalition activists made him a target, lost the IWA's customary first vice-president slot on the Fed executive to his long-standing rival, Art Gruntman of the Canadian Paperworkers Union.

The anticlimactic end to Operation Solidarity's unprecedented fight against the government has tended to shroud what was arguably one of the noblest chapters in the history of the BC labour movement. Lost in the activists' understandable anger over the failure of the Kelowna Accord to achieve anything on social issues was a trade union victory. The government's attempt to run roughshod over union rights was stopped in its tracks. By standing shoulder to shoulder, the labour movement forced the implacable Bill Bennett to back down on both Bill 2 and Bill 3. And although large numbers of layoffs did take place, all proceeded according to the terms of their union contracts. The province's teachers were also victors. By walking out in such numbers, risking legal punishment for what was an illegal strike, they earned their trade union stripes once and for all. The BCTF has been among the most militant of BC unions ever since.

Finally, Bennett took a big hit in popularity. The summer of chaos provoked by the breadth of his government's simultaneous attack on so many rights, followed by a near general strike, vexed the public, which tended to blame the premier more than Operation Solidarity for the turmoil. Confrontation fatigue set in. This, too, was a legacy of Operation Solidarity. For the many thousands of British Columbians who took part, they could look back with pride at being part of a people's movement that has come around only once in the province's history.

19 EXPO 86 AND A NEW PREMIER

B ILL BENNETT'S THIRD TERM CONTINUED to be difficult terrain for unions. While his government never quite found the gumption to bring in right-to-work legislation to end both the union and closed shop, the concept had more than a few adherents within the Social Credit caucus. They particularly detested the near monopoly held by the powerful building trade unions on all major

Giant Blockade by organized labor and the building trades of anti-union contractor Kerkhoff's False Creek construction site, March 12, 1984, Vancouver, BC.

construction projects in the province. These unions, whose origins went back to the nineteenth century, had weathered twenty years of W.A.C. Bennett and were more than holding their own under his son Bill.

But in 1982, J.C. Kerkhoff and Sons, a little-known construction company from Chilliwack, shocked the building trades by securing a $14 million contract to build the new provincial courthouse in Kamloops. It was the largest public project awarded to a non-union contractor in BC. Despite union protests and considerable skepticism that the company had the skill and expertise to do the job, the courthouse was finished ahead of time and under budget. At the official opening, local MLA and ardent right-to-work advocate Claude Richmond could not resist crowing, "People were abusive and told me point blank it couldn't be done. But Kerkhoff showed that non-union contractors can do anything done by the union sector, do it faster and for less money."

The driving force behind the company was chippy thirty-seven-year-old Bill Kerkhoff. With the help of like-minded concrete supplier Ewald Rempel, Kerkhoff displayed a single-mindedness in blazing a trail for non-union contractors that was underestimated by the building trades. He had hands-on support from many in government. Claude Richmond made that clear at the opening of the courthouse: "There's no question that Mr. Kerkhoff and I were in the trenches on this for quite a while."

In the spring of 1984, Kerkhoff took his crusade to Vancouver, emerging with the contract to build the final two-thirds of a large, luxury condominium project known as Pennyfarthing in False Creek. Enraged to find Kerkhoff on a site where they had worked two weeks earlier, the unions could not let this pass. "It was like a red flag in the face of the building trades," summed up Local 115 of the Operation Engineers in its account. A union blockade went up. The site became a daily magnet for hundreds of desperate, unemployed construction workers

Vancouver photographer and cultural narrator Henri Robideau took this panoramic picture on March 12, 1984, of the building trades' fierce battle at Pennyfarthing against non–union contractor Bill Kerkhoff. *Courtesy Henri Robideau.*

The 1980s decade was a difficult time for BC's tough construction unions. Government-backed non-union contractors began to take more and more work away from the unionized sector.
In March 1984, the building trades took a stand against this trend by blockading the non-union Pennyfarthing condominium development at False Creek.
Dan Keeton photo, Image MSC160-947-04A, Pacific Tribune Photo Collection, Simon Fraser University Library.

After a court injunction and the threat of crippling fines ended the building trades' confrontation at Pennyfarthing, they moved on to a much bigger prize, Vancouver's forthcoming world's fair, Expo 86, demanding assurances that all fair construction would be built by union contractors.
Dan Keeton photo, Image MSC160-988-07, Pacific Tribune Photo Collection, Simon Fraser University Library.

haunted by the lack of available jobs during BC's grim recession. Close to downtown and the popular Granville Island market, and a short stroll from the city's two newspapers, Pennyfarthing was big news.

Tantalizingly visible just across the

waters of False Creek was another reason for the union stand. There sat the vast site for Expo 86, an ambitious world's fair scheduled to welcome visitors in little more than two years. Pennyfarthing was a warning by the building trades of their determination and capacity to fight to ensure the fair's massive amount of construction would be the exclusive preserve of union contractors. "We've got to convince Bennett that we can screw up Expo," BC and Yukon Building Trades Council president Roy Gautier told a heated rally at Pennyfarthing. Stoked by such talk, protesters confronted anyone who challenged their illegal blockade.

On March 19, Kerkhoff and Ewald Rempel decided to do just that. When Rempel purposefully drove up to the site, his Ford Ranger was quickly surrounded, rocked back and forth, pelted with a foul-smelling material no one wanted to ask too much about, and its tires were slashed. A truck loaded with lumber was similarly attacked and disabled. A week later, Kerkhoff had a court injunction allowing unimpeded access to Pennyfarthing. "We didn't want to get six months into the contract and have all this happen," he gloated. "So we sent someone in right at the beginning to provoke a confrontation." The strategy worked. Already hit with a $30,000 fine by the courts, the unions' month-long blockade came down.

But the building trades had served notice of the chaos that could erupt over any attempt to allow non-union contractors a share of the construction jewel across the water. Expo 86 had ballooned into an ambitious $800 million venture planned on 175 acres of industrial land laced by sawmills, railway tracks and a Victorian-era barrel factory. It was a lot of construction, and the fair had to be finished on time. Gautier and other building trades leaders were adamant that Expo would be an all-union site or not get built.

Notwithstanding the Kamloops courthouse, only the building trades had the numbers and range of skills essential for a big job. Proud and militant, the building trades also knew how to undermine a project. If the wrong person was assigned a certain task, if there was a slight bending of a safety rule, if there was even a single non-union tradesman on site, work would stop. With that kind of clout, how could Expo risk work stoppages that might imperil the fair opening on time? Nevertheless, the building trades were willing to sign a no-strike pact, as they had with W.A.C. Bennett for his big dam projects in the 1950s and 1960s, on condition that they received all the work.

Gautier was discussing such a pact as early as 1982 with his Expo counterpart Jimmy Pattison, the brash business dynamo from East Vancouver who had agreed to serve as president of Expo 86 for a dollar a year. But their best of intentions went awry with the post-election ascendancy of anti-union hawks in the Bennett government. The new government appointee to the Expo board was none other than Claude Richmond, still relishing his success against the building trades in the Kamloops courthouse skirmish. Bennett made it clear that Expo would be an open construction site. Contracts would be awarded to the lowest bidder regardless of union status. Bennett hailed non-union firms as the free market at work, "a gale of competition in a previously insulated environment." In a pointed reference to Pennyfarthing, the premier told British Columbians that "the front-line mentality must be replaced by the bottom-line mentality." He gave Pattison ten days to reach a deal with Gautier and the building trades. After that, Pattison was to recommend whether or not Expo 86 should be cancelled.

The prospect of Expo 86 not going ahead brought a wave of public pressure down on Gautier. But the tall, taciturn, resolute Scotsman had a powerful weapon in the form of the construction unions' long-established non-affiliation clauses. These gave the trades the right to refuse to work beside any construction worker not belonging to the BC and Yukon Building Trades Council. Gautier said they would be willing to forego their non-affiliation clauses, but only if non-union contractors were obligated to pay a "fair wage" that would cut into their ability to win contracts by shortchanging their workers.

Trying to set that "fair wage" turned into the most excruciating and ultimately frustrating experience in the building trades' long history. Time and again, Gautier and Pattison reached a deal, only to have it jettisoned by the Expo board or higher up by the ideologically driven government. It happened twice just during the short ten days Bennett had given Gautier and Pattison to forge an agreement.

With no pact in place, Pattison advised the premier to stop the fair. The risk of labour disruption was too great. Bennett ignored the recommendation, albeit insisting he still wanted a deal. That didn't stop the cabinet from nixing yet another agreement, providing a minimum rate of just over $19 an hour—about $4 an hour less than the union rate and $5 an hour more than what non-union contractors generally paid. At a time when the construction industry was riddled with 50 percent unemployment, the government seemed unconcerned that desperate workers were willing to work for almost anything that would provide more than an unemployment insurance cheque did.

On May 8, the government introduced significant amendments to the labour code. In addition to further restrictions on secondary picketing and enhancing the ability of employers to resist unionization, the changes administered a blow to the solar plexus of the building trades and their critical non-affiliation clauses. The government gave itself power to declare "special economic development projects" like Expo where non-affiliation clauses would simply not apply.

At the end of May 1984, Kerkhoff won his first Expo contract, his bid just $45,000 lower than the nearest union bid. When the Chilliwack contractor turned up, the building trades walked out. The crisis produced still more meetings between the dogged Gautier and Pattison, who by then might have been joined at the hip with all the hours they spent together seeking something, anything, that would pass government muster. Proposed "fair wage" rates, including a whimsical suggestion by Gautier of $19.86 an hour, bounced around like a ping-pong ball. Every time, the government or Expo said no.

Finally, the two managed a deal brokered by deputy labour minister Graham Leslie that almost everyone, even Kerkhoff, thought would fly. But Claude Richmond railed against it, and that was that. Thunderstruck, Gautier called this latest double-cross "absolutely incredible," a sign he'd been negotiating, he said, "in a sea of dishonesty and duplicity." The *Vancouver Sun* sympathized with his exasperation. "Every time he makes a concession to cut a deal on the use of non-union contractors, the Expo directors throw it back in his face," the newspaper wrote. "Are they mad, or just following orders from someone who is?"

The final showdown came in August when a second non-union contract was awarded. Marabella Pacific Enterprises, a cobbled-together enterprise with Ewald Rempel as half-owner, won the contract with a $4.7 million bid that was only $20,000 less than the bid of a unionized company. The moment Marabella equipment moved in, out went the building trades once again. Bennett didn't wait for the labour board to rule on the walkout. The government quickly exerted its new power to proclaim Expo an "economic development zone" carved into fourteen union and non-union sites. Further, the premier warned that contracts would be taken away from any construction firm whose workers were off the job for more than three days. The hammer had come down with all the powers of law and government. Short of defying the courts and having their treasuries drained, there was little the once mighty construction unions could do.

In addition to myriad compromises by Roy Gautier, the building trades had fought back with every weapon they had. But their lanky leader had been whittled down like a piece of wood. Although the vast majority of construction at the fair subsequently wound up in union hands, Expo was a watershed event that changed the nature of the BC construction industry for good. Over the next six months, the share of non-union construction in BC went from 37 percent to

The Social Credit government headed by Bill Bennett was full of anti-union hawks who were equally determined to give a significant slice of the pie to the non-union construction sector. On July 26, 1984, the building trades made their message clear at a rally outside the Expo 86 offices. But the campaign did not end well.

Dan Keeton photo, Image MSC160-1026-06A, Pacific Tribune Photo Collection, Simon Fraser University Library.

54 percent. The figures would fluctuate from year to year, but the days when a job in major construction meant joining one of the building trades were at an end.

The building trades did get in a late lick at Expo's non-union contractors. A number of them had taken advantage of unemployed workers' desperation by stiffing them on overtime and paying less than the $15.25 minimum wage eventually established by the government. The carpenters' union took up their cause, running large newspaper ads calling on shortchanged workers to contact the union. Scores did. Many said they had no idea of the mandated rate, since Expo had refused to post it at construction sites and failed to monitor compliance. Some were paid as little as $7 an hour.

As these horror stories came to light, the Employment Standards Branch assigned ten full-time officers to investigate. By the end of February 1986, non-union contractors had been forced to pay out more than $110,000 in back wages. Diedrich Gerbrand was one who benefited. An experienced carpenter, he'd been paid $8 an hour with no overtime. "But what could I do? I've got four kids to feed. I'd been off work for quite a while," he said. So much for fairness in Bill Bennett's "new economic reality."

The fight with the construction unions was Bennett's last as premier. Shortly after Expo 86 opened, on time and on budget, "the tough guy" resigned after a stormy eleven years as premier, his lingering unpopularity from the 1983 confrontation with Operation Solidarity making re-election uncertain at best. His surprise successor was former Social Credit cabinet minister Bill Vander Zalm, the perpetually smiling gardening guru from Surrey. Parlaying his photogenic charisma and effective glad-handing into a "faaaaan-tastic" election victory over the NDP's bland new leader Bob Skelly, Vander Zalm promised an end to the bitter divisions of the Bill Bennett era. It was not to be, as foreshadowed by something that happened even before voting day.

The flags were set by the podium with care, in hopes that the premier soon would be there. It was early evening, October 3, 1986, and Bill Vander Zalm was about to get a lesson in labour relations. The new premier had taken a highly publicized break from the current election campaign, convinced he was about to settle one of BC's most challenging and costliest strikes, a showdown between the IWA, its largest private-sector union, and the coastal forest industry, its largest employer. The dispute was then into its third month. Aides scurried about, affixing the BC seal to a hotel room podium and setting up a pair of BC flags to adorn what was expected to be the grand announcement. Reporters sat waiting before the vacant podium. The hours ticked by. No premier. Well past midnight, a bewildered, bleary-eyed Vander Zalm emerged briefly from shuttling between the dug-in parties, musing to reporters, "Strange business, this negotiating ..." At 3 a.m. the premier, who seemed to think his legendary charm was all that was needed for peace to break out between two sides at odds for months, gave up. The seal and flags were packed away, and Vander Zalm scuttled back to the campaign trail, humiliated.

Only later did it emerge just how ineffectual the premier's intervention had been. In his autobiography, IWA leader Jack Munro recounted an early-morning plea by Vander Zalm for union negotiators to be more flexible. The blunt Munro said he was tired of the premier's "yapping." He suggested that Vander Zalm tell the industry to move. "But Jack," said Vander Zalm, "they won't move." Exhausted, exasperated and feeling he was being used as an election ploy, Munro snapped, "You're the fucking premier. Act like one!"

The dispute ran two more months. When it was over, twenty thousand woodworkers had waged the most prolonged shutdown ever experienced by BC's coastal forest industry. And it had nothing to do with money. It was all about jobs. For four and a half months, an angry Jack Munro and his unyielding membership fought what at times seemed an unwinnable strike for protection against the contracting out of IWA jobs. Munro's bitterness over the companies' attitudes ruptured his long understanding and quasi-friendship with his counterpart on the industry side of the negotiating table, Forest Industrial Relations (FIR) president Keith Bennett. The two didn't speak to each other for another year.

At their first bargaining session, FIR tabled four pages of contract concessions. For his part, Munro was single-minded: there would be no agreement without effective restrictions on contracting out. As companies opted to hire cheaper contract crews for work formerly performed by union members, too many IWA jobs were "going down the tubes," said Munro. In early July 1987 he removed all IWA issues from the table but two: pensions and contracting out. The fight was now clear, and it soon moved to war. On July 25, IWA members walked out at logging and sawmill operations up and down the coast.

Going on strike in the midst of an industry downturn on a non-monetary issue was not for the faint of heart. As a skilled negotiator, Munro was under no illusion of the difficulties. Rather than shutting everyone down, he reached out to operators agreeable to the unions' contracting-out demands. To FIR's annoyance, the industry found itself being whipsawed. When the union signed deals with employers in the northern Interior and four coastal companies—Doman, Whonnock, Nova Lumber and Westar—FIR responded with large newspaper ads accusing the IWA of "economic terrorism."

Less than two months in, however, the IWA's strike fund was down to $17. Munro asked the labour movement for help. The response was overwhelming. The CLC provided an immediate loan of $1 million by taking out a mortgage on its own building in Ottawa. "What good is a building when people are getting their asses kicked on the streets?" said CLC president Shirley Carr. The BCGEU also handed over $1 million. CUPE and Local 40, the Bartenders Union, coughed up big bucks too. Union dock workers, often at political odds with Munro, voted to personally donate the equivalent of an hour's pay each. The ninety-nine-member projectionists' union threw in $50,000. Small individual cheques came in from everywhere. IWA members still working contributed $5 a day. The shutdown continued.

IWA leader Jack Munro at his podium–pounding best at the union's annual convention in Nanaimo in September, seven weeks into their 1986 strike against coastal forest companies.
Dan Keeton photo, Image MSC*160–1358–11,* Pacific Tribune *Photo Collection, Simon Fraser University Library.*

In mid-September, the IWA got another boost. A non-binding report by BC Supreme Court Justice Henry Hutcheon concluded that the union was justified in its contracting-out concerns. Although FIR rejected his report, it shored up union morale and public opinion. As Vander Zalm discovered, however, there was no bend in the industry's willingness to ride out the dispute as long as it could. Mediator Don Munroe tried and failed to end the impasse, now stretching into November. The IWA seemed to have nowhere to go.

But one more settlement attempt, this one by former IWA officer Stuart Hodgson and forestry expert Peter Pearse, tipped the balance. Their recommendations were so bad, so far below the IWA's realm of settlement that it rejuvenated the membership. After more than four months on strike and suffering financially, their vote to reject the report was higher than their original strike vote. The strike took on new life. Mass pickets defied court injunctions at a non-union logging operation. Munro delivered a barn-burner speech at the BC Fed convention. The growing anger prompted the influen-tial Truck Loggers' Association to reach an understanding with the fired-up IWA and pressure the large coastal forest firms to do the same. It worked. FIR agreed to a letter of understanding that the companies would not contract out IWA jobs, pending the findings of a one-person commission by lawyer Ken McKenzie. Based on McKenzie's report, the two sides reached a deal on contracting out that was acceptable to the IWA. The union also won pension improvements, including the right of long-time workers to retire at sixty, and a small wage increase.

With few cards to play other than their solidarity and fortitude, twenty thousand woodworkers had taken on the most powerful industry in BC for seventeen tough weeks on a matter of job security, not money, and scored a victory. Looking back, Munro pointed to the assistance from other trade unions. "We were able to borrow $8 million basically on our word," he said. "I don't think anything like that has ever happened in Canada." By assessing all members $5 a day, the union was able to pay back every cent in less than four months.

Three years after many had questioned

The IWA's strike in 1986 against the contracting out of union jobs was perhaps the most difficult in the union's history in BC. These IWA members are picketing their BC Forest Products sawmill on day one, July 25. They would not be back at work for another four months. *Dan Keeton photo, Image MSC160–1349–30A, Pacific Tribune Photo Collection, Simon Fraser University Library.*

his trade union bona fides over the Kelowna Accord, Jack Munro demonstrated what had always been true. In the BC labour movement, he was a moderate, believing in compromise whenever possible. But when left with no option but to fight, the province's most high-profile trade unionist proved a working-class warrior. The next year IWA members in Canada joined the labour movement's growing nationalization. They left their international union in an amicable separation to form an all-Canadian union, IWA-Canada.

On the eve of Social Credit's re-election, Bill Vander Zalm had mused to the Rotary Club of Vancouver how great it would be if labour and management could sit down and work things out without strikes and lockouts. The premier committed himself to a tripartite forum for ongoing consultation among business, labour and government. "We'll show there is a better way." Like many politicians before and after him, once in office, Vander Zalm's shiny election promises became yesterday's news.

Vander Zalm was even duplicitous about his vow to seek industrial relations harmony. While rookie labour minister Lyall Hanson and his deputy Graham Leslie dutifully set out to consult with labour, management and the public about possible changes to the labour code, Vander Zalm convened a cabal of lawyers and others to draw up legislation for his own reforms. Hanson knew nothing about it. Still piqued by the failure of his ham-fisted intervention in the IWA strike and obsessed with union rights that didn't allow organized businesses to do whatever they wanted, the premier was planning yet another Social Credit assault on the province's trade unions.

In the meantime, with a strong push from Leslie and private arbitrator Joe Weiler, labour and business leaders were behind closed doors coming close to a milepost agreement to set aside their differences and work together to improve the province's investment climate. Leading labour's side

of the talks was the new president of the BC Federation of Labour, Ken Georgetti. He had run unopposed in late 1986 to replace the battle-weary Art Kube. The thirty-four-year-old Georgetti had spent most of his working life as a pipefitter at the Cominco smelter in Trail. There, he rose to prominence as president of the Steelworkers' large Local 480 during a spirited but ultimately unsuccessful raid by Steel's archrival CAIMAW.

The mustachioed Georgetti was young, energetic and moderate, with little time for table-thumping rhetoric. He would preside over the Fed for the next thirteen years before making the leap to leader of the Canadian Labour Congress, a post he held for another fifteen years. Eager to put an early stamp on his provincial leadership, Georgetti was receptive to the idea of a structured forum of consultation and consensus with business. After a series of meetings, Georgetti, Graham Leslie, Business Council president Jim Matkin and Darcy Rezac of the Vancouver Board of Trade tentatively agreed to set up the Pacific Institute of Public Policy, with a goal of working together to improve business and labour practices. The Canadian Labour Market and Productivity Centre promised $1 million in funding.

This hard-won spirit of good will and co-operation was soon blown out of the water. At the beginning of April 1987, Vander Zalm brought in Bill 19, one of the most comprehensive, one-sided pieces of legislation to hit the province's trade unions. The new Industrial Relations Act replaced the NDP government's groundbreaking Labour Code, much of which had remained intact under Bill Bennett. Unlike Bennett's restraint measures aimed at the public sector, Bill 19 was directed primarily at BC's private-sector unions.

The Labour Relations Board was sent packing, replaced by an all-powerful Industrial Relations Council (IRC) headed by Ed Peck. The former overseer of Bennett's wage-control program was given broad powers to intervene in any strike or lockout deemed to be affecting "the public interest" or a threat to the economy; impose lengthy cooling-off periods; order essential services maintained even in private-sector strikes; and institute binding arbitration. These were unprecedented powers for an unelected individual, taking Peck from "wage czar" to "labour czar." (Subsequent amendments transferred some of these powers to the cabinet, but the essential arbitrariness of the legislation remained unchanged.)

"Hot" declarations, secondary picketing and most union successorship rights were done away with. The building trades' vital non-affiliation clauses were restricted. Unionized companies were allowed to set up non-union branches, a practice known as "double-breasting." Employers would now be able to order votes on their "final offers," they were given more freedom to campaign against union organizing drives directly in the workplace and they could sue unions in the courts without prior permission from the labour board, now the IRC. The government's public hearings and vaunted consultations had been nothing but a sham.

Reaction was swift. Georgetti called the package "a flagrant insult." Jack Munro thundered, "It's just insanity." New NDP leader Mike Harcourt said the Socreds had moved labour relations back fifty years. Key employers also objected to the bill, criticizing its interference in free collective bargaining. Graham Leslie, the government's respected deputy labour minister with a long history of bargaining for municipalities, soon resigned. In a startling open letter to the premier, he denounced the legislation as an attempt to de-unionize the province and predicted confrontation ahead. "The bill was ... the product of too few and too narrow minds," he told Vander Zalm through the pages of the *Province*.

At an overflow union meeting in Vancouver, Fed secretary-treasurer Cliff Andstein said many in the room might have to go to jail for defying the legislation. To tumultuous applause, he declared, "If that's the case, so be it." As its first protest, labour withdrew from all joint government-business-union initia-

tives, including apprenticeship programs, a drug and alcohol task force and the fledgling Pacific Institute of Public Policy, dashing what Leslie called a "once-in-a-lifetime opportunity" to improve BC's adversarial industrial relations. Next there were threats to boycott the IRC, swelling protest rallies and a work-to-rule campaign, plus a ban on overtime set to begin May 21. On the eve of the overtime ban, ten thousand trade unionists gathered in Vancouver's Robson Square to hear a call to arms. Georgetti announced that members had voted 91.6 percent to back the Federation's action plan, which included the possibility of a general strike. "Bill 19 goes, or we fight," said the BC Fed leader.

The Robson Square rally included many teachers, who had already been out on the picket lines to protest another piece of anti-labour legislation. Introduced at the same time as Bill 19, Bill 20 gave teachers full bargaining rights, with the right to strike, for the first time. But the package also included some poison pills. Attesting to Vander Zalm's conviction that the BCTF did not represent the views of rank-and-file teachers, the bill ended the organization's compulsory membership and dues check-off. Teachers in each individual district would now have to reorganize and apply for certification. Principals and vice-principals were unilaterally removed from the union. Teacher certification, discipline and professional development were taken from the teachers and given to a new, multilateral College of Teachers.

The BCTF wasted little time striking back. On April 28, 1987, the vast majority of the province's twenty-eight thousand teachers ignored Vander Zalm's threats and stayed away from work on a one-day strike. Under the leadership of Elsie McMurphy, teachers continued their protest with an instruction-only campaign, withdrawing from all extra-curricular activities for the rest of the school year and into the fall. The BCTF was also fully supportive of the Federation of Labour's action plan, even if that meant more time off the job.

Bill 20, a companion piece to Bill 19, targeted the BC Teachers' Federation, ending its compulsory membership and removing principals and vice-principals from the union. BCTF president Elsie McMurphy spoke to a large union rally opposing both bills at Robson Square on May 20.
Sean Griffin photo, Image MSC160–1466–08, Pacific Tribune Photo Collection, Simon Fraser University Library.

The day after the Federation's defiant rally, Georgetti and Andstein spent an astounding nine hours closeted with Vander Zalm and Lyall Hanson going through Bill 19 clause by clause, spelling out their objections. Afterward, Georgetti told the media, "We did all the talking. [Vander Zalm] did all the listening." A few days later, Hanson tabled forty-eight amendments to Bill 19. Although some provisions were softened, the thrust of the legislation remained. "This is the final package," insisted Vander Zalm. The next day, accusing the premier of choosing confrontation over co-operation, Georgetti declared a one-day general strike by all organized labour in BC on Monday, June 1.

The Fed's careful preparation and pent-up union anger produced a historic walkout. More than a quarter of a million workers in every corner of the province stayed home. Ferries, trains and buses didn't run. Mills and

mines were shut down. Construction sites and newspaper presses were stilled. All public services including schools were closed. Non-Fed affiliates such as the Teamsters and unions in the Confederation of Canadian Unions went out too. It was, summarized CAIMAW leader Jess Succamore, "an unprecedented demonstration of solidarity within the BC labour movement."

In response, the government seemed to lose its collective marbles. Attorney General Brian Smith went to court seeking an injunction to prevent future illegal walkouts, which were characterized in overblown language as an attempt to resist "legislative change, showing Her Majesty has been misled or mistaken in her measures, [and] pointing out errors in the government of the province." The *Vancouver Sun* retorted that while "Her Majesty" was safe, it was democracy that was in trouble. Georgetti, McMurphy and eight

At the large early–evening rally, BC Federation of Labour president Ken Georgetti roused the thousands on hand with vows of a general strike if the legislation was not withdrawn.
Sean Griffin photo, Image MSC*160–1466–13, Pacific Tribune Photo Collection, Simon Fraser University Library.*

other union leaders were cited for conspiring to advocate the use of force "as a means of accomplishing a governmental change." This followed the Criminal Code definition of sedition, prompting one of those named to hide in the closet when he heard a knock at the door.

The overreaction to the peaceful one-day protest was ridiculed everywhere and strongly criticized in the media. The *Province* splashed the word *Sedition!* all over its tabloid front page, adding in an editorial that BC was threatening to turn into "an unnerving version of [apartheid] South Africa." The BC Supreme Court wasted little time dismissing the government's legal action.

After the June 1 blowout, the labour movement focused its attention on boycotting the Industrial Relations Council. Seeking amendments that would forestall the boycott, Vander Zalm's key aide David Poole

met secretly with Georgetti and Andstein. Although they came close, they couldn't close the deal. Bill 19 became law after the longest debate on a single bill in legislative history. The labour boycott was on. The protest was not as complete as labour's shunning of the Mediation Commission nearly twenty years earlier. Unions still had to use the IRC for such matters as certifications, strike votes and fighting employer applications. Although it was far less active than the former Labour Relations Board, the council was able to struggle along until consigned to the trash bin by the new NDP government.

Despite failing to head off Bill 19, labour's strong opposition dealt the first real body blow to a premier who was presiding over an increasingly disastrous, chaotic administration. As for the teachers, they demonstrated just how little Vander Zalm knew about the depth of their support for the BCTF. They rejoined the organization in massive numbers in every district in the province. Not only did they get their union back, they now had local bargaining and the right to strike.

Vander Zalm's gospel-like adherence to untrammelled free enterprise carried over into the public sector as well. Out of the blue, the government privatized the province's bridge and maintenance system. For-profit, private companies were invited to bid for contracts in twenty-eight districts, leaving thousands of government employees facing an uncertain future with no union protection. An innovative bid by the BC Government Employees' Union to take over the entire system and run it on a non-profit basis was dismissed by the government. Although diligent organizing eventually brought most of the former highways employees back under the union's umbrella, the process awakened BCGEU leaders to the need to be more than a government employees' union. Governments were downsizing. Services were being contracted out and bargaining

units fragmented. The union responded with a commitment to reach out to workers beyond the direct arm of the provincial government, wherever they were providing services, including the private sector.

The shift meant altering the union's long-established component bargaining structure, designed for a single employer—the government—and there was strong membership resistance. The matter was thrashed out at the union's two-day convention in 1989. Debate was long and passionate, stretching into the evening on both days. When the final gavel sounded at 8 p.m. on day two, four hours past adjournment time, delegates had narrowly voted down several proposed component mergers and president John Shields had barely retained his job. But these, as Shields pointed out, were details. With a few changes, the union's course was set.

To better reflect its growing non-government membership base, in 1993 the union changed its name to the BC Government and Service Employees' Union, while

A one-day general strike against Bills 19 and 20 took place on June 1, 1987. It was a resounding success. Most of BC was shut down for twenty-four hours. The picket line at New Westminster city hall included BC CUPE president Mike Dumler (centre) and secretary-treasurer Bernice Kirk (on his immediate left). *CUPE BC.*

retaining its BCGEU acronym. By 2016, the union had over seventy thousand members—only twenty-seven thousand of them employed directly by the government—and 550 separate bargaining units. A quarter of the membership worked in BC's health sector. Another ten thousand were employed in community-based social services. Others worked in credit unions, casinos, community colleges and hotels. Two years earlier, social services worker Stephanie Smith had become the union's first woman president. She was also its first elected leader to have not worked directly for government.

As the turbulent decade of the 1980s drew to a close, labour found itself fighting another adversary—free trade. In the 1988 federal election, unions poured all the resources they could muster to campaign against the Canada-US Free Trade Agreement. They feared huge job losses to low-wage areas of the United States and an inevitable lowering of their own wages and benefits. But a massive propaganda blitz by Canadian business in the final two weeks helped Brian Mulroney's pro–free trade Progressive Conservative government romp home with a reduced but comfortable majority. The pact came into effect on New Year's Day, 1989. Five years later, Canada signed on to the North American Free Trade Agreement (NAFTA), a new free trade pact that included Mexico.

Although some sectors did better, the Canadian Centre for Policy Alternatives estimated that Canada lost 334,000 manufacturing jobs over the first six years of free trade, while the income gap between rich and poor widened significantly. In BC, free trade signalled a distinct shift away from highly paid industrial jobs, where unionization was high, to the service sector, where it was low.

Free trade also contributed to the decimation of the unionized BC fishing industry.

The United Fishermen and Allied Workers' Union had parlayed a 1980s boom to negotiate record fish prices and solid contracts for cannery workers, including clauses to alleviate the impact of technological change. In the meantime, set off by the Prince Rupert Co-op's purchase of Alaska-caught herring roe for processing in Canada, US companies challenged Canada's ban on the export of its own unprocessed fish. A General Agreement on Tariffs and Trade (GATT) ruling in late 1987 ordered an end to the restriction, threatening BC coastal cannery jobs. Despite a vigorous campaign by the UFAWU, including a one-day shutdown of the fishing industry, the GATT decision became part of the US-Canada free trade deal.

Cancelling plans for new fish plants, companies used the ruling to demand sweeping concessions from the union. In the summer of 1989, the UFAWU took a stand. Declaring "a free trade strike," union fishermen tied up for what UFAWU president Jack Nichol called a "historic confrontation to protect Canadian resources, fish prices, working conditions and jobs." Angry members intercepted trucks crammed with unprocessed, non-union-caught fish as they headed across the border toward American fish plants, and vigilant picket squads did their best to block non-union fishermen. After sixteen days, the union won a concession-free contract for shore workers and fishermen, which included a pension plan still providing benefits today. But they could not escape their fate. With free trade allowing raw fish to move freely across both borders, BC fishermen lost their clout. Within a few years, minimum pricing agreements disappeared and processing switched increasingly to US plants, where wages and benefits were lower. Free trade had done its job.

20 WAR AND PEACE UNDER THE NDP

T HE VOLATILE VANDER ZALM YEARS, which had British Columbians and Canadians across the country shaking their heads over some of the antics that went on, came to an end in 1991. After forty years as a fixture in BC politics, Social Credit soon disappeared, mourned by no one in the trade union movement. Decades of fighting the Socreds' anti-union policies had unions looking forward to an era of progress and relative harmony under the NDP and the province's new premier Mike Harcourt, a former activist lawyer and popular mayor of Vancouver.

In the meantime, the face of the labour movement had changed. As public services expanded and private-sector unions saw their membership reduced by workplace automation, free trade and other pressures, public-sector unions were moving to the forefront. Women, who constituted a large part of the public sector, took on an increasingly prominent role. These trends were apparent in a big way ahead of the change in government during the seventeen-day BC Nurses' Union (BCNU) strike in the summer of 1989.

The tumultuous nurses' strike rocked the province and permanently changed their union. For years, nurses tended to believe that patient care was too saintly a task to be sullied with demands for more pay. Rather than being rewarded for their dutifulness, however, nurses found their wages falling further and further behind those of other professions. Only when they began to embrace the collective advantages of a union did their employers cough up better pay and improve working conditions. BC nurses began negotiating through their professional association, the Registered Nurses Association, but it was not a satisfying arrangement.

In 1976, the RNABC established a separate Labour Relations Division headed by Nora Paton to bargain formally for the province's nurses. Separation became complete

The BC Nurses' Union and the Hospital Employees' Union were united during the nurses' enthusiastic strike in June 1989, as shown by this march to a large rally outside Vancouver General Hospital on June 21. *Dan Keeton photo, Image* MSC160–1795–05, Pacific Tribune *Photo Collection, Simon Fraser University Library.*

five years later when two hundred nurses congregated at the Empress Hotel in Victoria to form the BC Nurses' Union. Although conditions and wages subsequently improved, the restraint programs of successive Social Credit governments had kept their pay levels below nurses in other provinces. As bargaining for a new contract covering 17,500 hospital nurses got under way in 1989, the membership's mood was militant, as shown by a lofty 94 percent strike vote. Beset by a nursing shortage they believed was caused by inadequate wages, nurses were determined to boost rates to a level commensurate with bottom-line industrial workers.

"We have been undervalued for years, and we believe our time has come," said BCNU president Pat Savage. The union called for a 33 percent wage increase over two years. Job action began in late May with a ban on cleaning, housekeeping and other non-nursing duties. It took two more weeks for the hospitals' Health Labour Relations Association (HLRA) to table its first wage offer: an increase of 18 percent over three years. Spurning the proposal, nurses began walking off the job on June 14. Within days, their strike had spread to all public hospitals

All three health-care unions, the BCNU, HEU and the Health Sciences Association, were irked by the role of the Vander Zalm government's controversial Industrial Relations Council in the June 1989 hospital dispute. *Dan Keeton photo, Image* MSC160–1797–30, Pacific Tribune *Photo Collection, Simon Fraser University Library.*

in the province. Hospital workers belonging to the Hospital Employees' Union and the paraprofessional Health Sciences Association respected the nurses' picket lines.

While essential services were provided by all three unions, the strike was the most

extensive labour disruption to hit BC hospitals. Elective surgeries were cancelled, patients were discharged where possible, and managers were forced to prepare meals, make beds and do the laundry. HEU members officially joined the picket lines on June 22 with their own strike. At the HEU's strike rally, where secretary-business manager Sean O'Flynn vowed his members would "wipe the smiles off management's face," Pat Savage told the many nurses in the crowd, "We are making progress in turning up the heat. So keep it up!"

Four days later, BCNU negotiators announced they had a tentative agreement providing a wage increase of 29.5 percent over three years. The deal did not go over well. Their determination and expectations rising with every day on the picket line, many nurses reacted to the news with anger. The next day, more than seven hundred crowded into a large Vancouver hotel room to demand answers from Pat Savage, the only member of the bargaining committee to show up. The BCNU president was booed and heckled. In the heat of the moment, Savage agreed to change the recommendation to accept the pact, a decision she rescinded in the calm of the following day.

Two days later, 150 nurses stormed a union executive meeting, tearing up copies of Pat Savage's press release and insisting on renewed negotiations to get a better contract. "I was in the office when they stormed in," said Fernie executive member Andy Wiebe. "I thought they were going to rip the office apart. It was pretty awesome, let me tell you. Members wanted to have their voices heard and they did." One embittered nurse explained, "This strike was to get nursing up to a professional level, beyond the blue-collar worker. Well, this offer isn't going to do it."

Two nurses from Vancouver General Hospital emerged as leaders of the growing dissident movement: Debra McPherson and Bernadette Stringer. With strong membership support, the two set out to defeat the tentative contract. In addition to unhappiness over the terms themselves, nurses also felt the wishes of the membership had been given short shrift by the BCNU's paid staff, whom they accused of doling out little information and running the union as a fiefdom. "Their refusal to talk to the membership was disrespectful," recalled McPherson. "We got disrespect from the employer. We didn't need it from our union."

The nurses' picket lines came down on July 1 and the ratification fight began. At a large, enthusiastic "no" meeting, attendees donated $5,300 to send Stringer and McPherson on a province-wide tour to urge nurses to vote down the deal. It was a throwback to the days of grassroots organizing. Billeted in members' homes, the duo spoke at impromptu membership meetings in the Okanagan, the Kootenays, northern BC and on Vancouver Island. All told, they travelled sixteen hundred kilometres by car, listening to nurses' concerns and explaining why they should vote no. BCNU president Pat Savage also toured the province but found it tough slogging.

With a 77 percent turnout, nurses voted 65 percent to reject their union's recommended agreement. As much as anything, the success of the protest movement was a matter of membership empowerment. Nurses had wanted more. They felt their

WAR AND PEACE UNDER THE NDP

leaders hadn't listened to them. But there now seemed no way for the parties to settle the dispute on their own. The parties agreed to binding arbitration by Vince Ready. The labour fixer decided on a two-year contract with a total wage increase of 20.9 percent, a slight hike in the annual pay package from the original three-year agreement.

The membership may not have been pleased with the result, but the strike and rejection campaign were pivotal events for the union. No longer were members willing to accept a union that appeared to be controlled by its paid staff with little input from the rank and file. Kathy Bonitz, a Burnaby Hospital shop steward, said the "no" camp demonstrated you couldn't ignore the membership. "Since then, BCNU has become much more of a member-driven, grassroots organization. And that's a very good thing." The strike also led to a fundamental change in leadership. Debra McPherson used her experience in the "no" campaign to run successfully for president of the nurses' union a year later. She wound up heading the BCNU for a total of eighteen years.

Despite the NDP victory in 1991 and the glow from Harcourt's "Let's boogie!" invitation on election night, there was no immediate difference for public-sector unions at the bargaining table. For twenty-nine thousand frustrated members of the Hospital Employees' Union, the same employers' attitude that had earlier provoked such anger among BC nurses carried on. After twelve months without a contract, the hospitals' wage offer remained stuck at 2 percent a year, well below other public-sector settlements. At the same time, Social Credit's prescription of bed closures, layoffs and contracting out continued as if nothing had changed.

Faced with growing cost pressures and a large deficit inherited from the Socreds, the Harcourt government seemed loathe to intervene. NDP health minister Elizabeth Cull was booed when she spoke to HEU protesters outside the legislature. Their mood was not improved when the HLRA's confron-

tational president Gordon Austin headed off job action by applying to the detested Industrial Relations Council, which had not yet been replaced, for a special mediator.

Renewed bargaining improved the employer's offer, but there was no provision for a key union demand, pay equity for women. By April 23 a series of small rotating strikes had turned into picket lines at selected hospital departments across the province. Finally the government stepped in. After meeting with the union, labour minister Moe Sihota appointed former LRB chair Don Munroe as a special conciliator. Munroe recommended a three-year contract containing improved wage increases, pay equity adjustments and rate comparability with the BCGEU by October 1, 1994, all of which led to a large raise for the union's lower-paid women workers. Members voted overwhelmingly in favour.

In the meantime, the NDP was grappling with recommendations by the Royal Commission on Health Care and Costs established by Social Credit in 1989. The commission's well-received report concluded the health-care system was too centred on costly acute care in hospitals. Both care and the bottom line would be enhanced if there were fewer hospital beds and more resources siphoned into long-term care, community health centres and home care. But cutting acute-care beds would also mean the loss of thousands of union jobs. Early in 1993, assistant deputy health minister Peter Cameron was assigned to see what could be worked out with the HEU, the BC Nurses' Union and the Health Sciences Association.

Cameron showed the unions how many jobs were likely to disappear under the government's ambitious goal to reduce patient days in acute-care hospitals. His charts convinced the unions to buy in and reopen their existing collective agreements. After forty-four gruelling days of negotiations, including some sessions lasting well into the night, the parties produced an agreement that was unparalleled in scope. Covering more than

ON THE LINE: A HISTORY OF THE BRITISH COLUMBIA LABOUR MOVEMENT ❖ 247 forty-five thousand health-care workers, it recognized their job security while paving the way for slashing up to 10 percent of the hospital workforce.

The Health Labour Accord attracted national attention, hailed by public-sector unions across the country as a landmark social contract in government-employee relations. Under the accord, unions accepted the government's plan to eliminate two thousand acute-care beds with an estimated loss of as many as forty-eight hundred jobs. Most were members of the Hospital Employees' Union. In return for their co-operation, the unions won guarantees of job security, retraining, a role in hospital decision-making and a reduction in the workweek from 37.5 to 36 hours a week with no loss of pay. Employees losing their hospital jobs were to be offered equivalent positions elsewhere in the system. It was hoped many replacement jobs would be found in non-hospital facilities, where the government aimed to put more and more of its dollars. Early-retirement incentives and attrition were also part of the package.

"It means our people can move with the switch from acute care to community care," said Carmella Allevato, secretary-business manager of the HEU. Predictably, the opposition, editorial writers, business leaders and the hospitals themselves assailed the package as a "sweetheart deal" with the unions. Wild costing figures were tossed about, none of which stood up to scrutiny. The HLRA failed to ratify the package, provoking impromptu, one-hour study sessions by health-care unions at five BC hospitals. Finally, after the government threw some extra money into the hospitals' pot, the accord went ahead.

It was tested right off the bat when the government decided to close the aging, three-hundred-bed Shaughnessy Hospital in Vancouver. Twelve hundred employees shifted seamlessly along with specific Shaughnessy services to other locations. But 439 employees saw their positions disappear altogether. The accord's newly established Health Labour Adjustment Agency managed to find jobs for all who were willing to accept them within the health-care system. Three hundred managers were not so fortunate. With no union contract, they were simply let go. Overall, the Shaughnessy closure saved the government nearly $40 million a year, with no loss of union jobs.

Similar results occurred wherever there were bed closures. The government was able to reduce costs, few health-care employees lost their jobs, and a difficult transition was managed without serious bumps and bruises. Originally expected to be temporary, the accord was so effective that its core feature, the Employment Security Agreement, was written permanently into the health unions' collective agreements in 1996.

Replacing Vander Zalm's ideologically based Industrial Relations Reform Act (Bill 19), a centrepiece of the party's election campaign, was another early task of BC's first NDP government in sixteen years. Emulating the course of its NDP predecessor, the Harcourt government appointed a troika of experts to recommend measures for a new labour code. Instead of Bill King's "three wise men," however, they became known as "the three amigos": mediator Vince Ready and experienced labour lawyers John Baigent and Tom Roper. Pulling together and fine-tuning proposals from a nine-member committee, they produced a 125-page report that would form the basis of the new labour code.

The IRC was scrapped in favour of a reconfigured Labour Relations Board. The right to secondary picketing, though still subject to LRB approval, was restored, as was the legality of "hot" declarations. Automatic union certifications, based on a majority of the workforce signing union cards, were back. And BC became the second province in Canada, after Quebec, to proclaim a so-called anti-scab law, banning the use of strikebreakers during a strike or lockout. Strikebreakers do nothing but prolong labour disputes and induce picket-line violence, said labour minister Moe Sihota.

Ending mandatory union certification votes was a boon to organizing. During the eight years Social Credit had required a vote every time a union applied to represent a bargaining unit, the average number of annual certifications fell by 45 percent. With the return of sign-up certifications, which eliminated the opportunity for employers to intimidate workers and campaign against the union in the run-up to a vote, newly organized workers more than doubled to an average of 8,762 a year.

However, Sihota disappointed the labour movement when he declined to follow the amigos' recommendation to bring in sectoral bargaining. That would have allowed unions to win a few certifications in a hard-to-organize industry such as retail, negotiate a master agreement and then use that contract to gradually claim other certifications until most of the industry was unionized. Small business would have "gone berserk," Sihota explained. "We had a mandate to bring in a new labour code … that made it easier to unionize. [But] we made a conscious decision not to swing the pendulum [too far] and have another government come in and reverse it."

The NDP also raised the minimum wage to $7 an hour, the highest in the country, and further enhanced working conditions with a new **Employment Standards Act**. For the first time, farm workers, live-in nannies, taxi drivers, artists, security guards, fishermen and newspaper carriers were brought under the legislation. And as the Barrett government had done, the Harcourt government brought in a fair-wages act to ensure that union rates, or close to them, were paid on all government projects.

Despite the NDP's many moves to improve matters for workers and the labour movement, there were still disputes with unions who felt the government should do more. Yet whenever it did anything perceived as friendly to labour, the government faced a chorus of attacks, denounced for "caving in" to unions. BC Fed president Ken Georgetti

was termed the "nineteenth cabinet minister," as if working people having access to government was a bad thing. "We don't have our way all the time, despite what most of the media claims," Georgetti said. "But we do know that when the government makes a decision, our views [are] considered. And that is a significant breakthrough."

As it was, Georgetti was irked that two large, union-backed developments he vigorously promoted were killed by the government. The ambitious Bamberton housing project north of Victoria and a controversial convention centre, hotel and casino development on the Vancouver waterfront were to be financed largely by union pension funds and create thousands of jobs. But hostile community pressure prompted a thumbs-down from the NDP government. Teachers also found themselves in conflict. Flexing their new right to strike acquired under Bill Vander Zalm, over thirty BCTF locals hit the bricks from 1988 to 1994, winning good wage increases and in most cases, limits on class size.

But the government seemed to grow tired of seeing classrooms behind picket lines. In 1993, the province legislated an end to protracted strikes in Surrey and Vancouver, and the following year put a stop to local-by-local negotiations that teachers found so beneficial. The **Public Education Labour Relations Act** imposed province-wide negotiations for all major issues, severely limiting what could be negotiated at local bargaining tables. There would be no more strikes in individual school districts. Teachers were incensed by the change, but there was no rolling it back.

The Harcourt government did manage a compromise with public-sector unions, which had threatened to disrupt the NDP's 1995 convention over a proposed 1.2 percent cap on wage increases. The unions agreed to accept restraint, provided that money was channelled to lower-paid workers and that the government reviewed public-sector wages. "We have acknowledged that there is just so much money to go around," said BCGEU president John Shields.

It sometimes seemed as if the Harcourt government spent almost all its energy trying to steer a middle course through a minefield of problems left behind by Social Credit. No issue sparked more attention, controversy and emotion than the government's attempt to resolve growing demands by environmentalists and First Nations for the preservation of Vancouver Island's remaining old-growth rainforests. For the labour movement and particularly the IWA, whose members stood to lose good-paying union jobs for every stand of timber saved from the chainsaw, this was a frustrating matter beyond the realm of collective bargaining. This time, no indomitable strike could stem the tide, as the union had against contracting out in 1986.

The IWA was paying the price for a rapacious forest industry that had had its way for years under Social Credit, clear-cutting, damaging sensitive watersheds and skimping on reforestation. With BC dubbed "Brazil of the North," the anti-logging campaign was on. The previous decade had already witnessed some high-profile skirmishes. First Nations and green activists had halted

logging on Meares Island near Tofino and Lyell Island on Haida Gwaii. More protests preserved half the Carmanah Valley on Vancouver Island for parkland. Conscious of the growing clamour, the NDP made sustainable development a key plank in its election campaign, vowing to end valley-to-valley conflict by striking a balance between preserving jobs and preserving the best of the province's precious rainforests. But a temporary truce between the factions did not last, and confrontations resumed.

They came to a head in "the War in the Woods" at Clayoquot Sound, 260,000 hectares of mostly unharvested, pristine rainforest on the west coast of Vancouver Island. In April 1993, the government enraged environmentalists by leaving up to two-thirds of the lush area open to selective logging, albeit under the most restrictive regulations ever imposed on the forest industry. In what was termed the largest act of mass civil disobedience in Canadian history, environmental groups marshalled waves of protesters that summer to blockade the main logging road, in defiance of a court injunction. More

than eight hundred individuals, from grandmothers to kids, were arrested and charged with criminal contempt of court. Many were jailed for up to sixty days.

With the War in the Woods garnering global attention amid worrisome boycotts of BC-cut wood, a new set of rules were applied to logging in Clayoquot Sound that were light years from the haphazard cutting of the past. Environmentalists were pleased. But the IWA estimated that the new cutting restrictions and park preservation would cost its members at least fourteen hundred jobs. Feeling like "the meat in the sandwich" between environmentalists, First Nations' land claims and the government, twenty thousand angry woodworkers and their supporters marched on Victoria in a noisy demonstration to bring attention to their pending unemployment.

The NDP was sympathetic. Established as a Crown corporation to retrain and find jobs for laid-off woodworkers and funded by a bump in stumpage fees, Forest Renewal BC provided some employment relief. Later however, a Jobs and Timber Accord, trumpeted as a "social contract for the woods," foundered with the dramatic revenue loss from the collapse of the Asian economy. IWA frustration boiled over when two Greenpeace vessels docked in Vancouver Harbour on their way up the coast to more logging protests. Turning the tables, the union kept the ships tied up for a week with a blockade and picket line of its own. "The issue is [Greenpeace] imposing its will on our members and their families," said IWA president Dave Haggard.

By the time the NDP government was defeated in 2001, it was recognized worldwide for its environmental record, preserving millions of hectares of wilderness, doubling parkland in the province and installing a long-awaited Forest Practices Code with real teeth. Still, the many union jobs lost in the process would never return. It wasn't easy coping with so many conflicting interests, acknowledged former environment minister Moe Sihota. "You have to deal with the real-

As environmentalists stepped up their campaign to preserve large tracts of old-growth rainforests, members of the IWA found themselves fighting to preserve their jobs. Organized by the union, pro-job rallies were common at the legislature during the first half of the 1990s.
Alberni Valley Museum, PN17811.

There are fewer happier times than a wedding, but this new bride in Nelson didn't forget her brothers and sisters on the line during the province-wide Safeway strike by members of the United Food and Commercial Workers in 1996. Accompanied by her husband, she took time off from the wedding celebration to hoist a picket sign.
Courtesy UFCW Local 1518.

ity of jobs, the reality of wood running out, the reality of communities that have always voted for you up in arms, and the reality of others that have looked to you—environmentalists, Natives—up in arms as well."

These years also saw the beginning of new labour awareness of Indigenous issues. Unions strongly supported the controversial 1998 Nisga'a Treaty, the first BC treaty signed in a hundred years. That same year, a comprehensive task force on First Nations education by the BCTF led to the hiring of a full-time Indigenous staff person and a reaching out to Indigenous educators to improve graduation rates and the teaching of Indigenous history. The BCGEU succeeded in organizing employees of two First Nations governments, although opposition from some Indigenous leaders prompted the union to set up an Aboriginal council to try to foster understanding.

(Such moves have continued in the 2000s. The BC Federation of Labour meets with Indigenous organizations and has actively promoted reconciliation over the tragedies of residential schools and missing and murdered Indigenous women. Some unions have included Indigenous customs within their contracts, including a right to seasonal leave without losing seniority and easing seniority to provide more apprenticeships. And midway through 2017, the Labourers' International Union, Canada's largest construction union, with eight thousand BC members, inked a pact with the Assembly of First Nations to encourage training and employment of Indigenous workers on big projects. "The potential is incredible," said union vice-president Joseph Mancinelli.)

Tension between unions and the NDP did not magically disappear under Harcourt's successor, Glen Clark, who pulled off an unexpected come-from-behind election win in 1996. Clark, a former union organizer, was helped immeasurably by strong support from organized labour. Unions were particularly offended by Liberal leader Gordon Campbell's vow to scrap the anti-scab law, and encouraged by Clark's direct appeal to blue-collar workers. The United Food and Commercial Workers, for example, sent letters reminding each of its twenty-five thousand members about Campbell's scab promise. On election day, the union organized carpools to ensure all members at its many organized supermarkets got to the polls, the kind of initiative considered critical to the party's narrow victory.

Ironically, a few months later the UFCW professed unhappiness over Glen Clark's perceived role in ending the union's six-week strike against the province's supermarket chains. The BCGEU took out ads lambasting the government for trying to make small reductions in the civil service to balance the budget. In 1999, unionized community social services workers staged a hard-fought eleven-week strike to bring their wages up to the level of community health workers. And many teachers objected when BCTF president Kit Krieger and his executive reached a controversial deal directly with the premier's office that provided class size limits and class composition standards in a master provincial agreement. In return, teachers accepted the government's wage restraint pattern of 0, 0 and 2 percent over three years. At the next BCTF convention, arguing that Krieger was too close to the government, David Chudnovsky from the militant Surrey local ran against him for president and won.

The BC Federation of Labour struck a chord with its humorous send–up of the Fraser Institute's controversial Tax Freedom Day in June by proclaiming a Corporate Tax Freedom Day in January, arguing that was how long it took for corporations to earn enough to cover their taxes for the rest of the year. In 1996, an inflated "corporate pig," shown off by Fed communications director Bill Tieleman (left), who thought up the spoof, and Chris Gainor of the Hospital Employees' Union, highlighted the day. *Courtesy Bill Tieleman.*

The fall of 1994 had also seen a throwback to the old days of labour defiance and punishment in Port Alberni. Trouble flared when MacMillan Bloedel brought in a non-union contractor to work on an addition to its Alberni pulp mill, work that had always been done by BC's unionized building trades. Hundreds of union members converged on the site to take a stand. For several months, mass pickets barred entry to the site, including a violent confrontation when the contractor tried to drive through. Court injunctions eventually did the trick and the way was cleared. But many chose arrest over stepping aside. Tears streaming down his face, pipefitter Ron Gehring told the *Vancouver Sun*'s Val Casselton, "I'm proud of what I'm doing. I can look [my family] in the face and tell them that." All told, one hundred picketers were convicted of contempt of court and sentenced to fourteen days in jail or electronic monitoring. Cells filled up, and authorities ran out of monitoring bracelets. Minus a bracelet, former building trades president Bill Zander was told not to leave home for fourteen days. He complied. "I did a lot of gardening," Zander said.

Overall, however, despite an up-and-down economy and ongoing difficulties for unions in the private sector, labour did well under the NDP. Extending basic health and safety standards at last to the province's toiling agricultural workers was a real breakthrough. Under Glen Clark the NDP went further, setting up a hands-on Agricultural Compliance Team (ACT). With representatives from employment standards, the WCB, the motor vehicle branch and federal agencies, the ACT took a proactive approach to inspections and enforcement, providing the best protection BC farm workers had ever had. Changes and standards that unions had sought for years were now in place, and labour's voice was heard at the cabinet table.

There was even opportunity for humour. Chuckles abounded over the BC Federation of Labour's effective and funny "Corporate Tax Freedom Day," a stunt dreamed up by

the Fed's communications director Bill Tieleman to counter the Fraser Institute's vaunted Tax Freedom Day. The latter was the dubious date, usually in June, on which the right-wing think-tank claimed an average Canadian family had earned enough money to pay all its myriad taxes for the year. The BC Fed proclaimed "Corporate Tax Freedom Day" in early January to illustrate how little tax corporations paid. The share of federal revenue from corporate taxes had declined from 21.5 percent in 1960 to just 7.5 percent in 1990. The first Corporate Tax Freedom Day was staged on the top floor of a downtown hotel on January 27, 1993. Disguised labour types celebrated in tuxedos and fancy dresses. The highlight was a "Race to the Trough" featuring ten battery-operated, oinking toy pigs emblazoned with logos of Canada's major corporations. The TV cameras loved it. When a fuming Fraser Institute denounced the well-covered event, the Federation was overjoyed. But far more serious matters lay ahead as the NDP's ten years in office came to a shattering close with a 77–2 shellacking at the hands of Gordon Campbell's Liberals in the spring election of 2001.

Not surprisingly, with an NDP government in place, the 1990s proved a better time for BC workers after sixteen years of Social Credit. Among the beneficiaries were the province's agricultural workers, finally included under basic health and safety regulations, with a laudable hands–on approach to inspections and enforcement. *Craig Berggold photo.*

21 PICKING ON THE PUBLIC SECTOR

THE BC LIBERALS WHO TOOK OVER GOVERNMENT from the NDP had little in common with their federal Liberal namesakes. They were a centre-right coalition united, like the BC Social Credit Party, by a common desire to keep the NDP in opposition and promote free enterprise. Their leader Gordon Campbell, a three-term mayor of Vancouver, was committed to dramatically lowering taxes and significantly reducing government.

During the 1996 election campaign, which he had lost to Glen Clark, Campbell had vowed to scrap the Health Labour Accord, the landmark deal between the NDP and health unions to protect jobs during hospital downsizing. But just before the 2001 campaign, he surprisingly reversed himself. Asked point-blank by HEU communications director Stephen Howard whether he still wanted the accord gone, Campbell replied, "I don't believe in ripping up agreements. I said I disagreed with [it]. That's just the way it was. I am not tearing up any agreements."

Then, shortly after taking office, the Liberals did precisely what Gordon Campbell had promised they would not do. Without the slightest notice to the union, the Liberal government rammed through legislation stripping key contracting-out protections from the Hospital Employees' Union's collective agreement. Hospitals were now free to contract out and privatize the jobs of thousands of hospital employees. More than 80 percent of the positions affected were held by women. They included many women of colour, older women and immigrants. When the premier and his government had finished using their massive majority to enact Bill 29 just before dawn on January 28, 2002, the HEU's contract lay in tatters.

Gone was the celebrated Health Accord, including the Health Labour Adjustment

Agency, which had done such an efficient job of retraining laid-off workers for positions elsewhere in the system. Gone were seniority bumping rights dating back to the days of W.A.C. Bennett. And gone too were restrictions against contracting out that were first negotiated under Bennett's son Bill. It was, said *The Globe and Mail*, an act of "legislative vandalism." Hospitals wasted little time taking advantage of the opportunity to ditch the union and contract out services. Almost overnight, in Vancouver and the Fraser Valley, long-term service contracts were signed with multinational corporations who made their large profits by squeezing workers.

Laundry, dietary and housekeeping employees who had been earning $18 an hour found themselves on the street. If they wanted to keep working, they were forced to reapply for their old jobs, now non-union and paying about $10 an hour, with no guarantee they would be hired. The hospitals were cheered on by health minister Colin Hansen and other ministers who said there was no justification for paying hospital support workers $18 an hour. Ten dollars an hour was fine.

At the same time, the government began closing long-term care facilities, where staff knew and cared for the residents, forcing seniors into a vaguely defined future of assisted-living facilities where demand exceeded supply. Heart-wrenching stories filled the media about couples married for decades being separated by the transition. The Liberals' pre-election promise to create fifty-five hundred more long-term care beds proved as hollow as Gordon Campbell's pledge not to rip up agreements. Not even the venerable May Bennett Home in Kelowna, named after the wife and mother of BC's two Bennett premiers, escaped the chopping block. Meanwhile, HEU members at the long-term care homes were losing their jobs.

Community pressure sometimes stalled the process, and occasionally there was a change of heart. But mostly the closures rolled forward. *Province* columnist Mike Smyth observed, acidly, "This government is desperate to kick old people out of nursing homes to save money."

HEU members fought back against the loss of unionized laundry, kitchen and housekeeping services to low-paying, non-union private corporations with protests, short-term occupations, picketing and large, spirited rallies. Secretary-business manager Chris Allnutt, president Fred Muzin and financial secretary Mary LaPlante were arrested for taking part in a union blockade that put bales of hay across the road at a Chilliwack industrial park where trucks full of dirty laundry were scheduled to roll to Calgary. Given a ten-year private contract to provide clean laundry for four Fraser Valley hospitals with no local facility, K-Bro Linen Systems had to truck millions of tons of laundry hundreds of kilometres to Calgary and back, taking forty-three local union jobs with them.

The BC Children and Women's Hospital in Vancouver was so anxious to shed union jobs that they awarded a housekeeping contract to an American company owned by Cecilia von Dehn, an ardent anti-abortionist with a long history of harassing abortion clinics. Fine, except that abortions were performed at the hospital. After a public outcry, health minister Colin Hansen admitted due diligence had not been done. The contract was cancelled with ninety days' notice. Until then, extra security was hired to ensure the safety of women seeking abortions and of staff.

Over time, an estimated eight thousand HEU members would be bumped from their jobs by private non-union contractors. It was the most extensive privatization of health services in Canada and, some said, the largest mass layoff of women workers since the end of World War II. In a controversial effort to ease the bleeding, HEU leaders worked out a tentative deal to accept major mid-contract concessions, including deferment of scheduled 4.4 percent wage increases, lengthening the workweek to 37.5 hours with no hike in pay (effectively, a 4 percent pay cut), and a

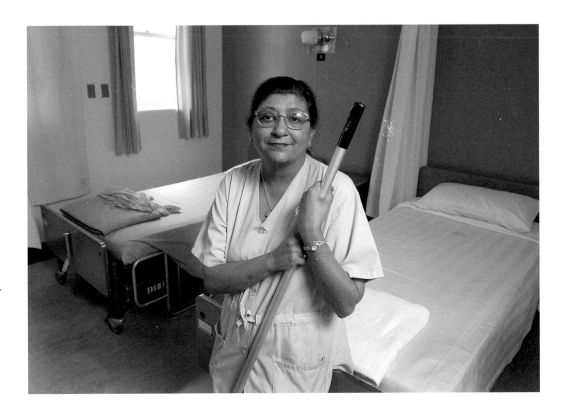

When the Gordon Campbell government broke its pre–election promise and unilaterally stripped contracting-out protection from members of the Hospital Employees' Union in 2002, thousands of hospital laundry, dietary and housekeeping employees lost their decently paid union jobs. Many of them were immigrants. *Hospital Employees' Union.*

two-year extension of the current contract to 2006. In return for these payroll savings of $500 million, health employers agreed to better severance and bumping rights for laid-off workers and to cap the number of contracted-out jobs at a still substantial thirty-five hundred full-time positions. This was nevertheless a big improvement over the government's original target of twenty thousand jobs, according to union leader Allnutt.

But he was unable to sell the so-called Framework Agreement. Members unaffected by contracting out were less than thrilled by the prospect of working longer hours for less pay. Others felt the union was giving up too much for too little. The package was voted down by 57 percent. In the meantime, a little-noticed constitutional challenge to Bill 29 by the HEU and allied health unions was beginning to wind its way through the courts. The unions argued that the unilateral removal of contract provisions by the government violated their right to freedom of association guaranteed by the Canadian Charter of Rights and Freedoms. The BC Supreme Court dismissed the unions' case,

as did the BC Court of Appeal. Without a lot of hope, the unions appealed to the Supreme Court of Canada.

After the collapse of the Framework Agreement, the pace of layoffs quickened. The largest privatization took place at Vancouver General Hospital, where 950 union housekeeping positions disappeared, replaced by a now familiar contingent of low-paid, non-union employees hired by the US-based multinational Aramark Corp. By the time bargaining for a new HEU contract reached a head in the spring of 2004, twenty-five hundred more members had been shown the door. Among them was Deanna Graham. In an emotional letter to the HEU's *Guardian* periodical, the veteran cleaner at Vancouver General decried her fate: "Despite popular opinion, I do not believe eighteen dollars an hour is substantial after twenty-five years of labour. $9.50 an hour is not only insulting, but impossible to raise a family on." Bill 29 did more than strip away their contract rights, she said. "It attacked our very identity. I am not an overpaid cleaning lady pushing a broom. I am a dedicated employee, a team

In 2004, the BC Liberals' back–to–work legislation and two–year contract imposed on striking members of the Hospital Employees' Union, already devastated by government–sanctioned contracting out of thousands of their jobs, prompted threats of a general strike and the largest May Day march in Vancouver in years. *Kim Stallknecht photo, Province newspaper.*

player, a loving mother, and a compassionate human being."

At the bargaining table, the HEU offered wage rollbacks similar to those in the Framework Agreement, but with better security, bumping rights and severance pay. When employers responded with demands for even more concessions, union members' frustration and rage boiled over. Following a massive 89 percent strike vote, picket lines went up at hospitals across the province on April 25. Three days later, the government brought in back-to-work legislation. Passed at six o'clock the next morning, Bill 37 imposed a two-year contract on the hospital workers and ordered an end to their strike.

Its terms might have been drawn up by Ebenezer Scrooge. Union members were thumped with a wage cut of 11 percent plus a longer workweek, amounting to another 4.4 percent reduction in their hourly rate. There was no cap on layoffs, no provisions for severance pay. To rub more salt into the wounds, the wage rollbacks were retroactive to April 1, meaning members would owe the government money on their return to work.

The HEU instructed its members to maintain their picket lines. Outside Vancouver General, Allnutt told cheering strikers, "We undertake this because the government has introduced legislation that is unprecedented, is draconian, and is taking away the fundamental freedoms and rights that we have in a free and democratic society." Geraldine Ross, a sixty-two-year-old unit clerk at Women's Hospital, said Bill 37 would cut her wages by $3.50 an hour with no job security. When a manager tried to serve her with a warning of disciplinary action, she turned her back. "We consider ourselves part of the health-care team," Ross told a *Vancouver Sun* reporter. "What we get paid, we earn. This legislation is demeaning. It's like a kick in the stomach."

The harshness of the legislation and the HEU's decision to defy it spurred spontaneous outbreaks of industrial action. As the weekend approached, thousands of CUPE members walked out, shutting down municipal, school and library services around the province. "The government stepped over the line, and it's time we stand up for what we believe in," said Vancouver garbage collector

Doug McNicol. Some sawmills, a pulp mill, a power-generating plant and scattered transit services were also struck. The BC Federation of Labour was swamped by phone calls from other unions clamouring to join in.

The result was a hastily cobbled-together action plan leaked to BCTV's Keith Baldrey and the *Vancouver Sun* that threatened mass walkouts of public- and private-sector workers in the week ahead. Emblazoned across the top of the *Sun*'s Saturday edition was the headline, "Blueprint for havoc." For the first time since the days of Operation Solidarity more than twenty years earlier, the province was facing the spectre of a general strike. Saturday was also May Day. The pending confrontation produced the largest, most spirited "workers' day" rallies in years. Trade unionists were fired up and ready to go.

Not for the first time, the threat of a wide-scale, militant labour response, coupled with pressure from a worried BC Employers' Council, tempered the BC government's previously inflexible approach. On Sunday, last-ditch talks took place to try to settle the bitter dispute before Monday's D-Day. Adding to the urgency for the union was a rare Sunday decision by the BC Supreme Court finding the HEU guilty of contempt of court for defying the back-to-work order. The court threatened the union with punitive fines if its members remained off the job.

Shortly before midnight, Allnutt and BC Federation of Labour president Jim Sinclair announced that the union had a deal. The government agreed to cap the number of lay-offs at six hundred over the next two years, eliminate employee paybacks by moving the effective contract date up to May 1, and provide a new $25 million severance fund for those let go. Given the uncertainties of waging an all-out illegal strike, the two union leaders decided these improvements over Bill 37 were enough. With less than nine hours to go, the solidarity walkouts, along with the strike, were called off. "This was the best we could achieve," said Allnutt. "We were faced with a law and a government

determined to privatize health care. We have limited that, and that is a victory for working people and patients in this province."

But the abrupt end to a swelling protest movement, when emotions had been building all weekend in anticipation of Monday's "big bang," angered some HEU members, who were particularly furious that the settlement left their pay cut and longer work-week intact. "I feel betrayed," said medical lab technician Susan Barron, sobbing bitterly as she returned to work. "We've been sold out by the government and our leaders." At Royal Jubilee Hospital in Victoria, single mother Jade Cabico collapsed into the arms of a colleague, venting her anguish at the settlement and the likelihood of losing her job in the fall. "I'm not going to go begging for my job back. I give up. I'm sick of it."

Dissident pickets closed HEU offices for the day, while protest lines at some hospitals stayed up well into the afternoon. Six weeks later, for the union's several days' defiance of the back-to-work order, Supreme Court Justice Robert Bauman fined the HEU $150,000, then the largest fine imposed on a union in BC history. Not long afterward, Chris Allnutt was replaced by Judy Darcy, who had moved to BC after twelve years at the national helm of CUPE, the largest union in Canada. Darcy restored calm and unity to the fractured labour organization.

A feature of the HEU's resistance had been strong community support, even in Liberal-leaning areas like the Cariboo. Diana French, a columnist for the *Williams Lake Tribune*, touched on why. "In a small community like ours," she wrote, "the HEU workers aren't the faceless 'unskilled, overpaid workers' the government wants us to believe they are. Most of us know them as good, decent, caring and hard-working citizens. They are our friends, our relatives, our neighbours."

In Quesnel, one hundred kilometres farther north, as many as five thousand people walked out on Monday, despite the settlement. Schools, mills, government offices, non-essential hospital services and even major grocery stores were affected. "We're just sick of the government," explained local CUPE president Dan Weiman. Local teachers' union president Brian Kennelly said Quesnel had been hit hard under the BC Liberals. "We've lost social workers, forestry workers, highways people, hospital workers," said Kennelly. "We're losing jobs, we're losing families. There are empty houses. We even lost our Zellers store."

The HEU set about organizing the thousands of non-union workers hired by the multinational corporations. It was not easy. The corporations filed countless complaints to the LRB. The union and privatized workers also had to battle against owners like those at Nanaimo Seniors Village. Whenever its employees organized, the owners ended their contract. Care aide Sheil Niehaus told a reporter she had suffered three firings in four years. Each time, she was hired back to do the same job for a different contractor for less money. In the Lower Mainland, 450 health aides employed by private contractors were

dismissed after they joined the HEU and won higher wages. But the union persevered.

When certification votes were eventually tallied, the HEU won almost all by lopsided margins. Hard bargaining, including a brave, seven-week strike by fourteen hundred dietary, cleaning and other support staff against the French multinational Sodexo nudged wages over $13 an hour, $3 more than most workers had been earning. Ten years later the HEU represented the vast majority of hospital employees working for the big four corporations: Sodexo, Aramark, Axiona and Compass. Succeeding rounds of negotiations managed to raise wages up to $16 an hour with significantly improved benefits.

Although it was the main government target, the HEU wasn't the only victim of Bill 29. Unionized community social services workers were also swept into the Health and Social Services Delivery Improvement Act, a euphemism of the first order. With memories still fresh of their long strike during the last term of the NDP, they found their hard-won contract

For four days, members of the Hospital Employees' Union thumbed their noses at the government's harsh contract and back–to–work order (Bill 37) passed on April 28, 2004, with escalating support from the rest of the trade union movement, before the union reached a settlement just hours before a wealth of further solidarity walkouts were to take place.
Hospital Employees' Union.

gains wiped out, their job security imperilled and their union successorship rights cancelled. And the province's teachers had their own union-busting act to contend with.

Throughout the first fifteen years of Liberal government, no union was targeted more than the BC Teachers' Federation. At times, especially during Christy Clark's time as education minister during the early years of the Campbell administration, it appeared almost personal. Just months after chalking up their massive majority against the dispirited NDP, the Campbell government had proclaimed education an essential service, making it difficult for teachers to launch an effective legal strike. Teachers retaliated by refusing all voluntary administrative and supervisory duties.

The government did not take long to strike back. In late January 2002, at the same time Bill 29 came down the pike, the teachers were hit by Bills 27 and 28. The first imposed a three-year contract, providing minimal annual increases of 2.5 percent. But that was a mere glancing blow compared to the knockout punch delivered by the Public Education Flexibility and Choice Act (Bill 28), surely labelled by someone with a macabre sense of humour. As they had with health-care unions and community services workers, the government stripped key rights from the teachers' existing contract with no notice or attempt to negotiate.

The teachers lost negotiated limits on class size, stipulations on class composition, support for students with special needs and staffing ratios for librarians, counsellors and ESL instructors, plus the right to negotiate them at all. If that were not galling enough, these were rights the teachers had won under the NDP by accepting a virtual wage freeze in their last agreement. Now they were without both the improved working conditions and the money they surrendered to achieve them.

In just a few days, the government had wiped out the work and struggle of a generation of teachers—many of whom had gone on strike to win similar conditions when there was local bargaining with individual school boards. Their fight to regain them would be prolonged and arduous. For the next decade and a half, there was no more persistent adversary of the Liberal government than the BCTF and its tenacious membership. And in the end there would be the best of victories.

The day Bill 28 became law, teachers walked off the job for a one-day protest. At a pumped, packed rally at the PNE Agrodome, BCTF president David Chudnovsky told thousands of cheering teachers, "This is not a one-day protest. This is day one of the protest." Rather than charging out on an illegal strike, however, the BCTF opted to bide its time and prepare for the long haul. Membership meetings provided information and gathered feedback. Dues money financed a Public Education Advocacy Fund. The BCTF joined the BC Federation of Labour in 2003 and the Canadian Labour Congress two years later. The organization also launched an expensive but effective public information blitz during the run-up to the 2005 provincial election, highlighting the impact of school closures, teacher layoffs and funding restrictions in other areas. And the teachers initiated a constitutional challenge to Bill 28 as other unions did with Bill 29.

Teachers had also been flexing their muscles elsewhere. When CUPE support workers in twenty-nine school districts went on strike in 2000, nearly every teacher honoured their picket lines. In 2003, when education minister Christy Clark provocatively took steps to remove teachers' control of the professional College of Teachers, BCTF members refused to pay their College fees. The government backed down.

By the time talks for a new contract fell apart in the fall of 2005, teachers were primed to take the government on, hardened by the treatment they had received over the previous four years. The BCTF began job action with a ban on administrative duties. That was to be followed by rotating district walkouts and a full-scale strike October 24.

They didn't have to wait that long. In early October, for the second time in less than four years, the Liberals foisted a collective agreement on the teachers. Following the pattern of other public-sector contracts, Bill 12 froze their wages for two years while providing nothing in better classroom working conditions.

Furious at the government's sledgehammer, teachers crowded hastily arranged membership meetings across BC. After careful warnings about the implications of illegal job action, members voted overwhelmingly to defy Bill 12 and go on strike. The 90.5 percent vote was higher than the first strike vote. A pre-emptory ruling by the BC Labour Relations Board that a strike would be illegal and the filing of a back-to-work order in BC's Supreme Court were ignored. Teacher picket lines went up on Friday, October 7, just before the Thanksgiving weekend.

At the helm of the defiance was the BCTF's fifty-three-year-old president, Jinny Sims. Born in a tiny village in the Punjab region of India, Sims was the first woman of colour to head a major union in BC. After her family emigrated to England, she was a good student, a community activist and an athlete, winning medals in fencing and a black belt in judo. Sims took up teaching. But the policies of then education minister Margaret Thatcher prompted Sims and her husband, also a teacher, to try Canada. The couple wound up in Nanaimo in 1977, where Sims established her career as a high school teacher and counsellor.

Sims was motivated to become active in the BCTF by the anti-teacher actions of the Vander Zalm government, dubbed "Vanderlism" on thousands of political buttons. In a few years, she was local president, tearing up her NDP membership card after the Harcourt government imposed province-wide bargaining. "They decertified seventy local unions with a stroke of the pen," said Sims, still angry more than twenty years later. (Sims later rejoined the party, serving as an NDP MP in Ottawa and winning a seat for the NDP in the 2017 provincial election.) Gradu-

ally, she worked her way up BCTF leadership ranks until her election as president in 2004.

As such, she found herself the public face and leader of a province-wide illegal strike by thirty-eight thousand teachers. The stakes were upped right away. In the midst of the holiday weekend, BC Supreme Court Justice Brenda Brown found the BCTF guilty of contempt of court for defying the back-to-work order. If citizens could choose which court orders to obey and which to flout, "anarchy cannot be far behind," Justice Brown intoned. She put off penalties for the teachers until Thursday. "My mother was petrified I was going to be in jail," Sims recalled.

But there was no weakening of resolve. "We are taking a stand against the unjust and punitive legislation of this government," Sims maintained. "Sometimes a law is bad and we as citizens have to take a stand." While the media and cabinet ministers thundered about the bad example teachers were showing their students by disobeying the law, polls showed a majority of the public supported them. This remained true throughout the strike, confounding the Liberals, who expected an anti-teacher public backlash.

On Thursday, October 13, BCTF leaders

The teachers' 2005 illegal strike was solidly supported by its members throughout the province, including this spirited group of teachers in the Bulkley Valley taking advantage of some rare October shirt–sleeve weather up north. CUPE school board workers joined them on the picket line. *Courtesy BCTF.*

BC teachers take their cause to the steps of the provincial legislature in Victoria during their 2005 strike that defied a back-to-work order for nearly two weeks.
Joshua Berson photo.

sat tensely in BC Supreme Court waiting for Justice Brown to hand down her punishment for their ongoing contempt of court. Instead, to their amazement, the judge moved against the BCTF's strike fund. She froze the organization's accounts, forbidding strike pay or any other financial assistance to teachers on the picket line. It was a continuation of Justice Brown's surprising reluctance to fine or imprison union leaders while the dispute lasted. It was as if she were giving a signal to the parties to settle it themselves. Most teachers took the cut in stride. "This isn't about wages or strike pay," said French immersion teacher Erin Fitzpatrick. "If I wanted money, I wouldn't be a teacher." As the rain poured down outside her East Vancouver school, Grade 4 teacher Sylvia Seto echoed, "Fifty dollars a day [strike pay] is not what it is all about. We are here for public education and for the benefit of our province."

For some, however, losing their strike pay after a wageless summer was a monetary blow. But the judge's unusual order prompted an outpouring of support from other unions and members of the public. So

much donated food showed up on the picket line that some teachers reported gaining weight. In Dawson Creek, there was dismay when it seemed the local Tim Horton's had run short of donuts, a staple of the picket line. It turned out a local car dealership had bought up most of the supply to distribute to the picketers themselves. In affluent West Vancouver, chauffeurs were reportedly delivering trays of catered hot food to the line. College faculty associations handed out $50 food vouchers, and a much-appreciated Hardship Fund was set up by the Canadian Teachers' Federation for those in need.

The next day, a week into the strike, organized labour threw its collective weight behind the striking teachers. Flanked by fourteen union leaders, BC Federation of Labour president Jim Sinclair announced that other unions would walk off the job Monday, October 17, in Victoria for a mass protest on the lawn of the legislature. If the government maintained its steadfast refusal to talk with the teachers as long they continued their illegal strike, he vowed further action.

Withstanding a drenching rain, more

than twelve thousand people rallied in front of the legislature on the big day. Much of Victoria was shut down. CUPE went even further, calling fifteen thousand members off the job on Vancouver Island and four thousand the following day in the north. Maple Ridge teacher Mary Johnston woke at 4 a.m. to board a crack-of-dawn bus to the rally. "We don't feel like we're breaking the law, because it's a bad law," she told a reporter. Premier Campbell's plea to obey the law was ridiculed by signs displaying the premier's mug shot from his well-known drunk-driving escapade in Hawaii. "This is what illegal looks like," said one. A second sign read, "Bill 12, another example of impaired judgement."

In an uncompromising speech, Jinny Sims told Campbell to call off his threats. "Stop trying to divide us. It will not work. We will not be broken!" She defended the illegal walkout as civil disobedience. "There is a big difference between breaking a law and having a law created to break you," she told the energized crowd. Another sympathy strike was scheduled for Wednesday in the Kootenays, with a resounding show of union support set for the end of the week in Vancouver.

Still hoping to rein in the teachers with the long arm of the law, the government appointed Leonard Doust as a special prosecutor to consider laying criminal contempt-of-court charges against BCTF leaders. His appointment followed a remarkable decision by Crown prosecutors not to pursue the matter because of a possible conflict of interest arising from their own labour tussle with the government. Public support remained solid. A poll released during the strike's second week found only 37 percent opposed to the teachers' illegal walkout. On Wednesday, as planned, thousands of public- and private-sector workers in the Kootenays walked out in support of the teachers. The much larger walkout planned for Friday in Vancouver was ready to go.

But the prospect of growing labour tumult, now involving the private sector, had persuaded the Liberals to drop their long-held demand that teachers lift their picket lines before agreeing to talk. Troubleshooter Vince Ready was brought in to facilitate an end to the strike, while Gordon Campbell sent over trusted adviser Ken Dobell to represent the government. After a round of his patented marathon bargaining, Ready opted to issue his own recommendations, which was enough to put the Vancouver sympathy strike on hold.

Although he kept the government's basic wage freeze, Ready threw in a lot of other money for the teachers and their issues: a major improvement in pay for teachers on call, $40 million to compress salary grids in the province, a one-time payment of $40 million to pad the teachers' long-term disability fund and $20 million to help address class size and assist students with special needs. These were significant increases over the stringent contract imposed by Bill 12, but the government grasped Ready's recommendations with relief, eager to extract themselves from the pit they had dug for themselves. The BCTF took its time. Some thought Ready's proposals were not enough. In the end, a majority of the negotiating committee recommended that members accept the deal. They did, by 77 percent.

On Monday, October 24, the province's teachers returned to their classroom duties with heads high. They had fought a two-week illegal strike against an intractable government and claimed a measure of victory. Although the wage freeze remained and former limits on class size and composition were not restored, few could deny the gains teachers achieved by fighting back against Bill 12. Almost lost in the end-of-strike bustle was the whopping fine ultimately handed down by Justice Brown for the BCTF's defiance of the court: half a million dollars, one of the largest fines levied ever against a union in Canada.

Jinny Sims's unyielding demeanour had played a big part keeping morale high during the difficult strike. Looking back, she said she was sustained through the trying times by starting every morning on the picket line. "There, I would talk to the teachers. That gave me strength, so I never felt like giving up. Jinny Sims didn't lead that strike. The members led that strike." Sims also credited the labour movement and the BC Federation of Labour for their mobilization. "When you're right in the middle of something like this, that kind of support is overwhelming." In addition to job action by private-sector workers and thousands of CUPE school workers who respected teacher picket lines, CUPE BC president Barry O'Neill called other members off the job for one-day walkouts on Vancouver Island, the Kootenays and northern BC, where "CUPE Day" saw fifteen thousand members in fifteen communities rallying to the teachers' cause. "We thought we were going to be out there alone," said appreciative Terrace teacher Veralynn Munson. "We cannot say enough about the role of Barry O'Neill. They were at our side right from the beginning. I will remember it for my lifetime."

The strike was followed by a five-year respite from hostilities, thanks to a rare even-handed approach by the government and the teachers' willingness to accept an unprecedented lengthy agreement. The deal, part of finance minister Carole Taylor's pre-Olympics largesse, provided a 16 percent wage increase over its five years. Each teacher also received a $4,000 bonus. It proved a welcome calm before the storm resumed.

The 2006 softening of the government's hard-hearted approach to public employees, including teachers, may have been prompted by the NDP's strong electoral comeback the previous year. Under new leader Carole James, the NDP had rebounded from its devastating defeat in 2001, gaining thirty-one seats and boosting its share of the popular vote by 20 percent. The Liberals' popularity dropped nearly 12 percent. Much of that could be attributed to the BC union movement.

During the Liberals' first term, with the NDP reduced to two fighting but lonely MLAs in a sea of seventy-seven Liberals, labour had

functioned as an unofficial opposition, taking on the government over its anti-union policies and rallying public support. Unions were heavily involved in the 2004 municipal elections, supporting candidates who swept Vancouver and won nearly two hundred council seats across the province. And the BC Federation of Labour's million-dollar fund for grassroots organizing among rank-and-file union members brought many back to the NDP fold.

Although the Liberals still won a thirteen-seat majority, few doubted that the fight against their harsh policies had caused a rethink, at least for the moment. The government also had a healthy surplus thanks to a comeback in natural gas and resource revenues, after record deficits caused by its startling 25 percent cut in income tax. The result was finance minister Carole Taylor's billion-dollar bonus for nearly three hundred thousand public-sector workers. Noting that they had paid an economic price for the government's restraint program, Taylor said they should be rewarded now that budgetary times were better. Union members who reached new four-year contracts before their existing agreements expired, strategically taking them beyond the next election and the 2010 Olympics, would receive signing bonuses of around $4,000 each. This was more than chump change. Not a single public-sector union failed to meet Carole Taylor's clever deadline in order to cash in.

Unions also took advantage of Taylor's emphasis that there would be no "one size fits all" template to address built-up grievances. For the battered HEU, that meant annual wage increases of 2.6 percent, adjustments for those in high-demand positions, renewed limits on contracting out and the Taylor bonus, especially appreciated by those at the low end of the wage scale.

Then came the sweetest payback of all. Almost unnoticed, the health unions' constitutional challenge to Bill 29 had made it to the Supreme Court of Canada. After the case was argued in February 2006, led by constitutional lawyer Joseph Arvay, it would be another sixteen months before the justices of the Supreme Court of Canada handed down their ruling. When they did, on June 8, 2007, the decision was a blockbuster. Nearly five and a half years after Bill 29 was rammed through the legislature, the Supreme Court struck down critical sections of the bill as a violation of the Canadian Charter of Rights and Freedoms. By a solid 6–1 majority, the court agreed with the union that unilaterally removing protection against contracting out, eroding employee bumping rights and slicing layoff notices from six months to sixty days contravened the charter's guarantee of freedom of association.

For the first time, Canada's highest court enshrined collective bargaining as a constitutional right. The justices shredded Bill 29 because the Campbell government had made no attempt to negotiate with the unions before taking a legislative meat cleaver to their contracts. In clear, unmistakable language, the court declared, "Recognizing that workers have the right to bargain collectively as part of their freedom to associate reaffirms the values of dignity, personal autonomy, equality and democracy that are inherent in the Charter."

This right was now constitutionally protected under the charter. In one of those great ironies occasionally delivered up by history, the unprecedented catastrophe for the HEU had culminated in the most significant legal victory for unions in Canadian history. No longer would governments be able to impose contract conditions willy-nilly on a union without first trying to reach a settlement through meaningful bargaining. The BC Federation of Labour has since proclaimed June 8 as Collective Bargaining Rights Day in British Columbia.

The Hospital Employees' Union could scarcely believe the result. After so many dark days, so many members privatized onto unemployment lines in favour of workers paid barely half the union rate, it was truly a victory to savour. "I can tell you, my phone, my

email, people coming into the building … they are jubilant," secretary-business manager Judy Darcy told reporters. "They jump for joy, they cry, they shriek… They have been through absolute hell." The Supreme Court provided the Liberals a year to set things right with the HEU and other involved unions.

Seven years to the day that Bill 29 received royal assent, the unions announced they had reached a settlement with the government. The package included $70 million for the thousands of workers who had lost their jobs through Bill 29, $5 million for retraining workers laid off within the current contracting-out cap, restored bumping rights, at least sixty days' notice of further planned privatizations, and the right of health-care unions to propose alternatives in order to keep services in-house. This was the kind of fairness that had been missing in action in 2002, and HEU members voted overwhelmingly to accept it. There were more critical decisions to come. But after all those decades of courts giving workers the short end of the stick, who would have expected the Supreme Court of Canada to emerge as trade unionism's great defender?

Union president Jinny Sims, speaking to the teachers' mass rally at the legislature, never wavered in her strong leadership of the BCTF throughout its risky, high–stakes illegal strike in 2005.
Joshua Berson photo.

22 BACK TO SCHOOL

T HE EXTRAORDINARY COURT VICTORY BY the health-care unions gave great heart to BC teachers. They too had had their contract ripped open by the Campbell government. But their court challenge to Bill 28 had been on hold while the health-care unions proceeded with their constitutional case. When Bill 29 was struck down and collective bargaining established as a constitutional right, the BCTF confidently resurrected its own challenge. Sure enough, in April 2011, more than nine years after Bill 28 had become law, BC Supreme Court Justice Susan Griffin tossed it out. The judge found that the bill violated the teachers' charter right to collective bargaining and was aimed at saving the government an estimated $275 million a year rather than improving the education system. She gave the province a year to rectify the situation.

Instead, the government embarked on a "consultation" process with the BCTF that involved its own remedy to the Griffin decision: a three-year $165 million "Learning Improvement Fund" to address class composition issues. This didn't come close to meeting the class size and composition strictures teachers had before Bill 28. The teachers fought back with a full year of job action involving a ban on such administrative responsibilities as report cards, staff meetings and playground supervision, and a three-day province-wide strike. In the midst of it all, the government trod its well-worn path to legislation.

Introduced in March 2012, Bill 22 banned further job action until September, imposing a mediation process that specifically prohibited improvements in wages and class size. With hostility between the two sides such that they could barely be in the same room together, mediator Charles Jago described his task as "mission impossible." But at the end of the troubled school year, having achieved some improvement in benefits and seniority, fatigued members of the BCTF reluctantly accepted a two-year agreement largely on the government's terms. Further confrontation was put off until the next round of contract talks.

In 2013 the BCTF presidency passed from Susan Lambert to Jim Iker, a teacher from the small north-central BC community of Topley. Under his leadership, the teachers would be severely tested once again, tossed about by a roller coaster of good and bad news and challenged by an exceptionally difficult strike. Their hopes for catch-up wages were hampered early on by modest agreements negotiated by other public sector unions in late 2013 and into 2014. The Health Sciences Association settled first, followed by the BCGEU and most of the rest of the public sector. Reached before their current contracts expired, the agreements provided a 5.5 percent wage increase over five years plus a formula that promised a bit more money if the BC economy surpassed projections. (In fact, this did produce an extra 1.25 percent over the contracts' first three years.)

The unions felt long-term stability outweighed minimal pay hikes. With public-sector unions and their pension plans under mounting pressure across Canada, the new contracts guaranteed no concessions or pension plan reductions for the next five years. But the wage pattern was set. As much as teachers argued for a substantial wage increase, given how far their salaries had fallen behind those in other provinces, there was virtually no chance of breaking the previously set wage pattern for the public sector. It would take the BCTF a long time to accept this.

When contract talks stalled, with the parties predictably far apart, the BCTF embarked on its familiar pattern of job action: a ban on administrative duties, followed by rotating walkouts, then a province-wide strike. This time there was a difference. Premier Christy Clark had been the unexpected winner of the 2013 election after the NDP and its leader Adrian Dix squandered a huge lead in the polls. Part of her election platform was a promised "ten-year deal" for teachers. To pursue this pipe dream, she and her new education minister Peter Fassbender took control of bargaining from school trustees. Peter Cameron was swiftly appointed as the government's lead negotiator to front the tough approach. This was the same Cameron who had spent years as a leader of the militant, independent Canadian union CAIMAW

before engineering the 1993 social accord with BC health-care unions as a public servant in the NDP government.

When teachers launched their first minimal job action, the government cut off their benefits and began deducting 10 percent from their paycheques. Fassbender made it clear the government had no intention of legislating an end to the dispute. Regardless, with ten days left in the school year, the BCTF launched a full-scale walkout on June 17, 2014. Veteran mediators Vince Ready and Stephen Kelleher both rejected invitations to become involved, concluding there was insufficient inclination by either party to bridge the gap between them, the cumulative result of more than thirteen years of fractious dealings.

Complicating negotiations was another court victory by the BCTF at the beginning of 2014. The same BC Supreme Court judge who struck down Bill 28 threw out its successor, Bill 22. Justice Susan Griffin found the Liberals had not only failed to meet the court's mandate to bargain class size and class composition in good faith, they had strategically tried to provoke the BCTF into a strike to win public support for a legislated settlement. She ordered the old 2002 class size limits back into the contract and fined the government $2 million for its failure to address her previous decision. It was a stinging rebuke, but the government managed to get the judgment stayed while it appealed Justice Griffin's no-nonsense ruling. Given the cost implications, the government preferred to take its chances with the Court of Appeal rather than reach an expensive deal at the bargaining table.

After a summer break, BCTF picket lines went back up August 25. The biggest stumbling block remained the never-ending fight over class size and composition. Teachers argued passionately that smaller classrooms and more assistance for students with special needs were better for their workload and the quality of education. As the strike continued past the opening of school on September 3,

Teachers on the line with a CUPE supporter at the Vancouver Education Centre on Sept. 3, 2014 as the new school year prepared to open with public schools still shut down by members of the BC Teachers' Federation.
Courtesy Stephen Hui.

the BCTF ran out of strike pay. Similar to its support for the IWA in 1986, the labour movement pitched in with $8 million in loans to ensure teachers would not be forced back to work by lack of money. Still, the mood on the picket line was tense.

When the government spurned Jim Iker's desperate call for binding arbitration, backed by 99.4 percent of a worried membership, it began to seem as if the province's half a million students would never be back in school without the BCTF running up a white flag. In mid-September, however, the government began to feel pressure from exasperated parents. Sparked by a chance encounter

with CLC president Hassan Yussuff, Premier Christy Clark met face-to-face with Yussuff and Jim Iker. The logjam was broken. Over a weekend, the government withdrew a contentious proposal that would have undone the teachers' court successes, increased the money to settle past grievances and agreed to a new education fund for hiring more teachers. The teachers accepted the government's small wage package, spread over a record six years. Early on the morning of September 16, they had a deal. Resignedly and with a sense of relief, teachers voted more than 85 percent to end their demanding five-week strike, by far the longest in their history. High school teacher Nick Smith spoke for many when he told *The Globe and Mail*, "It isn't great, but for most of us, it's good enough."

With classrooms reopened, both sides waited for the courts to resolve the teachers' Herculean struggle for class size and composition limits once and for all. The next round went to the government. Singling out Justice Susan Griffin for searing criticism, the BC Court of Appeal overturned her finding that the government had failed to bargain in good faith, ruling that Bill 22 was a justified use of legislation. The decision was not unanimous. Ian Donald, the senior member of the BC Court of Appeal, who long ago as a labour lawyer had won SORWUC's historic victory that banks could be organized branch by branch, issued a vigorous, meticulously argued dissent. "[If] the government could declare all further compromise in any context to be untenable, pass whatever it wants,

and spend all 'consultation' periods repeatedly saying 'sorry, this is as far as we can go,' [that] would make a mockery of the concept of collective bargaining," Donald wrote.

On November 10, 2016, the matter came before the Supreme Court of Canada for a final verdict. After a morning of argument, the court spent a mere twenty minutes considering its decision before returning to the courtroom and delivering a quick oral judgment. By 7–2, the court rejected the judgment of the BC Court of Appeal and restored Justice Griffin's finding "substantially for the reasons of Justice Donald." Class size and composition limits were back in the teachers' contract for the first time since 2002. It was a total victory for the province's teachers, and a resounding defeat for a government that had spent so many years stifling the teachers' right to free collective bargaining. For those in the courtroom and teachers

In 2014, BC teachers struggled through a difficult five-week strike, their longest province-wide walkout by far. But spirited rallies, like this one, co-sponsored by the BC Federation of Labour in Vancouver, helped maintain morale.

Mark van Manen, PNG.

Vancouver high school teachers celebrate on Nov. 10, 2016, moments after watching the Supreme Court of Canada deliberate for only twenty minutes before ordering the BC government to restore contractual class size and composition limits they had stripped from BC teachers way back in 2002.

Courtesy Vancouver Secondary Teachers' Association, Terry Stanway photo.

watching back in BC, there was a moment of stunned silence, before an outpouring of joy. Along with the cheers, many tears were shed by those who had fought so long and hard for their rights as a union against a resolute, anti-union government.

This time, the government didn't fool around. Complex negotiations to restore the 2002 contract language concluded in March 2017. To cope with smaller classrooms, the government committed to hiring twenty-six hundred new teachers, at an estimated cost of $330 million. "It took fifteen years, but we are now on the verge of having our language back and restoring what was wrongfully taken away," said new BCTF president Glen Hansman as he thanked teachers for their unwavering tenacity. It was fought in different ways, in a different time, but the teachers' long battle for their rights could stand with any of the noble confrontations of BC labour's rich past.

THE GOLDEN TREE AND FIGHTING FOR WORKPLACE SAFETY 23

BEYOND MAKING ORGANIZING MORE DIFFICULT and gutting apprenticeship programs, the Campbell government did little to hammer unions in the private sector as they had those in the public sector. Even the NDP's controversial anti-scab law remained in place. In part, this may have been because the private-sector unions were no longer the force they were, struggling with the impact of free trade, low-wage competition from other countries, a downturn in the resource economy and ramped-up technology on the production floor wiping out large numbers of good-paying jobs. Part-time employment claimed an increasing share of the workforce, while the real incomes of British Columbians lagged.

As the new century proceeded, the percentage of BC workers in a union, once the highest in Canada, fell to sixth-lowest, trailing even rural Prince Edward Island. It was difficult for private-sector unions to make meaningful gains at the bargaining table. Mostly they fought to hold their own, fending off employer attacks on benefits and pension plans while avoiding hard-to-win strikes. Between 2007 and 2012, an average of just fifteen hundred workers a year took up picket signs.

Yet private-sector unions did not disappear into the woodwork. Many began to focus on issues besides strikes and take-home pay. The United Steelworkers were among them. Under the leadership of its veteran director Stephen Hunt, the Steelworkers pushed the fight, with other unions and the Federation of Labour, for both a safe workplace and curbs on the influx of temporary foreign workers, often exploited by employers and seen by some as taking the jobs of British Columbians.

Hunt was passionate about worker safety. He had been part of his union's sustained campaign to amend the Criminal Code of Canada to make employers more liable for workplace fatalities. The drive was spurred by the 1992 tragedy at the Westray coal mine in Nova Scotia when a lethal accumulation of methane gas exploded into a giant fireball, killing all twenty-six underground miners on the night shift. Although a commission of inquiry judge found that the disaster was the result of "incompetence, mismanagement, bureaucratic bungling, deceit, ruthlessness, coverups, apathy, expediency and cynical indifference" by the company and provincial safety officials, no mine manager, no CEO, no environment regulator was held responsible.

Eventually passed on March 31, 2004, after prolonged union pressure, additions to the Criminal Code known as the "Westray law" imposed new legal responsibility on employers to ensure workplace health and safety. They were now criminally liable for violations resulting in injuries or death. Since then, however, except in a few scattered cases, authorities have almost wilfully declined to use the law. Their reluctance belies the fact that more than nine hundred Canadian workers continue to die on the job every year.

In BC, when the Crown refused to charge Weyerhaeuser over the death of Lyle Hewer at its New Westminster sawmill in November 2004, Hunt launched the Steelworkers' own prosecution. Hewer perished after a supervisor, ignoring "confined space regulations," ordered him inside an enclosed hopper to clean out clogged wood waste, despite worker complaints that it was hazardous. The waste collapsed and Hewer was asphyxiated. Finding the company negligent, Work-SafeBC hit Weyerhaeuser with what was then a record fine of $297,000. After their own investigation, police recommended charges of criminal negligence against the company under the Westray bill. The Crown refused. (The Workers' Compensation Board changed its name to WorkSafeBC in 2005, a branding exercise criticized by the labour movement for removing "workers" from the title and seeming to downgrade employers' responsibility to ensure "safe work.")

Enraged, the union hired top criminal lawyer Glen Orris to prosecute Weyer-haeuser on behalf of the union. After a three-day hearing, provincial court judge Therese Alexander cleared the way for the case to go forward. But it was not to be. The criminal justice branch awoke from its slumber to reassert control of the prosecution. Months later, the Crown decided for a second time not to proceed. Hunt assailed the decision. "A man died here in one of the most egregious cases of workplace negligence," he said angrily. "To say we are disappointed would be an understatement." The union's mettle would soon be tested even more severely in a deadlier workplace tragedy.

Up north, oblivious to the global warming that had allowed the voracious pine beetle to claim vast stretches of BC forests, the winter of 2012 was still cold enough to freeze the bells off a hippie. At the Babine Forest Products sawmill in Burns Lake, fans that sucked dust outside were turned off and windows shut tight to keep workers warm as they worked long shifts to cope with the stepped-up harvesting of dead pine trees. The reduction in ventilation, plus less time for clean-up duties, led to abnormally large accumulations of fine, dry dust from the cut pine wood. But the consensus of Work-SafeBC and the forest industry was that dust levels mattered only if they affected workers' breathing.

On the night of January 20, 2012, a huge explosion rocked the sawmill, sending enormous balls of fire racing through the plant. Workers staggered out into the cold. Twenty were burned or otherwise injured. Lead hand Robert Luggi and cut-off saw operator Carl Charlie didn't make it. The blast seemed unfathomable. There had never been an explosion like that in the history of the BC forest industry.

Two days later, however, welder Bruce Disher singled out dust as a problem at the mill. Careful to note that he had no idea whether that caused the explosion, Disher said the dryness of the pine-beetle wood had produced "a fair amount of dust in the air. It's 90 percent of what we've been cutting for

Lakeland Mills sawmill on the outskirts of Prince George exploded and burned. As at Burns Lake, two workers died in the inferno: Glenn Roche and supervisor Alan Little. Co-worker Don Zwozdesky told a coroner's inquest of seeing Roche emerge from the burning mill, his clothes seared off. "He said, 'I'm still on fire, man … I can feel it.'" Increasingly worried about dust levels at the mill after the Babine fatalities, Roche had foreseen it happening again. Zwozdesky recalled him saying, "You watch, this place is going to bloody blow up." Management ignored his concerns. Roche's wife testified that he told her of extinguishing a fireball that had erupted right in front of him at work just before the explosion.

The day after Lakeland Mills went up, labour minister Margaret MacDiarmid belatedly ordered all BC sawmills to conduct "top-to-bottom" reviews of sawdust buildup. An exhaustive investigation by WorkSafeBC into the Babine explosion concluded that it had indeed been triggered by the ignition of accumulated sawdust in the mill's basement, sparking a chain of dust-fed fireballs that roared through the premises. The agency recommended four charges against the mill

An unidentified woman is comforted at the entrance to the Babine Forest Products sawmill in Burns Lake the morning after an explosion and series of ensuing fireballs levelled the mill on January 20, 2012, killing two workers and injuring nineteen others.
Jonathan Hayward photo, The Canadian Press.

the last three to four years, and it's really dry. The dust factor [was] phenomenal." Despite such speculation and an earlier WorkSafeBC inspection also reporting unsafe dust levels at the mill, no action was taken to check accumulation at other sawmills. Surely it was just one of those things.

It wasn't. Three months to the day that Babine Forest Products was flattened, the

Three months after the Babine mill went up, a similar fireball explosion destroyed the Lakeland sawmill in Prince George, also claiming two lives.
Brent Braaten photo, Prince George Citizen.

owners, including a failure to prevent hazardous levels of dust. To the dismay of the victims' families and the Steelworkers union, which represented workers at both mills, the Crown declined. Prosecutors concluded that WorkSafeBC itself had fatally damaged the case by botching its investigative procedures.

The same thing happened to the agency's recommendation of charges against the owners of Lakeland Mills. Disheartened, exasperated and angry, the Steelworkers and the victims' families pressed the government for an independent public inquiry into the explosions. That, too, was rebuffed. "We can't go back. We need to go forward," said labour minister Shirley Bond. WorkSafeBC did levy fines of $1 million and $725,000 against Babine and Lakeland Mills for violating the Workers' Compensation Act, but both companies appealed the penalties. Lucy Campbell, sister of victim Carl Charlie, said Babine owners should pay and apologize rather than whining about the fine. "They had control over this mill. It's a little wee penalty. No amount of money will ever replace my brother."

Stephen Hunt reached an emotional tipping point during the coroner's inquest into the explosions. Midway through, the Steelworkers walked out. They had lost confidence that WorkSafeBC would be held accountable for its failure to look after the safety of the mill workers, said Hunt. The Steelworkers continued to press for an independent inquiry into what had gone wrong, where witnesses would be compelled to testify under oath. The government continued to say no.

As at Westray, aggrieved families were left to mourn loved ones lost through company neglect, with no one paying a price. At an emotional ceremony by the banks of the Fraser River on the 2014 National Day of Mourning for workers killed on the job, surviving sisters and widows of the victims renewed their plea for a public inquiry and prosecutions under the Westray amendments. Robert Luggi's widow, Maureen,

recalled her husband's last activity at home, making dinner for their son. "Then he went to work and was killed," she said. She lamented that no one was held accountable for his "brutal death ... in an unsafe workplace." For the United Steelworkers and other unions who have taken up the cause, emotional moments like these fuel their unstinting drive for workplace accountability. Their slogan is blunt: "Kill a Worker, Go to Jail."

The BC Federation of Labour has also been heavily involved in the campaign for workplace safety and holding negligent employers to account. At the Federation's 2016 convention, president Irene Lanzinger choked back tears recounting the death of Kelsey Ann Kristian. Only twenty-two years old with little training, on her second day of work at a quarry near Mission she was assigned to operate a thirty-one-thousand-kilogram Caterpillar truck with no supervision. Improperly parked, the heavy vehicle rolled downhill and flipped, crushing its young driver. Eight long years after the 2007 fatality, charges of criminal negligence causing death were laid against Stave Lake Quarries and two company personnel. It was the first time such a charge had been laid in BC over an industrial fatality. But the judge imposed a fine of $100,000 rather than jail. "That employer deserved a prison sentence," an emotional Lanzinger said.

The torch had been passed to Lanzinger by her predecessor Jim Sinclair. He had pursued workplace safety with a passion throughout his unprecedented fifteen years in the Federation's top job. He first embraced the cause in 1982 when he was sent by the fishermen's union newspaper, *The Fisherman*, to report on a ghastly fish-plant injury. Twenty-year-old Scott Patterson lost both legs when he slipped into the path of the grinding blades of an ice auger. Sinclair discovered that a protective safety grate had been removed to allow the auger to operate more efficiently. He took on the issue and within eighteen months, the fishing industry had a permanent safety director and all

DAY OF MOURNING

If a police officer or firefighter dies in the line of duty, their memorials are marked by stirring marches of hundreds of uniformed counterparts from across North America, with full media coverage. And rightly so. But when an "ordinary" worker is killed, beyond grieving by friends, family and his or her workplace colleagues, society rarely takes notice. Yet every year, close to a thousand Canadians die on the job or from work-related disease. In BC, fatalities hover around 150 a year, not to mention the distressing annual total of those injured on the job. Now, thanks to the labour movement, there is at least some recognition of Canadians who are killed or hurt simply doing what it takes to earn a pay cheque.

The idea of a Workers' Day Memorial was hatched in 1983 by CUPE's national health and safety director Colin Lambert and safety advocate Ray Sentes of the Alberta Federation of Labour, who was later to die tragically of asbestosis. The CLC soon endorsed it. And in 1991, after concerted labour lobbying, Parliament proclaimed April 28 a National Day of Mourning for workplace victims, ordering federal flags to be flown at half-staff across the country. Acceptance has accelerated ever since, the one day of the year politicians, employers, safety officials, workers and their unions come together in common reflection.

In BC, the Day of Mourning has been extended into the province's high schools. "Our society places much importance on Remembrance Day, but more people die on the job in Canada," said teacher John Decaire, who originated the program at Cariboo Hill Secondary in Burnaby. Besides observing a school-wide moment of silence, students are reminded that young workers from fifteen to twenty-four years of age are twice as likely to

Canada's annual day of mourning to commemorate workers killed or injured on the job is always a solemn occasion.
Courtesy Rod Mickleburgh.

be hurt or killed on the job as older workers. Abetted by a powerful video telling the story of Matthew Bowcott, a young restaurant worker who suffered horrendous burns in a preventable kitchen accident, students are also told of their right to refuse unsafe work. Bowcott makes it clear: he doesn't want any young worker to learn their lesson the way he did.

auger grates were permanently bolted down. "It changed my view of the world," Sinclair told *The Globe and Mail*'s Justine Hunter.

At the Fed, Sinclair paid special attention to non-union workplaces. When young gas station worker Grant De Patie suffered an excruciating death during a "gas and dash" robbery in March 2005, Sinclair helped

his heartbroken father Doug campaign for changes to prevent similar incidents. At the Fed's urging, WorkSafeBC investigated 366 gas stations across the province. All but a few were in contravention of regulations to identify and protect employees from a risk of violence. The efforts of the Fed and De Patie drew widespread support from the public and the sympathetic ear of BC labour minister Olga Ilich, who promised changes. In 2008, BC became the first province in Canada to require gas station customers to pay before filling up. The province also mandated at least two employees on shift between 10 p.m. and 6 a.m., or a barrier to prevent physical contact with customers. These amendments to the province's Occupational Health and Safety Regulations became known as Grant's Law.

There was more tragedy to come in the Fraser Valley. The morning of March 7, 2007, as rain came down in sheets, Sarbjit Kaur Sidhu said goodbye to her three small children and clambered into a large van. She was one of sixteen South Asian women being picked up for transport to the greenhouses of RHA Enterprises in Chilliwack, where they had work. On the rain-slicked Trans-Canada highway just outside Abbotsford, the owner's van hydroplaned out of control, flipped over and landed on the highway's concrete

Corrine and Doug De Patie, parents of twenty-four-year-old Grant De Patie, who was killed in a cash-and-grab robbery at a late-night gas station, received strong support from the BC Federation of Labour in their successful quest for better safety regulations for late-shift employees working alone. The resulting changes became known as Grant's Law.
Joshua Berson photo.

median. Thirteen passengers and the driver were injured, many seriously. Three were dead. Among them was Sarbjit Kaur Sidhu. Also killed were Sukwinder Kaur Punia and Amarjit Kaur Bal, the latter on the way to her first shift at the greenhouses.

The van had been full of wooden benches, not seats. There were only two seat belts, neither of which had been used. The tires were worn and underinflated, the brake lines frayed, and the driver did not have a proper licence. Yet two weeks earlier the van had passed a safety inspection. "This is nothing new," said Charan Gill, a Fraser Valley farm workers' advocate for more than thirty years. "Every year, I have to offer condolences to farm worker families." He put the blame squarely on the provincial government. Since their election in 2001, the BC Liberals had significantly loosened labour standards in the agricultural industry. A laxer attitude prevailed toward labour contractors who skirted the rules. Roadside inspections became almost non-existent, and the effective multi-pronged enforcement body set up under the NDP, the Agriculture Compliance Team (ACT), had been scrapped.

The Abbotsford tragedy was the worst but not the first van mishap to befall farm workers. An overloaded van carrying nineteen passengers blew a tire and crashed in 2004, killing farm worker Mohindar Kaur Sunar. Two months later another van overturned, injuring fourteen farm workers. Mark Thompson, UBC professor emeritus of industrial relations, noted that growers and labour contractors wielded "a lot of political power" within the government. "When the Liberals shut down the ACT, they sent a message that it would back to business as usual." In 1999, under the NDP, 885 orders were issued against labour contractors. By 2003, the number was down to fifty-two.

As the families of the three dead farm workers mourned, the labour movement demanded action. Amid a public outcry over the deaths, the BC Federation of Labour, family members and Charan Gill presented

a list of thirty recommendations to labour minister Olga Ilich and agriculture minister Pat Bell, calling for a return to previous labour standards and vastly stepped-up enforcement. "We came to this meeting for future protection," said Harsharan Bal, son of Amarjit Kaur Bal. "We don't want to see what happened to us happen to others."

WorkSafeBC released sobering statistics on the hazards of helping put food on the table for British Columbians. Between 2001 and 2005, twenty BC farm workers were killed on the job, 183 seriously injured. Prodded by the Fed, the government conducted a series of unannounced roadside inspections. More than a third of the 180 farm-worker vans inspected were taken off the highway for failing to meet safety standards. In May, the government responded. Seat belts became mandatory for all passengers in a moving vehicle. Ilich also announced increased farm inspections, continued spot checks and the hiring of more inspectors. Sinclair welcomed the changes while observing, "It's a sad comment on our society when people have to die before the right thing is done." WorkSafeBC

subsequently fined the company $69,000, but not a dime was collected, since it was already out of business. A coroner's inquest brought some comfort to the families when the government adopted most of the jury's eighteen strong recommendations.

The tragedy has not been forgotten. Besides sharing an annual candle-lit vigil with family members on each anniversary, the labour movement contributed nearly half the $310,000 cost of a hauntingly beautiful and inspiring memorial to the victims. In the form of a sculpted apple tree covered in gold leaf, images of three women are featured on the branches. Known as *The Golden Tree*, the sculpture was placed in Abbotsford's contemplative International Friendship Garden behind the library. It has proven to be a place of healing. "Now, when my father is having a hard time, he can sit there and relax under the memorial," said Harsharan Bal.

Eighteen months after the van fatalities, Sinclair and the Federation were plunged into another farm-worker tragedy that affected even more lives. On the Friday afternoon of September 5, 2008, two workers struggled

An evocative sculpture of a golden tree, financed in large measure by the labour movement, commemorates three Fraser Valley farm workers fatally injured in an accident while being transported to their jobs in an unsafe van. *Michael Lanier photo.*

to clear a clogged pipe in the small, enclosed pumphouse of a Langley mushroom and compost business. When they managed to open the pipe, toxic gases spewed out, sucking oxygen from the air. In no time they were unconscious, their lives ebbing away. Unaware of the danger, three workmates rushed to rescue them. They too were overcome. Ut Tran, Jimmy Chan and Han Pham died at the scene. Thang Tchen and Michael Pham were unconscious, maintaining only a flicker of life. Paramedics arrived to pandemonium. Bodies lay on the ground, agonized screams of other workers shattered the darkness. There was nothing the team could do. "I think it will stay with us for the rest of our lives," paramedic Matthew Nasseri told a coroner's inquest. "It's very hard to stand there and watch people die." With three deaths and two other victims unable to function, thirteen children were left to grow up without their fathers or their active presence.

As with the van accident, this was not happenstance. The mushroom farm was run as if safety regulations and legalities did not exist. There were no health and safety programs for employees. The owners had no idea of WorkSafeBC's detailed "confined space" regulations, nor did they or their workers know of deadly hazards they might face. Yet no one twigged to the dangers. There were records of only two WorkSafeBC inspections. In neither case did inspectors see the deadly pumphouse, which was being built at the time of their last visit.

Sinclair and the Federation reached out to the devastated families. Six weeks after the deaths, they joined together to call for a public inquiry into farm-worker safety in BC. Through an interpreter, Trieu Thi Nga said that her husband, Han Pham, had told her the pumphouse shed was dangerous. "He said if his boss asked him to go in there, he would quit," she said. "So why did he end up dying there?" Their emotional plea for an inquiry was rejected.

The eventual coroner's inquest detailed a long history of missteps, failures, ignored warning signs and lack of concern by the operators for the basics of health and safety that culminated that fateful September day. Lead investigator Mohinder Bhatti testified that the workers were unaware of possible dangers from toxic hydrogen sulphide when they tried to unclog the pipe. No engineers were consulted on building the composting facility. It was planned, he said, "on the back of a cigarette pack."

At a meeting with BC cabinet ministers at the end of the summer of 2009, attended by family survivors of five workplace tragedies, Sinclair accused Crown prosecutors of continuing to give negligent employers "get out of jail free" cards. Families of the mushroom farm victims expressed bitterness that the owners were charged with safety violations rather than under the Criminal Code. Further, the heavy fines assessed were never paid after the owners declared bankruptcy. "This sends a message that your life isn't worth as much as you thought," said the tearful young daughter of victim Tracey Phan. "I want the employers to go to jail until my dad comes out of his coma."

While death claimed Fraser Valley farm workers, Local 1518 of the United Food and Commercial Workers was valiantly trying to organize them. Since the sporadic success of the Canadian Farmworkers' Union in the late 1970s and 1980s, farm workers had remained almost impossible to organize on a consistent basis. The UFCW, representing a quarter of a million Canadian workers mostly in the food industry, began their difficult national venture in the 1990s.

In British Columbia, the union's mission was heightened in 2004 when migrant farm workers began coming to the Fraser Valley under the federal Seasonal Agricultural Worker Program (SAWP). Many were from Mexico, snapped up by growers who claimed they could not hire enough local workers. Under the SAWP, migrant workers were flown in for growing and harvesting, then transported back when the season was over. They were to be paid the same wages as Canadian workers, provided with health and medical benefits, plus accommodation. There was no shortage of migrants eager for the chance to earn money in Canada. "This is a good job for me and my family," said Jose Guadalupe of his seasonal work at Cedar Rim Nursery.

But there were cases of Mexican workers being exploited and treated poorly by their employers, who controlled whether they would be hired back the following year. In 2008 workers at Greenway Farms in Surrey took the courageous step of joining Local 1518. "The treatment by the boss was not good," explained one farm worker. "We don't have adequate housing and the water situation is bad. People were getting sick." After winning a vote, the union was granted BC's first certification of migrant SAWP farm workers. It didn't take long for the seasonal nature of the work to dash the union's hopes. The next year Greenway hired back only twelve of the original thirty-five workers from Mexico. The rest were replaced with local employees who applied successfully for the UFCW bargaining unit to be decertified.

Despite the setback, Local 1518 persevered, setting up assistance centres for migrant workers and hiring Mexican native Lucy Luna as a full-time organizer. The local managed to organize SAWP farm workers at two more greenhouse operations: Floralia Plant Growers in Abbotsford and Sidhu and Sons Nursery in Mission. A long, arduous journey ensued, through countless hearings at the Labour Relations Board and legal battles in the BC Supreme Court and the Court of Appeal—costing a small fortune in legal fees. In the process, the UFCW won a key LRB ruling that SAWP employees could be a distinct bargaining unit within a larger group of farm workers doing the same jobs for the same employer. The differences between migrants and local farm workers toiling beside them are "marked and real," the board found. After Local 1518 won a narrow certification vote, forty SAWP employees at Sidhu and Sons finally secured a first contract late

in 2010. The landmark deal included seniority rights, paid breaks, better vacation pay, a small wage increase, a grievance procedure and recall rights so that those who wanted to return were given priority the following year. (A lesser agreement had been negotiated at Floralia in 2009.)

But the struggle was far from over. The local Mexican consul in Vancouver couldn't stand the thought of victimized Mexican workers joining unions to improve their lot. He began to single out union supporters at Sidhu and Floralia, arranging for their visa applications to be blocked when they applied to return next season. The matter blew wide open after private government documents detailing the consul's blacklisting of union sympathizers were leaked to the UFCW. When the union brought the matter to the LRB, accusing Mexico and its Vancouver consul of unfair labour practices, Mexico claimed diplomatic immunity. It took an LRB appeal panel to firmly reject Mexico's claim. After hearing extensive evidence detailing Mexican interference, the Labour Relations Board tossed out decertification applications pending at both locations.

Farm workers were not the only target of the government's drive to reduce employment standard regulations in the interest of "cutting red tape." Children were also singled out. Replacing child employment measures that had been in place since 1948, Bill 37 amended the **Employment Standards Act** in 2003 to allow the hiring of twelve- to fourteen-year-olds if they had a letter of approval from one parent.

For the previous fifty-five years, employers had required a permit from the Employment Standards Branch before being allowed to hire youngsters under fifteen. A labour standards officer then determined the suitability of the job for a young employee. Permit applications were often amended to ensure better conditions, while 20 percent were turned down flat. Bill 37 ended such oversight. Two years after the bill passed, the Canadian Centre for Policy Alternatives

found that 58 percent of twelve- to fourteen-year-olds in the workplace did not even have the required written permission from a parent. Seventy percent said they had worked illegally without adult supervision.

More concerning was a rise in workplace accidents involving young employees. During the first five years of Bill 37, annual injury claims for twelve- to fourteen-year-olds increased tenfold. Individual claims dipped after that, but in 2011 WorkSafeBC paid out a record $212,000 in benefits to young workers injured on the job. Two youths under fifteen were permanently disabled. Despite strong anti-child-labour campaigns by the union movement, the Liberals continued to defend the regulations, leaving BC with the weakest protection for those under fifteen in the country. While the days of twelve-year-olds toiling in the mines are long gone, the situation in 2017 is a reminder that the battle against exploitation of young people in the workplace has not yet been won.

Asbestos was another health and safety matter that the labour movement took on. Unions had been battling since the 1970s for strict regulations in the use of asbestos and decent compensation for those stricken from exposure to its carcinogenic fibres. But awareness peaked in the 2000s as the number of workers succumbing from breathing asbestos dust long ago began rising at an alarming rate. In British Columbia, an unfortunate milestone of sorts occurred in 2009 when for the first time, the number of work-related death claims from industrial disease—primarily caused by exposure to asbestos—surpassed claims related to workers dying on the job.

Both asbestosis, a scarring of the lungs that can lead to death, and the incurable cancer mesothelioma take decades to develop. As a consequence, the annual total of asbestos-related death claims in BC has more than doubled since 2000, at the same time as use of the killer substance has been on a dramatic decline. By 2015, they totalled nearly seventy a year, more than a third of all death claims recognized by WorkSafeBC. And these grim figures represent only accepted cases. According to a UBC study headed by clinical professor Paul Demers, fewer than half of all identified mesothelioma cases received compensation from WorkSafeBC.

Many workers facing a mesothelioma death sentence have too much else to deal with to also tackle the stress of all the paperwork and rigmarole required for a claim.

Adding to its black mark for lessening protection of vulnerable farm workers and young employees, the government eliminated pensions for anyone stricken with asbestosis or mesothelioma after turning sixty-five. Given the length of time it takes for these diseases to show up, this was cruel and unusual punishment. Loretta Bulfone's husband, Eno, died from asbestos exposure at the age of seventy, angry at receiving no pension for himself or his family. "They're not compensating people who are dying from a workplace disease," she told the *Vancouver Province* in 2013. "There is no fairness in that." WorkSafeBC does pay for doctor visits and funeral costs.

Showing up late in life, long after any exposure, deaths from asbestos are partic-

ularly heartbreaking. Dirk Jansema, fit and active, was diagnosed with mesothelioma after years of working in BC pulp mills. "You get ripped off of your life," he told the *Province*. "It wasn't self-inflicted. Somebody else did this to me." The same thing happened to Doug Ford, who had been looking forward to a healthy, happy retirement following thirty-five years as a safety-conscious electrician at the large Powell River pulp mill. In 2006, doctors diagnosed his growing shortness of breath as mesothelioma. Eighteen months later, a few days after turning seventy, he was dead. "It was devastating," said his wife, Lesley, who has joined with daughter Tracy and BC building trades to found the Asbestos Research, Education and Advocacy Fund. "If someone had just told him to take steps to safeguard himself, he would have done it."

But for many years, the use of asbestos was a free-for-all. Despite warnings from

As early as 1971, concerned about growing evidence of the serious health risk posed by asbestos, members of the Heat and Frost Insulators and Asbestos Workers led a wildcat strike over the presence of asbestos at the Pacific Centre construction site in downtown Vancouver. *Dan Scott photo,* Vancouver Sun.

health specialists, BC did not establish its first regulations until 1978. Unions led the fight for change. Activists such as Lee Loftus and Tony Ceraldi of the Heat and Frost Insulators and Asbestos Workers, CAIMAW's Cathy Walker and Larry Stoffman of the United Food and Commercial Workers campaigned hard to heighten public awareness of asbestos hazards and pressure the government for compensation.

On the job, workers did their best. Knowing they were at risk, miners at the Cassiar Asbestos mine in northern BC staged a series of wildcat strikes during the 1970s to protest safety conditions. Heat and Frost Insulators members led a wildcat strike over asbestos exposure at downtown Vancouver's Pacific Centre construction site in 1971. CAIMAW members at Arrow Transport refused to work on containers contaminated with asbestos from Cassiar. Trail was another hot spot. After several town meetings, the United Steelworkers Local 480 identified nearly one hundred asbestos victims who had worked in the smelter before 1980. "Someone has to be responsible for the shortened lives and the pain and suffering families go through," said local president Doug Jones. "It just doesn't seem fair."

The BC Federation of Labour had demanded a national asbestos ban as early as 1984, followed ten years later by the CLC, which had to overcome strong objections from unions in Quebec, where asbestos mining continued. It still took until 2016 for Canada to finally ban the known carcinogen. That was six years after building trades and other activists placed one hundred BC-made mock coffins on the steps of Parliament. While Ottawa stalled, Social Credit's cursory regulations in BC had been thoroughly revamped by the NDP governments of the 1990s, reducing asbestos exposure limits and imposing aggressive regulatory controls.

Unions have kept up the pressure. WorkSafeBC successfully sought a sixty-day jail sentence for demolition contractor Arthur Moore for repeatedly exposing his workers—

many young recovering drug addicts—to asbestos without adequate protection. And a Lower Mainland asbestos-removal contractor was tagged with nearly $300,000 in fines for consistently violating safety regulations. The deadly legacy of asbestos, with no end in sight, ensures no letup in the labour movement's drive. "We continue to fight for the living, and mourn for our dead," said Larry Stoffman.

On another front, the federal Conservatives' victory in the 2006 election brought further challenges to the BC labour movement. In addition to an anti-union animus that led to onerous contracts being imposed in several labour disputes and passage of a punishing financial reporting bill applying only to unions, the Stephen Harper government accelerated use of the Temporary Foreign Worker Program (TFWP). The long-standing program allowed Canadian employers to bypass conventional immigration procedures and hire foreign workers on temporary work permits for a specific job and period of time when qualified Canadian workers could not be found.

As the new millennium proceeded, however, the program was increasingly abused. Requirements were eased, lower wages were permitted and enforcement virtually disappeared. Employers leaped at the chance to hire workers who were under their thumb, afraid to complain about their low wages or poor working conditions lest they be sent home. By 2011, fifty thousand more TFWs had been accepted into Canada than conventional immigrants.

A number of BC unions were in the forefront of opposition to the program's abuses. They went to great lengths defending the rights of victimized foreign workers and exposing unscrupulous employers. The BC Federation of Labour, insisted that temporary foreign workers should have the same rights as Canadian workers and a clear path to acquire permanent residency. "If you're good enough to work here, you're good enough to live here," said president Jim Sinclair.

A major skirmish took place during the

Top left: Magusig Mendoza of the Philippines waves to the crowd on March 2, 2008, as he emerges from the gargantuan tunnel–boring machine that carved out the underground portion of the Canada Line from downtown Vancouver to Richmond. The BC building trades objected to underpaid foreign workers being used on the project.
Richard Lam photo, The Canadian Press.

Below left: When the Labourers' International Union organized a number of Canada Line foreign workers in 2006, the union complained to the Labour Relations Board that its supporters had been threatened and bullied by their Italian company. Among the complainants were (from left) Luis Retes Anderson, Franklin Mora and German Cordero, all from Costa Rica.
Glenn Baglo photo, Vancouver Sun.

building of the high-profile Canada Line from downtown Vancouver to Richmond for the 2010 Winter Olympics. Tunnel boring was subcontracted by SNC-Lavalin to the Italian firm SELI Canada Inc., which imported a number of TFWs from Latin America. They were paid far less than European foreign workers also recruited by SELI. Overcoming formidable organizing hurdles, Local 1611 of the Labourers' International Union managed to win a historic certification to represent the aggrieved Latin American workers.

When negotiations went nowhere, the union hauled SELI before the BC Human Rights Tribunal on charges of wage discrimination. They won the case, but then had to fight five more years of company appeals, stalling tactics and court challenges before SELI agreed to pay the workers $1.25 million. One of the largest human rights settlements in Canadian history, the money compensated them for personal damages and the difference between what they were paid and the high wages and benefits European TFWs received. A union delegation travelled to Costa Rica to personally present individual cheques of $35,000 to thirty-five of the original workers.

The BC Fed won an even larger award on behalf of seventy-seven Filipinos employed by Denny's restaurants. They had been forced to pay recruiters for their jobs, charged travel costs to Canada, then denied overtime and other wage provisions of the TFWP. In response to a class-action suit launched by the Federation, Denny's agreed to a payout of $1.3 million, plus a large donation to charities that help Filipino immigrants.

Then came the case that catapulted the TFWP into the public eye and ultimately paved the way for sweeping reforms. In 2012, with twenty thousand Canadian miners out of work, HD Mining, a Chinese-controlled company, secured permits for two hundred TFWs from China to work at its fledgling Murray River coal mine at Tumbler Ridge. Public outrage greeted disclosure that Mandarin was listed as an employment requirement at the mine, along with knowledge of a mining method used nowhere else but in China.

The Labourers and International Union of Operating Engineers challenged the permits in court. The United Steelworkers released an investigative report pinpointing close ties between HD Mining and the Chinese government. Although work by the company continued, the union-raised furor prompted the federal government to question the company's permits.

When abuses by other employers surfaced, Ottawa brought in major changes to the program in 2013, curtailing the ability of employers to hire foreign workers at a time when 1.4 million Canadians were unemployed. To howls from the business community, immigration minister Jason Kenney advised them, "Don't just double, but triple your efforts to hire and train available Canadians." Although unhappy the program was not scrapped entirely, BC labour leaders were nonetheless pleased that on one issue at least, they had been heard in faraway Conservative Ottawa.

Workplace safety, poorly treated farm workers, child labour laws, abuse of temporary foreign workers—these were all matters pursued by unions away from the bargaining table, often costing them a bundle without adding a dime to their members' pockets and at a time when they were increasingly hard pressed. This is not the image of unions generally depicted in the media, but it goes to the heart of the labour movement's existence as agents of social change, beyond dollars and cents.

THE STRUGGLE CONTINUES 24

A FTER MORE THAN 150 YEARS OF STRUGGLE marked by death, hardship, sacrifice, many bitter defeats and eventually a long period of solid gains and achievements, the British Columbia labour movement has survived as a fighting force into the twenty-first century. But the challenges ahead are rife. As their percentage of the workforce has dipped, unions have declined in clout—particularly those in the private sector. According to Statistics Canada, BC experienced a six-point drop in the percentage of workers belonging to a union between 1996 and 2013, the biggest decline in the country. Mostly this is the result of a major fall in size of private-sector unions: from as high as 30 percent of all non-government workers several decades ago to about 18 percent today.

Changes in the workforce have made it challenging for unions to maintain their former footing. Employment in BC has shifted from once powerful manufacturing and resource-based industries that were mostly unionized to the service sector, where it is difficult for unions to make sustained inroads. Historic gains such as the eight-hour day, decent pensions and job security are under attack. More than 75 percent of all employed British Columbians are now service providers. Employee units are becoming smaller and harder to organize, compared with the large industrial plants of the past. More and more jobs are temporary, part-time, contract or self-employed. Heightened global competition, free trade and the fluidity of investment capital have also taken a toll. This increasingly competitive environment puts downward pressure on wages, making it harder for unions to pursue one of the chief rationales for their existence, better pay.

The climate is especially difficult for younger workers. Polls show many are interested in joining unions, but openings are not easy to find, as union workforces shrink. Younger workers often wind up in the expanding world of information technology—which has

UNITED WAY SOLIDARITY

Too often unions make the news only when they strike. Yet away from the public eye, many are actively involved in making their community a better place, without attracting a single headline. Look no further than the United Way. The far-reaching charity's strongest partner is none other than the BC labour movement. Workplace donations account for 80 percent of the more than $20 million the United Way takes in every year, making unions a key component of its annual fundraising drive. Labour representatives work there full-time, and union appointees are on its board of directors. "[United Way is] the one non-profit that also has access to the workplace [for donations]," says trade unionist Mervyn Van Steinburg, part of the organization for years.

The close relationship goes back to the late 1970s, when Art Kube, the Canadian Labour Congress's regional education director, set out to end labour's virtual boycott of the United Way. With some justification, BC unions considered the charity too corporate in its outlook. Kube prodded it to become more socially progressive and embrace union participation, not only for donations but for the values labour stood for. Both sides were receptive. A joint declaration steered the United Way toward more hands-on social services and permanent union involvement. The charity's first full-time union rep was the scrappy, diminutive Joy Langan, an executive officer of the BC Federation of Labour and the first woman printer

Joy Langan, Art Kube and Jack Munro attend the twenty-fifth anniversary of the labour movement's active participation in the United Way.
Courtesy Mervyn Van Steinburg.

at Pacific Press, which produced the *Sun* and *Province* newspapers.

The revamped United Way quickly showed the value of its new union partnership, paying added attention to such matters as domestic violence and other social problems. Shortly afterward, when the province was hit by a deep recession, United Way backing helped secure federal funding for thirty-two Unemployment Action Centres across BC, coordinated by Langan and run by local labour councils. The storefront operations were gathering places where unemployed workers could receive assistance or just a cup of coffee. Some functioned as nerve centres for Operation Solidarity in 1983. They also initiated a number of food banks during their five-year run.

At the CLC's annual Winter School at Harrison Hot Springs, the United Way sponsors courses on community activism and counselling workers on employee assistance. Due in no small measure to BC labour, the charity's ongoing efforts to make society a more caring place exemplifies unions' historic pledge: "What we desire for ourselves, we wish for all."

yet to be unionized in a meaningful way—or in poorly paid service jobs. As private-sector unions struggle, the underpinning of the labour movement has moved to the still heavily unionized public sector. More than three-quarters of all those employed by government and Crown corporations have union cards, making up more than 60 percent of the membership of the BC Federation of Labour. In spite of the strains, there is no sign of trade unions becoming extinct. They remain a key force protecting and advancing the cause of all workers in a no-holds-barred economy.

But labour leaders understand they need to do more to face the future and engage younger workers. In the fall of 2016, the Canadian Labour Congress organized the first-ever Young Worker Summit in Ottawa, which made news when delegates gave Prime Minister Justin Trudeau a rough ride. The United Food and Commercial Workers has a number of initiatives and internships aimed at youth, while the BC Federation of Labour, along with other large labour organizations, has an activist Young Workers' Committee open to anyone under thirty-one.

Long-established unions are merging to better combine their forces for the battles ahead. In 2013, the Canadian Auto Workers (CAW) and the Communications, Energy and Paperworkers Union joined together to form Unifor, the country's largest private-sector union, with more than three hundred thousand members. Earlier, even the fabled IWA, its membership hovering around twelve thousand, opted to cast its lot with the United Steelworkers. And before its merger, the CAW had already absorbed most of the independent Canadian unions.

The fifty-seventh convention of the BC Federation of Labour provided a convenient snapshot of the state of BC's unions in the fall of 2016. The changes, as well as labour's timeless travails, were on full display. There was history at the top. Welcoming the 950 delegates representing half a million workers was Irene Lanzinger, the first woman to head BC's voice of organized labour. Rather than congratulating the Federation, Lanzinger asked, rhetorically, "Why did it take so long?" Systemic leadership barriers to women remain, she said, pointing out that the presidents of twelve of BC's fourteen largest unions were men.

New people at the top; BC NDP leader John Horgan and BC Federation of Labour president Irene Lanzinger. The close ties between the NDP and organized labour continue, and in 2017 the province had its fourth NDP government, a welcome end to the tough slog unions had had during the previous sixteen years of BC Liberal rule.
Joshua Berson photo.

The labour movement has been in the forefront of the vigorous campaign for a minimum wage of $15 an hour, an example of unions fighting on behalf of workers because they are poorly paid, not because they are in a union. With NDP assuming government in 2017, there are expectations the long–sought goal will finally be realized.

Courtesy Rod Mickleburgh.

Lanzinger had replaced the shaggy-haired Jim Sinclair, the Fed's loud and passionate president of fifteen years. Controversial at times, Sinclair left his mark on the organization, championing causes outside the realm of contracts, working behind the scenes to try to resolve difficult disputes and articulating labour's beefs with fire and conviction. Lanzinger, a veteran of the BCTF, was the first member of a public-sector union to head the Federation. Illustrating just how far diversity has come, Lanzinger was also undoubtedly the first Fed president to cite labour as a movement "that vigorously engages in the battle against racism, sexism, ableism, homophobia, transphobia and xenophobia."

At the same time, problems cited by the Fed president would have been familiar to anyone attending a convention fifty years earlier: continued attacks on unions by those

she branded as "the rich and the powerful"; the ongoing fight to ensure safe workplaces; low wages and precarious employment; the failure of governments to reduce poverty, provide sufficient child care and establish an adequate minimum wage; and the need to elect political leaders committed to social issues. Lanzinger's ringing cry that "our response must be to build a movement that includes and fights for every member of the working class and the poor" could have been uttered at any time in labour's distant past.

And of course, there was division. The labour movement has never been short of strong opinions, and they don't always merge. As Lanzinger acknowledged, a split had deepened over jobs and the environment, epitomized by the Site C dam and Kinder Morgan pipeline. Construction unions are attracted by the thousands of jobs. Others in the labour movement oppose the projects for their potential damage to the environment.

What of the years ahead? In spite of the best efforts of business, media commentators and right-wing politicians to dismiss them as anachronisms in the modern, rapidly evolving gigabyte economy, unions aren't going away. Indeed, they are needed more than ever. Continuing to push the envelope of workers' rights, they are moving, however haltingly, into the difficult terrain of high-tech electronics and fields dominated by computers. In January of 2017, the International Alliance of Theatrical Stage Employees stepped up an organizing drive among Vancouver's many studio animators with what the union called "a major town hall meeting" at a location kept secret from studio managers. Unifor Local 2000, the former Newspaper Guild, has also been in the field trying to organize animators, visual-effects workers and video-game developers.

As 2017 progressed, despite ongoing economic uncertainty, strike votes were soaring: 99.5 percent by Kitimat smelter workers; 96 percent by four thousand housekeeping and dietary workers at BC hospitals; and 99.4 percent by more than a thousand workers at the River Rock Casino seeking a first contract after being organized in 2016 by the BCGEU. The summer of 2017 saw a return to power by the BC NDP, in a minority government with Green Party support, after sixteen years of Liberal government. Backed by strong union support, the NDP promised a substantial increase in the minimum wage to $15 an hour and less onerous rules for union organizing.

It will not be easy. It never is for unions. But the dream of a better society for working men and women keeps the movement going, long after so many other social movements have passed into the dustbin of history. The ringing words of labour's rousing anthem "Solidarity Forever," written by Wobbly Ralph Chaplin in 1915, have never gone out of style: "When the union's inspiration through the workers' blood shall run/ There can be no power greater anywhere beneath the sun/ Yet what force on earth is weaker than the feeble strength of one/ But the union makes us strong."

The next chapter awaits.

What have a hundred and fifty years of union struggle given us? Just a short list would include the eight–hour day, extra pay for overtime, weekends, paid vacations, sick leave, pensions, workplace health and safety, maternity leave, equal pay for equal work by women, an end to child labour, the minimum wage, workers' compensation, employee rights, unemployment insurance, the right to strike and free collective bargaining. As the sign says: THANK YOU, LABOUR UNIONS. *Joshua Berson photo.*

ACKNOWLEDGEMENTS

On the Line was commissioned by the BC Labour Heritage Centre, and I am grateful to members of the book's steering committee for their faith in me. Their comments were helpful and encouraging throughout. The committee members are Ken Novakowski (chair), Joey Hartman, Michelle Laurie, Irene Lanzinger, Jim Sinclair, Kendra Strauss and Mervyn Van Steinburg.

I did not do many personal interviews for the book, but those whom I did interview include Jackie Ainsworth, Peter Burton, Peter Cameron, George Davison, Ray Haynes, Stephen Kelleher, Steve Koerner, Art Kube, Anna Lary, Shirley Mathieson, Craig Paterson, Rajinder Pettakur, Stan Shewaga, Jinny Sims, Jim Sinclair, Colin Snell, Gary Steeves, Jess Succamore, Mervyn Van Steinburg, Cathy Walker and Bill Zander.

Although my name is on the cover, this account of BC's rich trade union history—stretching over a century and a half—could not have been written without the assistance of many others who willingly gave of their time, helped set me straight on any number of issues, were unfailingly constructive and, well, just helped. Among them were Jean Barman, Soren Bech, Elaine Bernard, Kim Bolan, Kate Braid, Rick Cash, Val Casselton, Marie Decaire, Jock Finlayson, Ashley Ford, David Frank, Bailey Garden, Terry Glavin, Sean Griffin, Gordon Hak, Stephen Howard, Stephen Hume, Stephen Hunt, Justine Hunter, Ben Isitt, Colleen Jordan, Paul Knox, Phillip Legg, Mark Leier, Lee Loftus, John Mabbott, John Mackie, Gary Mason, Dale McCartney, Geoff Meggs, Andrew Neufeld, Janet Nicol, Tom Sandborn, Lorne Slotnick, Carolyn Soltau, Norman Spector, Larry Stoffman, Roger Stonebanks, Wendy Stueck, Brooke Sundin, Bill Tieleman, Ron Verzuh, Sue Vohanka, Doug Ward, Patricia Wejr, Paul Yee and Henry Yu. Thanks also to the Vancouver Public Library and WorkSafeBC. Apologies to those I missed. Special thanks to Ray Haynes for his invaluable scrapbooks, which he kindly shared, and to David Yorke, for his priceless collection of union memorabilia and his deep fount of labour knowledge.

Several individuals were particularly critical to the book's completion. Researcher Robin Folvik kept me focused on key issues, drew my attention to events of which I knew little, and amassed and organized an abundance of photos, sources and information. My heroic editor Silas White left me deeply in his debt. He managed the difficult task of reducing a mass of material to a readable, manageable length, devised a coherent structure, kept my eye on the ball and tolerated my writing and work habits. Ken Novakowski, a beacon of perseverance, saw the project all the way through its many ups and downs. Using a patience and diplomacy that was a marvel to behold, he remained unfailingly positive that everything would work out in the end. Labour heritage in BC has no better friend. Donna Sacuta, executive director of the BC Labour Heritage Centre, came late to the book project, but her energy, dedication and archival research were vital to the final product. Nor can I thank enough the progressive, aptly-named Community Savings Credit Union; my publisher, the treasured Harbour Publishing; project editor Peter Robson and copy editor Arlene Prunkl.

Finally, I would like to thank my parents, who allowed me to grow up in a home where politics and unions were part of normal conversation and not creatures from outer space. And most of all, thanks to my steadfast partner, Lucie McNeill, who lived with this book from the beginning with enduring equanimity and love and was always there for me. Words are inadequate to express my immense gratitude.

BIBLIOGRAPHY

BOOKS

Abella, Irving M. *Nationalism, Communism and Canadian Labour: the CIO, the Communist Party, and the Canadian Congress of Labour, 1935–1956.* Toronto: University of Toronto Press, 1973.

Anderson, Robert, and Eleanor Wachtel. *The Expo Story.* Madeira Park, BC: Harbour Publishing, 1986.

Ayukaw, Michiko Midge. *Hiroshima Immigrants in Canada, 1891–1941.* Vancouver: UBC Press, 2008.

Baird, Irene. *Waste Heritage.* Toronto: Macmillan Company of Canada Ltd., 1973 (originally published in 1939).

Baldrey, Keith, and Gary Mason. *Fantasyland: Inside the Reign of Bill Vander Zalm.* Toronto: McGraw-Hill Ryerson, 1989.

Bank Book Collective, The. *An Account to Settle: The Story of the United Bank Workers (SORWUC).* Vancouver: Press Gang Publishers, 1979.

Barman, Jean. *The West Beyond the West: A History of British Columbia* (3rd edition). Toronto: University of Toronto Press, 2007.

Barrett, Dave, and William Miller. *Barrett: A Very Passionate Life.* Vancouver: Douglas & McIntyre, 1995.

Bech, Soren, and Mary Rowles. *Sisters & Brothers Fighting for Social Justice: The Story of the BCGEU, 1980–2002.* Burnaby, BC: Mitchell Press, 2011.

Bennett, William. *Builders of British Columbia.* Vancouver: Broadway Printers, 1937.

Bergren, Myrtle. *Tough Timber: The Loggers of British Columbia: Their Story.* Toronto: Progress Books, 1967.

Bernard, Elaine. *The Long Distance Feeling: A History of the Telecommunications Workers Union.* Vancouver: New Star Books, 1982.

Berton, Pierre. *The Great Depression 1929–1939.* Toronto: McClelland & Stewart, 1990.

Berton, Pierre. *The Last Spike: The Great Railway, 1881–1885.* Toronto: McClelland & Stewart, 1971.

Bowen, Lynne. *Robert Dunsmuir: Laird of the Mines.* Montreal: XYZ Publishing, 1999.

Braid, Kate. *Journeywoman: Swinging a Hammer in a Man's World.* Halfmoon Bay, BC: Caitlin Press, 2012.

Broadfoot, Barry. *Ten Lost Years: 1929–1939.* Toronto, McClelland & Stewart Inc., 1973.

Campbell, Peter. *Canadian Marxists and the Search for a Third Way.* Montreal: McGill-Queen's University Press, 1999.

Carrothers, A.W.R. *The Labour Injunction in British Columbia.* Toronto: CCH Canadian Ltd., 1956.

Duff, Wilson. *The Indian History of British Columbia: The Impact of the White Man.* Victoria: The Royal British Columbia Museum, 1997.

Dunaway, Jo. *We're Your Neighbours: The Story of CUPE BC.* Vancouver: the Canadian Union of Public Employees, BC Division, 2000.

Fukawa, Masako, with Stanley Fukawa. *Spirit of the Nikkei Fleet: BC's Japanese Canadian Fishermen.* Madeira Park: Harbour Publishing, 2009.

Gawthrop, Daniel. *High-Wire Act: Power, Pragmatism and the Harcourt Legacy.* Vancouver: New Star Books, 1996.

Green, Jim. *Against the Tide: The Story of the Canadian Seamen's Union.* Toronto: Progress Books, 1986.

Griffin, Sean, ed. *Fighting Heritage: Highlights of the 1930s Struggle for Jobs and Militant Unionism in British Columbia.* Vancouver: Tribune Publishing Company Ltd., 1985.

Hak, Gordon. *The Left in British Columbia: A History of Struggle.* Vancouver: Ronsdale Press, 2013.

Hinde, John. *When Coal Was King: Ladysmith and the Coal-Mining Industry on Vancouver Island.* Vancouver: UBC Press, 2003.

Howard, Irene. *Gold Dust on His Shirt: The True Story of an Immigrant Mining Family.* Toronto: Between the Lines, 2008.

Howard, Irene. *Helena Gutteridge: The Unknown Reformer.* Vancouver: UBC Press, 1992.

International Longshoremen's and Warehousemen's Union, Local 500. *"Man Along the Shore"! The Story of the Vancouver Waterfront.* Vancouver: ILWU Local 500 Pensioners, 1976.

Isitt, Benjamin. *Militant Minority: British Columbia Workers and the Rise of a New Left, 1948–1972.* Toronto: University of Toronto Press, 2011.

Jamieson, Eric. *Tragedy at Second Narrows.* Madeira Park, BC: Harbour Publishing, 2008.

Johnston, Hugh J.M. *The Voyage of the* Komagata Maru*: The Sikh Challenge to Canada's Colour Bar* (revised edition). Vancouver: UBC Press, 2014.

King, Al, with Kate Braid. *Red Bait! Struggles of a Mine Mill Local*. Vancouver: Kingbird Publishing, 1998.

Knight, Rolf. *Indians at Work: An Informal History of Native Labour in British Columbia 1858–1930*. Vancouver: New Star Books, 1996.

Lazarus, Morden. *Up from the Ranks: Trade Union VIPs Past and Present*. Toronto: Cooperative Press Associates, 1977.

Leier, Mark. *Where the Fraser River Flows: The Industrial Workers of the World in British Columbia*. Vancouver: New Star Books, 1990.

Lembcke, Jerry, and William M. Tattam. *One Union in Wood: A Political History of the International Woodworkers of America*. Madeira Park, BC: Harbour Publishing, 1984.

Leslie, Graham. *Breach of Promise: Socred Ethics under Vander Zalm*. Madeira Park, BC: Harbour Publishing, 1991.

Lutz, John Sutton. *Makúk: A New History of Aboriginal-White Relations*. Vancouver: UBC Press, 2008.

Mayo, Joan. *Paldi Remembered: 50 Years in the Life of a Vancouver Island Logging Town*. Duncan, BC: Priority Printing Ltd., 1997.

McCormack, A. Ross. *Reformers, Rebels, and Revolutionaries: The Western Canadian Radical Movement 1899–1919*. Toronto: University of Toronto Press, 1977.

McLean, Bruce. *A Union amongst Government Employees: A History of the B.C. Government Employees' Union 1919–1979*. Vancouver, BC: Government Employees' Union, 1979.

Meggs, Geoff. *Salmon: The Decline of the B.C. Fishery* (paperback edition). Vancouver: Douglas & McIntyre, 1995.

Meggs, Geoff, and Rod Mickleburgh. *The Art of the Impossible: Dave Barrett and the NDP in Power 1972–1975*. Madeira Park, BC: Harbour Publishing, 2012.

Mitchell, David J. *Succession: The Political Reshaping of British Columbia*. Vancouver: Douglas & McIntyre, 1987.

Mitchell, David J. *W.A.C. Bennett and the Rise of British Columbia*. Vancouver: Douglas & McIntyre, 1983.

Mouat, Jeremy. *Roaring Days: Rossland's Mines and the History of British Columbia*. Vancouver: UBC Press, 1995.

Munro, Jack, and Jane O'Hara. *Union Jack*. Vancouver: Douglas & McIntyre, 1988.

Neufeld, Andrew. *Union Store: The History of the Retail Clerks Union in British Columbia, 1899–1999*. Vancouver: United Food and Commercial Workers Union, Local 1518, 1999.

Neufeld, Andrew, and Andrew Parnaby. *The IWA in Canada: The Life and Times of an Industrial Union*. Vancouver: IWA Canada/New Star Books, 2000.

Norton, Wayne, and Tom Langford. *A World Apart: The Crowsnest Communities of Alberta and British Columbia*. Kamloops: Plateau Press, 2000.

Ormsby, Margaret A. *British Columbia: A History*. Vancouver: Macmillan Company of Canada Ltd., 1958.

Palmer, Bryan D. *Solidarity: The Rise and Fall of an Opposition in British Columbia*. Vancouver: New Star Books, 1987.

Penner, Norman. *Winnipeg 1919: The Strikers' Own History of the Winnipeg General Strike* (2nd edition). Toronto: James Lorimer & Company, 1975.

Persky, Stan. *Fantasy Government: Bill Vander Zalm and the Future of Social Credit*. Vancouver: New Star Books, 1989.

Persky, Stan. *Son of Socred*. Vancouver: New Star Books, 1979.

Peterson, Jan. *Black Diamond City: Nanaimo—The Victorian Era*. Surrey, BC: Heritage House Publishing Co. Ltd., 2002.

Phillips, Paul. *No Power Greater*. Vancouver: BC Federation of Labour, Boag Foundation, 1967.

Plecas, Bob. *Bill Bennett: A Mandarin's View*. Vancouver: Douglas & McIntyre Ltd., 2006.

Robin, Martin. *Radical Politics and Canadian Labour* (paperback edition). Kingston, Ontario: Industrial Relations Centre, Queen's University, 1971.

Robin, Martin. *The Rush for Spoils: The Company Province 1871–1933*. Toronto: McClelland & Stewart, 1972.

Roy, Patricia. *A White Man's Province: British Columbia Politicians and Chinese and Japanese Immigrants 1858–1914*. Vancouver: UBC Press, 1989.

Sandborn, Tom. *Hell's History*. Vancouver: United Steelworkers, 2016. https://www.usw.ca/act/activism/health-safety-and-environment/resources/body/Hells-History_web2.pdf.

Scott, Jack. *Plunderbund and Proletariat: A History of the IWW in B.C.* Vancouver: New Star Books, 1975.

Sheils, Jean Evans, and Ben Swankey. *Work and Wages! A Semi-Documentary of the Life and Times of Arthur H. (Slim) Evans*. Vancouver: Trade Union Research Bureau, 1977.

Steedman, Mercedes, Peter Suschnigg, and Dieter K. Buse, eds. *Hard Lessons: The Mine Mill Union in the Canadian Labour Movement*. Toronto: Dundurn Press, 1995.

Stevens, Homer, and Rolf Knight. *Homer Stevens: A Life in Fishing*. Madeira Park, BC: Harbour Publishing, 1992.

Stonebanks, Roger. *Fighting for Dignity: The Ginger Goodwin Story*. St. John's, NF: Canadian Committee on Labour History, 2004.

Tennant, Paul. *Aboriginal Peoples and Politics*. Vancouver: UBC Press, 1990.

Waiser, Bill. *All Hell Can't Stop Us: The On-to-Ottawa Trek and Regina Riot*. Calgary: Fifth House Ltd., 2003.

Warburton, Rennie, and David Coburn, eds. *Workers, Capital and the State in British Columbia*. Vancouver: UBC Press, 1988.

Webb, Patricia G. *The Heart of Health Care: The Story of the Hospital Employees' Union—The First 50 Years*. Vancouver: The Hospital Employees' Union, 1994.

Webster, Jack. *WEBSTER!* Vancouver: Douglas & McIntyre, 1990.

Wejr, Patricia, and Howie Smith. *Fighting for Labour: Four Decades of Work in British Columbia, 1910–1950*. Victoria: Province of British Columbia, 1978.

Whitaker, Reg, and Gary Marcuse. *Cold War Canada: The Making of a National Insecurity State, 1945–1957*. Toronto: University of Toronto Press, 1994.

White, Howard. *A Hard Man to Beat: The Story of Bill White: Labour Leader, Historian, Shipyard Worker, Raconteur*. Madeira Park, BC: Harbour Publishing, 2011.

Willcocks, Paul. *Dead Ends: BC Crime Stories*. Regina: University of Regina Press, 2014.

ARTICLES AND OTHER SOURCES

Atherton, Patricia Gwen. "CAIMAW – Portrait of a Canadian Union." Master's thesis, University of British Columbia, 1981. https://open.library.ubc.ca/cIRcle/collections/ubctheses/831/items/1.0095449

Binning, Sadhu, and Sukhwant Hundal. "Darshan Singh Canadian: Ten Years in Canada." *Watan*, 1989. http://watanpunjabi.ca/pdf/darshan-singh-canadian-english.pdf.

Bush, Murray, and the Canadian Farmworkers' Union. "Zindabad! B.C. Farmworkers' Fight for Rights, 1994–1995." http://www.vcn.bc.ca/cfu/.

Campbell, Peter. "Making Socialists: Bill Pritchard, the Socialist Party of Canada, and the Third International." *Labour/Le Travail*, vol. 30 (Fall 1992). http://www.lltjournal.ca/index.php/llt/article/view/4852/5725.

Chaklader, Anjan. "History of Workers' Compensation in BC: A Report to the Royal Commission on Workers' Compensation in BC." May 1998. http://www.qp.gov.bc.ca/rcwc/research/chaklader.pdf.

Chapleau, J.A., and John H. Gray. "Report of the Royal Commission on Chinese Immigration: Report and Evidence." 1885. https://archive.org/details/cu31924023463940.

Creese, Gillian. "Exclusion or Solidarity? Vancouver Workers Confront the 'Oriental Problem.'" *BC Studies*, no. 80 (Winter 1988–89). http://ojs.library.ubc.ca/index.php/bcstudies/article/view/1295/1337.

Dobbin, Murray. "I am the BCTF: The Story of the 2005 BC Teachers' Strike." Commissioned by the BC Teachers' Federation, 2006. http://bctf.ca/uploadedFiles/HistoryMuseum/Rooms/Bargaining/I_Am_the_BCTF.pdf.

Dooley, Michael Kevin. "Our Mickey: The Story of Private James O'Rourke, VC.MM (CEF), 1879–1957." *Labour/Le Travail*, vol. 47 (Spring 2001). http://www.lltjournal.ca/index.php/llt/article/view/5223/6092.

Drent, Jan. "Labour and the Unions in a Wartime Essential Industry: Shipyard Workers in B.C., 1939–1945." *Northern Mariner Journal of the Canadian Nautical Research Society* (Canada), no. 6 (October 1996). https://www.cnrs-scrn.org/northern_mariner/vol06/tnm_6_4_47-64.pdf.

Elkins, David. "Politics Makes Strange Bedfellows: The BC Party System in the 1952 and 1953 Provincial Elections." *BC Studies*, no. 30 (Summer 1976). http://ojs.library.ubc.ca/index.php/bcstudies/article/view/879/919.

First Call: BC Child and Youth Advocacy Coalition. "Child Labour Is No Accident: The Experience of BC's Working Children." May 2013. http://firstcallbc.org/wordpress/wp-content/uploads/2015/08/Child-Labour-Is-No-Accident-FirstCall-2013-05.pdf.

Gray, Stephen. "Woodworkers and Legitimacy: The IWA in Canada, 1937–1957." PhD history thesis, Simon Fraser University, 1989. summit.sfu.ca/system/files/iritems1/5561/b15120156.pdf.

Howard, Irene. "The Mothers' Council of Vancouver: Holding the Fort for the Unemployed, 1935–1938." *BC Studies*, nos. 69–70 (Spring/Summer 1986). http://ojs.library.ubc.ca/index.php/bcstudies/article/view/1234/1278.

International Union of Operating Engineers. "Firing Iron: A History of IUOE Local 115." Compiled for the local union's Diamond Jubilee, December, 2006. https://www.iuoe115.ca/wordpress/wp-content/uploads/2016/04/IUOE-115-Firing-Iron-2006.pdf.

Isitt, Benjamin. "Searching for Workers' Solidarity: The One Big Union and the Victoria General Strike of 1919. *Labour/Le Travail*, vol. 60 (Fall 2007). http://www.labourheritagecentre.ca/wordpress/wp-content/uploads/2017/05/GVTA-1919-Strike-Final_web.pdf.

Isitt, Benjamin, and Melissa Moroz. "The Hospital Employees' Union Strike and the Privatization of Medicare in British Columbia." *International Labour and Working-Class History*, no. 71 (Spring 2007). https://www.cambridge.org/core/journals/international-labor-and-working-class-history/article/div-classtitlethe-hospital-employeesandapos-union-strike-and-the-privatization-of-medicare-in-british-columbia-canadadiv/7670BDC8BDCB7E7386CD116BF463B051.

Kealey, Gregory S. "1919: The Canadian Labour Revolt." *Labour/Le Travail*, vol. 19 (Spring 1984). www.lltjournal.ca/index.php/llt/article/download/2600/3003.

Klausen, Susanne. "The Plywood Girls: Women and Gender Ideology at the Port Alberni Plywood Plant, 1942–1991." *Labour/Le Travail*, vol. 41 (Spring 1998). http://www.lltjournal.ca/index.php/llt/article/view/5103/5972.

Knox, Paul Graham. "The Passage of Bill 39: Reform and Repression in British Columbia's Labour Policy." Master's thesis, University of British Columbia, 1972. https://open.library.ubc.ca/media/download/pdf/831/1.0099887/1.

Lang, Dr. Ronald W. "Open Letter on Wage Controls and the CLC." 2010. http://arts.uwaterloo.ca/~rneedham/documents/WageControlsandTheCLC.pdf.

Langford, Tom, and Chris Frazer. "The Cold War and Working-Class Politics in the Coal Mining Communities of the Crowsnest Pass, 1945–1958." *Labour/Le Travail*, vol. 49 (Spring 2002). http://www.lltjournal.ca/index.php/llt/article/view/5253/6123.

Lennon, Elizabeth J. Shilton. "Organizing the Unorganized: Unionization in the Chartered Banks of Canada." *Osgoode Hall Law Journal*, vol. 18, no. 2 (August 1980). http://digitalcommons.osgoode.yorku.ca/cgi/viewcontent.cgi?article=2041&context=ohlj.

Loosmore, Thomas Robert. "The British Columbia Labour Movement and Political Action, 1879–1906." Master's thesis, University of British Columbia, 1954. https://open.library.ubc.ca/cIRcle/collections/ubctheses/831/items/1.0107058.

Marcuse, Gary. "Labour's Cold War: The Story of a Union That Was Not Purged." *Labour/Le Travail*, vol. 22 (Fall 1988). http://www.lltjournal.ca/index.php/llt/article/view/4698/5571.

McCandless, R.C. "Vancouver's 'Red Menace' of 1935: The Waterfront Situation." *BC Studies*, no. 22 (1974). http://ojs.library.ubc.ca/index.php/bcstudies/article/view/804/847.

McCartney, Dale Michael. "A Crisis of Commitment: Socialist Internationalism in British Columbia during the Great War." Master's thesis, Simon Fraser University, 2010. summit.sfu.ca/system/files/iritems1/9970/etd5879.pdf.

McDonald, Ian. "Class Conflict and Political Factionalism: A History of Local 213 of the International Brotherhood of Electrical Workers." Master's thesis, Simon Fraser University, 1986. summit.sfu.ca/system/files/iritems1/6361/b16608768.pdf.

Mouat, Jeremy. "The Politics of Coal: A Study of the Wellington Miners' Strike of 1890–91." *BC Studies*, no. 77 (Spring 1988). http://ojs.library.ubc.ca/index.php/bcstudies/article/view/1281/1323.

Nicol, Janet Mary. "Unions Aren't Native: The Muckamuck Restaurant Labour Dispute, Vancouver, B.C. (1978–1983)." *The Journal of Canadian Labour Studies*, vol. 40 (Autumn 1997).

Parker, Peter. "We Are Not Beggars: Political Genesis of the Native Brotherhood, 1931–1951." Master's history thesis, Trent University, 1987. summit.sfu.ca/system/files/iritems1/3813/b14263452.pdf.

Parnaby, Andy. "We'll Hang All Policemen from a Sour Apple Tree!: Class, Law, and the Politics of State Power in the Blubber Bay Strike of 1938–39." Master of Arts thesis, Queen's University, 1993. summit.sfu.ca/system/files/iritems1/6743/b17572988.pdf.

Rajala, Richard A. "Pulling Lumber: Indo-Canadians in the British Columbia Forest Industry, 1900–1998." *British Columbia Historical News*, vol. 36, no. 1 (Winter 2002–03). http://www.library.ubc.ca/archives/pdfs/bchf/bchn_2002_03_winter.pdf.

Ralston, Keith. "The 1900 Strike of Fraser River Sockeye Salmon Fishermen." Master's thesis, University of British Columbia, 1965. https://open.library.ubc.ca/cIRcle/collections/ubctheses/831/items/1.0105476.

Rosenthal, Star. "Union Maids: Organized Women Workers in Vancouver 1900–1915." *BC Studies*, no. 41 (Spring 1979). http://ojs.library.ubc.ca/index.php/bcstudies/article/view/1011/1049.

Roy, Patricia. "The Preservation of the Peace in Vancouver: The Aftermath of the Anti-Chinese Riot of 1887." *BC Studies*, no. 31 (Autumn 1976). ojs.library.ubc.ca/index.php/bcstudies/article/download/896/936.

Seager, Allen. "Socialists and Workers: The Western Canadian Coal Mines, 1900–1921." *Labour/Le Travail*, vol. 16 (Fall 1985). https://journals.lib.unb.ca/index.php/LLT/article/viewFile/2471/2874.

Smith, Julia Maureen. "Organizing the Unorganized: The Service, Office and Retail Workers' Union of Canada (SORWUC), 1972–1986." Master's thesis, Simon Fraser University, 2007. http://summit.sfu.ca/item/9826.

Tam, April. "CAW History 2301: 55 Years of History from the Workers' Voices." History project, 2009. http://www.caw2301.ca/files/Projectforweb.pdf.

Verzuh, Ron. "The Underpants Speech: How an Angry Speech Paved the Way to Canada's Communist Labour Purges of the 1950s." June 14, 2014. http://www.ronverzuh.ca/wordpress/wp-content/uploads/2014/07/The-Underpants-Speech.pdf.

White, Jim. "The Early History of the Pulp, Paper and Woodworkers of Canada," 1982. https://www.ppwc.ca/ppwchist01.pdf

Williams, Jeanne Myers. "Ethnicity and Class Conflict at Maillardville/Fraser Mills: The Strike of 1931." Master's thesis, Simon Fraser University, 1982. http://summit.sfu.ca/item/6142.

In addition, many newspaper articles, particularly from the *Vancouver Sun*, *Vancouver Province*, *Vancouver Daily World* and labour's early paper, the *BC Federationist*, provided a rich source of material.

INDEX